WRITINGS The
FOR A Tom
DEMOCRATIC Hayden
SOCIETY Reader

WRITINGS FOR A DEMOCRATIC SOCIETY

The Tom Hayden Reader

City Lights Books
San Francisco

For permissions information see page 568.

Cover photograph of Tom Hayden by Paul Sequeira; the photo was taken some-time during the Chicago Eight Conspiracy Trial.

Cover design: Pollen

Text design: Gambrinus

Library of Congress Cataloging-in-Publication Data

Hayden, Tom.
 Writings for a democratic society : the Tom Hayden reader.
  p. cm.
 Includes index.
 ISBN 978-0-87286-461-0 (pbk.)
 1. United States—Politics and government—1945-1989. 2. United States—Politics and government—1989–3. California—Politics and government—1951–4. World politics—20th century. 5. World politics—21st century. 6. Protest movements—United States. 7. Hayden, Tom—Political and social views. I. Title.

JK1726.H394 2008
320.530973—dc22

2007044961

City Lights Books are published at the City Lights Bookstore,
261 Columbus Avenue, San Francisco, CA 94133.
Visit our Web site: www.citylights.com

Contents

IV. DIGGING FOR ROOT CAUSES: ENDING GANG VIOLENCE

V. PERSONAL ROOTS: THOUGHTS ON IRELAND

VI. PERSONAL LIFE

VII. PROTECTING THE ENVIRONMENT

VIII. LESSONS LEARNED: PROGRESSIVE POLITICS AND FOREIGN POLICY

IX. REFLECTIONS ON THE 1960s

X. FROM CHICAGO TO SEATTLE AND BEYOND: WRITINGS
ON THE GLOBAL JUSTICE MOVEMENT

XI. WRITING AGAINST THE IRAQ WAR

1

On Writing

January 2008

I AM DEEPLY HONORED that City Lights, and its editor, Greg Ruggiero, would decide to publish these fifty years of my writings. Since I first hitchhiked west and visited the City Lights bookstore in 1960, I have revered it as a sanctuary of the word, and as a fountain of the nonconformity that not only broke and survived the icy 1950s, but announced the coming of the 1960s. I am thankful to Greg for his dedication and incisive mind, to Eliot Katz for his loyalty to the cultural legacy of the 1960s, and to Carolyn Stanley for her perseverance in handling permissions.

I was a high school sophomore when Allen Ginsberg first read "Howl," a graduating senior when *On the Road* was published in 1957. My hometown was Royal Oak, Michigan, one of the nation's early suburbs. In 1954, unknown to me, Royal Oak's business elite promoted our town as "virtually 100 percent white."[1] This was a rare public admission in those silent times. The quote never came to my attention until the author David Freund unearthed and published it in 2006. It took a writer to fill in this gap in my identity. I was blind to the reality in which I lived. During my high school years I thought that the civil rights struggle was only in Montgomery, Alabama, and Little Rock, Arkansas, but not in suburban hometowns.

I realized that the cure to this blindness somehow involved the power of perception, the ability to discern "the evidence of things not seen" (the quote is both from James Baldwin and the Bible). In today's bureaucracies, it is called "thinking outside the box." The writer's task was to discover, observe and report on unnoticed events that might be important to living or even become History. I joined the staff of my high school paper as a sports writer, and advanced to editor-in-chief. When I went to university,

I was drawn into the culture of the *Michigan Daily*, a paper that we "put to bed" in the early hours of every morning. The *Daily* became an alternative university for me, one where ideas seemed to matter more than in the classroom.

> *"For the native, objectivity is always directed against him."*[2]
> —*Frantz Fanon*

I have always struggled with objectivity. I was deeply independent and critical, leaving me a loner as exciting events were unfolding all around me. When I interviewed Martin Luther King Jr. at the Democrats' 1960 convention, my inner contradictions were swirling. I wanted to identify with the new civil rights movement, but I felt awkward putting down my notebook and holding up a picket sign. I thought, too, reporting Dr. King's words might advance my career in journalism.

I also wrote about Kennedy's nomination with ambivalence: "He has inspired this convention with the promise of political victory, with the promise of vigorous and tenacious party leadership, with the promise of youth. He has not yet inspired everyone with his ideas and the firmness of his commitment to those ideas."[3]

I straddled too, reporting from Los Angeles on the birth of the new student movement, as if it was a thing apart from me, to be carefully examined:

"If a fear of the profound complexity of modern life forces the majority of students to withdraw into conservatism, what is it in life which magnetizes the minority of students into quite fearless rebellion?

"The student seems to have reached a point where it is so self-humiliating not to assert himself that he is impelled to cry out at any material cost so that he may somehow preserve the integrity of his personality. I do not profess to know if this is the final answer. In fact, no one seems to know at the moment. But 500 students will picket the Democratic convention today."[4]

I could not remain neutral, however. I realized that the very people and events that I was covering were changing me. I was moving within my inner self. At the time, investigative reporting was not a recognized field of journalism. Editorials were opinion pieces written by the editors. News, even news analysis, was sanitized of opinion. My models were Tom Paine's revolutionary pamphlets and Albert Camus' passionate essays on resistance. I evolved into an impassioned college editor who exposed that the dean of women was snooping on co-eds, and who wrote some of the first articles covering the emergence of the new student movement which drew considerable concern from university administrators and left me feeling unsure of my own journalistic boundaries. I took the further activist step of promoting a student political party, called Voice, that eventually became a chapter of Students for a Democratic Society (SDS). I gradually chose activism over a journalistic career, but never ceased to write, becoming at first a pamphleteer drafting broadsides from the South. In late 1961 I was asked by the SDS to write the founding manifesto, the *Port Huron Statement* (*PHS*), which I began scribbling furiously from a jail cell in Albany, Georgia. The *PHS* recognized the need for writers and intellectuals in building a New Left movement: "In a time of supposed prosperity, moral complacency, and political manipulation, a new left cannot rely on only aching stomachs to be the engine force of social reform. The case for social change, for alternatives that will involve uncomfortable personal efforts, must be argued as never before."

From that point forward, I thought of myself primarily as a community organizer and activist, my writing linked to causes. But the deeper truth was this: I took activist leadership where it seemed necessary, but I could never, ever stop digging for the truth and writing it down.

These writings collected here are my own witness to fifty years of American history (unbelievably, at 67 years old, I have lived one-fourth of our country's history!). There is an arc, a story line of sorts, discernible in the selections chosen for this book:

➤ In my period of youthful radical idealism (1960–68), the writings are like wake-up calls, attempting to inspire the readers to action on behalf of southern blacks, student empowerment, and above all to stop the Vietnam

War. In mainstream terms, the peak moment of "success" came on November 13, 1967 when the *New York Times* published an article about me as an "improbable radical" who symbolized the insurgency of the New Left. Suddenly there was widespread interest in what I was writing. The *New York Review of Books* and Random House solicited me for articles and books. Robert Silvers of the *New York Review* was either gutsy or giddy enough to publish on the journal's cover a drawing of a Molotov cocktail along with my 90,000-word story about the Newark riot. Random House rushed to publish the text as *Rebellion in Newark*. But as my writings seemed to defend campus takeovers and ghetto riots, my star plummeted among the "the New York intellectuals" and other cultural-literary circles in general. Irving Howe detected a Stalinist authoritarian bent. Hannah Arendt weighed in against the intruders on university property. The *Review* retreated from its radical flirtations, never asked me to write again, and later condemned my book *Irish on the Inside* for being soft on violence. All the distinctions between advocating for, defending, and understanding violence vanished as the openings of the 1960s closed and the neoconservative grip tightened.

Perhaps more ominous were the Pentagon-sponsored counterinsurgency manuals identifying me as "one of the masters of terrorist planning," divulged by Congressman Joseph Kennedy years later. At first I thought this was a smear or a mistake, but reading further I realized that it seemed forbidden, unacceptable, for an American writer to even suggest a logic of violence. The training manual points out that "many terrorists are very well trained in subversion of the democratic process and use the system to advance their causes." At the time the manual was circulating, I was an assemblyman working in Los Angeles with refugees from the civil war and death squads that the U.S. government fostered in El Salvador. The counterinsurgency experts apparently saw me as well trained in subversion of the democratic process because of my being elected by the voters. (See Lisa Haugaard, "Latin American Working Group," *In These Times*, October 14, 1996.)

As a politician and an author, the accusation of being "soft on violence" has haunted me as for decades. If, as Clausewitz wrote, violence is politics by other means, then I believe we must use the nonviolence of the word to explore openings which make political change an alternative to violence. Where peaceful reform is impossible, as John Kennedy said, violent rebellion becomes inevitable.

➤ In my two-decade period of electoral politics (1976–2000), the writings are more purposeful and programmatic, though eclectic, including ruminations on building a progressive political movement and commentaries on concrete issues like educational reform, rebuilding cities, or phasing out cancer-causing chemicals. There came another peaking of legitimacy in the 1980s when I was elected to office and was associated with the likes of Jerry Brown, Gary Hart, and Michael Dukakis. The *Los Angeles Times* published nearly any column I sent them as long as I held an electoral mandate, an era of access which closed when I left office in 2000 and ownership of the paper changed hands. During this period my writings were published in the *Wall Street Journal*, the *New York Times*, the *Washington Post*, and the *Boston Globe*.

➤ In my current reflective period (circa 1998–present), the writings turn back to social movements and larger concerns of my youth, beginning with Seattle in 1999, the growing anti-globalization movement of young people in the nineties, the moral challenge of the environmental crisis, many pieces on stirrings in Central and Latin America, and finally the war in Iraq. During this period I became a member of the *Nation's* editorial board, learned to blog for the *Huffington Post* Web site and I wrote five books for independent publishers. Also during this period, I wrote many op-eds in opposition to the Iraq war which the *New York Times* rejected on the grounds that I wasn't "qualified," though they did seek my reflections on the street protests outside the 2004 Republican national convention.

I learned from these experiences that a writer's success, at least in quantifiable terms, depends on the mood swings of public opinion as gauged by the media and publishing gatekeepers who determine the boundaries of "legitimate" editorial opinion. What is legitimate is too often politically determined. It is commonplace that propagandistic, even mindless, articles by public officials are published—articles which are written by their staffs. The spectrum of what is considered legitimate editorial opinion has drifted far to the right since the Reagan and Bush eras, even when public opinion moves to the left. The resulting gap is being increasingly filled by the blogosphere.

City Lights has been a steady exception to this rule. And who knows, a new generation of young people may get turned on to the searching, openness, struggle and vibrant counterculture which City Lights brought to society's attention fifty years ago. The year 2008 will mark the fortieth anniversary of the Chicago conspiracy trial, and two films on the subject are already planned for release. In 2010 we will begin the fiftieth anniversary of everything that happened in the decade of the 1960s. As a cultural war over the control of memory, it will be a critical period for reflection and debate as the last survivors of the 1960s fade away.

The arc I notice in these fifty years of writings is this: in this third and current phase I return to my early roots as an awakened eyewitness to new social movements, but now with the experience of having worked within the system I originally desired to change. Where I began in Mississippi, I was now writing about Chiapas and Bolivia. Where I began as a chronicler of the American student movement, I was now writing about the globalized protests of a new generation. Where I began writing as a Northern student about the American South, I now felt myself drawn into the rising of the global South. Where I once wrote endlessly about the Vietnamese, I was now witnessing the suffering and struggles of Iraq. It seems like a circle, ever enlarging, but returning always to its own beginnings. Los Angeles, where I have lived for three decades, seemed a logical place from which to see the global refracted in virtually everything local and vice versa, from the immigration of Central American war refugees and Mexican campesinos, to the globalization of capital and the resistance to its reach, to the "Latino-ization" of the United States and its backlash, to the wars on drugs and gangs and the growth of the prison-industrial complex, to the rise of mega-cities with their sweltering ghettos and barrios alongside the lifestyles of the rich and famous made possible by the lethal draining of distant environmental resources. In Los Angeles one could stare with experienced eyes at the miles of electrical lights and, with a proper understanding, really grasp the polluting of the Grand Canyon, the draining of great rivers and the cutting of great ancient forests that made all this imperial affluence possible.

As I fell away from leadership roles in politics and organizations, I began to feel a renewed purpose as an observer, interviewer, writer and teacher. Sociologists call the technique "participant observation," but I prefer the notion of being an engaged and reflective human being and writer, a participatory witness. The divisions between the objective and subjective have faded. As the Jesuits insist, contemplation in action is the ideal. To understand events, one must participate in them while critically observing others and oneself at the same time. And so, like learning and reporting what I learned in Georgia and Mississippi in 1961, now I felt an urgency to experience Seattle or the other anti-globalization uprisings first hand, not as a leader but as a writer surprised at the unexpected birth of a new activism. Action, involvement, participation all create a kind of evidence that cannot be seen before it occurs. The subjective changes the objective. That seminal observer, writer and rebel, Henry David Thoreau, said this long ago with great brevity: "Action from principle—the perception and the performance of right—changes things and relations; it is essentially revolutionary and does not consist wholly with any thing which was."[5]

I also notice the passage of time, the stages of life, in these fifty years of writings. In the beginning, there is more vision and impatience, even utopianism, the great qualities of the young and inexperienced. In the middle period, there is more responsibility, as everything is written by one holding a gavel of office, writing for achievable results. In the later period, the writings contain qualities of both, the idealism of new beginnings but also an unavoidable filter of experiences, and the beginning of another path of inquiry, the path toward reflection on larger meanings. There is a sense now that I am witnessing new and original stages in a process of change and struggle 500 years old, one which began with conquest, crusades, imperialism, the Inquisition, slavery, and the rise of European capitalism. I know I will not live to see it end, and that is a feeling radically different than the dreams of my youth. Already many brilliant young writers, Naomi Klein, Susan Faludi, Arundhati Roy and Jeremy Scahill among them, are chronicling the new experience and vision of their own generation. I learn from such young engaged writers. I know where I fit. I know the meaning of being asked to publish fifty years of writing. I will continue to write as long as curiosity keeps me alive, as notes from a past to a future I welcome. Nearly fifty years ago, James Baldwin looked ahead to an unknown time. I have tried to live by the words he wrote:

> One writes out of one thing only—one's own experience . . . The difficulty, then, for me . . . was the fact that I was, in effect, prohibited from examining my own experience too closely by the tremendous demands and the very real dangers of my social situation . . . the most crucial time in my own development came when I was forced to recognize that I was a kind of bastard of the West.[6]

Baldwin realized that he was both an African and an American who couldn't return to his past. He would "have to appropriate these white centuries" and refuse to let the white world "have a murderous power over me," or he could not write authentically at all. In a similar way, I have found it necessary to embrace my alienation as the only way to discover radical traditions usually hidden from white Americans. Otherwise, I would have adjusted to the system's relentless demands long ago, and as a writer, would be a stranger to my own estrangement. I agree with Baldwin's conclusion, that "I consider that I have many responsibilities, but none greater than this: '*to last*,' as Hemingway says, '*and get my work done.*'"[7]

NOTES

1. David M. P. Freund, *Colored Property, State Policy and White Racial Politics in Suburban America*, University of Chicago, 2006, p. 243.
2. Fanon, *The Wretched of the Earth*, Grove Press, 1963, p. 77 in "Concerning Violence."
3. *Michigan Daily*, July 15, 1960.
4. *Michigan Daily*, July 9, 1960.
5. Henry David Thoreau, *On Civil Disobedience*, Dover, 1993, p. 7.
6. Baldwin, "Autobiographical Notes," in *Baldwin, Collected Essays*, Library of America, 1998, p. 8.
7. Baldwin, p. 9. (Italics added for emphasis.)

I

Building a New Left
Student Activism &
Civil Rights in the Early 1960s

2

A Letter to the New (Young) Left

Originally published in the Activist,
Oberlin College, Winter 1961.

Part speech and part essay, this text was originally drafted to inspire students to join Students for a Democratic Society (SDS). The title must have been taken from C. Wright Mills' influential essay in New Left Review. *The Activist was written and published by students at Oberlin College, where SDS founders Rennie Davis and Paul Potter, among others, formed one of the earliest student political parties, the precursor of an SDS chapter. This essay was a rehearsal for the drafting of the* Port Huron Statement, *which followed not long after. The tone is one of idealism, an awakening of feelings that were growing among an increasing number of activist circles on campuses around the country. There is the fearlessness of inexperience, naïveté—casting off the fetters of all previous thought and ideology to express a new mood and vision. What I find interesting, beneath the apocalyptic tone, is the persistent emphasis on testing and learning from experience itself, not ideologies or paradigms. If there is a dogmatic quality, it is an* antidogma dogma, *embracing doubt and taking action nonetheless. It is existential, spiritual and practical, seeking a unity of human identity in the face of specialization.*

◆　　◆　　◆

IN A PUBLICATION such as the *Activist*, written and read by a community sharing some degree of consensus regarding political values, it should not be necessary to labor in detail over the several challenges confronting the peoples of the world, and especially confronting those who claim to be of the Left. However, in part:

Internationally, the growing power and even higher expectations of the "underdeveloped" nations; the numerous issues directly relating to man's nuclear arsenal; the population problem; the influence of the Cold War conflict on seemingly every private and public facet of the common life; the polarizing effects of the Cold War; the disintegration of easily grasped categories like "democratic," "undemocratic," "neutral"; the evolution from Stalinism to ? in Russia; the hazy and threatening future of China; the movement of power away from the West in the United Nations; the development of outer space; the coming of new communications systems. . . .

Domestically, the failures of the welfare state to deal with the hard facts of poverty in America; the drift of decision-making power away from directly representative, legislative or executive institutions into corporate and military hands neither checked by nor responsible to the courted "public"; the persistence of a racism that mocks our principles and corrupts everyday life; the encroachment upon our civil liberties seen in the intellectually masked "balancing" theory of the five Supreme Court judges as well as in the naked paranoia of our most rabid communist-phobes; the resurgence of a leaderless McCarthyism raising the flag and fist in every city across the land; the near-total absence of left position in an incredibly conservative Congress; the growing dominance of the military over formerly civilian decisions; the decline of already-meager social welfare legislation in the face of larger defense appropriations; the squandering and continuous—though somewhat checked—exploiting of our natural resources; the ugliness and ill-planned nature of our cities; the development of a technology great in its potential. . . .

Educationally, the endless repressions of free speech and thought, the stifling paternalism that infects the student's whole perception of what is real and possible and enforces a parent-child relationship until the youth is suddenly transplanted into the "the world;" the sterility of the student government and the general student community; curriculums conspicuously anachronistic in the fields of Africa, Asia and Latin America; whole new areas of study in astronomy and nuclear physics. . . .

The problems are immense. We of the Left, however, find no rest in theory, and little hope in leadership. Liberal philosophy has dealt inadequately with the twentieth century. Marx, especially Marx the humanist, has much to tell us but his conceptual tools are outmoded and his final vision implausible. The revolutionary leaders of the rising nations have been mostly non-ideological, either forced to be so or preferring (as is the case of Guevara) to forge their political views in the heat and exigencies of revolution and the present. The American intellectuals? C. Wright Mills is appealing and dynamic in his expression of theory in the grand manner, but his pessimism yields us no formulas, no path out of the dark, and his polemicism sometimes offends the critical sense. The others? There is, I find, an inhibiting, dangerous conservative temperament behind the facade of liberal realism which is so current: Niebuhr in theology; Kornhauser, Lipset, and Bell in political science and sociology; the neo-Freudians in psychology; Hofstadter in history; Schlesinger and others of the ADA mind in the Democratic Party. Their themes purport to be different but always the same impressions emerge: Man is inherently incapable of building a good society; man's passionate causes are nothing more than dangerous psychic sprees (the issues of this period too complex and sensitive to be colored by emotionalism or moral conviction); ideals have little place in politics—we should instead design effective, responsible programs which will produce the most that is realistically possible. . . . Here and there, from the pages of *Dissent* or from isolated radicals and scholars, including Mills himself, come cries: No! You false liberals are suffering from the failure of your youthful dreams; you are eviscerating the great optimistic tradition of liberalism from the Enlightenment to the twentieth century; you are justifying disinterest in morality; you are eliminating emotion, dissent, outrage and, yes, the wellsprings of life itself.

So here we stand, limp, questioning, even scared. Our jokes run something like the cover of a recent *Liberation*: scrawled in the manner one finds covering restroom walls is the question "What can we do now?" and the huge, bold answer, "Get ready to die." It is not as though we can dismiss the world; some of us know people who already have contracted radiation disease. It is not as though we can change things; Mills was pretty accurate with his description of the monolithic power elite. It is not as though we even know what to do: we have no real visionaries for our leaders, we are not much more than literate ourselves. And it is not as though, I also fear, we even know who we are. What has made me so strangely sensitive when my brothers seem so acquiescent, what has made me call insane what the experts call the "hard facts of power politics," what has made me feel we are on the threshold of death when others excitedly say we are on the New Frontier, and why have I turned with trembling and disgust from the Americans who do recognize peril and recoil into shelters full of the comforting gadgets the culture has produced? A more blinding situation is difficult to imagine. War, ironically, would be cathartic—though the release would be grimly brief.

In the unpredictable meantime, there are classes to attend; there are drinking bouts ahead, new friendships to be formed, loves to be experienced, parents to relate to—in short, lives to be led, no matter what the tension.

But there are more than normal lives for us to lead. The felt truths of this age call us to incorporate new dimensions into our existence. Those dimensions will constitute our response to the challenges of modernity I have briefly mentioned. Here a fundamental point should be made: "challenge" implies not only threat but opportunity. We have access to more knowledge, more potential and actual and varied power than ever before, and in the endlessness of change lies always the possibility of making new and revolutionary departures.

How, then, shall we respond? I should like here to separate style of response from program of response and claim that both our style and our program can tend toward either a defeating dogmatism or a hopeful radicalism.

By dogmatism of style is meant the style which employs stereotypes, untested concepts, easy answers, ritualistic language. Red-baiting, especially the loose use of "stalinoid" and "stalinist" is usually either paranoiac or begs the central question: it attacks motivation or psychology without substantively addressing whatever issue is really at hand, e.g. whether or not democratic social control is evolving in the Soviet Union, whether or not the Hungarian revolution was a fascist-inspired uprising. Red-baiting is no more or less dogmatic, I should add, than its current opposite, "anti-anticommunism," or "issues orientation," which tends to seal off critical, freewheeling discussion in the worthless name of "group unity." The "issues orientation" tendency says essentially: let us join together in action wherever we agree upon the specific, isolated issue, regardless of our differences over any other issues; let us find an ideology "inductively," through group action, rather than starting with an ideology and running off into sectarian corners to spar. The danger in this course of action has not been, as fearful persons would allege, "fellow travelling" and "fronting," but, more concretely, the subversion of the possibility of lending a persuasive, insightful intellectual content to protest. "Ban the bomb" is a sentiment we all share intestinally, but it makes a movement appear mindless to the decision-makers. Furthermore, it communicates no challenge to the Rand or NATO intellects, and most important, it has no permanent educational effect upon participant, audience, and society.

The radical style, on the other hand, takes as its presupposition Dewey's claim that we are free to the extent that we know what we are about. Radicalism as a style involves penetration of a social problem to its roots, to its real causes. Radicalism presumes a willingness to continually press forward the query: Why? Radicalism finds no rest in conclusions; answers are seen as provisional, to be discarded in the face of new evidence or changed conditions. This is, in one sense, a difficult mental task and, in a more profound moral sense, it represents a serious personal decision to be introspective, to be exposed always to the stinging glare of change, to be willing always to reconstruct our social views. Who likes to understand himself, or be without his personal Bible, be it that of Marx, Freud, Darwin, or Christ? Radicalism of style asks us to go beyond the State Department lies about the U-2, or the simplistic view that Khrushchev dropped the fifty-megaton bomb for purposes of pure terror, or that democratic socialism solves all the problems of individual development. In its harshest condensation, radicalism of style demands that we oppose delusions and be free. It demands that we change our life.

All this circumlocution is not intended to suggest that simple moral statements or concerns are meaningless. On the contrary, I think most persons who lean to the left politically are moved by quite important feelings of solidarity for the impoverished, the oppressed, the debased, and all of suffering mankind; by a commitment to the general ideals of Western humanism, particularly, the freedoms of speech, thought, and association;

by a distrust of selfish, competitive individualism operating in the economic sphere (or any other); by a belief in cooperation and collective planning balanced against the necessity for individual consent; and so on. These, however enthralling, are not worthy of our allegiance as abstraction. It is their infusion into practical life which gives them true content and determines the extent to which we shall value them. The things we are for or against are quite simple at the level of abstraction; it is in the test of their practical meaning that we must make our judgment—not between good and evil, but the more difficult distinction between better or best, or the hardest choice of all, that of the necessary evil. Radicalism, it seems to me, does not exclude morality; it invites and is given spirit by the quality of *reflective commitment,* the combining of our passion and our critical talents into a provisional position. To remove an idea from the plane of abstraction, it should be added, means to inject its meaning into our total life—to send telegrams of support to Southern students means to *live one's solidarity with them,* not to belie glorious phrases by private selfishness or tolerance of local discrimination.

Radical program is simply the radical style as it attempts to change the practical life. As with style, a radical program is not one that rests before it has plumbed to the basis of the problem it confronts. We should not be satisfied with going by "back door" methods (however "realistic") to persuade President Kennedy to wire a telegram of encouragement to a jailed Martin Luther King. That is problem-mitigating, not problem-solving. That is useful, preventive, and even opinion-changing, but not radical for it in no sense identifies and deals with the underlying political-economic-historic-psychological bases of the problem.

All this is not to say we should diminish our urgency or reduce our passions—we should not. This is not to say we should go off in corners to study "both sides of the issue"—we should, but not exclusively. This is simply to say that the student movement which has rejected so many institutions and instruments of social change—the Southern courtrooms, by and large the Democratic Party, the military, often the Congress—has invented no substitute save a noble morality and in some cases a commitment to non-violence that will dissipate soon if not secured in new social structures. An essential phase of radicalism is the decision to disengage oneself entirely from the system being confronted (segregation for example) so that the structure sustained by our former attitudes can no longer endure. Another essential, however, is that we visualize and then build structures to counter those which we oppose. This extends from the concrete formation of a national student organization to the conceptual—for the time being—formation of a different society.

Instead of this we find ourselves making the understandably frequent mistake, for example, of confusing target with goal. This is true of the campaign to abolish the House Committee on Un-American Activities. HUAC is surely no more than a target, but our passions have made its abolition, in fact, a goal. The danger here is that in our failure to formulate a comprehensive personal vision of a social goal beyond the abolition of HUAC, abolition itself may not carry with it a scourging effect on the society. The deeply rooted strands of nationalism, fascism, and racism will be newly woven in new HUAC's by our fearful public. Similarly, the lunch counter sit-in movement has been forced to develop a broader, more complex vision of the future—interrelating targets with goals—to remain successful.

Thus far we have been quick to know what we oppose: racism, militarism, nationalism, oppression of mind and spirit, unrestrained capitalism, provincialism of various kinds, and the bombs. It has been an almost instinctive opposition. We have been hurt by what exists, and we have responded in outrage and compassion. However, the times are too threatening for us to respond simply as comforters of the oppressed. Keeping sentiments as our base, we must move ahead concertedly with our goal—the changing of society, not the assuaging of its continuous ills. That means politics as well as sentimentality. That means writers and theoreticians as well as organizers and picketers. That means drawing on what remains of the adult labor, academic and political communities, not just revolting in despair against them and the world they have designed for us. Contrary to what our passions demand, our struggle will not be brief and cataclysmic—unless terminated in the roaring climax of nuclear war. Our gains will be modest, not sensational. It will be slow and exhaustingly complex, lasting at the very least for our lifetimes. For many of us it will not and cannot be a college fling, a costless, painless tugging at our liberal sentimentality. It will be longer, and the cost great.

What is desperately needed, I think, is the person of vision and clarity, who sees both the model society and the pitfalls that precede its attainment, and who will not destroy his vision for short-run gains but, instead, hold it out for all to see as the furthest dream and perimeter of human possibility. I am beset by doubt at this point; so, perhaps, are we all. We doubt our ability to effect change, we doubt our ability to understand enough, we doubt the validity of time-honored liberal notions, we doubt the right and wrong of it. I do not recommend that we banish doubt and rush forth under the banal slogan "where there is a will there is a way," but I would suggest that it is possible and necessary to begin to think and act—provisionally yet strongly—in the midst of our doubts. We must begin to see doubt, not as a reason for inaction—that way leads to intellectual sterility. We must see it as a reminder that infallibility is not the property of any single man and, moreover, that compassion for enemies is not simply a heroic show, but a manifestation of our deepest moral anxiety.

3

SNCC in Action
Dignity for the
Enslaved and for Us All

Fall 1961

When the student civil rights movement began, I traveled to the South to write about the Student Nonviolent Coordinating Committee's (SNCC) second region-wide meeting, in October 1960. It was there I fell in love with the movement and with Sandra Cason, a poetic graduate student from Austin, Texas. I asked to be the SDS southern field secretary, married Casey and moved to Atlanta in 1961. The marriage sadly collapsed in two years, partly because I was not ready at that age (few relationships lasted through those liberating days). She remained a major figure in both SNCC and in the birth of the women's movement in 1964; today she lives with her husband and children in New Mexico.

My mission for SDS was to witness the sit-in movement and write about it for a growing audience of Northern students, which I did through the Michigan Daily, *the* Progressive *and, believe it or not,* Mademoiselle *magazine.*

In September 1961, I traveled clandestinely to rural Mississippi with my close friend Paul Potter, an SDS leader who was then vice president of the National Student Association. Paul and I rented a car in Jackson, and drove two hours to tiny McComb, where we had to transfer cars and hide on backseats before meeting with Bob Moses, Charles McDew, Bob Zellner and a few others in a basement with blankets draped across all the windows. We also met openly with the local sheriff and newspaper editor, who railed against the outside agitators suddenly assaulting their way of life. The sheriff knew who we were and whom we had visited the night before.

Later that day, Paul and I drove alongside about 100 high school students marching in protest against segregated conditions. They were singing, holding signs, acting in an orderly manner, when suddenly all hell broke loose. Our car doors were ripped open and we were dragged to the ground, punched and kicked by a local man, an electrician named Carl Hayes. After it ended, with no police in sight, a photographer whispered to me that we should leave our motel to avoid being taken that night. The police then arrived, took us through a screaming mob at City Hall, and brought us face to face with a representative of the state's Sovereignty Commission, a secretive alliance whose mission was to preserve the racist state. He told us we had a choice, be jailed for "vagrancy" or immediately leave the state. We left. We flew to Atlanta, where we were interviewed by suspicious FBI agents, and then traveled to Washington for meetings with the Justice Department. I was shocked when the respected Deputy Attorney General Burke Marshall encouraged me to ask the SNCC organizers to leave Mississippi before they were killed. The lesson that registered was that constitutional protections did not extend to where they were most needed. Marshall later changed his mind, but I had formed an impression.

◆　　◆　　◆

A LITTLE OVER TWO WEEKS after the beating of John Hardy, Mississippi terrorism reached a peak in the killing of a 52-year-old Negro man, Herbert Lee. (The following information has been obtained from several private sources.) Lee was a member of the Amite National Association for the Advancement of Colored People (NAACP). When SNCC came to Mississippi, Lee became an active, dedicated worker, assisting Bob Moses in meeting people and arranging get-togethers. He lived on a farm just outside of Liberty, near the Louisiana line. On the morning of September 25, he arose early, prepared to go to Liberty to gin cotton. As Lee drove his truck into Liberty, he was followed by Mississippi State Representative Eugene Hurst. Hurst and Lee had known each other for quite some time. Lee's brother, Frank, had apparently once purchased some of Hurst's land in Louisiana. In 1956 Hurst helped Lee get a cut in the cost of some land which Lee wanted to purchase. (The reduction was from $9,000 to $7,000.) Lee in turn promised Hurst a "tip" of some $500 upon completion of Lee's payments on his land. On September 25, Lee had paid more than $6,500 on the land and was carrying a total of $287 in his pocket.

There had reportedly been a recent economic crackdown in the whole area. The white community was circulating a list of names of those Negroes seriously involved in the voter registration or NAACP "movements." Many were being cut off from basic commodities. Mr. Steptoe, the NAACP head in Amite, received a letter, for instance, telling him to pay off his debts. . . . Such was the situation that morning in Liberty, Mississippi. When Lee stopped his truck this morning, Hurst, who is the father-in-law of Billy Jack Caston, did the same. Hurst got out of his truck, and approached Lee, carrying a .38 in his hand. Lee remained in the cab of his truck. An argument ensued, partly about debts owed, partly about the .38, and partly about a tire tool Lee was alleged to be holding in the cab. Apparently the two challenged each other to put down their respective weapons. Hurst put his gun inside his belt. Lee edged across the seat, attempting to get out on the far side of the truck, which caused Hurst to run around the front of the truck. There Hurst is alleged to have said, "You didn't use the tire tool when you had it, and you're not going to use it now." Two motions followed, both by Hurst. The second motion was a downward thrust of the arm, a shot, and Lee was on his stomach with a .38 bullet in his brain. Hurst left the scene. Lee was left on the ground fully two hours before he was taken to the Negro coroner in McComb. A tire tool was near his body. A coroner's jury, after hearing whites but no Negro witnesses, ruled that the killing was in self-defense, and thereby a justifiable homicide. Hurst was never booked, charged, or tried.

In a county such as Amite, its caste system uninfluenced by the movement of ideas in the rest of the United States and the world, the tradition identified in 1937 by John Dollard (Caste and Class in a Southern Town) is still relevant: "One of the best ways for a politician to get notoriety was to kill a Negro; such an act would speed him on the way to getting office and reveal that his sentiments on the race question were sound." When appraising the effect of the Lee killing, it is well to bear in mind that it happened at a moment when the Negro's hope of gaining the vote was rising once again, that it was executed with apparently the full support of the white caste's law enforcement agency, legal system, and public opinion, that the privileged assailant is himself a symbol of the enthroned political power which the Negro vote would presumably seek to undercut, and that he is a symbol connected with a historic pattern of killing for political reputation. All of these factors influence the effect of the slaying regardless of whether or not Hurst actually killed Lee deliberately for his part in voter registration.

A week later a little scrawled but mimeographed sign went out:

Bulletin
Mass Meeting for Voter Registration
Oct. 2nd, Tuesday
Guest Speaker
Rev. Charles Jones
From Charlotte, N.C.
Masonic Hall 630 Warren
7:30
Collection will be taken for the
wife and ten children of
Mr. Herbert Lee.

The Pike County Non-Violent Movement, perhaps the youngest and most challenged in the South, was resuming operation. Five sit-inners had returned to jail. On October 3, the mass meeting was held. Parents attended and spoke. People stressed that the corrupt governments which permitted Lee's death could only be eliminated if Negroes registered. A total of $81 was collected for Lee's wife and ten children. An unarticulated decision was made: if Brenda Travis and Ike Lewis were not readmitted to Burgland High School, the students would protest. On the next day, the Negro high school principal, Commodore Dewey Higgins, ruled that the two would not be readmitted to Burgland High School. For personal reasons, Lewis, 20 years old, had decided not to return to school. Brenda, however, had demanded entrance.

THE STUDENT WALKOUT

Chaos . . . during the previous day Martin Luther King sent an open telegram to President Kennedy protesting a "reign of terror" in McComb, and calling the Executive's attention to recent beatings. Several new SNCC people, returning from a successful national trip in quest of funds for bond for the sit-inners, had arrived in McComb on the morning of the 4th. Among those arriving was Robert Zellner, a white man from Alabama who, as a white, was even more susceptible to mob hostility than a Negro, though in no sense could the Negro SNCC representatives feel secure.

The students—remember, one hundred under eighteen years of age—spent the midday preparing signs, and at about 2:30 p.m., they started to march downtown. Never before in McComb—never before in an area so rural, so violent—never before *anywhere in the South* with students so very young. One of them, thirteen years old, has been charged with "assault with intent to kill" because she ran over the foot of a white woman in a supermarket with a push-cart, and, subsequently, the two slapped each other. That is simply an example. The others, while a little older, suffer the same system and are moved by the same courage. And so they went downtown—with 119 in all, including nineteen students over age eighteen—and Bob Moses, Charles McDew and Robert Zellner. They walked through the Negro neighborhoods where families watched from the windows and steps and yards, through the downtown business district, down to the edge of McComb, and back up to City Hall. There the march halted. Elmer Haynes, one of the original McComb sit-inners, began to pray on the steps. Three times the police asked him to move on. He refused and was arrested. Then it was Lewis, Robert Talbert, and 16-year-old Brenda, in order, all arrested—Brenda violating juvenile parole. Each individual in the march stood quietly, waiting to be arrested. Moments before, a white man had tried to run over them with his automobile; now there were whites on foot, yelling, cursing. And each of the 114 left was quietly standing. Too much time was being taken up, so the police blew their whistles and pronounced everyone under arrest.

The whole march started up the stairs, on its way to be booked. As they did, a local white citizen reached out for Zellner and began to beat him. Hurting Zellner with the first punch, the man then grabbed him around the neck and began choking him and gouging his eyes. Then Bob Moses and Charles McDew were there, one holding the white's wrists, one clasping Zellner in protection. Moses and McDew were struck and dragged into the station by police, who then pulled in Zellner. The first statement inside the police chief's office, according to Zellner, was, "Ought to leave you out there." Everyone was arrested and placed in jail. The nineteen over eighteen years of age were arraigned on October 5, after a night in Pike County Jail. Before Judge Robert W. Brumfield of McComb's Police Court, they pled innocent to charges of disturbing the peace; bond was $100 each. Nine also pled innocent to the charge of contributing to delinquency of minors; bond was $200 each. Trial was set for 9:00 a.m., October 23.

The nine charged on both counts were:

Curtis E. Hayes	Hollis Watkins	Donald Gadson
Isaac Lewis	Robert Moses	(John) Robert Zellner
Stephen Ashley	Charles McDew	Robert Talbert

The high school students, meanwhile, refused to compromise their stand, as announced in the statement which they distributed:

> We the Negro youth of Pike County, feel that Brenda Travis and Ike Lewis should not be barred from acquiring an education for protesting an injustice. We feel that as members of Burgland High School, they have fought this battle for us. To prove that we appreciate their having done this, we will suffer any punishment they have to take with them.
>
> In the schools we are taught democracy, but the rights offered by democracy have been denied us by our oppressors; we have not had a balanced school system; we have not had an opportunity to participate in any of the branches of our local, state, and federal government; however, we are children of God who makes our fellowmen to love rather than hate, to build rather than tear down, to bind our nation with love and justice without regard to race, color, or creed.

Why only 100 students in a school of 600? A few of the others perhaps were opposed to change in the community. Many more, however, were clearly sympathetic with the revolt but either afraid or in conflict with parents, or tied economically to the white system.

And as for those who went to jail? "You get kind of hard," said McDew, "after two or three days without eating, lying on the floor with the window busted out. It is cold in McComb at night." Beyond the question of physical health hazards, the crucial problem was the threats on the lives of McDew, Moses and Zellner. By this time, everyone in the city knew them; they'd been photographed, facial close-ups appearing in the *Enterprise-Journal,* and now, in jail over the night, not far from the area where Charles Mack Parker was emasculated and lynched two years ago, they sat in their cells, confronted for four hours by a steady run of staring, muttering white visitors. "Do you believe in Jesus Christ?" was the question of a hostile local minister. "Do you believe that God is love?" was the question in return. "You don't believe in Jesus Christ, do you, you son-of-a-bitch; you'll go to hell and I'm going to see you get there soon." Four hours of threats and hatred.

The night passed, without death. The SNCC members were released on bond, and the next day the students solidified their commitment.

Brenda Travis, having broken parole by committing an offense within thirty days of her last one, is sentenced to one year in Colored Girls Industrial School, a detention home near Oakley, Mississippi. Until she is readmitted, the students claim, they will not reenter high school.

First they were told to return to school—after signing the following affadavit:

> This is to advise that I am aware of the regulation of the McComb School Board concerning student walkouts in the McComb school system. This is to further advise that I have participated in such a walkout and am now asking for re-admission on probation. I also acknowledge that should I participate in a second school walkout that I shall be automatically expelled for the next school year.

They refused. They were a little scared; they felt odd without any history of Negro protest with which to identify because the sovereign state of their birth does not tell history honestly. They were almost all without planned futures. They were even giggling like kids that age do in Northern suburbs, but they refused—again and again.

On October 12, Moses and McDew taught them classes in their new "non-violent high school," the Negro Masonic Temple. The next week SNCC people taught other subjects: history, for example, which the Mississippi school system presents in a thick book with a Confederate flag on one cover and the capitol of Mississippi on the other, and which tells of the "War of Northern Aggression," the positive aspects of slavery, and the heroism of the Ku Klux Klan in the South's series of crises.

The high school administration has declared that any student who has not signed the affadavit is thereby expelled for the rest of the year. Unless I miss my guess, most will not sign those slips. They'll take classes from SNCC or go to school elsewhere, and perhaps they'll petition the white school for admittance, and they'll take it to the courts, and someday they will win.

Perhaps this situation cannot be adequately conveyed. Does it become more real in noting that a white man connected with the broadcasting system there sees the solution to the problem in "throwing those little niggers in one bag, castrating them, and dropping the bag in the river?" Does it become more real in visualizing Herbert Lee lying on his face for two hours? Does it become real in recognizing that those Negroes are down there, digging in, and in more danger than nearly any student in this American generation has faced? What does it take? When do we begin to see it all not as remote but as breathing urgency into our beings and meaning into our ideals? James Baldwin said last year that these kids are the only really free people in the country; perhaps he is right. They have decided not only to protest but to seek social transformation as well, and that is revolution. They have decided it is time right now—not in a minute, not after this one more committee meets, not after we have the legal defense and the court costs promised—to give blood and body if necessary for social justice, for freedom, for the common life, and for the creation of dignity for the enslaved, and thereby for us all.

4

Excerpts from the Port Huron Statement of the Students for a Democratic Society

June 1962

Much has been said of this founding document, named after the United Auto Workers camp on the shores of Lake Huron and published in June 1962. The story of the sixty-some twentysomethings who collectively reviewed, revised and adopted the document can be found in my books Reunion *(1988),* Rebel *(2000), and* The Port Huron Statement *(2005). Also see Kirkpatrick Sale's* SDS.

The five-day Port Huron experience was deeply inspirational, a sense that is still conveyed by the document. The statement we wrote was originally conceived as a recruiting tool for SDS but later became widely viewed as a defining political document of the sixties. Some of our elder leftist sponsors reviled the document, mainly on the grounds that its criticism of the Cold War implied a rejection of their fierce anticommunism, which it did. For our generation, the Cold War—especially the nuclear arms race—was an apocalyptic framework that controlled our past, present and future. We were threatened with nuclear war twice in the early 1960s, over Berlin and Cuba. While we stated our democratic opposition to the Soviet bloc, we wanted both sides to turn toward peace, a view which came to be expressed in public by President John Kennedy only weeks before his death.

The core purpose of the Port Huron Statement *was to inspire people to break out of apathy and to join the growing civil rights and student movements in a campaign to shift national priorities from the Cold War to issues of democracy at home and around the world, especially among the so-called Third World bloc of nations just liberating themselves from colonialism. The* Port Huron Statement *espouses "participatory democracy," a concept inherited from John Dewey through a University of Michigan professor of mine, Arnold Kaufman. This notion gives coherence to the experience of the new movements which are excluded from "representative" democracy. SDS favored building social movements whose political impact would be the realignment of the Democratic Party into a more progressive party without its white segregationist wing.*

The PHS *was radical in the sense that we wanted to extend democratic participation and regulation to the corporate economy and challenge the military-industrial powers. It was disturbing to the status quo of the Democratic Party at the time. It bridged the divides between those who were more movement-oriented and those ultimately seeking political solutions.*

But the PHS *was also realistic in the sense that we were grounded in actual movements that were shaking the status quo every day, and in its confidence that we could evolve from the status of a prophetic minority to build a new, progressive governing coalition not seen since the New Deal.*

It may have happened. But JFK was murdered, then Lyndon Johnson invaded Vietnam after pledging not to. The promise of Port Huron became our road not taken. Within five years, SDS revolutionaries condemned the PHS *as "reformist," which it was. Yet, fifty years later, the* Port Huron Statement *is the most-cited and widely-studied document of the New Left. Sometimes I believe this is due to a certain nostalgia for what might have been. But the doctrine of participatory democracy is openly embraced by millions of engaged people as well, from bloggers working hard through their Web sites to realign the Democratic Party and end the war, to democracy movements around the world, whether students in China or indigenous communities in Latin America.*

◆   ◆   ◆

INTRODUCTORY NOTE

This document represents the results of several months of writing and discussion among the membership, a draft paper, and revision by the Students for a Democratic Society national convention meeting in Michigan, June 11–15, 1962. It is represented as a document with which

SDS officially identifies, but also as a living document open to change with our times and experiences. It is a beginning: in our own debate and education, in our dialogue with society.

INTRODUCTION: AGENDA FOR A GENERATION

We are people of this generation, bred in at least modest comfort, housed now in universities, looking uncomfortably to the world we inherit.

When we were kids the United States was the wealthiest and strongest country in the world: the only one with the atom bomb, the least scarred by modern war, an initiator of the United Nations that we thought would distribute Western influence throughout the world. Freedom and equality for each individual, government of, by, and for the people—these American values we found good, principles by which we could live as men. Many of us began maturing in complacency.

As we grew, however, our comfort was penetrated by events too troubling to dismiss. First, the permeating and victimizing fact of human degradation, symbolized by the Southern struggle against racial bigotry, compelled most of us from silence to activism. Second, the enclosing fact of the Cold War, symbolized by the presence of the Bomb, brought awareness that we ourselves, and our friends, and millions of abstract "others" we knew more directly because of our common peril, might die at any time. We might deliberately ignore, or avoid, or fail to feel all other human problems, but not these two, for these were too immediate and crushing in their impact, too challenging in the demand that we as individuals take the responsibility for encounter and resolution.

While these and other problems either directly oppressed us or rankled our consciences and became our own subjective concerns, we began to see complicated and disturbing paradoxes in our surrounding America. The declaration "all men are created equal . . ." rang hollow before the facts of Negro life in the South and the big cities of the North. The proclaimed peaceful intentions of the United States contradicted its economic and military investments in the Cold War status quo.

We witnessed, and continue to witness, other paradoxes. With nuclear energy whole cities can easily be powered, yet the dominant nation-states seem more likely to unleash destruction greater than that incurred in all wars of human history. Although our own technology is destroying old and creating new forms of social organization, men still tolerate meaningless work and idleness. While two-thirds of mankind suffers undernourishment, our own upper classes revel amidst superfluous abundance. Although world population is expected to double in forty years, the nations still tolerate anarchy as a major principle of international conduct and uncontrolled exploitation governs the sapping of the earth's physical resources. Although mankind desperately needs revolutionary leadership, America rests in national stalemate, its goals ambiguous and tradition-bound instead of informed and clear, its democratic system apathetic and manipulated rather than "of, by, and for the people."

Not only did tarnish appear on our image of American virtue, not only did disillusion occur when the hypocrisy of American ideals was discovered, but we began to sense that what we had originally seen as the American Golden Age was actually the decline of an era. The worldwide outbreak of revolution against colonialism and imperialism, the entrenchment of totalitarian states, the menace of war, overpopulation, international disorder, supertechnology—these trends were testing the tenacity of our own commitment to democracy and freedom and our abilities to visualize their application to a world in upheaval.

Our work is guided by the sense that we may be the last generation in the experiment with living. But we are a minority—the vast majority of our people regard the temporary equilibriums of our society and world as eternally functional parts. In this is perhaps the outstanding paradox: we ourselves are imbued with urgency, yet the message of our society is that there is no viable alternative to the present. Beneath the reassuring tones of the politicians, beneath the common opinion that America will "muddle through," beneath the stagnation of those who have closed their minds to the future, is the pervading feeling that there simply are no alternatives, that our times have witnessed the exhaustion not only of Utopias, but of any new departures as well. Feeling the press of complexity upon the emptiness of life, people are fearful of the thought that at any moment things might be thrust out of control. They fear change itself, since change might smash whatever invisible framework seems to hold back chaos for them now. For most Americans, all crusades are suspect, threatening. The fact that each individual sees apathy in his fellows perpetuates the common reluctance to organize for change. The dominant institutions are complex enough to blunt the minds of their potential critics, and entrenched enough to swiftly dissipate or entirely repel the energies of protest and reform, thus limiting human expectancies. Then, too, we are a materially improved society, and by our own improvements we seem to have weakened the case for further change.

Some would have us believe that Americans feel contentment amidst prosperity—but might it not better be called a glaze above deeply felt anxieties about their role in the new world? And if these anxieties produce a developed indifference to human affairs, do they not as well produce a yearning to believe there is an alternative to the present, that something can be done to change circumstances in the school, the workplaces, the bureaucracies, the government? It is to this latter yearning, at once the spark and engine of change, that we direct our present appeal. The search for truly democratic alternatives to the present, and a commitment to social experimentation with them, is a worthy and fulfilling human enterprise, one which moves us and, we hope, others today. On such a basis do we offer this document of our convictions and analysis: as an effort in understanding and changing the conditions of humanity in the late twentieth century, an effort rooted in the ancient, still unfulfilled conception of man attaining determining influence over his circumstances of life.

VALUES

Making values explicit—an initial task in establishing alternatives—is an activity that has been devalued and corrupted. The conventional moral terms of the age, the politician moralities—"free world," "people's democracies"—reflect realities poorly, if at all, and seem to function more as ruling myths than as descriptive principles. But neither has our experience in the universities brought us moral enlightenment. Our professors and administrators sacrifice controversy to public relations; their curriculums change more slowly than the living events of the world; their skills and silence are purchased by investors in the arms race; passion is called unscholastic. The questions we might want raised—what is really important? can we live in a different and better way? if we wanted to change society, how would we do it?—are not thought to be questions of a "fruitful, empirical nature," and thus are brushed aside.

Unlike youth in other countries we are used to moral leadership being exercised and moral dimensions being clarified by our elders. But today, for us, not even the liberal and socialist preachments of the past seem adequate to the forms of the present. Consider the old slogans: Capitalism Cannot Reform Itself, United Front Against Fascism, General Strike, All Out on May Day. Or, more recently, No Cooperation with Commies and Fellow Travelers, Ideologies Are Exhausted, Bipartisanship, No Utopias. These are incomplete, and there are few new prophets. It has been said that our liberal and socialist predecessors were plagued by vision without program, while our own generation is plagued by program without vision. All around us there is astute grasp of method, technique—the committee, the ad hoc group, the lobbyist, the hard and soft sell, the make, the projected image—but, if pressed critically, such expertise is incompetent to explain its implicit ideals. It is highly fashionable to identify oneself by old categories, or by naming a respected political figure, or by explaining "how we would vote" on various issues.

Theoretic chaos has replaced the idealistic thinking of old—and, unable to reconstitute theoretic order, men have condemned idealism itself. Doubt has replaced hopefulness—and men act out a defeatism that is labeled realistic. The decline of utopia and hope is in fact one of the defining features of social life today. The reasons are various: the dreams of the older left were perverted by Stalinism and never recreated; the congressional stalemate makes men narrow their view of the possible; the specialization of human activity leaves little room for sweeping thought; the horrors of the twentieth century, symbolized in the gas-ovens and concentration camps and atom bombs, have blasted hopefulness. To be idealistic is to be considered apocalyptic, deluded. To have no serious aspirations, on the contrary, is to be "toughminded."

In suggesting social goals and values, therefore, we are aware of entering a sphere of some disrepute. Perhaps matured by the past, we have no sure formulas, no closed theories—but that does not mean values are beyond discussion and tentative determination. A first task of any social movement is to convenience people that the search for orienting theories and the creation of human values is complex but worthwhile. We are aware that to avoid platitudes we must analyze the concrete conditions of social order. But to direct such an analysis we must use the guideposts of basic principles. Our own social values involve conceptions of human beings, human relationships, and social systems.

We regard *men* as infinitely precious and possessed of unfulfilled capacities for reason, freedom, and love. In affirming these principles we are aware of countering perhaps the dominant conceptions of man in the twentieth century: that he is a thing to be manipulated, and that he is inherently incapable of directing his own affairs. We oppose the depersonalization that reduces human beings to the status of things—if anything, the brutalities of the twentieth century teach that means and ends are intimately related, that vague appeals to "posterity" cannot justify the mutilations of the present. We oppose, too, the doctrine of human incompetence because it rests essentially on the modern fact that men have been "competently" manipulated into incompetence—we see little reason why men cannot meet with increasing skill the complexities and responsibilities of their situation, if society is organized not for minority, but for majority, participation in decision-making.

Men have unrealized potential for self-cultivation, self-direction, self-understanding, and creativity. It is this potential that we regard as crucial and to which we appeal, not to the human potentiality for violence, unreason, and submission to authority. The goal of man and society should be human independence: a concern not with image of popularity but with finding a meaning in life that is personally authentic: a quality of mind not compulsively driven by a sense of powerlessness, nor one which unthinkingly adopts status values, nor one which represses all threats to its habits, but one which has full, spontaneous access to present and past experiences, one which easily unites the fragmented parts of personal history, one which openly faces problems which are troubling and unresolved; one with an intuitive awareness of possibilities, an active sense of curiosity, an ability and willingness to learn.

This kind of independence does not mean egoistic individualism—the object is not to have one's way so much as it is to have a way that is one's own. Nor do we deify man—we merely have faith in his potential.

Human relationships should involve fraternity and honesty. Human interdependence is contemporary fact; human brotherhood must be willed, however, as a condition of future survival and as the most appropriate form of social relations. Personal links between man and man are needed, especially to go beyond the partial and fragmentary bonds of function that bind men only as worker to worker, employer to employee, teacher to student, American to Russian.

Loneliness, estrangement, isolation describe the vast distance between man and man today. These dominant tendencies cannot be overcome by better personnel management, nor by improved gadgets, but only when a love of man overcomes the idolatrous worship of things by man. As the individualism we affirm is not egoism, the selflessness we affirm is not self-elimination. On the contrary, we believe in generosity of a kind that imprints one's unique individual qualities in the relation to other men, and to all human activity. Further, to dislike isolation is not to favor the abolition of privacy; the latter differs from isolation in that it occurs or is abolished according to individual will.

We would replace power rooted in possession, privilege, or circumstance by power and uniqueness rooted in love, reflectiveness, reason, and creativity.

As a social system we seek the establishment of a democracy of individual participation, governed by two central aims: that the individual share in those social decisions determining the quality and direction of his life; that society be organized to encourage independence in men and provide the media for their common participation.

In a participatory democracy, the political life would be based in several root principles:

➤ that decision-making of basic social consequence be carried on by public groupings;

➤ that politics be seen positively, as the art of collectively creating an acceptable pattern of social relations;

➤ that politics has the function of bringing people out of isolation and into community, thus being a necessary, though not sufficient, means of finding meaning in personal life;

➤ that the political order should serve to clarify problems in a way instrumental to their solution; it should provide outlets for the expression of personal grievance and aspiration; opposing views should be organized so as to illuminate choices and facilitate the attainment of goals; channels should be commonly available, to relate men to knowledge and to power so that private problems—from bad recreation facilities to personal alienation—are formulated as general issues.

The economic sphere would have as its basis the principles:

➤ that work should involve incentives worthier than money or survival. It should be educative, not stultifying; creative, not mechanical; self-directed, not manipulated, encouraging independence, a respect for others, a sense of dignity and a willingness to accept social responsibility, since it is this experience that has crucial influence on habits, perceptions and individual ethics;

➤ that the economic experience is so personally decisive that the individual must share in its full determination;

➤ that the economy itself is of such social importance that its major resources and means of production should be open to democratic participation and subject to democratic social regulation.

Like the political and economic ones, major social institutions—cultural, education, rehabilitative, and others—should be generally organized with the well-being and dignity of man as the essential measure of success.

7896543

In social change or interchange, we find violence to be abhorrent because it requires generally the transformation of the target, be it a human being or a community of people, into a depersonalized object of hate. It is imperative that the means of violence be abolished and the institutions—local, national, international—that encourage nonviolence as a condition of conflict be developed.

These are our central values, in skeletal form. It remains vital to understand their denial or attainment in the context of the modern world.

THE STUDENTS

In the last few years, thousands of American students demonstrated that they at least felt the urgency of the times. They moved actively and directly against racial injustices, the threat of war, violations of individual rights of conscience and, less frequently, against economic manipulation. They succeeded in restoring a small measure of controversy to the campuses after the stillness of the McCarthy period. They succeeded, too, in gaining some concessions from the people and institutions they opposed, especially in the fight against racial bigotry.

The significance of these scattered movements lies not in their success or failure in gaining objectives—at least not yet. Nor does the significance lie in the intellectual "competence" or "maturity" of the students involved—as some pedantic elders allege. The significance is in the fact the students are breaking the crust of apathy and overcoming the inner alienation that remain the defining characteristics of American college life.

If student movements for change are rarities still on the campus scene, what is commonplace there? The real campus, the familiar campus, is a place of private people, engaged in their notorious "inner emigration." It is a place of commitment to business-as-usual, getting ahead, playing it cool. It is a place of mass affirmation of the Twist, but mass reluctance toward the controversial public stance. Rules are accepted as "inevitable," bureaucracy as "just circumstances," irrelevance as "scholarship," selflessness as "martyrdom," politics as "just another way to make people, and an unprofitable one, too."

Almost no students value activity as citizens. Passive in public, they are hardly more idealistic in arranging their private lives: Gallup concludes they will settle for "low success, and won't risk high failure." There is not much willingness to take risks (not even in business), no setting of dangerous goals, no real conception of personal identity except one manufactured in the image of others, no real urge for personal fulfillment except to be almost as successful as the very successful people. Attention is being paid to social status (the quality of shirt collars, meeting people, getting wives or husbands, making solid contacts for later on); much too, is paid to academic status (grades, honors, the med school rat race). But neglected generally is real intellectual status, the personal cultivation of the mind.

"Students don't even give a damn about the apathy," one has said. Apathy toward apathy begets a privately constructed universe, a place of systematic study schedules, two nights each week for beer, a girl or two, and early marriage; a framework infused with personality, warmth, and under control, no matter how unsatisfying otherwise.

Under these conditions university life loses all relevance to some. Four hundred thousand of our classmates leave college every year.

But apathy is not simply an attitude; it is a product of social institutions, and of the structure and organization of higher education itself.

The extracurricular life is ordered according to *in loco parentis* theory, which ratifies the Administration as the moral guardian of the young.

The accompanying "let's pretend" theory of student extracurricular affairs validates student government as a training center for those who want to spend their lives in political pretense, and discourages initiative from more articulate, honest, and sensitive students. The bounds and style of controversy are delimited before controversy begins. The university "prepares" the student for "citizenship" through perpetual rehearsals and, usually, through emasculation of what creative spirit there is in the individual.

The academic life contains reinforcing counterparts to the way in which extracurricular life is organized. The academic world is founded in a teacher-student relation analogous to the parent-child relation which characterizes *in loco parentis*. Further, academia includes a radical separation of student from the material of study. That which is studied, the social reality, is "objectified" to sterility, dividing the student from life—just as he is restrained in active involvement by the deans controlling student government. The specialization of function and knowledge, admittedly necessary to our complex technological and social structure, has produced an exaggerated compartmentalization of study and understanding. This has contributed to an overly parochial view, by faculty, of the role of its research and scholarship; a discontinuous and truncated understanding, by students, of the surrounding social order; a loss of personal attachment, by nearly all, to the worth of study as a humanistic enterprise.

There is, finally, the cumbersome academic bureaucracy extending throughout the academic as well as extracurricular structures, contributing to the sense of outer complexity and inner powerlessness that transforms so many students from honest searching to ratification of convention and, worse, to a numbness to present and future catastrophes. The size and financing systems of the university enhance the permanent trusteeship of the administrative bureaucracy, their power leading to a shift within the university toward the value standards of business and the administrative mentality. Huge foundations and other private financial interests shape under-financed colleges and universities, not only making them more commercial, but less disposed to diagnose society critically, less open to dissent. Many social and physical scientists, neglecting the liberating heritage of higher learning, develop "human relations" or "morale-producing" techniques for the corporate economy, while others exercise their intellectual skills to accelerate the arms race.

Tragically, the university could serve as a significant source of social criticism and an initiator of new modes and molders of attitudes. But the actual intellectual effect of the college experience is hardly distinguishable from that of any other communications channel—say, a television set—passing on the stock truths of the day. Students leave college somewhat more "tolerant" than when they arrived, but basically unchallenged in their values and political orientations. With administrators ordering the institutions, and faculty the curriculum, the student learns by his isolation to accept elite rule within the university, which prepares him to accept later forms of minority control. The real function of the educational system—as opposed to its more rhetorical function of "searching for truth"—is to impart the key information and styles that will help the student get by, modestly but comfortably, in the big society beyond.

THE SOCIETY BEYOND

Look beyond the campus, to America itself. That student life is more intellectual, and perhaps more comfortable, does not obscure the fact that the fundamental qualities of life on the campus reflect the habits of society at large. The fraternity president is seen at the junior manager levels; the sorority queen has gone to Grosse Pointe; the serious poet burns for a place, any place, or work; the once-serious and never-serious poets work at the advertising agencies. The desperation of people threatened by forces about which they know little and of which they can say less; the cheerful emptiness of people "giving up" all hope of changing things; the faceless ones polled by Gallup who listed "international affairs" fourteenth on their list of "problems" but who also expected thermonuclear war in the next few years: in these and other forms, Americans are in withdrawal from public life, from any collective effort at directing their own affairs.

Some regard these national doldrums as a sign of healthy approval of the established order—but is it approval by consent or manipulated acquiescence? Others declare that the people are withdrawn because compelling issues are fast disappearing—perhaps there are fewer breadlines in America, but is Jim Crow gone, is there enough work and work more fulfilling, is world war a diminishing threat, and what of the revolutionary new peoples? Still others think the national quietude is a necessary consequence of the need for elites to resolve complex and specialized problems of modern industrial society—but, then, why should business elites help decide foreign policy, and who controls the elites anyway, and are they solving mankind's problems? Others, finally, shrug knowingly and announce that full democracy never worked anywhere in the past—but why lump qualitatively different civilizations together, and how can a social order work well if its best thinkers are skeptics, and is man really doomed forever to the domination of today?

There are no convincing apologies for the contemporary malaise. While the world tumbles toward the final war, while men in other nations are trying desperately to alter events, while the very future qua future is uncertain—America is without community, impulse, without the inner momentum necessary for an age when societies cannot successfully perpetuate themselves by their military weapons, when democracy must be viable because of its quality of life, not its quantity of rockets.

The apathy here is, first *subjective*—the felt powerlessness of ordinary people, the resignation before the enormity of events. But subjective apathy is encouraged by the *objective* American situation—the actual structural separation of people from power, from relevant knowledge, from pinnacles of decision-making. Just as the university influences the student way of life, so do major social institutions create the circumstances in which the isolated citizen will try hopelessly to understand his world and himself.

The very isolation of the individual—from power and community and ability to aspire—means the rise of a democracy without publics. With the great mass of people structurally remote and psychologically hesitant with respect to democratic institutions, those institutions themselves attenuate and become, in the fashion of the vicious circle, progressively less accessible to those few who aspire to serious participation in social affairs. The vital democratic connection between community and leadership, between the mass and the several elites, has been so wrenched and perverted that disastrous policies go unchallenged time and again.

THE COLONIAL REVOLUTION

While weapons have accelerated man's opportunity for self-destruction, the counter-impulse to life and creation are superbly manifest in the revolutionary feelings of many Asian, African and Latin American peoples. Against the individual initiative and aspiration, and social sense of organicism characteristic of these upsurges, the American apathy and stalemate stand in embarrassing contrast.

It is difficult today to give human meaning to the welter of facts that surrounds us. That is why it is especially hard to understand the facts of "underdevelopment": in India, man and beast together produced 65 percent of the nation's economic energy in a recent year, and of the remaining 35 percent of inanimately produced power almost three-fourths was obtained by burning dung. But in the United States, human and animal power together account for only one percent of the national economic energy—that is what stands humanly behind the vague term "industrialization." Even to maintain the misery of Asia today at a constant level will require a rate of growth tripling the national income and the aggregate production in Asian countries by the end of the century. For Asians to have the (unacceptable) 1950 standard of Europeans, less than $2,000 per year for a family, national production must increase 21-fold by the end the century, and that monstrous feat only to reach a level that Europeans find intolerable.

What has America done? During the years 1955–57 our total expenditures in economic aid were equal to one-tenth of one percent of our total Gross National Product. Prior to that time it was less; since then it has been a fraction higher. Immediate social and economic development is needed—we have helped little, seeming to prefer to create a growing gap between "have" and "have not" rather than to usher in social revolutions which would threaten our investors and our military alliances. The new nations want to avoid power entanglements that will open their countries to foreign domination—and we have often demanded loyalty oaths. They do not see the relevance of uncontrolled free enterprise in societies without accumulated capital and a significant middle class—and we have looked calumniously on those who would not try "our way." They seek empathy—and we have sided with the old colonialists, who now are trying to take credit for "giving" all the freedom that has been wrested from them, or we "empathize" when pressure absolutely demands it.

With rare variation, American foreign policy in the fifties was guided by a concern for foreign investment and a negative, anticommunist political stance linked to a series of military alliances, both undergirded by military threat. We participated unilaterally—usually through the Central

Intelligence Agency—in revolutions against governments in Laos, Guatemala, Cuba, Egypt, Iran. We permitted economic investment to decisively affect our foreign policy: fruit in Cuba, oil in the Middle East, diamonds and gold in South Africa (with whom we trade more than with any African nation). More exactly: America's "foreign market" in the late fifties, including exports of goods and services plus overseas sales by American firms, averaged about $60 billion annually. This represented twice the investment of 1950, and it is predicted that the same rates of increase will continue. The reason is obvious: *Fortune* said in 1958, "foreign earnings will more than double in four years, more than twice the probable gain in domestic profits." These investments are concentrated primarily in the Middle East and Latin America, neither region being an impressive candidate for the long-run stability, political caution, and lower-class tolerance that American investors typically demand.

Our pugnacious anticommunism and protection of interests has led us to an alliance inappropriately called the "Free World." It includes four major parliamentary democracies: ourselves, Canada, Great Britain, and India. It also has included through the years Batista, Franco, Verwoerd, Salazar, De Gaulle, Boun Oum, Ngo Diem, Chiang Kai Shek, Trujillo, the Somozas, Saud, Ydigoras—all of these non-democrats separating us deeply from the colonial revolutions.

Since the Kennedy administration began, the American government seems to have initiated policy changes in the colonial and underdeveloped areas. It accepted "neutralism" as a tolerable principle; it sided more than once with the Angolans in the United Nations; it invited Souvanna Phouma to return to Laos after having overthrown his neutralist government there; it implemented the Alliance for Progress that President Eisenhower proposed when Latin America appeared on the verge of socialist revolutions; it made derogatory statements about the Trujillos; it cautiously suggested that a democratic socialist government in British Guiana might be necessary to support; in inaugural oratory, it suggested that a moral imperative was involved in sharing the world's resources with those who have been previously dominated. These were hardly sufficient to heal the scars of past activity and present associations, but nevertheless they were motions away from the fifties. But quite unexpectedly, the president ordered the Cuban invasion, and while the American press railed about how we had been "shamed" and defied by that "monster Castro," the colonial peoples of the world wondered whether our foreign policy had really changed from its old imperialist ways (we had never supported Castro, even on the eve of his taking power, and had announced early that "the conduct of the Castro government toward foreign private enterprise in Cuba" would be a main State Department concern). Any heralded changes in our foreign policy are now further suspect in the wake of the Punta Del Este foreign ministers' conference where the five countries representing most of Latin America refused to cooperate in our plans to further "isolate" the Castro government.

Ever since the colonial revolution began, American policy makers have reacted to new problems with old "gunboat" remedies, often thinly disguised. The feeble but desirable efforts of the Kennedy administration to be more flexible are coming perhaps too late, and are of too little significance to really change the historical thrust of our policies. The hunger problem is increasing rapidly mostly as a result of the worldwide population explosion that cancels out the meager triumphs gained so far over starvation. The threat of population to economic growth is simply documented: in 1960–70 population in Africa south of the Sahara will increase 14 percent; in South Asia and the Far East by 22 percent; in North Africa 26 percent; in the Middle East by 27 percent; in Latin America 29 percent. Population explosion, no matter how devastating, is neutral. But how long will it take to create a relation of trust between America and the newly-developing societies? How long to change our policies? And what length of time do we have?

The world is in transformation. But America is not. It can race to industrialize the world, tolerating occasional authoritarianisms, socialisms, neutralisms along the way—or it can slow the pace of the inevitable and default to the eager and self-interested Soviets and, much more importantly, to mankind itself. Only mystics would guess we have opted thoroughly for the first. Consider what our people think of this, the most urgent issue on the human agenda. Fed by a bellicose press, manipulated by economic and political opponents of change, drifting in their own history, they grumble about "the foreign aid waste," or about "that beatnik down in Cuba," or how "things will get us by" . . . thinking confidently, albeit in the usual bewilderment, that Americans can go right on like always, 5 percent of mankind producing 40 percent of its goods.

ANTICOMMUNISM

An unreasoning anticommunism has become a major social problem for those who want to construct a more democratic America. McCarthyism and other forms of exaggerated and conservative anticommunism seriously weaken democratic institutions and spawn movements contrary to the interests of basic freedoms and peace. In such an atmosphere even the most intelligent of Americans fear to join political organizations, sign petitions, speak out on serious issues. Militaristic policies are easily "sold" to a public fearful of a democratic enemy. Political debate is restricted, thought is standardized, action is inhibited by the demands of "unity" and "oneness" in the face of the declared danger. Even many liberals and socialists share static and repetitious participation in the anticommunist crusade and often discourage tentative, inquiring discussion about "the Russian question" within their ranks—often by employing "stalinist," "stalinoid," trotskyite" and other epithets in an oversimplifying way to discredit opposition.

Thus much of the American anticommunism takes on the characteristics of paranoia. Not only does it lead to the perversion of democracy and to the political stagnation of a warfare society, but it also has the unintended consequence of preventing an honest and effective approach to the issues. Such an approach would require public analysis and debate of world politics. But almost nowhere in politics is such a rational analysis possible to make.

It would seem reasonable to expect that in America the basic issues of the Cold War should be rationally and fully debated, between persons of every opinion—on television, on platforms and through other media. It would seem, too, that there should be a way for a person or an organization to oppose communism *without* contributing to the common fear of associations and public actions. But these things do not happen; instead, there is finger-pointing and comical debate about the most serious of issues. This trend of events on the domestic scene, towards greater irrationality on major questions, moves us to greater concern than does the "internal threat" of domestic communism. Democracy, we are convinced, requires every effort to set in peaceful opposition the basic viewpoints of the day; only by conscious, determined, though difficult, efforts in this direction will the issue of communism be met appropriately.

ALTERNATIVES TO HELPLESSNESS

The goals we have set are not realizable next month, or even next election—but that fact justifies neither giving up altogether nor a determination to work only on immediate, direct, tangible problems. Both responses are a sign of helplessness, fearfulness of visions, refusal to hope, and tend to bring on the very conditions to be avoided. Fearing vision, we justify rhetoric or myopia. Fearing hope, we reinforce despair.

The first effort, then, should be to state a vision: what is the perimeter of human possibility in this epoch? This we have tried to do. The second effort, if we are to be politically responsible, is to evaluate the prospects for obtaining at least a substantial part of that vision in our epoch: What are the social forces that exist, or that must exist, if we are to be at all successful? And what role have we ourselves to play as a social force?

1. In exploring the existing social forces, note must be taken of the Southern civil rights movement as the most heartening because of the justice it insists upon, exemplary because it indicates that there can be a passage out of apathy.

This movement, pushed into a brilliant new phase by the Montgomery bus boycott and the subsequent nonviolent action of the sit-ins and Freedom Rides has had three major results: first, a sense of self-determination has been instilled in millions of oppressed Negroes; second, the movement has challenged a few thousand liberals to new social idealism; third, a series of important concessions have been obtained, such as token school desegregation, increased administration help, new laws, desegregation of some public facilities.

But fundamental social change—that would break the props from under Jim Crow—has not come. Negro employment opportunity, wage levels, housing conditions, educational privileges—these remain deplorable and relatively constant, each deprivation reinforcing the impact of the others. The Southern states, in the meantime, are strengthening the fortresses of the status quo, and are beginning to camouflage the fortresses by guile where open bigotry announced its defiance before. The white-controlled one-party system remains intact; and even where the Republicans are beginning, under the pressures of industrialization in the towns and suburbs, to show initiative in fostering a two-party system, all Southern state Republican Committees (save Georgia) have adopted militant segregationist platforms to attract Dixiecrats.

Rural dominance remains a fact in nearly all the Southern states, although the reapportionment decision of the Supreme Court portends future power shifts to the cities. Southern politicians maintain a continuing aversion to the welfare legislation that would aid their people. The reins of the Southern economy are held by conservative businessmen who view human rights as secondary to property rights. A violent anticommunism is rooting itself in the South, and threatening even moderate voices. Add the militaristic tradition of the South, and its irrational regional mystique, and one must conclude that authoritarian and reactionary tendencies are a rising obstacle to the small, voiceless, poor, and isolated democratic movements.

The civil rights struggle thus has come to an impasse. To this impasse, the movement responded this year by entering the sphere of politics, insisting on citizenship rights, specifically the right to vote. The new voter registration stage of protest represents perhaps the first major attempt to exercise the conventional instruments of political democracy in the struggle for racial justice. The vote, if used strategically by the great mass of now-unregistered Negroes theoretically eligible to vote, will be decisive factor in changing the quality of Southern leadership from low demagoguery to decent statesmanship.

More important, the new emphasis on the vote heralds the use of political means to solve the problems of equality in America, and it signals the decline of the short-sighted view that "discrimination" can be isolated from related social problems. Since the moral clarity of the civil rights movement has not always been accompanied by precise political vision, and sometimes not even by a real political consciousness, the new phase is revolutionary in its implication. The intermediate goal of the program is to secure and insure a healthy respect and realization of constitutional liberties. This is important not only to terminate the civil and private abuses which currently characterize the region, but also to prevent the pendulum of oppression from simply swinging to an alternate extreme with a new unsophisticated electorate, after the unhappy example of the last Reconstruction. It is the ultimate objectives of the strategy which promise profound change in the politics of the nation. An increased Negro voting rate in and of itself is not going to dislodge racist controls of the Southern power structure; but an accelerating movement through the courts, the ballot boxes, and especially the jails is the most likely means of shattering the crust of political intransigency and creating a semblance of democratic order, on local and state levels.

Linked with pressure from Northern liberals to expunge the Dixiecrats from the ranks of the Democratic Party, massive Negro voting in the South could destroy the vice-like grip reactionary Southerners have on the Congressional legislative process.

2. The broadest movement for *peace in* several years emerged in 1961–62. In its political orientation and goals it is much less identifiable than the movement for civil rights: it includes socialists, pacifists, liberals, scholars, militant activists, middle-class women, some professionals, many students, a few unionists. Some have been emotionally single-issue: Ban the Bomb. Some have been academically obscurantist. Some have rejected the System (sometimes both systems). Some have attempted, too, to "work within" the System. Amidst these conflicting streams of emphasis, however, certain basic qualities appear. The most important is that the "peace movement" has operated almost exclusively through peripheral institutions—almost never through mainstream institutions. Similarly, individuals interested in

peace have nonpolitical social roles that cannot be turned to the support of peace activity. Concretely, liberal religious societies, anti-war groups, voluntary associations, and ad hoc committees have been the political unit of the peace movement, and its human movers have been students, teachers, housewives, secretaries, lawyers, doctors, clergy. The units have not been located in spots of major social influence, the people have not been able to turn their resources fully to the issues that concern them. The results are political ineffectiveness and personal alienation.

The organizing ability of the peace movement thus is limited to the ability to state and polarize issues. It does not have an institution or the forum in which the conflicting interests can be debated. The debate goes on in corners; it has little connection with the continuing process of determining allocations of resources. This process is not necessarily centralized, however much the peace movement is estranged from it. National policy, though dominated to a large degree by the "power elites" of the corporations and military, is still partially founded in consensus. It can be altered when there actually begins a shift in the allocation of resources and the listing of priorities by the people in the institutions which have social influence, e.g., the labor unions and the schools. As long as the debates of the peace movement form only a protest, rather than an opposition viewpoint within the centers of serious decision-making, then it is neither a movement of democratic relevance, nor is it likely to have any effectiveness except in educating more outsiders to the issue. It is vital, to be sure, that this educating go on (a heartening sign is the recent proliferation of books and journals dealing with peace and war from newly developing countries); the possibilities for making politicians responsible to "peace constituencies" becomes greater.

But in the long interim before the national political climate is more open to deliberate, goal-directed debate about peace issues, the dedicated peace "movement" might well prepare a *local base,* especially by establishing civic committees on the techniques of converting from military to peacetime production. To make war and peace *relevant* to the problems of everyday life, by relating it to the backyard (shelters), the baby (fallout), the job (military contracts)—and making a turn toward peace seem desirable on these same terms—is a task the peace movement is just beginning, and can profitably continue.

3. Central to any analysis of the potential for change must be an appraisal of *organized labor*. It would be ahistorical to disregard the immense influence of labor in making modern America a decent place in which to live. It would be confused to fail to note labor's presence today as the most liberal of mainstream institutions. But it would be irresponsible not to criticize labor for losing much of the idealism that once made it a driving movement. Those who expected a labor upsurge after the 1955 AFL-CIO merger can only be dismayed that one year later, in the Stevenson-Eisenhower campaign, the AFL-CIO Committee on Political Education was able to obtain solicited $1.00 contributions from only one of every twenty-four unionists, and prompt only 40 percent of the rank and file to vote.

As a political force, labor generally has been unsuccessful in the postwar period of prosperity. It has seen the passage of the Taft-Hartley and Landrum-Griffin laws, and while beginning to receive slightly favorable National Labor Relations Board rulings, it has made little progress against right-to-work laws. Furthermore, it has seen less than adequate action on domestic problems, especially unemployment.

This labor "recession" has been only partly due to anti-labor politicians and corporations. Blame should be laid, too, to labor itself for not mounting an adequate movement. Labor has too often seen itself as elitist, rather than mass-oriented, and as a pressure group rather than as an 18-million-member body making political demands for all America. In the first instance, the labor bureaucracy tends to be cynical toward, or afraid of, rank-and-file involvement in the work of the union. Resolutions passed at conventions are implemented only by high-level machinations, not by mass mobilization of the unionists. Without a significant base, labor's pressure function is materially reduced since it becomes difficult to hold political figures accountable to a movement that cannot muster a vote from a majority of its members.

There are some indications, however, that labor might regain its missing idealism. First, there are signs within the movement: of worker discontent with the economic progress, of collective bargaining, of occasional splits among union leaders on questions such as nuclear testing or other Cold War issues. Second, and more important, are the social forces which prompt these feelings of unrest. Foremost is the permanence of unemployment, and the threat of automation. But important, too, is the growth of unorganized ranks in white-collar fields. Third, there is the tremendous challenge of the Negro movement for support from organized labor: the alienation from and disgust with labor hypocrisy among Negroes ranging from the NAACP to the Black Muslims (crystallized in the formation of the Negro American Labor Council) indicates that labor must move more seriously in its attempts to organize on an interracial basis in the South and in large urban centers. When this task was broached several years ago, "jurisdictional" disputes prevented action. Today, many of these disputes have been settled—and the question of a massive organizing campaign is on the labor agenda again.

These threats and opportunities point to a profound crisis: either labor continues to decline as a social force, or it must constitute itself as a mass political force demanding not only that society recognize its rights to organize but also a program going beyond desired labor legislation and welfare improvements. Necessarily this latter role will require rank-and-file involvement. It might include greater autonomy and power for political coalitions of the various trade unions in local areas, rather than the more stultifying dominance of the international unions now. It might include reductions in leaders' salaries, or rotation from executive office to shop obligations, as a means of breaking down the hierarchical tendencies which have detached elite from base and made the highest echelons of labor more like businessmen than workers. It would certainly mean an announced independence of the center and Dixiecrat wings of the Democratic Party, and a massive organizing drive, especially in the South to complement the growing Negro political drive there.

A new politics must include a revitalized labor movement; a movement which sees itself, and is regarded by others, as a major leader of the breakthrough to a politics of hope and vision. Labor's role is no less unique or important in the needs of the future than it was in the past; its numbers and potential political strength, its natural interest in the abolition of exploitation, its reach to the grass roots of American society, combine to make it the best candidate for the synthesis of the civil rights, peace, and economic reform movements.

The creation of bridges is made more difficult by the problems left over from the generation of "silence." Middle-class students, still the main actors in the embryonic upsurge, have yet to overcome their ignorance, and even vague hostility, for what they see as "middle-class-labor" bureaucrats. Students must open the campus to labor through publications, action programs, curricula, while labor opens its house to students through internships, requests for aid (on the picket line, with handbills, in the public dialogue), and politics. And the organization of the campus can be a beginning—teachers' unions can be argued as both socially progressive, and educationally beneficial; university employees can be organized—and thereby an important element in the education of the student radical.

But the new politics is still contained; it struggles below the surface of apathy, awaiting liberation. Few anticipate the breakthrough and fewer still exhort labor to begin. Labor continues to be the most liberal—and most frustrated—institution in mainstream America.

4. Since the Democratic Party sweep in 1958, there have been exaggerated but real efforts to establish a liberal force in Congress, not to balance but to at least voice criticism of the conservative mood. The most notable of these efforts was the Liberal Project begun early in 1959 by Representative Kastenmeier of Wisconsin. The Project was neither disciplined nor very influential but it was concerned at least with confronting basic domestic and foreign problems, in concert with several liberal intellectuals.

In 1960 five members of the Project were defeated at the polls (for reasons other than their membership in the Project). Then followed a "post mortem" publication of *The Liberal Papers*, materials discussed by the Project when it was in existence. Republican leaders called the book "further out than Communism." The New Frontier administration repudiated any connection with the statements. Some former members of the Project even disclaimed their past roles.

A hopeful beginning came to a shameful end. But during the demise of the Project, a new spirit of Democratic Party reform was occurring: in New York City, Ithaca, Massachusetts, Connecticut, Texas, California, and even in Mississippi and Alabama where Negro candidates for Congress challenged racist political power. Some were for peace, some for the liberal side of the New Frontier, some for realignment of the parties—and in most cases they were supported by students.

Here and there were stirrings of organized discontent with the political stalemate. Americans for Democratic Action and the *New Republic*, pillars of the liberal community, took stands against the president on nuclear testing. A split, extremely slight thus far, developed in organized labor on the same issue. The Rev. Martin Luther King, Jr. preached against the Dixiecrat-Republican coalition across the nation.

5. From 1960 to 1962, the campuses experienced a revival of idealism among an active few. Triggered by the impact of the sit-ins, students began to struggle for integration, civil liberties, student rights, peace, and against the fast-rising right-wing "revolt" as well. The liberal students, too, have felt their urgency thwarted by conventional channels: from student governments to Congressional committees. Out of this alienation from existing channels has come the creation of new ones; the most characteristic forms of liberal-radical student organizations are the dozens of campus political parties, political journals, and peace marches and demonstrations. In only a few cases have students built bridges to power: an occasional election campaign, the sit-ins, Freedom Rides, and voter registration activities; in some relatively large Northern demonstrations for peace and civil rights, and infrequently, through the United States National Student Association whose notable work has not been focused on political change.

These contemporary social movements—for peace, civil rights, civil liberties, labor—have in common certain values and goals. The fight for peace is one for a stable and racially integrated world; for an end to the inherently volatile exploitation of most of mankind by irresponsible elites; and for freedom of economic, political and cultural organization. The fight for civil rights is also one for social welfare for all Americans; for free speech and the right to protest; for the shield of economic independence and bargaining power; for a reduction of the arms race which takes national attention and resources away from the problems of domestic injustice. Labor's fight for jobs and wages is also one against exploitation of the Negro as a source of cheap labor; for the right to petition and strike; for world industrialization; for the stability of a peacetime economy instead of the instability of the war economy; for expansion of the welfare state. The fight for a liberal Congress is a fight for a platform from which these concerns can issue. And the fight for students, for internal democracy in the university, is a fight to gain a forum for the issues.

But these scattered movements have more in common: a need for their concerns to be expressed by a political party responsible to their interests. That they have no political expression, no political channels, can be traced in large measure to the existence of a Democratic Party which tolerates the perverse unity of liberalism and racism, prevents the social change wanted by Negroes, peace protesters, labor unions, students, reform Democrats, and other liberals. Worse, the party stalemate prevents even the raising of controversy—a full Congressional assault on racial discrimination, disengagement in Central Europe, sweeping urban reform, disarmament and inspection, public regulation of major industries; these and other issues are never heard in the body that is supposed to represent the best thoughts and interests of all Americans.

An imperative task for these publicly disinherited groups, then, is to demand a Democratic Party responsible to their interests. They must support Southern voter registration and Negro political candidates and demand that Democratic Party liberals do the same (in the last Congress, Dixiecrats split with Northern Democrats on 119 of 300 roll-calls, mostly on civil rights, area redevelopment and foreign aid bills; the breach was much larger than in the previous several sessions). Labor should begin a major drive in the South. In the North, reform clubs (either independent or Democratic) should be formed to run against big city regimes on such issues as peace, civil rights, and urban needs. Demonstrations should be held at every Congressional or convention seating of Dixiecrats. A massive research and publicity campaign should be initiated, showing to every housewife, doctor, professor, and worker the damage done to their interests every day a racist occupies a place in the Democratic Party. Where possible, the peace movement should challenge the "peace credentials" of the otherwise-liberals by threatening or actually running candidates against them.

THE UNIVERSITY AND SOCIAL CHANGE.

There is perhaps little reason to be optimistic about the above analysis. True, the Dixiecrat-GOP coalition is the weakest point in the dominating complex of corporate, military and political power. But the civil rights and peace and student movements are too poor and socially slighted, and the labor movement too quiescent, to be counted with enthusiasm. From where else can power and vision be summoned? We believe that the universities are an overlooked seat of influence.

First, the university is located in a permanent position of social influence. Its educational function makes it indispensable and automatically makes it a crucial institution in the formation of social attitudes. Second, in an unbelievably complicated world, it is the central institution for organizing, evaluating, and transmitting knowledge. Third, the extent to which academic resources presently are used to buttress immoral social practice is revealed first, by the extent to which defense contracts make the universities engineers of the arms race. Too, the use of modern social science as a manipulative tool reveals itself in the "human relations" consultants to the modern corporation, who introduce trivial sops to give laborers feelings of "participation" or "belonging," while actually deluding them in order to further exploit their labor. And, of course, the use of motivational research is already infamous as a manipulative aspect of American politics. But these social uses of the universities' resources also demonstrate the unchangeable reliance by men of power on the men and storehouses of knowledge: this makes the university functionally tied to society in new ways, revealing new potentialities, new levers for change. Fourth, the university is the only mainstream institution that is open to participation by individuals of nearly any viewpoint.

These, at least, are facts, no matter how dull the teaching, how paternalistic the rules, how irrelevant the research that goes on. Social relevance, the accessibility to knowledge, and internal openness—these together make the university a potential base and agency in a movement of social change.

1. Any new left in America must be, in large measure, a left with real intellectual skills, committed to deliberativeness, honesty, reflection as working tools. The university permits the political life to be an adjunct to the academic one, and action to be informed by reason.

2. A new left must be distributed in significant social roles throughout the country. The universities are distributed in such a manner.

3. A new left must consist of younger people who matured in the post-war world, and partially be directed to the recruitment of younger people. The university is an obvious beginning point.

4. A new left must include liberals and socialists, the former for their relevance, the latter for their sense of thoroughgoing reforms in the system. The university is a more sensible place than a political party for these two traditions to begin to discuss their differences and look for political synthesis.

5. A new left must start controversy across the land, if national policies and national apathy are to be reversed. The ideal university is a community of controversy, within itself and in its effects on communities beyond.

6. A new left must transform modern complexity into issues that can be understood and felt close-up by every human being. It must give form to the feelings of helplessness and indifference, so that people may see the political, social and economic sources of their private troubles and organize to change society. In a time of supposed prosperity, moral complacency and political manipulation, a new left cannot rely on only aching stomachs to be the engine force of social reform. The case for change, for alternatives that will involve uncomfortable personal efforts, must be argued as never before. The university is a relevant place for all of these activities.

But we need not indulge in illusions: the university system cannot complete a movement of ordinary people making demands for a better life.

From its schools and colleges across the nation, a militant left might awaken its allies, and by beginning the process towards peace, civil rights, and labor struggles, reinsert theory and idealism where too often reign confusion and political barter. The power of students and faculty united is not only potential; it has shown its actuality in the South, and in the reform movements of the North.

The bridge to political power, though, will be built through genuine cooperation, locally, nationally, and internationally, between a new left of young people, and an awakening community of allies. In each community we must look within the university and act with confidence that we can be powerful, but we must look outwards to the less exotic but more lasting struggles for justice.

To turn these possibilities into realities will involve national efforts at university reform by an alliance of students and faculty. They must wrest control of the educational process from the administrative bureaucracy. They must make fraternal and functional contact with allies in labor, civil rights, and other liberal forces outside the campus. They must import major public issues into the curriculum—research and teaching on problems of war and peace is an outstanding example. They must make debate and controversy, not dull pedantic cant, the common style for educational life. They must consciously build a base for their assault upon the loci of power.

As students for a democratic society, we are committed to stimulating this kind of social movement, this kind of vision and program is campus and community across the country. If we appear to seek the unattainable, it has been said, then let it be known that we do so to avoid the unimaginable.

5.

Newark Rebellion

July 1967

These writings are a blend of notes and on-site reporting made during the July 1967 Newark rebellion and later published in the New York Review of Books *and* Rebellion in Newark *(Random House, 1967). For the best account at the time, see Ron Porambo,* No Cause for Indictment: An Autopsy of Newark *(Holt, Rinehart, Winston, 1971). For an eye-opening PBS documentary film forty years later, see* Revolution 1967 *by Marylou and Jerome Bonjorno.*

Brad Parks of the Newark Star-Ledger wrote a retrospective article on July 9, 2007, summarizing with documents and interviews that there was no evidence of black snipers as widely reported at the time. On the other hand, the Newark Police Department never accounted for the number of bullets they fired, but the New Jersey State Police shot 2,905 rounds and the New Jersey State Troopers fired 10,414. Parks also named as an FBI informant one "Colonel Hassan" who suddenly arrived in our midst with a purported "black liberation army" a few months before the events. My assumption was that a police/FBI counterintelligence operation was active in Newark at the time.

I left Newark, reluctantly, for two reasons: first, Stokely Carmichael's persuasive call for black power made interracial organizing problematic, and second, it was clear that I could be more useful organizing against the Vietnam War. I left Newark for Chicago in May 1968.

It was a painful decision, since I had organized my life around living in Newark four years earlier, in the summer of 1964. Several of those I worked with, like Junius Williams and Robert Curvin, remained for the long haul. The community organizing project, I believe, played an important role in challenging the city's old guard and mobilizing a new generation of black activists from poor and working-class backgrounds. But Newark itself was abandoned by Vietnam spending through the 1970s and by the corporate de-

*industrialization that shattered many cities with large African American pop-
ulations through the Reagan era. In this context, the final sentence of this
section—"peace returned"—referred only to the withdrawal of state troopers that day, not the arrival of social justice.*

◆　　◆　　◆

ON A SWELTERING DAY in July 1964—a few weeks before the Democratic
convention—I stepped out of a car after an all-night drive from Ann Arbor
and found myself looking for the first time at the black ghetto of Newark:
Scores of furniture stores, foul-smelling markets, and cheap record shops
lined the baking streets of tar. Young people carrying schoolbooks in one
hand and holding radios to their ears with the other crossed the street.
Mothers carried large bags of groceries while trying to keep trailing children out of the traffic. A few men stood outside a bar in animated
argument. A police car slowly cruised by, the officers glancing at me, the
only white who was clearly not a merchant. Off this commercial street ran
several red-brick streets into a residential community of fifty-year-old
wood-frame houses with dirt front yards that had been a white district
only ten years before.

The sight of the neighborhood, which would be my home for the next
four years, left me unbalanced. None of my reading or class work prepared
me to know the ghetto, or know concrete economic realities, or know the
real operation of political machines. And here I was to organize, as if I
knew something that those living here didn't know. I was twenty-four
years old and preparing to lead the poor in an assault on the downtown
power structure. But first I had to get a street map, then an apartment, and
some savvy—quick.

I had arrived on this Newark street corner as part of a new and unprecedented event in the history of American students: the migration of
hundreds, and ultimately thousands, into organizing projects in impoverished communities from Harlem to Appalachia. Instead of choosing
conventional careers and the benefits of middle-class life, students were
settling in ramshackle houses in the Mississippi Black Belt, or apartments

in Chicago's Uptown, in attempts to organize society's outcasts. The spirit of this effort, which would soon see a pale and token reflection in the federal government's VISTA and antipoverty programs, was one of transformation, from book-carrying students to American *kibbutzniks* dedicated to organizing the poor for power. We who bore witness to squalor in the midst of affluence would ultimately be ignored. This failure would come to be a *missed opportunity,* a road tragically not taken, as American society flirted briefly with a "war on poverty" only to consume its generosity in a war on Vietnam. Had the nation been able to focus on its internal agenda, students might have triumphed as catalysts to channel the frustrations of poverty into constructive reform. Instead the cities, and soon the campuses, were lit by what James Baldwin forecast as "the fire next time."

During the critical juncture of 1963–64, the early SDS leaders decided to organize the poor. There are nineteen people in a black-and-white group photo of that early SDS leadership taken at the end of a September 1963 national meeting in Bloomington, Indiana. The men are dressed mostly in the short-sleeved, button-down shirts of the time. Rennie Davis and Robb Burlage have briefcases, and Todd Gitlin wears a sports jacket with a Harvard insignia. Our hair is uniformly close-clipped. The women are wearing dresses or skirts, with one exception in tight-fitting khaki slacks. I am standing to one side with my shirt hanging over my pants, more disheveled than the others. All of us, however, are raising clenched fists.

It was at this meeting, shortly after the march on Washington, that we finalized our plans for developing a northern parallel to SNCC, sending student organizers into slums to organize the poor. Evolving independently from SDS, which would still organize the campuses, we called ourselves the Economic Research and Action Project (ERAP—"EE-rap"). Knowing of SNCC's emerging plan for a Mississippi Summer, we decided to recruit and send hundreds of young people into urban areas at the same time, though for longer than a summer, in an attempt to organize the white as well as the black poor. The program was ambitious. Walter Reuther, thanks to Mildred Jeffrey, sent a five-thousand-dollar check to help us get started in 1963. Rennie Davis, one of our best organizational minds, was chosen to direct the national ERAP office in Ann Arbor. A young student named Joe Chabot was dispatched to Chicago to get a "feel" for unemployed youth. SDS chapter leaders scouted possibilities for storefront projects in cities across the country. Our confidence was fueled by President Johnson's announcement in January 1964 of an "unconditional war on poverty in America." We knew that the ultimate official effort would be a token in comparison with the real needs. Instead of calling for the more radical "participatory democracy," for example, the government's programs set as its goal "maximum feasible participation" of the poor in self-help programs, leaving the practical control in the hands of local authorities. But to us, it seemed that our movements were again setting the agenda—as we had in civil rights—and the government was responding, giving us legitimacy and a sense of effectiveness.

Not everyone in our circle shared this enthusiasm. In our first serious difference, Al Haber strongly opposed the ERAP and what he called its "cult of action." He felt it was still more important to intellectually define a "radical agenda" and prepare people to be radicals in their professional careers. To me, he represented an inconclusive intellectualism that was frustrating the birth of SDS as an active force. The ERAP concept was far from a leap into "mindless activism," as he bitterly charged. If anything, ERAP was a product of intense thinking about the intertwined issues of race and poverty and how to bring them to center stage in a nation consumed by the Cold War. Todd Gitlin, the new SDS president, and I helped draft a statement on the "triple revolution" of nuclear weapons, industrial automation, and civil rights at Princeton University in early 1964. Key sponsors of the "triple revolution" statement included Robert Oppenheimer, Gunnar Myrdal, and economist Robert Theobald, as well as United Auto Workers officials. We exuberantly felt we were heading in the right direction, intellectually as well as personally. Nuclear weapons made warfare increasingly obsolete, the Cold War was receding, and the combination of new technologies with rising expectations dictated the necessity of a new focus on jobs and economic issues.

By spring 1964, there were plans for organizing ERAP projects in cities as diverse as Chicago, Cleveland, Newark, Boston, New Haven, Philadelphia, Oakland, Baltimore, Louisville, and Hazard, Kentucky (deep in Appalachia). While finishing my graduate work in Ann Arbor and trying to decide where to go after June, I was impressed with Carl Wittman, one of the moving forces behind ERAP, who already had formed an effective project in the Chester, Pennsylvania, ghetto near the Swarthmore campus. Together, we wrote an ERAP strategy paper entitled *Toward an Interracial Movement of the Poor?*, a cumbersome document arguing the imperative of organizing across racial lines to win the support of a majority of Americans. We still believed in the integrationist philosophy of SNCC and Dr. King, but both of us were impressed by the deep appeal of Malcolm X in the northern ghettos. Carl, Vernon Grizzard, Connie Brown, and other Swarthmore students encountered Malcolm in the Philadelphia area and felt the urgency to prove that at least some whites were not "devils." I had a brief but similar experience in Ann Arbor when the Muslim leader lectured to an overflow crowd. Afterward, I attended a private dialogue that turned into an intense argument. I found myself liking Malcolm for his dignity, passion, and intelligence, and I thought as a young and opinionated journalist that he enjoyed sparring with me. The argument became vociferous over whether whites are racist at birth or merely conditioned to their prejudice. Like Carl, I wanted to prove in action that an integrationist perspective stressing common economic interests could still work. So when Carl suggested that I join the budding Newark ERAP project, I was interested. I'd never been to Newark before, but I'd heard an airplane stewardess describe it as the "armpit of the world." That was good enough for me.

When I told my parents of this new mission, they politely suggested I was throwing my life away. My father had just remarried (his new wife, Esther, was also a Chrysler employee) and become a father again in late 1963. I visited Detroit in early 1964 to meet my 1-year-old sister, Mary, who was curly-haired, playful, and adorable. As she posed for photos on my lap, I tried to explain my decision to go to Newark. My father was already disturbed that I had passed up a journalism career to go south. The breakup with Casey added to his sense of my instability; now came Newark. "I don't know, Tom, how you got involved in these things," he said, keeping his temper but shaking his head. "It certainly wasn't the way we raised you."

My mother, still living in Royal Oak, already accepted the fact that I was following my own lights, but she felt hurt as well. My sojourn to the South had seemed dangerous but at least temporary. There was still time for me to return to journalism or law school, she believed. The commitment to Newark seemed to give away the third decade of my life and promised to fill their middle years with trauma, confusion, and a foreboding sense of parental failure. My father was beginning to assume that he'd lost a son to bizarre radical influences; my mother was more trusting, but nonetheless baffled at my behavior.

When I arrived, Newark was the only major American city with a black majority. Viewed from a national political perspective, the city was defined as a liberal Democratic stronghold. Its officeholders, led by Mayor Hugh J. Addonizio, were for voting rights, social welfare, and all the "good things" the "Dixiecrat" wing of the party opposed. Over a half century, as many as 100,000 black families had migrated from the South in search of those "good things" in this northern city. But on arrival, they found a different reality than the image of the liberal North. The city's elected government included only one black official, an aging, patronage-oriented councilman named Irvine Turner. White or black, city officials were widely perceived as corrupt. Construction costs on city contracts were higher than anywhere in the United States. Gambling was the city's biggest business, and the narcotics trade flourished. Anthony "Tony Bananas" Caponigro and Anthony "Tony Boy" Boiardo were among the mayor's biggest campaign contributors. Ordinary people were the casualties. With a total population of 400,000 people, Newark ranked highest in the country in crime, maternal and infant mortality, tuberculosis, and venereal disease. Unemployment citywide was 15 percent, and much higher in the black community. One third of the city's children dropped out of school, and less than 10 percent achieved normal reading levels. In 1960, 32.5 percent (41,430) of its housing units were officially substandard. Nearly 30,000 of those dwellings lacked internal heating systems, and 7,000 had no flush toilets. There were 5,000 totally abandoned units and 13,000 public housing units—more per capita than any American city.

The thirteen of us who signed up for Newark were a cross section of the activist generation, coming primarily from middle-class homes and major campuses like Michigan, Swarthmore, Amherst, and Howard. Only one of us was black, a highly talented organizer named Marv Holloway, though we were soon joined by two others, Junius Williams and Phil Hutchings, later a SNCC chairman. Faulty preparation misled us into believing that the Clinton Hill neighborhood was racially integrated in makeup. Carl Wittman had received a misleading picture from the white liberals in the Clinton Hill neighborhood who had agreed to sponsor our presence. In fact, the whites tended to be middle class and lived on the avenues high on the hill, while the blacks were poor and lived at the bottom. The city's poor whites lived in the East Ward; we were in the South. We decided to stay in Clinton Hill, regardless of our being mainly white, and made long-range plans to target the East Ward, plans which were ultimately carried out in the late sixties. These were the years before "black power," the years when television carried regular news of white civil rights workers in the black South; there was still some degree of black identification with young white activists. One young black girl told her parents that I looked like one of the Beatles (a flattering, if far-fetched, observation). At any rate, we believed—correctly, it turned out—that we would recruit new staff out of the black community.

The ERAP spirit was one of voluntary poverty and simple living. We believed you could not organize poor people without living on their economic level in their neighborhood. Sharing shelter and meals was also the only way to pay for a large project on a small budget. ERAP projects in different cities would enthusiastically compete for the lowest food budget; for a time, the Newark staff was eating for fifty cents a meal per person. We could not subsist on guilt, however, and soon the expenditure rose, though never beyond poverty levels.

We rented two or three apartments in the ghetto; each apartment housed as many as eight or ten of us. We dressed casually, usually a khaki version of the SNCC jeans "uniform." There was little privacy—as time went by only a few of the permanent people, or an occasional couple, were allocated rooms of their own. Even then, the bed, study table, and chairs were crammed into a tiny space. Others, less fortunate because their status was transitory, slept on couches or floors—often for weeks. One person even built a bed in a closet to achieve a little privacy.

There was not a lot of monogamy in this self-sacrificing community. It was a time of questioning for all traditional relationships, placing collective needs above personal ones and exploring new ways to relate in an open atmosphere. Couples tended to be respected, but were not even given special dispensations like taking meals together.

In the fall of 1964, Casey arrived in Newark for a two-week stay. The Atlantic City convention had been exhausting. SNCC was beginning to feel a serious tension over whether educated and qualified whites were unconsciously interfering with the leadership development of local blacks. A power struggle was casting shadows on the community of love, with advocates of greater structure and discipline arrayed against decentralists like Bob Moses. For Casey, after the failure of the huge Freedom Democratic Party effort, there seemed nothing to do. She came to Newark to explore ERAP and, less explicitly, to see what remained of our marriage. There was nothing there but the awkward friendliness that besets former lovers. She stayed in my room off the kitchen, but we couldn't recreate our former intimacy, and she soon began going into Manhattan to see Willie Morris. Finally, she returned to Mississippi to live in a freedom house in Jackson with Mary King.

I visited a Mississippi SNCC retreat as winter began and found the participants wearied, tense, and searching for direction, totally unlike the intense élan of only three years before. Blacks were withdrawing from whites, who were reacting with painful defensiveness, and the memory of Atlantic City—as well as the shadow of Vietnam—hung over the future menacingly.

As SNCC fell into these internal divisions, Casey and others increasingly became stoned. Not long after we formally divorced, represented by an Atlanta civil rights lawyer who had defended us during the sit-ins. It cost sixty-three dollars and seemed logical.

After nearly a year in Newark, I became involved with another staff organizer. A diminutive, shy, and quiet Swarthmore graduate, Connie Brown seemed out of place in the ghetto streets. But her soul was caring, her sense of individual psychology acute, and she became an excellent organizer, forming a welfare rights organization.

Connie and I came together one gray day in February 1965, returning in a bus from the National Poor People's Conference in Cleveland. A radio announced the news of Malcolm X's murder in Harlem. Both of us had encountered Malcolm, she in the Chester, Pennsylvania organizing project, and we had followed with enthusiasm his recent evolution away from diatribes against "white devils." He had been a hopeful bridge between the efforts of SNCC and ERAP. Now he was dead, at the hands of his former Muslim brothers.

As the news sank in, Connie and I leaned against each other on the backseat of the bus, filled with fifty somber blacks and a few whites, as it rolled along the freezing interstate. Discovering intimacy, we stayed together after that. It was almost impossible to live as a couple amid the stress generated by ten organizers. In search of privacy, we tried living in a single-room abandoned tool shop. The cement structure was just behind the two-story, wood-frame house the staff rented at 227 Jelliff Avenue. Our "home" lacked a bathroom and heat, and the Newark winters were freezing. I went to absurd lengths to make the place warm, installing a potbelly stove and scaffolds of blankets for insulation. We were alone at last, but unable to survive the winter without an indoor toilet, we gave up and moved back into a single room of the chaotic front house.

Amid the bedlam of the time, there were relatively few liaisons between staff and community people. They were not allowed as a matter of principle (unless they were deemed "serious" and "responsible"). This wall of separation, erected for organizational reasons, only intensified the need for what affection and intimacy was possible among ourselves. There even appeared, very discreetly, a few gay and lesbian relationships—a phenomenon I still did not understand. When I learned that a woman I'd slept with was lesbian, I was shocked. Upon discovering that Carl Wittman was gay (I don't recall the term used then), I noticed a tendency in myself to withdraw from him. It was all very unspoken. When Carl decided to move to Hoboken to begin a project of his own, we never discussed his real feelings, nor mine.

Our spartan life-style offended some white liberals and even certain blacks who thought we were "slumming," and in the end it was too demanding of people, but I am convinced that we affected most of the people we were trying to reach with our willingness to sacrifice. Our acts separated us clearly from any other would-be organizers, missionaries, or social workers these poor had ever seen. Instead of looking down on them, we tried to apply our skills in a process of "looking up," searching for answers from their experience instead of from experts.

The goal of our organizing plan was for people to overcome their fears and self-doubts and go on eventually to become their own community organizers and leaders. Every morning about nine-thirty we held a staff meeting. Between ten and twelve, and again in the afternoon, we went out in two-person teams to what we called "the blocks." The neighborhood was divided by streets, each to be organized door by door into block associations. We went to each house asking people their grievances and talking up the need to form an organization. About one out of every ten or fifteen people would be interested; at that rate, you had to talk with 150 people to get a house meeting of fifteen or twenty people, the minimum size we defined as a real group. The common grievances were dilapidated housing, high rents or property taxes (for the few on each street who were homeowners), lack of streetlights and effective garbage collection, welfare, and police abuse. This neighborhood process did not lend itself to organizing around job issues. We tried, with only limited results, to organize hospital workers into a union by recruiting workers to attend house meetings, but it was difficult to unify them.

Petty, emotional differences often kept people from working together: parental hostility toward the lifestyle of young people, for example, or a homeowners' tendency to blame welfare mothers for their problems. There was a pervasive pattern of blaming individual weakness as the cause of social ill. Most people lived inside the narrow "personal milieu" C. Wright Mills had described; our task was to penetrate that isolated web and replace it with a *social* one. To accomplish this, we found a process that worked quite naturally. We would encourage one person after another at meetings to talk about specific problems until they were all shaking their heads in agreement and a *system* of collective abuse had become apparent. Thus, the first step was in transferring blame from oneself to institutions. In addition, through the therapeutic experience of speaking out after so many years of voicelessness, a sense of pride and ability could begin to grow. Our work was to encourage this process, through which the people we had organized became organizers themselves. Our leadership had to be transformed into theirs.

It was hard but rewarding work. Hard because we were rejected nine out of ten times at the door, often by people who needed help the most. But it was rewarding, because that 10 percent could develop into a large number of committed people—and did. In a few weeks, we had 250 people meeting in about fifteen block groups. We began knitting them into a neighborhood-wide organization so that people from each block would see their common problems in larger perspective. We held weekly meetings of the block leaders, which led to a neighborhood leadership body. We opened a storefront office on a seven-day basis. Soon our mimeos were pouring out leaflets announcing meetings and demonstrations or outlining in simple terms such subjects as tenants' rights and where to get legal aid. We encountered friction with some of the white liberals who had helped invite us to Newark and were now becoming threatened by the emergence of a grassroots organization of black poor people they couldn't control. From that rift, so similar to the conflicts between SDS and the League for Industrial Democracy old guard, we concluded that we would have to form an organization of our own rather than joining a coalition with more traditional forces in the city. We named ourselves the Newark Community Union Project (NCUP, pronounced EN-cup) embodying the idea that people in communities controlled by outside and downtown interests had to form unions just as they did in the workplace to contend with the front office.

One day I received an invitation to Washington from the Peace Corps, which was then headed by Frank Mankiewicz. They asked me to "explore" working together on a common project, but wouldn't give more details.

Curious, I flew from Newark Airport to hear what they had in mind. Ever the organizer, I think I was wearing a red-and-black wool jacket on top of the usual khakis. I met with Mankiewicz after a long preliminary meeting with an aide and was startled to hear him ask if I would be interested in training Peace Corps volunteers in Latin America. The Andes could be mine, he said, laughing. I said, no, I didn't think so, but made a counter-offer that NCUP train VISTA volunteers in American slums, barrios, and hollows. VISTA was the federal government's response to SDS and SNCC organizing, providing an opportunity for volunteer service in poverty areas. While the VISTA volunteers were more moderate and conventional in approach than, say, NCUP organizers, many of them were motivated by strong idealism and compatible objectives. My proposal was serious, and we agreed on an informal training arrangement. After a few more meetings, the idea lapsed; but ironically, the Campaign for Economic Democracy (CED), which I formed twelve years later in California, did train VISTA workers on a grant from the Carter administration.

Official recognition of poverty had been triggered by Mike Harrington's *The Other America,* but the real impetus for federal action was the threat of violence and radicalism in the cities. The federal troubleshooter assigned to Newark, Father Theodore Gibson, acknowledged as much in an interview with the local paper when he said he was "convinced that the antipoverty program was the key to racial peace in Newark this summer." Even members of the most militant groups, he said, "were so busy working on antipoverty projects that they had little time to stir up dissension."

Instead of trying to contain these ghetto energies, I believed it was necessary to release the potential of people who were bottled up by the system. Contrary to the image of unstable and dangerous ghetto culture, I was impressed by how many people responded quickly and enthusiastically to positive incentives and how many were personally well-organized and responsible individuals in spite of the pressures of being made marginal. I found countless people in Newark who truly were "the salt of the earth," living decent and caring lives in spite of a system that minimized their potential. . . .

THE FIRE NEXT TIME: JULY 1967

When the Newark riot began on July 12, 1967, I was playing football.

This minor fact turned out to be quite important in saving me from a conspiracy indictment. The police were sure that an outside mastermind had to be manipulating events that week. They tried for weeks to blame me for the riot, but were stopped cold when a secretary, herself the wife of a policeman, confirmed that I indeed was playing football. She knew because her employer, attorney Leonard Weinglass, was throwing passes to me in front of his office.

Besides football, my friend Len liked his human-scale law practice, teaching property law to Rutgers students, and his memories of Yale Law School and Air Force service in Greenland. We first met inside a Newark tenement building. A close friend of his, a VISTA volunteer who knew me slightly, brought us together in what became a long friendship. I persuaded him to take some court cases involving rent strikers and welfare mothers. He was a few years older than I was, balding and affable, a character out of a Philip Roth novel. His strong sense of morality, even guilt, combined with his sincerity and intelligence, made him a very effective courtroom advocate for unpopular clients. He might have made an excellent candidate for office, but he was never much for politics. He was good company. When downtown, I would often drop by his office—across the street from Rutgers Law School—for conversation, a break, some football in the street, as I did on that particularly hot night in July.

While I kept trying to catch passes over my head by streetlight, a phone call came to Len's office indicating that "trouble" was starting in the Central Ward. We jumped in his car and drove ten minutes to the lower economic pits of Newark's ghetto.

We parked amid the tall housing projects, which looked like a ghostly gathering of prisons, and walked quickly toward the Fourth Police Precinct, an aging brick building, where hundreds of people were milling around. It looked like the Bastille during the French Revolution.

Moments after we arrived, a Molotov cocktail hit the wall of the police station and broke into a long spiraling column of flame. The people cheered. Len gasped, half smiling in awe. It was the opening shot in a rebellion which, along with the one in Detroit the following week, would be the largest of those violent years. In five days, twenty-six people were killed, a thousand injured, fourteen hundred arrested and sixteen million dollars' worth of damage done to property, as nearly six thousand police, state troopers, and national guardsmen tried to restore order.

The roots of the violence lay tangled in years of blind neglect by the authorities. Newark's officials were confident that their city was immune to the wave of urban riots occurring throughout America. In May, a city official told the *New York Times* that only a "few agitators" wanted any violence; in June, Mayor Hugh J. Addonizio declared that his "open door" administration had the confidence of the black community. It was not the first time I would hear pompous proclamations from high officials blindly on the brink of their political graves.

The immediate cause of friction was the behavior of Newark's virtually all-white police department. The police force reflected the white ethnic groupings—mainly Italian and Irish—that dominated Newark's government in the generation before transition to a black majority. Seeing themselves as defenders of a way of life on the decline, many of the officers were overflowing with resentment. Their hostility and defensiveness was expressed in a five-day, five-thousand-strong demonstration in 1965 in response to local civil rights marches against police brutality. While fiercely opposing a civilian review board, the Newark police offered no convincing alternative for dealing with widespread citizen complaints against their officers. An in-house complaint-referral system lacked the confidence of the community and, when occasionally used, didn't deter irresponsible behavior. Of a meager sixty complaints lodged against police in the six years before July 1967, the police investigators substantiated the claim of brutality only twice, meting out only minor discipline in both cases. Under increasing community pressure in 1965, the mayor agreed to forward certain complaints to the FBI; but of seven cases reported by July 1967, no action was taken by the federal authorities either.

The explosion was set off by a routine incident on the night of July 12. Two policemen arrested a black cab driver for tailgating and driving the wrong way on a one-way street. The cab driver, John Smith, was badly beaten in the course of the arrest, leaving him with broken ribs and a split scalp. Community people saw Smith being dragged into the Fourth Precinct. The rumor spread that the police had beaten the cab driver, and angry people began to assemble on the streets. Civil rights leaders, hearing of the beating, arrived at the police station in time to see Smith's condition and lodge complaints of unnecessary force. But this night would not end with a mere exchange of words on a picket line. The "moment" had arrived, the Molotovs flew, and in an hour, the looting of nearby white-owned stores was under way.

There were thousands of people on the streets taking advantage of the temporary police paralysis, ripping iron bars off storefronts, smashing windows, and loading their arms with tape recorders, toasters, televisions, clothing, and bottles of liquor. There were well-dressed middle-class couples, no doubt on their way to a party or movie, shiftless young street people, hustlers, groups of neighbors, even people driving trucks up to the inviting windows. There was exhilaration and no sense of guilt; after all, it was felt, the store owners had been ripping off the ghetto for years. Most interesting, there was an order of sorts within this "breakdown of law and order." As I wandered through the stores and streets for two hours, I saw no one injured, trampled, or cut by flying glass, no one fighting over property, no one criticizing the events. There were a very few people totally crazed by the excitement, starting fires in certain stores, throwing Molotovs onto factory roofs, and taunting the police.

FBI MEMORANDUM

The patrolman questioned Hayden as to why he was not attacked by the mob, the patrolman not knowing who Hayden was, why Hayden had stopped there to talk with him and he talked to them. . . . It should be pointed out that this was at the height of the riot and the rioters were particularly anti-white, and here was a white man, Thomas Hayden, able to move among them without any difficulty whatsoever.

I didn't even find the rioters to be especially anti-white. They seemed surprised to see me and other whites from NCUP in the streets, but there was no open hostility that first night. The rebellion was against racism, against the system, against indifferent politicians, but it was strangely color-blind on a personal level. Looked at from the inside, this apparently irrational explosion was a classic case of a "festival of the oppressed." I began to understand that beneath the image of disorder, and beyond the traditional debates over nonviolence, there was another dimension here: the riot was a rite of passage from feelings of servitude to the proud psychic independence of "black power."

When Governor Richard Hughes rolled into Newark after the second night with four thousand virtually all-white National Guardsmen and five hundred state troopers to relieve Newark's thirteen hundred police, a grim weekend of military occupation and terror began. Until that point, despite the widespread looting, no one was dead. Now, however, an eerie tension settled on the streets, as people backed into their homes or stores and watched the circling convoys of police cars, jeeps, and military trucks patrolling the ghetto. Bayonets were attached to the guards' M-1 rifles or .30-caliber carbines, which they carried in addition to .45-caliber pistols. Armored personnel carriers weighing eleven tons, as well as trucks with mounted machine guns, joined the patrol by Friday afternoon. By that night, the police or military had killed ten blacks, and wounded one hundred with gunshot; another five hundred were treated at City Hospital for various injuries. By the end of the weekend, another ten were dead, at least fifty wounded, and over five hundred arrested. I spent most of my time with NCUP staff, poverty program attorneys, and news reporters trying to piece together the stories of the killings. I sensed an indiscriminate violence against innocent people—several of them mothers looking out their windows—as I interviewed shaken witnesses in their homes and cross-checked details with other investigators.

For instance, 19-year-old James Rutledge was killed on Sunday afternoon. According to police, he was caught in a looted tavern, pulled a knife, and had to be shot. The body of James Rutledge had forty-two holes in the head and upper torso.

Rose Abraham, a domestic worker, was shot by police as she searched for one of her six children in the streets. She was not operated on for six hours after her husband brought her to the city hospital.

Ted Bell, 28, an employee in a looted bar, told people not to run if police started shooting. A moment later a police bullet killed him. There was Leroy Boyd, with six .38-caliber bullets in his body and a bashed-in head; Rebecca Brown, a mother of four, killed when the military fired into her apartment building while she attempted to snatch her two-year-old away from a window; William Furr, 35, shot in the back in broad daylight for carrying a six-pack of beer down the street, as a *Life* magazine photographer clicked off the sequence; Hattie Gainer, killed by a police bullet fired into her apartment as her three grandchildren watched; Richard Taliaferro, 25, wounded and then "finished off," according to eyewitnesses, one week before his induction into the U.S. Army.

In the course of this mayhem, one policeman and one fireman were also killed by bullets that could have been fired by blacks but just as possibly by guardsmen. Though *Life* magazine sensationally reported a "secret meeting with the snipers," I believed they were being set up, and one account later noted that the journalists paid money for the interview. Months later, Newark's police chief told an investigating commission that "it was so bad that guardsmen were firing on police and police were firing back at them. I think a lot of the reports of snipers were due to the, I hate to use the word, trigger-happy guardsmen, who were firing at noises and firing indiscriminately."

"Where are you going, nigger?" "Kill that nigger bitch." "Get moving or I'll take that camera and wrap it around your head." "You son of a bitch, I'll fix you so you don't drive any more cabs." "Where do you think you're going, you black bastard?" "Kennedy's not with you now." These were typical of the hundreds of verbal police attacks our investigators recorded. The police additionally smashed approximately one hundred black-owned stores that had been spared by looters. They simply shot into the windows marked SOUL BROTHER or broke in with rifle butts.

The jails were overflowing by Sunday. Over fourteen hundred blacks were detained, on bail ranging from $1,000 to $10,000. Most were charged with looting, only three with attempted arson, and none for shooting and bombing. Except for 150 juveniles, no one arrested was fed until Saturday, many not until Sunday.

While white suburbanites read of looting, arson and snipers, the truth was that the looting was essentially dying down *before* the massive military buildup began. Arson, while frequently reported, was actually limited to twenty-five cases, nearly all before Saturday. The troops were not protecting the downtown business district or the white suburbs by patrolling the inner city. From a pure crowd-control standpoint, had the black areas been cordoned off, they would have cooled down by the weekend. Instead, the troops were provoking and intimidating people.

Governor Hughes declared that the "line between the jungle and law and order might as well be drawn here as anyplace in America," adding for good measure that blacks "had better choose sides" because "the side of law and order has joined this to the finish." Perhaps carried away as commander-in-chief, he also announced a "thrill of pride in the way state police and the National Guard have conducted themselves." His words sounded more like those of a Rhodesian military governor than a liberal Democratic politician. To the black community, the governor's purpose seemed not to restore order in the most efficient way, but to teach a lesson: that anarchic rebellion, even against years of empty promises, would be forcibly punished and that white authorities would kill human beings for stealing property.

In this grim setting, we at NCUP had long discussions about what to do. Once the military occupation began, we were in serious danger, like everyone else, if we went out on the streets at night, even to our office. We watched the endless military patrols racing down the street with automatic weapons pointed at the houses. We observed the daily confrontations between poorly trained National Guardsmen and unpredictable swarms of black teenagers taunting them at bayonet point. We tried to collect as much food and medical supplies as possible from outside the community, having great difficulty with the logistics. (One of the shipments came from a community store in New York run by a zany, passionate former civil rights worker named Abbie Hoffman—the first time our paths crossed.) I worked relentlessly on collecting the detailed, eyewitness complaints.

One night, as I worked at the Legal Services office, a phone call came from Furman Templeton, a young, black governor's aide who had attended Newark Law School. His message was that Governor Hughes was finally beginning to search for an alternative to the military occupation, but that serious debates were still raging between "hawks" and "doves" within his circles. Templeton asked if I would come, as an eyewitness, to make a presentation. Also invited was a close friend of mine, Bob Curvin of CORE. I immediately agreed. It would be weird to meet the man whose decisions were leading to all the grief I was documenting on my desk, but I would do anything to help end the madness.

Shortly, a state troopers' car pulled up outside the Legal Services office. As I got inside, four troopers were standing outside the vehicle at military attention with automatic weapons drawn. We were going only a short way to the Federal Building, but for security reasons the troopers drove in a long, whipping circle around the outside of the city to get there. Most troopers came from conservative downstate New Jersey towns, and at the time all but five of the twelve hundred were white. Sitting between these uniformed musclemen in the back seat, racing through the dark streets with lights low and weapons drawn, listening to the hysterical chatter of the radio system, seeing fire engines, armored cars, flashing lights, all reinforced by the original mind-set which the men themselves brought to the ghetto, I could see how they believed themselves to be at war. They had no human contact. Each group of blacks turning the corner might be the enemy. None could be talked to or trusted. It was an urban Vietnam. These men, I realized, were the governor's official point of contact with the community during the crisis.

The vehicle slowed cautiously at the Federal Building, and the troopers leaped out and pointed their weapons at the rooftops. I was escorted inside the building and entered a suite of offices which seemed to be used as a headquarters or crisis center for officials. I saw a bewildered Bob Curvin immediately, then the other figures began taking shape, until I at last saw the governor, a strangely cheery, curly-haired, ruddy man who motioned us to be comfortable. The "doves" present included Furman Templeton as well as an "urban specialist" from the Ford Foundation, Paul Ylvisaker. The "hawks" were mainly the police, trooper, and National Guard officials sitting grim-faced along one side of a mahogany table.

I didn't feel comfortable in the isolated "war room," sitting there red-eyed, wearing a faded shirt and Levi's, talking about the mechanized terror in the streets. I had no exact idea why we had been called, but I assumed that our task was to convince the governor to withdraw his troops. As with Vietnam, he was worried about a possible "bloodbath" if they withdrew and also about a political backlash if the rioting then continued.

"Governor," I began, "there is a massacre going on outside in the streets, and it is caused primarily by the presence of the troops. In the first two nights people rioted and looted, yes, but the violence did not get directed against people until you brought the troops here. Now there has been so much brutality against so many innocent people that you have radicalized the whole community into a hatred. If you don't get the troops out, some people might really start firing on them. If you don't get them out, you could have twice as many dead in two days, and no end in sight. You should leave the people alone, let them bury their dead, heal the injured, take back the prisoners, let the normal fabric of life be restored. Nothing is likely to happen if you withdraw, but if you stay it will only get worse." Bob Curvin said much the same thing, containing his anger and concentrating on the need for a solution.

The "hawks" at the table complained that their men were being fired on and had to fire back for protection, that a withdrawal would be followed by more ransacking and bloodletting. The "doves," in their turn, wanted steps toward peace through negotiations. The governor asked what we thought of an enclave theory—the withdrawal of troops from one neighborhood and, if no violence followed, more withdrawals later. Bob and I looked at each other, then I said, "It's not necessary to test the water. You should just withdraw. But if it would give you greater security, you should begin in our neighborhood, Clinton Hill. Let it begin there, and the rest will follow."

I didn't expect much. Here we were, sitting in a command post, telling the governor that the reality in the heads of his military advisers was either crackpot or fabricated. In moments we would return to the streets, where the patrols roamed like sharks and the sounds of confrontation continued. We ended the meeting feeling pointless, confused by the governor's charming manner. He shook our hands firmly as we left and asked if there was anything he could do for us. I remember Bob Curvin blinking and requesting, with irony, protection from the Newark police. The governor laughed, reached for his card, and scribbled a note on the back. Mine was inscribed *To Tom, Good Luck, Dick Hughes.*

To my surprise the governor announced a complete troop withdrawal the next morning. Peace returned.

II The Vietnam War, the Antiwar Movement, and the Chicago Eight

6

The Other Side: Hanoi, 1965

From Reunion: A Memoir *(Random House, 1988)*

Vietnam today is at the forefront of nations working toward self-determination in a world of corporate globalization. In the absence of a "socialist camp," it must be difficult for Vietnam to come to terms with old foes like Japan and the United States. The Vietnamese, with their proud and independent history, must wish for more than serving as a cheap labor pool for other countries. They are among many nations, from China to Latin America, striving to peacefully change the balance of power and inequality across the world. After all they have been through, one can only wish them well.

People in the United States have largely forgotten Vietnam. Our government and elites have no interest in perpetuating the memory of defeat. The anti-Vietnam War movement will have to write itself into memory and history or face oblivion in mainstream histories to come. Among the things we learned from Vietnam are:

1) It is impossible to militarily defeat an independent nationalist culture;

2) Trying to conquer a popular nationalist movement inevitably requires torture and repression abroad, and the limiting of democracy at home;

3) Social movements have a role to play in complicating and eventually stopping foreign occupations, checking the tendency toward the imperial executive, and forcing a refocusing on domestic priorities.

All my life my aspiration toward making our country better has been invaded by forces seeking their global empire at our domestic expense. When Vietnam began, I was a civil rights worker and community organizer. When the Central American wars commenced, I was an elected member of the state legislature. When Iraq was invaded, I was immersed in fair trade and police reform issues in Los Angeles. The lesson of my experience is that democracy and empire don't mix.

The text that follows combines notes I wrote in 1965 (when I was 25 years old) with my 1988 retrospective, and still represents my feelings today.

◆   ◆   ◆

IN NOVEMBER 1965, while still immersed in Newark, my life suddenly took another direction. As the shadow of the Vietnam War cast its darkness over my hopes, I was drawn toward the shadow's mysterious source. I became one of the first of the few hundred Americans to visit and have contact with North Vietnam during the war. What began as an exercise in amateur diplomacy taught me more than I could imagine about war and revolution, inflicting unhealed scars, not to mention political baggage, that I still carry today.

It began with a phone call from Staughton Lynd. He and his wife, Alice, whom I knew well, were among the few remaining advocates of nonviolence as a way of life. Quakers by faith, they were drawn to the South to contribute to the civil rights movement; Staughton had directed the freedom schools in Mississippi in 1964. About a decade older than I, he looked trim and professional in his white shirts and ties, and his manner was caring and gentle. His parents, Robert and Helen Lynd, were pioneering sociologists who had authored *Middletown,* a well-known study of community power structures of Muncie, Indiana. Robert Lynd had also written *Knowledge for What?,* a study which had influenced C. Wright Mills and younger sociologists like Dick Flacks. In the fall of 1965, when many whites left SNCC, Staughton took a history department appointment at Yale. Increasingly, he was absorbed with the agony of Vietnam and was a major speaker at rallies and teach-ins. "Brother Tom," he asked, when I answered the phone, "how would you like to go to Hanoi?"

I was stunned.

Barely able to control his emotion, Staughton explained that Herbert Aptheker, a Marxist historian, had been in Eastern Europe at a conference attended by several North Vietnamese, who invited him to visit their country and asked if he would bring with him two noncommunist Americans concerned with peace. Aptheker invited Staughton; as a Quaker, Staughton

saw himself as a potential peacemaker, and was hopeful of finding a negotiating bridge between our government and Hanoi. He was worried about
the public image of traveling with a communist, but there was no other
practical possibility. In addition, he asked me how could he call for peace
with a communist government but be unwilling to travel there with a
communist? He had insisted on one condition from Herbert: that he select
the third person.

Staughton's first choice was Bob Moses, who was beginning to connect
the civil rights and peace issues, but Bob couldn't or wouldn't go, perhaps
reasoning that it would be too much additional pressure for SNCC to bear.
Staughton turned to me.

I also worried about the smear campaign that would surely be aimed at
NCUP and SDS from the trip. I took the startling proposal back to a staff
meeting in Newark and several days of soul-searching followed. We sat
around the floor of the apartment trying to develop a rational approach
to an issue that was almost beyond our understanding. Few, if any of us,
had ever traveled outside the United States. Our involvement with the
Vietnam issue was confined to reading what we could and bringing several carloads of Newark people to demonstrations in Washington.

But in the end, the possibility of turning a corner of history outweighed
the dangers. I applied for a passport for the first time in my life, and raised
two thousand dollars for the trip from several liberal supporters of NCUP.
There was virtually no time, but I started to read and consult heavily. I
knew the most sensitive question would be, wasn't I supporting the enemy
against our boys? Being for peace was one thing, but traveling to Hanoi
was quite another. Was I an American or a traitor? In my innocence of
American political history, I thought that, in fact, the proposed trip was a
very American thing to do and that the best way to support American soldiers was to end the killing.

The fledgling antiwar movement was already becoming a serious problem for the government, and talk of repression of "unpatriotic" elements
was in the air. The cause of national division, as I saw it, was that the president, who promised in 1964 not to "send any American boys nine or ten
thousand miles away from home to do what Asian boys ought to do for

themselves," was doing just that. In 1964, the Democratic Party process had failed on two counts: it had rejected the Mississippi Freedom Democrats' credentials challenge and reneged on Johnson's pledge of "no wider war" in Vietnam. As a result, the turnout for the spring 1965 SDS march on Washington had been unexpectedly large. I was deeply impressed that day with three speakers: Bob Moses of SNCC, who said that Vietnam was a "mirror of America," Paul Potter, now SDS president, who said that the war was a "sharp razor" that would force us to "name the system" that was causing it, and Staughton Lynd himself, who compared the Vietnamese to figures being crucified. The huge march was followed a month later by massive and innovative teach-ins on college campuses and then in October by nationwide demonstrations involving over 100,000 people in nearly a thousand cities.

Draft boards were reclassifying certain protestors from II-S, which was a student deferment, to I-A. I vacillated between conscientious objection, although I didn't know whether I was an absolute pacifist, and the II-S deferment, although I didn't approve of the student privilege. When my number finally came up, I went to the induction center at Whitehall Street in lower Manhattan. I remember a great many very young and nervous men standing in naked embarrassment, a concentration-camp image that has never left my mind. I was classified I-Y, officially because of allergy problems, but I suppose in reality because the military wasn't taking any "maladjusted" protestors at the time. Shortly after, David Miller, a young Catholic pacifist, became the first person to burn his draft card, and the draft resistance movement began spreading.

Reading Kirkpatrick Sale's important 1973 book on SDS, I was reminded of how fiercely we were then opposed by Mississippi Senator John Stennis, chairman of the Armed Services Committee. Our segregationist foe was calling for the administration to "immediately move to jerk this movement up by the roots and grind it to bits before it has the opportunity to spread further." More important and crucial to understanding the New Left was the fact that liberal Democrats were ardent believers. Vice President Humphrey charged that the "international communist movement" had "organized and masterminded" the antidraft campaign. Senators who would later become doves, like Mike Mansfield and William Proxmire, were critical as well. James Reston of the *New York Times* attacked the peace movement for "not promoting peace but postponing it." Attorney General Nicholas Katzenbach declared that antidraft activity "begins to move in the direction of treason." The tone was set by President Johnson, who was convinced that a Soviet web of influence lay behind the emerging peace movement. Doris Kearns, a young, liberal White House intern who became a distinguished historian, later described him as raving about "communist conspiracies" threatening his administration. [All these claims were later refuted when a secret 1968 CIA report called "Restless Youth" was declassified thirty-plus years later.]

What became known as the "generation gap" stemmed from the very different world views of those of my father's era and my own. My father's generation believed—correctly—that they had defended democracy against *foreign* despotism; we believed we were defending democracy from its enemies at home. Chuck McDew, the first SNCC chairman, summarized the difference: our parents wanted to "make the world safe for democracy"; we felt compelled to "make democracy safe for the world." Second, our parents had seen a case of clear aggression across national boundaries by Nazi Germany in the late thirties, and it was met in the United States by calls for isolationism, peace pledges, negotiations, and worst of all, silent indifference—until it was too late for many victims. "Never again" was not only the postwar cry of the Jewish community, but also an instinctive response for Americans like my parents. In the wake of the world war, Soviet tanks rolled into Eastern Europe, and five years later the Korean War added new fears about foreign aggression, this time from the Chinese. It was predictable that my parents' generation would accept the official view that a "free" South Vietnam was being invaded by a northern aggressor with six hundred million Chinese waiting in the background. They were prepared to believe the logic of Lyndon Johnson that "the battle against Communism must be joined in Southeast Asia . . . or the United States must inevitably surrender the Pacific and pull out our defenses back to San Francisco." Or as the *New York Times* editorialized in 1950 "Indochina is critical—if it falls, all of Southeast Asia will be in mortal peril."

In retrospect, there is even something idealistic in my parents' generation's willingness to support a war against such unbelievable odds. Experience had taken them prisoner, and they failed to see Vietnam as a popular and nationalist struggle, with elements of a civil war, against the new foreigners, who happened to be Americans. In my generation's world view, the most apparent and unwanted invaders were our own armed forces—"white boots marchin' in a yellow land," as Phil Ochs sang—the very opposite of the dynamics of World War II.

Sadly, I had no chance to debate these diverging lessons of experience with my father. Perhaps I might have convinced him that the situation was not the same as in the days when I watched the San Diego skies for Japanese attackers. Perhaps not; for marine private Jack Hayden, *Semper fidelis* was an important commandment. My 1964 visit to my new sister was the last for a long time. As my life became more unconventional, and my image more notorious, my father stopped answering my letters. Our relationship descended into a complete break.

My relationship with my mother was different but no less troubled. Her loyalty was to her son, not to the U.S. Marines or any other institution, and she found the war incomprehensible. Years later, she would say "Indonesia" when referring to Indochina. But she made it painfully clear that my behavior caused her boundless embarrassment in her midwestern small-town circles. To maintain a relationship with me, she felt she had to cut her ties to her inquisitive neighbors.

I decided to go to Hanoi. I needed to know who this supposed enemy was. If my parents were wrong, the United States was making a disastrous mistake. If they were right, what did the U.S. government want to keep from the media and the American public by making travel to North Vietnam illegal by administrative directive? We were committing our human and economic resources to the discretion of a president who, in 1964, had pledged "not to send a single American boy." Was North Vietnam really invading South Vietnam, or was the United States itself intervening in an internal conflict? Was our government really only bombing "steel and concrete" military targets, as the president swore, or was the civilian population itself being assaulted? Was peace through military escalation just around the corner, or were conventional American military tactics futile against a popular guerrilla war? Was there really no hope for a negotiated settlement or was the United States escalating the war in a vain effort to impose a settlement from a position of strength? The journey would be a fact-finding mission. The war was too serious to let the facts be defined and monopolized by Lyndon Johnson and the Pentagon.

I also hoped that I could bring back an image of the Vietnamese as human beings. I was deeply disturbed by stereotypes of the "faceless Vietcong." Whether it was Lyndon Johnson as a congressman orating against being "bullied by any Oriental with a knife," or more sophisticated claims about Asian indifference to individual life, Americans were dehumanizing the enemy to make killing thousands of them easier.

Finally, there was an ethical imperative, the same one which Thoreau had argued with Emerson during the Mexican-American War (and which Casey had cited in the speech that affected me so deeply five years before): jailed for refusing to pay taxes in support of a war against Mexico, Thoreau spoke of the need to be "citizens of the world." In our time, C. Wright Mills had called for a "separate peace" between humanists in both Cold War blocs. We wanted to let the Vietnamese people know that napalm was not the monolithic message of American society, that there was "another America" that was not at war with them, and that there were Americans supportive of negotiations and a political settlement.

In preparation, I read *Man's Fate,* Andre Malraux's classic 1933 novel of revolutionary Asia, and was amazed to discover the history of anticolonialist Westerners in Indochina. In the 1920s, Malraux had been associated with the earliest Vietnamese revolutionaries and had even edited an anticolonialist paper in Saigon until it was shut down by the French government. On the way to Hanoi I read Malraux's novel, underlining the famous passage in which a police officer, about to put a young revolutionary to death, asks, "What do you call dignity? It doesn't mean anything." The doomed revolutionary replies, "The opposite of humiliation."

♦   ♦   ♦

On December 21, 1965—four years after being jailed in Georgia and conceiving the *Port Huron Statement,* and ten days after my twenty-sixth birthday—our two-engine Chinese passenger plane entered the airspace over North Vietnam. We had careened from plane to plane across the communist world, stopping in Prague, Moscow and Peking, where we were the first American travelers in many years. My quick impression from these first stops was that there was hardly a unified international communist "conspiracy" behind the Vietnamese. In fact, our brief discussions with Soviet and Chinese spokesmen showed they had national interests of their own in the Vietnam crisis. The Russians wanted nothing to interfere with a developing coexistence with the United States, and Herbert Aptheker echoed their view. But in Peking, we found leaders on the verge of Mao's Great Cultural Revolution who were eager to reject the "coexistence" thesis on behalf of a doctrine of permanent "people's war." In this view, any negotiations with the United States were a betrayal of the Vietnamese revolution, which the Chinese felt should continue to "total victory"—or the last drop of Vietnamese blood. These dialogues only increased my interest in whether Vietnam, as a small country, could find any independence in a world of such powerful blocs.

Now we were over the place itself; below was "enemy territory." The skies were thick with billowing clouds, and through them I could see green rice fields, carefully sustained by dikes and levees, a countryside nurtured through monsoons for four thousand years. The capital itself appeared lazily, a sprawling maze of low-scale yellowed buildings left behind by the French, surrounded by dense residential districts about five miles in diameter. There was occasionally a tiny hamlet or road crossing, but no signs of the "steel and concrete" the president claimed to be bombing, unless it was the lone railroad track rolling south of Hanoi. That narrow, two-lane road next to the tracks—a country lane by our standards—was indeed "Highway One," I was told.

According to U.S. State Department regulations, it was not "valid" to use a passport for travel to North Vietnam (or China, Cuba, Albania, or North Korea). Since this seemed to us to be an administrative tactic to interfere in freedom of travel, we decided upon a counter-technique: instead of using our passports, we traveled on visas issued by our hosts. A North Vietnamese soldier in olive-drab uniform came aboard the plane and waved us toward the terminal, a one-story, pale-green structure containing perhaps three rooms (it was bombed to rubble several years later). As I stepped to the ground, a Vietnamese man with a finely chiseled face, dressed in a suit and tie with a dark sweater, smiled and asked in a British accent, "Tom Hayden? Welcome to Vietnam."

He was Do Xuan Oanh, a representative of our host group, something called the Peace Committee. As with many things Vietnamese, the construction of his name was the exact reverse of ours, a cultural fact that I was struggling to understand. It meant that his last name (which was pronounced *weng*) was his first, or familiar name, and his first name was actually his last. While I was deciding which to address him by, Oanh kept unbalancing me with his formal British tone of speaking, which he had developed through listening to the BBC.

We drove on a rough road in two powerful black Russian-built Volgas, vehicles which look something like the limousines of American gangsters of the 1930's. Out the window I watched dozens of water buffalo guided by men, women and children through the deep mud of freshly irrigated fields. The people wore conical straw hats, faded old shirts, and rolled-up pants. Many were without shoes, while others wore "Ho Chi Minh sandals" made from scrap rubber. Children were everywhere, the little ones often carried on the hips of the slightly older. They held hands and clustered by the roadside to peer into our cars. I wondered who on earth they thought we were. If they were the quaking targets of the U.S. Air Force, it did not show. They seemed to be gossiping about us and would occasionally shout things that seemed to be funny.

The inner city was a visual flashback to French colonialism. The Vietnamese had seized it from the French in August 1945 when they declared an independent state, using quotes from the American Declaration of Independence. Aside from keeping the streets immaculately clean, it didn't look as if the former servants had spent much time refurbishing the previous master's buildings. The walls were invariably a faded plaster, the structures spacious and high-ceilinged with long, narrow windows open-ing out on little balconies.

We finally stopped at a several-story building, the former colonial Hôtel Métropole, now renamed the Thong Nhat, or Reunification Hotel. Inside there was a lobby with pillars along the sides and overhead fans, leading to an elegant little bar which was a historic watering hole for journalists and diplomats in this and previous wars. After a ritual glass of sweet rice wine, we were led to our upstairs rooms, each of which seemed large enough for a family, complete with four-poster beds covered with mos-quito netting, little tables brimming with fruit, candy, tea leaves, and thermos bottles of hot water. I was exhausted but couldn't rest.

Shortly after taking my first walk in the streets of the city, I rushed to set my impressions down in notes. Cars were almost completely absent, leaving a calm silence broken by an occasional trolley and the whirling, clicking sounds of thousands of bicycles. Often couples rode together, the woman or child seated sideways above the rear fender. Now and then a water buffalo tugging a cart of wood came plodding around a corner. Some people walked along with long bamboo poles suspended across their shoulders, on which hung baskets of bricks and belongings. Though many children had been evacuated to the countryside, a few played games in the street that resembled hopscotch and jump rope, eagerly tempting us to join. Some of the adults would show exasperation as bicycles plied through the streets, veering dangerously close to each other, but the overall impres-sion was of patience and harmony. There were no armed police visible anywhere, though I was sure they could be summoned. I saw no beggars.

In Hanoi's center was the Lake of the Restored Sword, referring to a leg-endary tale of national resistance. It was surrounded by a park and the trolley line. As I looked more closely at the streets, I was startled to see hun-dreds of individual bomb shelters, which looked exactly like manholes with covers, just large enough for an adult and an infant, or perhaps two cramped adults. On some of the park benches by the shelters, couples sat talking intimately, while on others people read or slept. Some children played in and around a larger bomb shelter, which looked like the outdoor restroom in an American park.

First impressions are very important to me, and the dawning sense I had that day in Hanoi was of fearlessness, calm determination, pride, even serenity. If the buildings were drab, the people's faces were not. They showed curiosity, sentimentalism, directness, gentleness, dignity. They were not faces I associated with a communist city. In later years, I would walk through East Berlin, for example; its surface seemed depressed in comparison with what I saw on my first strolls through Hanoi. Though I was fast succumbing to a romantic conception of the Vietnamese I met, my views of revolution and violence were still forming. In notes at the time, I rejected the stereotype of the Vietcong guerrilla as a "mean little man, living like a beast off berries in the jungle, occasionally disemboweling a villager to terrify others, so feebly endowed with personal values that he can be the torturer or the tortured without flinching." I was seeing with my own eyes that these were human beings before me, many of them inspired (and inspiring) because of their revolutionary experience. On the other hand, I wrote, "The Vietnamese revolution has not been pure; innocent people have been killed; decent men have been purged." But this revolution was also a fact, an objective force which could not be reversed by American violence, only hardened. Staughton and I concluded that "we believe in identifying with the revolutionary process and finding ways within one's limits to make it as humane as possible."

Most of my memories of the Vietnamese experience are collective ones, a whole society more than specific individuals. The language barrier and cultural modesty kept most of the individual Vietnamese we met from projecting any trademarks or idiosyncrasies. Perhaps it was Do Xuan Oanh I came to know best. Then forty-three years old, he was born aboard a fishing boat on the magical Halong Bay in the Gulf of Tonkin. As a youth, Oanh worked in the French coal mines; in spare hours, he studied music. In the war against the French, he joined the Vietminh army in the jungles. His wife had been seized and tortured by the French in Hanoi; because she still felt the effects of the cold, damp weather, we met the shy, smiling mother of two only briefly.

After the 1954 Geneva Accords, Oanh joined the Peace Committee, which, I learned, was a mechanism frequently used by communist governments to develop "fraternal" relations with peace movements or non-governmental visitors from other countries. In 1965, we were the committee's first American guests, a fact which kept Oanh and his friends continually anxious. I was intrigued at his dual task, which was not only to guide us through North Vietnam, but to educate his own country favorably about America. It was Oanh's intent to point out a "progressive" and "democratic" side of American life to the Vietnamese, who were under daily siege. As I was beginning to lose faith in precisely the American virtues that Oanh was determined to idealize, our relationship became one of intense discussion. When I first asked him why he was so interested in putting a positive face on the United States, Oanh remarked simply, "To reduce hatred." There were strategic reasons as well: North Vietnam wanted to affect American public opinion. That is why, I assumed, nearly every Vietnamese we met quickly and mechanically drew a distinction between the American government's policy and that of the "progressive and democratic American people."

But Oanh, in addition, seemed to be a genuine romantic. We discovered that he had recently published a song about Norman Morrison, an American Quaker friend of Staughton's who had burned himself on the steps of the Pentagon two months before. While the American press dismissed the suicide as that of a disturbed and demented individual, Oanh was fascinated that Morrison, an American, had chosen an Asian, and Buddhist, form of death. Oanh's widely published poem, which said that "Morrison's flame will enlighten life," made the Quaker protestor known to thousands in North Vietnam.

There was one thing that seemed even more touching than Oanh's focus on Morrison; we learned that Oanh had laboriously translated *The Adventures of Huckleberry Finn* into Vietnamese. Shortly before we arrived in the country, Hanoi newspapers had reported that a copy of Oanh's translation was found on the body of a schoolgirl killed by American bombs. Though obviously trusted to represent the Hanoi government faithfully, his personality ranged far beyond most bureaucratic boundaries. After so many years of hearing about faceless communist *apparatchiks*, his openness and Western ways were deeply disarming.

I also was impressed with the historic antiquity of revolutionary nation-alism in Vietnam and how little even "informed" Americans like myself knew of it. I understood the long resistance war against the French and the legendary military triumph at Dien Bien Phu reasonably well, but not the depth of betrayal the Vietnamese felt over the 1954 Geneva Accords, which were supposed to have been followed by internationally supervised, secret-ballot national elections two years later, elections which were never held. The United States opted to support the new Republic of South Vietnam, rather than risk the overwhelming likelihood that Ho Chi Minh would prevail at the ballot box. But the fact that *national* elections were agreed to—by all negotiating parties, including the French—meant that Vietnam was recognized as one country divided into two temporary zones, not two separate countries, as our government subsequently attempted to stress.

The Geneva Conference was only "yesterday" in the span of Vietnamese national history. As I visited one museum after another and interviewed several Vietnamese historians, the weight of a thousand years of resistance wars settled on me. There was the "people's war" of the thirteenth century, when the Vietnamese resisted 500,000 troops of Kublai Khan, culminat-ing in a surprise sinking of the Mongol ships in the Bach Dang River in 1288. There was the Tay Son peasant revolt at the time of the American Revolution, an insurgency that climaxed in a Tet offensive in 1789. Little bronze arrows said to be a thousand years old were given to us by a museum director who had fought at Dien Bien Phu. He cried when he said good-bye to us, one of many of these supposedly "stoic Orientals" who shed tears during the course of our conversations.

At night I carefully studied *The Tale of Kieu,* a long narrative poem by Nguyen Du. It was urged on me by a Vietnamese writer as a key to the Viet-namese identity. Written in the eighteenth century, it was the epic story of a young woman, Kieu, who was separated from her lover and who experi-enced constant degradation, betrayal, and attempts on her life until she met him once again. Kieu's search, my friend was trying to tell me, was that of every Vietnamese for unification. Her willingness (and theirs) to sacrifice everything for principle was set down in lines known to most Vietnamese: "It matters little if a flower falls if the tree can keep its leaves green."

What drew my attention equally was another poem by the same author about the fate reserved for the long series of rulers who tried to vanquish Kieu's Vietnam on behalf of their own imperial ambitions. It appeared that the Vietnamese had seen and survived all forms of foreign vanity:

> *There were those who pursued power and glory,*
> *Who dreamt of conquest and power . . .*
> *Their golden palaces crumbled,*
> *And they envied a humble man's lot.*
> *Power and riches make many enemies . . .*
>
> *There were those who lived in curtained palaces,*
> *Priding themselves on their wealth and beauty.*
> *Then the storm came and thrones changed bands . . .*
> *Broken are the hairpins and the flower vases,*
> *Gone the animated voices and the laughter . . .*
>
> *There were those who wielded great power,*
> *Whose red-ink characters decided men's fates,*
> *Who were fountains of knowledge and experience.*
> *But prosperity and power engender hatred.*
>
> *There were those who pursued riches,*
> *Who lost appetite and sleep*
> *With no children or relations to inherit*
>   *their fortunes,*
>
> *With no one to bear their last words.*
> *Riches dissipate like passing clouds.*
> *Living, they had their hands full of gold.*
> *Departing from this world, they could take*
>   *not a single coin . . .*

There were those at the head of proud armies
Who sacked palaces and overturned thrones.
In a display of might like storm and thunder,
Thousands were killed for the glory of one man.
Then came defeat, and the battlefield was
strewn with corpses.
The unclaimed bones are lying somewhere in a
far-away land.
The rain is lashing down and the wind howling,
Who will now evoke their memory?

As I tried to absorb all this history, I began to feel that we Americans—especially those fighting these people—were like the characters in Joseph Conrad's *Heart of Darkness,* losing their moorings by wandering ever more deeply into an alien and bottomless cultural quagmire. "Whom the gods would destroy, they first make mad": to which I would add, "Whom they would make mad, they first make ignorant."

Looking back, there were dimensions of Vietnamese history that our hosts neglected to mention. I wish I had known, for example, of their centuries of imperial expansion southward into the kingdoms of Champa and Cambodia. Between 1650 and 1750, the whole Mekong Delta was wrested from the Khmer people, a historic root of the tragic and incomprehensible war between Vietnam and Cambodia in the late 1970s. These vital omissions aside, what the Vietnamese told us was essentially true, a history hidden from American minds like mine.

I encountered more of my ignorance by the day. We toured a factory that produced agricultural implements, for example, but the factory had been decentralized into small shops underground for protection against bombing. It was built over the site of a former French prison and named after a Vietnamese leader who fought against Genghis Khan. Of course, I thought, why not? With a tape recorder, I asked the workers what difference the Hanoi government had made in their lives; over and over the answer was concrete: literacy, education, a better standard of living. One told me he supported the Vietminh (the organized resistance against the

French) by "following the factory to the forest," where it was reassembled and production resumed. This had been his "normal" life for most of twenty-five years.

When we visited Phu Dien cooperative near Hanoi, it was the same oral history: stories of fighting to preserve real gains of the past. In this six-acre village of one thousand people, we were told that 137 people starved to death in 1945 (which, again, was like yesterday for many of these people), part of a nationwide famine just prior to the coming to power of the Vietminh. Another forty-five were killed in the French reconquest effort of 1946. There was mass illiteracy at that time, along with a host of uncontrolled diseases; everyone, they said, carried bamboo poles on their shoulders. But now, they continued, 75 percent of the households had bicycles, flasks of boiled water, and mosquito nets. Half their land was plowed by tractors, not buffalo; 85 percent of the homes were brick; fewer shoulders were burdened, and everyone was attending school at least part-time.

When I asked these villagers about communism, however, there was a tendency to rhetoric, but only in the way that some Americans attribute all good things to free enterprise. I asked two young women, carrying rifles as many did, what they thought of the American argument that their regime was a dictatorship under Chinese influence. They were peasants as well as members of a local self-defense group; two nights weekly they studied history, literature, and chemistry. They smiled demurely and scoffed at my question: "We love the party and socialism because thanks to the party our country has been liberated," they replied. "As women, we are conscious of our duties, and that is why we do what we do, not because of orders from the party, or from our government, or from China. We do things ourselves, by our own consciousness, not relying on anyone else." I found something wooden in their answers, and didn't think it was simply the translation. But on the other hand, theirs were simple patriotic statements, not different from the replies most Americans might give to similar questions. Did they feel free to speak up directly to their government? "Yes, of course, if you have something to say to the government, you should say it directly."

Certainly in my later experiences in places like Moscow or Warsaw, such questions would provoke comments of a more cynical nature, even cause people to lower their voices and look over their shoulders before speaking. But not here. As dusk came to the village, someone placed a lantern on the table around which these villagers and I had gathered, and they began questioning me with a destabilizing simplicity. "Do the American people know that their government is escalating the war?" "Do they know the reality of our country?" "What do *you* think, now that you have visited our village, because your government says we are not free and we live in slavery?" It gradually struck me that while these people lived under a one-party state with a government-controlled press, they were not easily deceived on the life-and-death issues. Many of them had seen it before, and all of them could measure the bombs and rockets falling, the number of young men leaving the village for war, the casualties, the increasing economic burdens. They knew more about their reality than we did in democratic America.

I found it hard to answer them, trying to be truthful and sensitive. I said that although Americans valued the family, hard work, and patriotism, just as these villagers did, the American people, in ignorance of Vietnam, might believe the president and support a further escalation of the war. The faces in the candlelight were somber and interested as the translator explained my words.

A bell called people to school, breaking our dialogue. One of the village leaders took my hand and said, "We would like to extend our thanks for your calling on us, and we wish you to convey to the American people, particularly the laboring people, our best wishes." Oh, sure, I thought. Mom and Dad will be real pleased, and so will the folks at Chrysler.

During our ten-day visit, we rushed to the large bomb shelter in the lower quarters of the Thong Nhat several times, but U.S. planes never attacked. We sensed that the wheels of diplomacy were turning, though we had no idea whether peace negotiations were near.

One afternoon we left Hanoi in two jeeps heavily camouflaged with branches and leaves. As the sun set two hours later, we slowly bumped around a bombed-out bridge across a narrow river and entered Nam Dinh, a major textile center about a hundred miles south of the capital. With a population of ninety thousand, including a majority of Catholics,

Nam Dinh had been bombed repeatedly. So for security reasons, night became day: People reversed their normal schedules and, as darkness came, moved around with flashlights to do their shopping in dimly lit stores. Their tiny beams also lit the way for countless bicycles and knots of pedestrians. Many people gathered in little circles, enjoying the cool of the evening for a cigarette and conversation. We drove out to the edge of town where a nursery school had been devastated by bombs and rockets. Walking through the rubble, I could read a slogan on a shattered wall: LET US BRING UP HEALTHY CHILDREN, LET US EDUCATE GOOD CHILDREN.

A short distance away was a bombed pagoda. Great holes in its high walls and roof allowed the light of stars to shine through. Searching the floor, I found some fragments of religious statues and put them in my pocket to take home. A monk in saffron robes told us that plans were already made to rebuild the structure.

Finally, we visited a textile factory, or rather, that twenty-by-thirty-foot section of a factory which had not yet been removed to the forests. All was dark except for the beams right in front of the women working at the weaving looms. Rifles hung on the ends of the looms. They barely looked up to notice us with our notepads, cameras and tape recorders. I sensed they were either not in much of a mood for American visitors or simply tired and strained.

Our interpreter broke into this surreal scene. "In order to ensure your safety, we have to leave now," he evenly said. An American bomber was prowling nearby, and we were under instruction to leave the city. We quickly said good-bye to those hosts who had briefly emerged from Nam Dinh's shadows to help us understand their world, then began the blackened drive back to Hanoi. Though we were on the slender road that the United States attacked most frequently, I felt overprotected compared to the people we left behind. But, I said to an interpreter, they seemed to be calm. "They have no other way to be than calm," he replied. As we bounced along the road, we heard the muffled thunder of bombs in the distance for the first time. Before the war was over, Nam Dinh would be completely destroyed—several times.

At the same time as our visit, the Johnson administration launched a "peace offensive," an international effort to create an image of willingness to talk rather than bomb. Of Johnson's effort, columnist Joseph Alsop wrote that "domestic political considerations were the prime motives of the vast international vaudeville which the President staged." But in Hanoi, Staughton Lynd took the ray of hope seriously and endeavored to discover as much as possible about North Vietnam's bargaining position. We met with officials like Ha Van Lau and Nguyen Minh Vy; unknown to us at the time, they would play prominent roles in the negotiations with the United States a decade later. Then on January 5, the day before our departure, we went to meet Prime Minister Pham Van Dong, one of the legendary leaders of the Vietnamese revolution from its infancy.

We drove to the former residence of the French governor-general, where the prime minister held official meetings, a lovely executive mansion surrounded by an expanse of gardens and lawns. As we stopped at the base of a high stone staircase, Pham Van Dong appeared at the top step and walked down alone. Perhaps it was his historic aura, but he was among the most striking world leaders I have ever seen. He was taller than most Vietnamese, and the features of his face seemed somehow like an American Indian's. His skin was reddish brown, his lips thick, cheekbones wide and prominent, and above a high forehead was a dramatic shock of silver hair. He wore a gray Oriental suit with a high collar buttoned at his throat, circled by a scarf. At sixty years, his eyes carried both the sparkle of youth and the depth of age.

Unfortunately, our meeting was too formal. It was, I believe, the first time that a top Hanoi official had met with Americans in any capacity. Pham Van Dong's staff asked us to submit diplomatic questions in advance, which we did. Our discussion was largely confined to a cordial exchange of views. Even so, Pham Van Dong's emotions and sentiments— which I came to know better through several meetings in subsequent years—came through clearly enough in this forty-five-minute talk. Steering away from diplomatic detail, he spoke in broad strokes:

> The Vietnamese people feel that they are fighting for a just cause against barbarous aggression. That is the central reality. The same thing happened when you fought against the British. . . . The lib-

eration movement in South Vietnam has become stronger than we here [in Hanoi] expected. I personally could not have imagined it. I was very anxious and concerned about what would happen when 200,000 American troops came. . . . When we say that we will fight ten or twenty years longer, these are not the words of rhetoric. . . .

The world is one. It is becoming smaller and smaller. History makes us closer to each other. That is a tendency which nothing can prevent. . . . The great truth of our time is that we must be brothers, fraternal toward each other. The highest sentiment is fraternity. This is the age of that sentiment. That is a noble ideology. If you have the opportunity to meet President Johnson, will you please ask him: Why is he fighting against us? There is no reason for it. . . .

At the end of a cordial discussion along these lines, an aide presented us with Pham Van Dong's written answers to the diplomatic questions we had submitted. These were formulated in the more cryptic language of diplomatic negotiators. Pham Van Dong was not a dreamy sentimentalist; he also had been the chief Vietminh negotiator at Geneva. In this statement, he denied that North Vietnamese troops were in the South, a statement we believed with difficulty. Staughton's guess was that several thousand Vietminh troops, regrouped northward as part of the Geneva Accords, had returned to the South. He later felt that our hosts, in attempting to justify the rebellion, which was indigenous to the South, had not told us the whole truth. He was right. There was, of course, a Ho Chi Minh Trail, and North Vietnamese soldiers traveled it, perhaps returning to the South, perhaps not. Most visitors to Hanoi were similarly misled.

Pham Van Dong called for the creation of a "broad national democratic coalition administration" in South Vietnam, including the National Liberation Front (NLF), but neutral and non-aligned. Most important to Staughton, the North Vietnamese were not intransigently demanding an American military withdrawal *before* talks with the United States could begin, as the Johnson administration claimed. We were told that a withdrawal of some "newly arrived [American] units," coupled with some sign of recognition of the NLF, would be enough to begin a process of negotiations.

We thanked Pham Van Dong for consenting to see us and returned to our hotel for our last evening in Hanoi. Staughton was excited by the diplomatic discussions and went off to type up his notes. Too overwhelmed by the entire trip to sit in my room, I went down to the Thong Nhat bar to watch the waitress, whose name was Minh Tinh. After two glasses of rice wine, I decided she was the most beautiful woman in Vietnam, a judgment I might have reached soberly. She wore a white jacket over black silk pants and wooden shoes that clicked on the tiled floor. Knowing that I could not understand her, she sang and talked to me with a teasing smile (as one might with a pet, I thought). Minh Tinh was also the leader of the hotel's anti-aircraft militia, a medal-winning marksman and a national Ping Pong champion. Irresistible and incomprehensible, romantic yet hardened, close but untouchable—like Vietnam. If I could only really know her . . . But it was time to go home.

Nothing came of our diplomatic "clarifications." Staughton spent several hours with State Department experts going over our notes, in which they saw nothing new. At the same time, the media was full of right-wing calls for our prosecution under the Logan Act, which prohibits "unauthorized persons" from engaging in diplomacy on their own, or under U.S. codes regarding "misuse" of passports. After three weeks, the United States resumed its bombing. Two days later, on February 2, the State Department temporarily withdrew our passports, declaring that we had acted in a manner "prejudicial to the orderly conduct of foreign relations" (a federal court later reversed the department's action).

We did manage to persuade Hanoi to admit an American correspondent for the first time, Harrison Salisbury of the *New York Times*. Later that year, he caused a public sensation with fourteen front-page articles charging that civilian casualties in North Vietnam were massive.

The Hanoi visit definitely deepened my sense of isolation from an America at war. The effect on my family was severe. When the news of our trip broke, the Michigan papers ran articles spotlighting both my parents. The *Royal Oak Tribune* news lead described my trip as "controversial and illegal" and myself as "one of those people that nobody really knows well." It then went on to describe my parents as divorced for a decade and printed their separate addresses. "The father," the *Tribune* went on,

> surprised by his son's unauthorized trip into the world's current No. 1 trouble spot, has had only minimal contact with Thomas in recent years.... "Tom was never in the service," he said in answer to a reporter's question, "but I don't know why." Hayden said his son's interest in such fields as civil rights and anti-U.S. foreign policy movements hadn't begun to bud while the family was living together. "I think he picked all that up in college," the father speculated.
>
> The mother, Mrs. Gene I. Hayden, 1217 East Fourth, Royal Oak, probably knows more about her only child than anyone in the area. But she has skillfully evaded reporters since news of the Hanoi trip broke Tuesday. Mrs. Hayden, a film librarian, talked only briefly with reporters, saying she hopes her son returns safely and "brings back some useful information." Mrs. Hayden said she had heard 'many fine things' about Lynd. Then she locked herself in her office at Martin Road School, 2500 Martin, Ferndale. Janitors barred reporters from entering the building. She left the school in her car, accompanied by a pet poodle, Tuesday afternoon, and has not been located since. A neighbor said Mrs. Hayden has "left town."

In fact, my mother moved into a motel and didn't leave for a week. A few friends came by her house, knocked on the door without success, and left little notes which she saved and I found many years later:

> Gene dear,
>
> I've tried to call you—many times—so please, when you can, call me. I just wanted to tell you how much we're all thinking of you—and if we can do anything at all, let us know . . . We've been

friends for so long—18 years!—and I'd like to help if I can, when you must be distressed and worried. Herb is sick, with a strep throat, but the rest of us are well. Bruce is enjoying his Christmas presents so much. The living room is impossible! My thoughts are with you constantly . . .

Much love,

JANE

Came by to "hold your hand" and sit a spell—call me when you have a chance.

GLADYS

Dear Gene,

We called to no avail, and I can't blame you for not answering your phone! Hank and I wanted to offer you a "refuge" from the mob in case you were in need of a place. My prayers and Masses have been with you and Tommy all week. Thank God there are still a few people left in this world with the courage of their own convictions.

KATIE

I first saw the war as America invading and dividing Vietnam. Now it was Vietnam, like a malignant tumor, invading and dividing us.

FBI MEMORANDUM 1/3/66

. . . inquiry was made this morning of Department Attorney James Welden to determine whether the Department is actively considering prosecution when Aptheker, Lynd and Hayden return to the United States.

Welden said that the Department is extremely interested in prosecution.

FBI MEMORANDUM 2/11/66

The attached article, which appeared in the "New York Times," indicates that the Administration is deliberately refraining from immediate prosecutive action against Aptheker, Lynd or Hayden "for fear of upsetting its current peace offensive." The article states that both the Justice and State departments, "apparently acting on orders from the White House," have decided to go slow in taking any legal action on the case.

At approximately 3:40 p.m., 1/11/66, Yeagley called and said he had talked to the Attorney General and the Attorney General was concerned that the investigation might cause a "furor." Yeagley said in view of this, we should restrict our investigation to interviewing members of the press media who were known to be at the airport when Aptheker, Lynd and Hayden returned to the United States.

TO: DIRECTOR, FBI 3/10/66
FROM: SAC, NEWARK

In planning the future course of this investigation, consideration has been given to requesting Bureau authority to interview the subject.

Several factors indicate that this would be the next logical step. These factors include: statements made by Herbert Aptheker that he considers the subject to be mildly anticommunist, lack of any statements or activities of the subject prior to his trip to Hanoi indicating any disloyalty to the United States, possible intelligence information possessed by the subject as a result of his trip to Hanoi.

It is also felt that subject's trip to Hanoi and his statements since his return may qualify him for the Security Index . . . Prior to recommending subject's inclusion on the Security Index on this basis, an interview of the subject to explore his present attitude seems desirable.

(referred to CIA)

TO: SAC, NEWARK 4/1/66
FROM: DIRECTOR, FBI
THOMAS EMMETT HAYDEN
(referred to CIA)

With regard to your consideration that subject be interviewed, it is pointed out to you that the matter of subject's recent trip to Hanoi is still under prosecutive consideration by the Department of Justice and, therefore, no interview of the subject should be contemplated at this time.

You should submit your recommendations as to whether or not the subject should be included on either the Security Index or the Reserve Index.

FBI SECRET
TO: DIRECTOR, FBI
FROM: SAC, NEWARK 4/19/66
THOMAS EMMETT HAYDEN

RECOMMENDATION:
In view of subject's recent unauthorized trip to North Vietnam with Aptheker and Lynd, it is being recommended that he be placed on the Security Index of the Newark office.

ADDENDUM DOMESTIC INTELLIGENCE DIVISION 5/6/66
Central Intelligence Agency has advised that they have never had an operational interest in Hayden.

7.

Vietnam: The Struggle for Peace

Published as an Indochina Peace Campaign pamphlet, February 1973

In fall 1972, Jane Fonda and I, along with singer Holly Near, former POW George Smith, and Saigon prisoner Jean-Pierre Debris, spoke several times a day in 100 cities against the war. Politically, our long-shot hope for a George McGovern victory was destroyed when McGovern switched his vice-presidential candidate shortly after the nomination. Nevertheless, the Nixon administration was worried enough to negotiate the appearance of a peace agreement before the election, conveyed by Henry Kissinger's "peace is at hand" declaration in October. Promptly after winning reelection, Nixon unleashed the saturation bombing of Hanoi at Christmas, which he would claim forced the Vietnamese to release American POWs and recognize America's client state in South Vietnam. It turned out to be a face-saving retreat for the United States, who pulled American troops out of Vietnam while accepting the presence of thousands of North Vietnamese combat forces for what Kissinger called "a decent interval" in the South. Within two years, the Saigon government collapsed in the face of a renewed offensive.

◆　　◆　　◆

THE PEACE AGREEMENT of January 1973 formally brings to an end America's direct military involvement in Vietnam and charts a course for self-determination in that land. The Agreement marks the greatest victory of a Third World resistance movement against a great Western power yet, and it is a turning point in world history still not fully appreciated.

This pamphlet brings together several essays on the 1972 Vietnam offensive which led to the Peace Agreement; a copy of the Agreement itself; and several Vietnamese interpretations of their own accomplishment. The materials focus on the importance of events inside Vietnam itself, especially the offensive.

A mention—really, a further pamphlet—is necessary, however, on the role of the American anti-war movement in securing this Agreement. It is our victory, ours and Vietnam's, and not Richard Nixon's. Great changes in public opinion have occurred because of our movement, and these changes have weighed heavily on each Administration. Eight years ago only two senators would vote against Vietnam appropriations; this year, if the cease-fire was not signed, the Senate and possibly the House would have voted against the war. Opposition to U.S. policy has grown in every walk of life, perhaps most dramatically within the armed forces where tens of thousands have deserted and thousands more fill the stockades. We retired one president and forced another to make the unpopular war invisible and, that failing, formally terminate it. We made it impossible for the Executive to ask the Congress for war taxes and thus forced an economic crisis as a cost of the war. We created social costs—"the generation gap," "the credibility gap"—that moved many establishment figures to reconsider the Vietnam investment. We showed the Vietnamese and Third World people that an aggressive war will be met with broad resistance inside America, and thus created a modest beacon of hope for the world. Our own consciences were found, and our politics gradually revolutionized for the future.

We did not do enough. Millions suffered to make us do what we did. But we did enough to help impose a settlement on America's more arrogant and conservative leaders, Richard Nixon and Spiro Agnew, who have long sought not only domination of South Vietnam but also loyal obedience at home.

Our victory is real, but we have to understand it to make it meaningful. The Vietnamese attitude of providing a non-humiliating "way out" means they will not win in one dramatic blow. Nixon certainly has a stake in making the setback look like a victory. And even the attitudes of some of us make it difficult. Many people expected perhaps to see Madame Nguyen Thi Binh driven to Saigon in a captured American tank. We don't always identify with a step-by-step revolutionary process.

Change is not always gradual, as some wishfully believe, but neither is it instantaneous. Sometimes it is beneath the surface, in the villages instead of the city hotels, in people's minds instead of Pentagon computers. We are in such a time, when appearance blurs reality. The American people are feeling the change in varying ways—defensive righteousness, confusion, despair, distrust, the feelings of a nation whose official purposes are thwarted but not replaced.

We in the anti-war movement are perhaps the only force with rehabilitative power, because we ourselves have learned how to change our simple, childhood views of America and accept the fact that our country needs overhauling. Our task is to help others follow that path. We have to learn and teach the lessons of Vietnam well: It was not our war but it is our peace.

Of course, American involvement in Vietnam is not over, and of course the basis of re-escalated war is present there. That does not rob the Peace Agreement of its significance. The Agreement has brought peace and happiness to millions of people already, a fact that makes it more difficult to begin the war again. It has given America's Vietnamese "enemy" a new dignity, a change from the status of "bandits" to a revolutionary administration recognized by most countries of the world. And it gives the anti-war movement, which started as a fringe group attacking State Department "White Papers," the possibility of holding up an official Peace Agreement to use against any forces who intervene in Vietnam's affairs again.

Many of us have been so hardened by the prospect of lifelong struggle that we cannot easily savor victories when they come, especially a temporary victory for peace. Thus we are alienated from the fruits of our labor. In a world of injustice, peace cannot be expected for long. But peace itself is a value we should cherish, a value threatening to a system geared for war. We should cherish the thought that the skies of Vietnam are clearing, that the long-suffering guerrillas may embrace their families by day, that our machinery of death is being repelled and restrained. If we feel the happy possibilities of just this moment, we will fight all the harder to keep it this way forever.

North Vietnam Stands Defiant Under Storm of U.S. Bombs

Boston Globe, *January 1, 1973*

This article was written immediately after the Christmas bombing and before the signing of the peace agreement. It is clear that the Vietnamese revolutionaries envisioned, and the United States accepted, an indefinite phase of political struggle and coalition arrangements in the South. This was necessary, not only to provide a face-saving mechanism for the United States, but because the Vietnamese theoreticians believed that the two zones of Vietnam had evolved very differently since 1954, one as a socialist state and the other as an occupied neocolony of the United States. This model of revolution-in-stages became obsolete when the Saigon regime proved to be artificial and nonviable, leading to a North Vietnamese victory in the South and immediate reunification.

◆   ◆   ◆

TOM HAYDEN WROTE this article exclusively for *The Globe* last week, before the cessation of bombing on Saturday. He had spent December 18–26 in Oslo, Stockholm, Paris and London, meeting with antiwar organizations and representatives of the North Vietnamese and the Provisional Revolutionary Government (PRG).

◆   ◆   ◆

North Vietnamese negotiators in Paris still can conceive of a negotiated peace, but only if the United States stops bombing the Hanoi-Haiphong area and returns to the agreements reached in October between Henry Kissinger and Le Duc Tho.

They will not be bombed into any compromise of their fundamental national rights, they assert. The present saturation bombing of their cities will be repelled by their anti aircraft defense and world public opinion, they say, and it will be no more effective than the mining of Haiphong, the 1971 invasion of Laos, or the 1970 invasion of Cambodia.

Using B52s to stop a guerrilla war, they say, is like "using forks to eat soup."

"How can you have peace with honor and bomb the people of Hanoi?" one negotiator asked me. Real peace with honor, they maintain, must involve mutual compromise.

On their side is a willingness to recognize the "reality" of the U.S.-subsidized Thieu dictatorship. They are willing to shift their struggle against Thieu to the political level. But this requires a concession by the American side, to recognize the reality of the Provisional Revolutionary Government (PRG) in the political future of South Vietnam.

Having failed to eliminate the "Viet Cong" with 500,000 American troops and 15 million tons of bombs and shells, it was absurd for the Americans to hope for their disappearance through negotiations. And so, in October, a compromise was reached by both sides that would permit a "victory for peace" rather than guaranteed domination for either.

But after the U.S. elections, the Vietnamese contend, Kissinger returned to Paris with proposals that would undermine the basis of the compromise and guarantee continued war.

Mr. Nixon's election triumph, the Vietnamese say, was a kind of anesthesia that temporarily made the Administration feel its Vietnam burden was lighter.

From the North Vietnamese-PRG standpoint, Kissinger wanted to undermine the first and most important political meaning of the nine-point October accords—recognizing the "independence, sovereignty, unity and territorial integrity of Vietnam."

For the Vietnamese, this provision means their nation is one, as recognized by the 1954 Geneva Conference. The proposed new administration in the South would be transitional rather than permanent, even if final reunification is years away.

In the interim, it means that troops of northern origin now in the South can remain, and normal relations can exist between the northern and southern zones after the cease-fire.

This is the essence of self-determination, even if it must be realized in stages.

The concrete guarantee of these rights is the recognition of the PRG as one of two administrations shaping events in the South. This provision would make certain that South Vietnam will not become a separate American-supported state dominated by the Saigon generals.

The U.S. reluctance to accept these points could be gleaned even from Kissinger's October 26 "peace is at hand" press conference where, in the course of some 3,000 words, he referred to every one of the nine points but the first, and made not a single reference to the PRG.

But the U.S. position really became clear, the Vietnamese say, when Kissinger returned to Paris November 20 with a total of 126 proposed changes in the October accords, most of them substantive.

According the Vietnamese representatives in France and Scandinavia, Kissinger's new proposals in essence were these:

1. NORTH VIETNAMESE TROOPS IN THE SOUTH: The Vietnamese charge that under the pretext of representing Thieu's interests, Kissinger has not only reopened this question, but contends he cannot otherwise promise the release of thousands of prisoners in Thieu's jails.

2. U.S. MILITARY BUILDUP IN SOUTH VIETNAM: After an October agreement to withdraw all U.S. military advisers and personnel within sixty days, the United States has initiated plans to send military advisers under civilian "cover" in greater numbers than were present during the "counterinsurgency" program of John F. Kennedy. In addition, the United States has sent unprecedented amounts of military supplies to Thieu since October 26.

3. CEASE-FIRE SUPERVISION: Kissinger wants an armed, several-thousand strong supervisory force which the Vietnamese call a "new foreign occupation force" with authority greater than their own. The military provisions of the Geneva Agreements for regroupment of troops were carried out efficiently with only a 350-man supervisory force, the Vietnamese point out.

Just as today, the problem in 1956 came from the U.S. commitment to a Saigon regime that refused national elections. The control commission need not be large if the contesting parties agree to a real settlement.

4. DEMILITARIZED ZONE: Kissinger wants to affirm the DMZ as a demarcation line between two separate Vietnams, although the Oct. 20 agreements made no reference to the DMZ.

5. ROLE OF THE PRG: Kissinger wants to omit reference to the PRG as a legitimate governmental entity. He continues to refer to "South Vietnam" as if it were a sovereign area under Saigon's authority.

6. ROLE OF THE THREE-SEGMENT ADMINISTRATIVE STRUCTURE: The National Council of Reconciliation and Concord is a compromise from the Vietnamese demand for an immediate three-segment coalition government. According to the October agreement, the National Council was to have administrative power to help implement the agreements and organize general elections.

Kissinger wants to dilute and frustrate this power and also to prevent the National Council from existing at grassroots levels.

Minimizing the National Council would eliminate the only structured opportunity for neutralists to emerge as a political force after a cease-fire. Kissinger's attitude toward this "third force" is reflected in his position on the question of Thieu's prisoners, including thousands of neutralists.

In October, the Vietnamese granted a small concession on the timing of prisoner releases: U.S. prisoners would be released within two months, Vietnamese in three.

But while the October agreements speak of "all captured and detained personnel," Kissinger is trying to narrow the category to include only regular soldiers, while the other side means not only soldiers but hundreds of thousands of political prisoners whose lives are endangered under Thieu. The inhabitants of refugee camps must also be free from restraint if they wish to leave.

What about the U.S. claim that "difficulties in Saigon" have caused the reopening of the fundamental issues? The Vietnamese find it impossible to believe that Thieu is the obstacle to peace. If he is, they ask, why is the United States rushing even more weapons and planes to him? Kissinger, they say, described himself as representing Thieu as well as Nixon during the October negotiations.

Kissinger's standing as a reliable negotiator has been damaged and perhaps destroyed in Vietnamese eyes by the recent chain of events.

The optimistic rumors of peace, they assert, were leaked by the American delegation in Paris, and even the friendly handshakes for photographers were initiated by Kissinger. The Vietnamese had to listen to Kissinger gossip about American movie stars during breaks in the talks. The Vietnamese went along "out of courtesy."

Kissinger started threatening a possible renewal of the bombing, they said, during the first round of talks after the U.S. election. The threats rose to as many as six per day, they said.

After the second round, Kissinger proposed that neither he nor Le Duc Tho speak about the talks to the press. Le Duc Tho kept that agreement when he left Paris for Hanoi December 15, saying "Merry Christmas" to reporters at the airport.

The next day in Washington, Kissinger held a long press conference blaming the Vietnamese for the failure of the talks. Two days later, only a few hours after Le Duc Tho's return to Hanoi, the unparalleled saturation bombing began. The very streets in Hanoi where the negotiators live were bombed while Kissinger spent Christmas in Key Biscayne.

The Vietnamese told Kissinger in Paris that threats would not yield peace with honor. "Throughout our history," they told him, "the people of Vietnam have not submitted to threats. If we were afraid of the American arsenal, we never would have started our war of resistance."

Hanoi is not Hiroshima. The mass killing will not end the war. The shooting down of record numbers of B52s proves, they say, that "the Vietnamese people are not afraid of the B52s and we have the means to resist them." The strategic significance is clear also: "This proves that B52s are no longer formidable weapons of the U.S. armed forces."

Ho Chi Minh warned the Vietnamese people in 1966 that Hanoi, Haiphong and other cities might be destroyed, but he then asserted that "nothing is more precious than independence and freedom." The present North Vietnamese leadership has sworn an oath to carry out Ho's will.

They had prepared their antiaircraft defense for an eventual attack on Hanoi and laid careful plans for the near-total evacuation of the city's people to the countryside and mountains.

The Vietnamese believe President Nixon will be forced to return to negotiations because of B52 losses and world condemnation, but not before unbelievable destruction has taken place in their beloved Hanoi, the heart of Vietnam, a city which has been leveled several times by foreigners since its founding in 1010 A.D.

9

The Streets of Chicago: 1968

From Reunion: A Memoir *(Random House, 1988)*

This piece, from 1988, continues to represent my perspectives on Chicago.

◆　　◆　　◆

THE STUNNING EVENTS of the spring—LBJ's withdrawal, the Paris peace talks, the sudden deaths and the riots—left people depleted and plans for the convention protest in doubt. If the Paris talks signaled the beginning of peace, the war would no longer be a cause for marching; if the talks were a sham, what was the leverage on a president who already had withdrawn from the race? The big question was, what could we hope to achieve with RFK dead and McCarthy no longer viable? What was the point?

I felt the plans for protest should go forward, if only to continue opposing a war which the president was trying to wipe off the front page during the election year. It appeared to me that the war was escalating in a new way. In late May, the American media reported the existence of a secret U.S. directive calling for an "all-out offensive against the enemy" over the summer. Though U.S. bombing had been halted in most of North Vietnam, bombing missions sharply increased over the "panhandle," the narrow strip of the North stretching down to the seventeenth parallel. The overall tonnage of bombs dropped on North Vietnam now was greater than before the president's March 31st limitations. In July, the number of U.S. troops in South Vietnam increased by 19,000 to 535,000, and the *New York Times* reported that the "Pentagon's estimate of enemy troop strength has remained unchanged between 207,000 and 222,000 despite repeated charges of heavy enemy infiltration." These reports increased my paranoia about what Johnson's "peace plan" actually meant.

In July, the Vietnamese decided to release several POWs as a conciliatory gesture. I couldn't go to Hanoi because of the preparations for Chicago. But I decided to fly for forty-eight hours to Paris to set up the release and learn for myself how far apart the two sides were.

Three Americans were with me in Paris en route to Hanoi: Vernon Grizzard of ERAP; Stewart Meacham, a Quaker leader; and Ann Weills Scheer, a Berkeley radical and feminist. We met with Averell Harriman about the POWs. He argued that they be returned aboard U.S. military aircraft; we sharply disagreed, demanding that they return by commercial aircraft with the peace activists, which is what eventually happened. But one remark of Harriman's stayed with me. "The Vietnamese, you know, have a lower standard of morality than we do," he said, out of nowhere. I thought Anne was going to explode, but she controlled herself, and we let the comment pass. In fact, none of us could believe that we heard Harriman correctly until we compared notes later. So much for a thaw in U.S.-Vietnamese relationships, I concluded.

The vast differences between the two sides were not simply diplomatic, but were best symbolized in their living situations. Harriman's party was staying at the finest suite of the elegant Hôtel Crillon, while the NLF-PRG delegation was in a small compound outside Paris where they could care for their own chickens and gardens. After two days, I flew back to Chicago convinced that the war would continue.

Years later, I asked historian Doris Kearns about Lyndon Johnson's 1968 intentions. She was a White House intern in the sixties, a dove, and a symbol to Johnson of the younger generation that he was losing. The president became obsessed with Kearns, often arguing with her while also confessing his inner thinking. These conversations became a book on the Johnson years, *Lyndon Johnson and the American Dream,* and made Kearns one of the few experts on the president's personal view of the times.

After Robert Kennedy's death, according to Kearns, Johnson briefly and ambivalently considered getting back into the presidential race. Stopping Robert Kennedy had been paramount for him. After RFK's death, he worried about a "draft Teddy" movement. "The way he would talk about it was by saying that all sorts of politicians were asking him to run, telling him that with the war on a better footing, he was the only one who could win,"

Kearns said. While these were largely fantasies, Johnson at least wanted to be present at the convention for his sixtieth birthday, on August 27. "He wanted them to fête his accomplishments and, if the convention fell apart, crazy as it seems, he would be there, available."

In any event, after Kennedy's death, the possibility of antiwar forces defeating Hubert Humphrey, Johnson's handpicked successor, slumped to zero. Humphrey's effort was denounced by Jack Newfield as "undemocratic and illegitimate;" in retrospect, it is difficult to believe how closed the Democratic Party was. Of the 7.5 million Democrats who voted in the 1968 primaries, 80 percent voted for either Kennedy or McCarthy. Only 20 percent voted for Humphrey "stand-ins" in New York and California; RFK received 50 percent of the vote in South Dakota, Humphrey's native state. Yet according to the rules, most of the Democratic convention delegates were selected almost two years before the convention. They were already pledged to Lyndon Johnson's ticket and platform. Therefore the McCarthy campaign, viewed realistically, became little more than a protest within a closed system, although its idealistic stalwarts still believed in miracles.

On the Chicago activist front, nothing was going very well either. SDS had moved unrecognizably to the left: Bernardine Dohrn was elected to the national leadership at their June convention, declaring, "I consider myself a revolutionary communist," which meant a supporter of the NLF, the Cubans, and Third World revolutionaries in general. They continued to worry over the twin perils of repression and liberal reformism during convention week. The Yippies were having their troubles too; their local meetings and fundraising concerts were disrupted by Chicago police. Entertainers like Judy Collins began saying they could not perform in Chicago unless permits and sound systems were guaranteed. In New York, Jerry Rubin and Abbie Hoffman were privately debating a cancellation. The National Mobilization itself was internally divided and still had not issued an official call to Chicago by the summer, although Dave Dellinger was personally committed. In the official corridors of Washington and Chicago, there was hope that the protests could be squelched; in fact, a White House memo indicated that Democratic Party chairman John Bailey was "optimistic, and expects none of the major groups that originally planned demonstrations to go through with them. But precautions will be taken [and] those attending the convention will leave Chicago remembering it as a friendly city." To discount such rumors, Rennie, Dave and I held unilateral press conferences on June 29 declaring that the demonstrations *would* happen—even though the cumbersome National "Mobe" still had not acted.

Rennie was getting nowhere in trying to meet with city officials about securing permits. Having negotiated with government officials for permits before, however, he was convinced that the city would wait until the last few days before the convention, in order to keep the numbers of protestors down, and then grant the permits.

According to one exhaustive history, the city decided as early as April not to issue permits or to cooperate in any way. The mayor's longtime press secretary said, "Our idea was to discourage the hippies from coming." The city was "not to give a staging ground" to the protesters by providing permits. Why should permits be given, he asked, for outside agitators "to plop on the ground" and "be taken care of?"

Unaware that such attitudes were already determined, Rennie tried a new approach, involving the U.S. Department of Justice. The department contained a little-known branch called the Community Relations Service, headed by Roger Wilkins, Roy Wilkins's nephew and a talented negotiator whose assignments were usually to deal with mulish officials in southern cities. At Rennie's invitation, Wilkins flew to Chicago for a discussion of our plans and was asked to act as an intermediary with the mayor. Rennie told me after the meeting how much he liked Wilkins, as I did when I met him later.

After meeting with Rennie, Wilkins sent a private memo to Attorney General Ramsey Clark that described Rennie as "an honest, intelligent man who was being candid with me" and recommended that the president and vice president be apprised of the plans of the Mobilization, as we now know them, at the earliest possible time (and) one of them or someone clearly acting in their behalf call Mayor Daley to apprise him of that point of view and that the mayor be advised that I will be coming to Chicago next week to inform him of the Mobilization's plans and . . . to set up a continuing working relationship between the city officials and the Mobilization.

Ramsey Clark, as far as I know, did not talk to Johnson or Humphrey, but refused FBI Director Hoover's request for wiretaps on several of us. It was arranged that in the following week Mayor Daley would talk with Roger Wilkins. But, according to Wilkins's account, the mayor was not interested in hearing our plans and seemed offended that federal officials would try to intervene in his city's affairs. Daley ended the meeting after about ten minutes.

Not long after, Wilkins again met with Rennie, this time bringing several Justice Department officials. One of them was Thomas Foran, a former political appointee of the mayor and the U.S. attorney for Chicago who would later be the chief prosecutor in the Chicago Eight trial. Hearing from Wilkins that the mayor was opposed to any permits, Rennie made a direct appeal to Foran, the only official close to Daley, for help. Foran was noncommittal. But the very next day, Deputy Mayor Stahl (whom we jokingly called "Stall") called the Mobe office. He complained about our going to the Justice Department but agreed to meet informally with Rennie. Rennie's stratagem had worked; we were ecstatic and believed the city would now be forced to grant us permits. It already was August 2, just over three weeks from the opening ceremonies of the convention. Time was of the essence.

Our hopes were quickly subdued. Meeting at a downtown coffee shop, Stahl told us that public parks couldn't be used as campsites, and the long-proposed march to the amphitheater was impossible for "security" reasons. In addition to these capricious views, Stahl's most telling comment, because of its clear dishonesty, was that all decisions regarding permits would be made by the Parks and Sanitation Department along with the police. In fact, as both sides at the coffee table knew, all such decisions in Chicago were made by one individual, Mayor Daley, not by lower bureaucrats. There was one last attempt at a City Hall meeting with Stahl, on August 12; it too ended in fiasco. On the same day, Senator McCarthy, after a personal appeal from Mayor Daley, made a public call for demonstrators to stay away from Chicago because of the "possibility of unintended violence or disorder." Shortly after, the open-convention advocates, including Allard Lowenstein and Geoff Cowan, were denied a permit for a Soldier Field rally and called off their activities for Convention Week.

On August 7, Vice President Humphrey's executive aide, William Connell, telephoned the FBI to ask for political intelligence on the upcoming convention, as was provided President Johnson on the Mississippi Freedom Democrats in 1964. Hoover assistant Carla De Loach assured Connell that "the FBI's Chicago office is well prepared to gather intelligence and pass such intelligence on to appropriate authorities during the convention," and that "full preparations have been made by the Chicago Office to handle the matter of passing intelligence to the vice president and his aides."

Our hopes not only for permits but for large numbers of demonstrators were beginning to collapse. How many people were going to spend four or five days in Chicago with no assurance that they could participate in a rally, attend a concert, march to the convention, or unroll a sleeping bag in Lincoln Park? Meeting continually now, some Mobe leaders—Dave Dellinger in particular—held out their belief that a lawsuit combined with public pressure would bring permits at the last hour, as happened the previous October on the eve of the Pentagon demonstration.

My mood darkened. "They're just fucking around with us, stalling for time, and they have no intention of giving us permits," I argued in a late-night meeting. "They gave no permits to Rennie and Maced these people in April during a nonviolent peace march, and they're going to do the same thing now. They want to keep most people out of town and drive the rest of us off the streets. We can't back down. We're not just protesting the war. We have to fight for the streets. We have to fight just for our right to be here." The city's strategy was working effectively to reduce our numbers, but it would backfire, I thought, in another way—by building an American iron curtain around the convention and creating a police state in the streets.

I went out later for a beer with John Froines. John and his wife, Ann, had been through ERAP with me, and we shared a passion about Vietnam. Like many people, John wanted to devote himself to an academic career but felt pulled into the vortex of Chicago. John recalls my saying that night that twenty or twenty-five people could die in the convention protests. If I did, I have blanked it out, but I do remember thinking that it was time to prepare for the worst scenario. The experimental questioning of American society that began at Port Huron was yielding bitter evidence; America was turning out to be more like Mississippi than not. How much difference was there, after all, between Jackson, Mississippi, and Mayor Daley's Chicago? In the South, we could at least appeal to a higher, and arguably more tolerant, level of government; in this case, that higher level in Washington was fully aligned with Chicago City Hall. At Port Huron, we believed that apathetic individuals could be transformed into active, thinking citizens who could influence government by building local organizations. Here in Chicago, every organization we had tried to build— the JOIN Community Union, the April Twenty-seventh Peace Coalition, and many others—had been routinely harassed, raided, sprayed with Mace, attacked by police and denied even the smallest victories of the kind we were able to achieve in Newark. There was the shoot-to-kill, shoot-to-maim rhetoric. And now, by denying permits, the mayor—and the White House behind him—was smugly denying that the First Amendment should protect the rights of hippies to sleep in a park, or McCarthy workers to rally at Soldier Field, or the Mobilization to assemble at the amphitheater. I was convinced we had to lay aside whatever hopes we harbored for respectability, for career, for step-by-step reform. It was a time to risk our necks to take democracy back, a time no longer for visionary platforms but for suffering and physical courage. I told a New York audience that they should come to Chicago prepared to shed their blood.

Camus had warned against the politics of resentment I was beginning to embody, calling it an "evil secretion, in a sealed vessel of prolonged impotence." But I believed that I was still acting in the spirit of Camus' rebel, and partly I was. His rebel was never realistic, nor was I then. Rebellion, for Camus, was "apparently negative, since it creates nothing," but it turned out to be "profoundly positive, in that it reveals the part of man which must always be defended," the human dignity shared by all. We had to resist police and political oppression in Chicago, I felt, not because it was realistic but because it was important to act, if only because not acting meant succumbing.

The protest plan for the convention, now only twelve days away, was being refashioned constantly. We repeatedly tried to explain its outline to city officials:

AUGUST 24: A decentralized "people's assembly" at over a score of "movement centers," where individuals would receive a briefing about the week's schedule, and meet together for the first time;

AUGUST 25: Opening day of the convention: nonviolent and legal picketing on sidewalks outside delegates' hotels in the Loop;

AUGUST 26: Rallies and meetings in Lincoln, Grant and Hyde Parks;

AUGUST 27: Concert and rally at Coliseum, Yippie Festival;

AUGUST 28: Day of Humphrey's nomination: rally in Grant Park, march 10 miles to International Amphitheater;

AUGUST 29: Decentralized actions at institutions representing war and racism.

Despite the uncertainty, we planned to go ahead with the schedule. If the city gave us a last-minute permit, so much the better. If not, we would have to become very creative. One of the key factors in our survival now was the training of about a hundred Mobilization marshals who, in a situation without rules, would have to play an important leadership role on the streets. In past demonstrations, marshals were used mostly as "traffic directors," guiding people toward a rally site, keeping marchers in orderly lines, shouting instructions or chants over bullhorns. But Chicago had to be approached differently. Instead of a "vertical" organization with leaders in front and followers marching obediently behind, we would need a "horizontal" structure of small groups as the vital base of the Mobilization. There was too clearly a danger that leaders like ourselves would be arrested or hurt, cut off from the mass of activists. Further, as we wrote in the instructions to the marshals, the police were expected to "operate from a strategy of containment and mass arrest rather than indiscriminate brutality." This meant a danger of hundreds or thousands of people being encircled and removed from the streets before the convention came to its climax on the twenty-eighth. We wanted to fill the streets as much as possible, not be held in jails on exorbitant bail.

Therefore, it was necessary to improvise what we called "mobile tactics." During parts of convention week, small groups of fifty to a hundred demonstrators would picket at a decentralized site, for example, a draft board office. That way, if they were rounded up, thousands of others would remain at large. On the other hand, for situations when large assemblies would come together, the marshals were being trained to lead people out of the danger of mass arrest. The marshals awkwardly tried to mimic the "snake dances" used by Japanese students as a way to break out of police lines while avoiding either attacks by demonstrators on police or leaving isolated individuals behind. A few practiced karate self-defense moves, teaching techniques for protecting vital organs from clubs and boots. But it was amateur theater compared to the riot-control techniques that were efficiently being practiced against simulated long-haired demonstrators by the National Guard over the summer. What was deadly serious, however, was the training of our marshals in makeshift first-aid techniques against head wounds, serious bleeding, and tear-gas or Mace attacks. Marshals also studied by map and on foot most of the throughways, bridges, and alleys from Lincoln Park to Grant Park and to the amphitheater.

On August 22, the police shot and killed a seventeen-year-old American Indian named Jerome Johnson in Lincoln Park. Johnson, an early arrival for the Festival of Life, was said to have "threatened" the officers who killed him. The next day, Judge Lynch (another aptly named friend of the mayor's) rejected our appeal for permits; the National Guard was provided fifteen sites for sleeping and assembling. There was nothing further to negotiate. The sides were now assembled, as in a medieval battle. In their camp were 11,000 Chicago police on full alert; 6,000 National

Guardsmen with M-1 rifles, shotguns, and gas canisters; 7,500 U.S. Army troops; one thousand federal agents from the FBI, CIA, and army and navy intelligence services (one of every six demonstrators was an undercover agent, they would claim later). Electronic surveillance was conducted against the Mobilization, the Yippies, McCarthy headquarters, and the broadcast media. The amphitheater was secured with a two-thousand-foot barbed wire fence, roadblocks in every direction, a ban on low-flying aircraft, and electronic equipment to certify the identity of delegates. The convention police command was centralized in a secure headquarters at the amphitheater, complete with giant electronic maps of Chicago, video and radio links to every security unit, and hot lines to the White House and Pentagon.

On our side were approximately a thousand people, mainly in our early twenties, waiting nervously in a park, looking for places to sleep. It was Saturday morning, August 24, one day before the official opening of the convention. I was sleeping late. The bedroom door opened. Drowsily, I saw a naked woman who had risen earlier. Maybe she'll come back to bed, I was thinking, when she said quietly:

"There's a man outside with a gun."

Well. No need for coffee now. She went back to observe him through the front-room curtains while I dressed and composed a plan. Grabbing an apple, I jumped out the kitchen window of the apartment building in Hyde Park, ran several blocks, and hopped the El train to Chicago's Loop. There I made my way through thick crowds of shoppers to our Mobilization offices, high in an office building on South Dearborn.

FBI MEMORANDUM 9/27/68

******* assigned to Area 5, Chicago Police Department, advised that he and ******* at 2 AM on August 24, 1968, were assigned to conduct a physical surveillance on Tom Hayden at 6027 South Kimbark Avenue, Chicago. ******* stated his shift commenced at 2 AM, and lasts until 2 PM. each day during the Democratic National Convention.

******* stated that he had very little visual contact with Hayden during the weekend of August 24–25, 1968 while he stayed in the apartment.

(* Material deleted by the FBI)

When I left the elevator at the floor of our office, there was a beefy, casually dressed man with crossed arms, menacing eyes, and greased hair standing against the wall. A hit man, I thought, and quickly entered the office. Rennie was there already and asked, smiling, "Have you met yours yet?" He had first encountered the man now outside the office door on his apartment steps that morning.

Our two plainclothes tails were Chicago police officers named Ralph Bell and Frank Riggio, although they never introduced themselves formally. They were assigned to follow us at the fairly claustrophobic distance of about ten feet wherever we went. We went to the bathroom; they followed. We went to lunch; they sat glowering at the next table. We drove to a meeting; they lurched behind in their car. When close enough, they made remarks about "getting" us, or "arresting you every time you're in the streets." The larger of them, Bell, had a real habit of losing his temper, getting wild-eyed, moving close, and threatening to do away with me on the spot. A phone call notified us that Jerry and Abbie were being followed too.

If this is a preview, I thought, we are not going to be free to meet or plan, and we will be lucky to survive. The week's events were grim already; now we were being followed by characters usually found in cheap movies about the Soviet Union.

By the afternoon, more and more demonstrators were arriving, filling Lincoln Park, getting to know each other, looking over maps of the city, taking down the phone number for legal aid, mainly waiting apprehensively for some direction. As night fell, the Yippies, who had nominated a live pig for president the day before on a platform of "garbage," were urging compliance with the 11:00 p.m. curfew. Allen Ginsberg, chanting *om,* believed he could calm the tension with the police. At 11:00 p.m. promptly, the police surged through the park on motorcycle and foot, removing a few hundred people but with minimal arrests.

As the delegates arrived in their hotels the following day, the twenty-fifth, we felt that the curtain of uncertainty caused by the lack of permits had to be pulled back and tested in daylight. With Rennie carrying a bull-horn and taking the lead, we marched from Lincoln Park all the way to the Loop's hotels—without incident. However, uniformed and plainclothes officers, including Bell and Riggio, strode beside us all the way, quarreling over the details of the route, until we reached Grant Park, across from the Conrad Hilton Hotel, where we dispersed. We were pleased, but no more certain of where the police would draw the line.

Lincoln Park is always dark, but it was absolutely eerie, filled with the silhouettes of young dropouts, militant protesters, McCarthy volunteers, voyeurs, and undercover agents. This would be the night, I sensed, that the battle for Lincoln Park could get out of hand. The convention was beginning the next morning, most of the protestors had arrived, and the police would try to establish dominance. An anticipation of police harassment held the people together, allowing them to forget the relatively low turnout of a thousand or more. If the police had done nothing, the protest might have fizzled, directionless. But it wasn't to be.

Off and on during the past two days I had lost my police tails, only to have them show up at the next place or event: where they expected me. Tonight they found me in the park and began glaring from behind trees as I wandered through the crowd. If there was going to be a confrontation at eleven, I knew that Rennie and I would not survive it one minute if we were closely tailed. I also knew that I would get little sleep unless I could get away from these pursuers to a safe and quiet apartment for the rest of the night.

A plan took shape: Bell and Riggio had driven their unmarked car into the park before following us on foot. If a tire was deflated, they could be stopped cold. With mingled friends providing protection, I stepped out of sight, circled the park, and approached the darkened car. An accomplice named Wolfe Lowenthal took most of the air out of one tire when Bell and Riggio suddenly appeared out of the trees, saw Wolfe at work, and quickly grabbed him. I ran up, and they turned on me, holding me against the vehicle, trying to shove me inside. What saved me from taking a very rough ride in that unmarked car was a crowd that quickly gathered around the officers, chanting, "Let him go, let him go!" Bell and Riggio, sensing their loss of control, backed away. When I last looked back, they were stooped over, fixing their rear tire.

The police waited until an hour past eleven to enforce the curfew that night, then swept Lincoln Park with clouds of tear gas. Our precautions for the gas attack were minor; people were instructed to cover their faces with Vaseline and soaking handkerchiefs or towels, even the sleeves of their shirts if necessary. But the gas canisters did their job, turning the balmy night air into a jolting, choking, inescapable darkness. It was as if someone held me down and stuffed pepper in my mouth, nose, and eyes. The impact made everyone gradually give way, screaming at the police or throwing rocks at their shotguns, then running blindly in whatever direction promised relief from the clouds of gas. The streets around the park were jammed for hours, as the citizens of Chicago began to feel the presence of confrontation for the first time. Some motorists shouted their sympathy, but most were enraged at the tie-up or immobilized at the sight of police weaving on foot between cars, clubbing longhairs into the pavements. The police also unleashed a volley of hate toward the press, beating many reporters and photographers who were wearing their press badges and attempting to cover the melee.

Temporarily free of Bell and Riggio, I slept a few hours on the couch of Vivian and Richie Rothstein's apartment. The next day, Monday the twenty-sixth, the convention began formally. McCarthy supporters and dissident Democrats now held out no hope for derailing Humphrey, who, in addition to restating his allegiance to Johnson's policies, was making obsequious statements of support for the Chicago police. The only hope remaining to the progressive delegates calling for an open convention was a Vietnam peace plank they sought to add to the Democratic platform. The platform committee's draft endorsed Johnson's policies, however, despite the fact that a 53 percent majority of Americans in the Gallup Poll now thought the war was a "mistake," up from 25 percent two years before. The alternative peace plank, calling for cessation of the bombing of North Vietnam, a mutual troop withdrawal from South Vietnam, and a coalition government in Saigon, would have a lot of delegate appeal, I thought. It would also bring Lyndon Johnson all the way from the Pedernales River if necessary to crush it. "He called me at the convention, where I was with my antiwar friends," Doris Kearns remembered. "He wanted to come, was planning to come. He went on for fifteen minutes about how the country was rejecting him."

I went to Lincoln Park for a meeting of our marshals early that afternoon. Since it appeared that the police would continue their gassing, clubbing, and arrests to drive us away from the convention areas, we needed an emergency response plan. Our exhausted medical volunteers were working on the injured and supplying crucial advice on coping with tear gas. How could we keep the police from arresting them? Our legal teams were similarly swamped, between bailing people out of jail all night and taking down endless affidavits against police brutality. They were frustrated on many levels, for example, by the police practice of covering their identifying badges with tape before the clubbing began. Virtually all communication with city officials, police commanders, and Justice Department liaisons was over.

As we contemplated what to do, I noticed a police wagon and a second vehicle bouncing straight over the grass, coming our way, pulling to a stop less than a hundred feet from us. After a moment, Bell and Riggio, backed by several uniformed and club-wielding officers, jumped out. There was no escape, so I simply said to the marshals, "I'm going to be arrested right now." The officers grabbed me by the arms and marched me into the wagon along with Wolfe Lowenthal, and we took off on a bumpy and rapid ride downtown while a surprised and angry crowd gathered in our way on the grass.

"I oughta kill you right now," Riggio said as we rode in the cramped back compartment of the van. He was nervously dragging on a cigarette and staring at me as if I were an animal. I concentrated on what to do if he started carrying out his threat. "But you're gonna get it. You're gonna get federal charges and go away for a long time." There it is, I thought. He's already been given the big picture by someone. And this is only day one of Convention Week. They jailed me downtown. Several stories below me I could hear marchers shouting, "Free Hayden!" Another demonstration had been permitted, I happily thought. The rules were changing by the moment. I rested quietly in my cell, trying to plan how I was going to make it through this week on the streets outside. My thinking was interrupted by a jailer who unlocked the cell door, informing me that I was bailed out.

Relieved that it was not yet dark, I quickly left the station—only to discover a new man with a gun leaning against the wall of the precinct. As I groaned to myself, he said, "Well, I've finally caught up with you." He was the original tail, who had waited outside my apartment Saturday morning. I didn't catch his name, but he was indistinguishable from the others, a nastiness seething from and marring his ethnic, working-class face. He sauntered close behind me as I looked for Rennie to get a report on the day's events and the night's expected chaos. We reconnected, were surprisingly able to lose my newest tail in the Chicago traffic, and decided to cruise by Lincoln Park as curfew neared.

FBI MEMORANDUM 9/20/68

******* advised that he was one of the officers assigned to a surveillance team on Thomas Hayden during the daytime hours. During that four day period, ******* and his partner, *******, spent most of their time trying to locate Hayden, who actively made every effort to lose his police escort through that period. Due to the crowds, Convention, and demonstration-type activities, Hayden was successful in these efforts.

(* Material deleted by the FBI)

The second night was worse than the first. In addition to the heavy gas, the police fired salvos of blanks from shotguns at the crowd in Lincoln Park. Allen Ginsberg and his friends seemed to think they could blissfully vibrate the violence away, and I'm sure he was disappointed that so many of us were consumed with what he considered negative energy. At the time I thought, however, that Ginsberg was crazy, sitting lotus-like in the grass, eyes closed, chanting *om* over and over while the police lines tightened. I didn't think our "bad karma" was particularly responsible for what was happening. In retrospect, I can see now that my own hostility was partly self-fulfilling, but it was also an honest response to being choked by the gas, to doubling up with pain, to crawling or running for safety, and to rubbing blood, dirt and tear gas into one's eyes.

The scene was totally surreal; a cultural war between thousands of police and protesters just blocks, even doors, away from the exclusive Gold Coast section of Chicago, where the affluent citizens went about their "normal" lives, trusting the police to keep their existence sanitized. It was crazier still in the Loop, where convention delegates wearing straw Humphrey hats, festooned with candidate buttons, were partying in the lounges just a sidewalk away from the police lines and the ominous darkness of Grant Park.

I was watching the delegates return from the amphitheater to the Conrad Hilton about midnight, when I encountered Jack Newfield, Geoff Cowan, and Paul Gorman, the McCarthy speechwriter. They described how Hubert Humphrey that night had cemented his pact with the southern Democrats against the antiwar liberals in pushing for the status quo platform plank on Vietnam. I tried to explain how insane it was in the streets, but it was as if we were in two worlds, invisible to each other. They invited me into the Hilton, where they had rooms. I got as far as the revolving door, where a hotel officer held out his arm. "We don't want this man in here," he said. Bemused, my friends started arguing that I was their guest. I became jittery. Just across Michigan Avenue a line of police was confronting a new crowd of demonstrators. Suddenly, Riggio appeared at the edge of our circle, smoking a cigarette, staring at me, his boots pawing the ground. "Forget it," I said and started to cross the street, careful to move away from the confrontation brewing in the park.

Suddenly, I felt the hint of a tornado over my right shoulder. Out of nowhere came Bell, charging like a linebacker, crashing both of us to the street, beating my head, dragging me through the kicking boots of other police, twisting my arm in a karate hold, and slamming me into a police car.

It was just after midnight, and I was going back to jail for a second time.

TO: FBI WASHINGTON
FROM: FBI CHICAGO
2:48 AM URGENT 8/27/68 PAK
TO DIRECTOR (157-8489)
FROM CHICAGO (100-44963) IP
DEMCON

ADVISED THOMAS HAYDEN, COFOUNDER, STUDENTS FOR A DEMO-
CRATIC SOCIETY (SDS), WAS ARRESTED AT ZERO ZERO FIVE ZERO
HOURS, AUGUST TWENTY SEVEN INCIDENT AT NORTHEAST CORNER
BALBOA AND MICHIGAN AVENUES, CHICAGO. CHARGED WITH SIM-
PLE BATTERY AND RESISTING ARREST (SPITTING ON POLICE
OFFICERS). HAYDEN TRANSPORTED TO CHICAGO PD HEADQUAR-
TERS. ELEVENTH AND STATE. ATTORNEY (FNU) SPELLMAN
COUNSELED HAYDEN ALMOST IMMEDIATELY ON ARRIVAL. SPELL-
MAN WITH HAYDEN TWENTY MINUTES, THEN DEPARTED AND
HAYDEN PROCESSED BY CHICAGO PD.

ADMINISTRATIVE

SECRET SERVICE AND MILITARY FURNISHED TELETYPES.
U.S. ADVISED. CHICAGO WILL FOLLOW.

The atmosphere in the detention room was ugly. I noticed among the thirty or so prisoners the faces of many younger SDS members—Bill Ayers of Ann Arbor, Terry Robbins of Cleveland, Jeff Jones from the Columbia University student strike—who had worked in civil rights and community projects. Whereas my first taste of violence in the South allowed me to *hope* for a response from the national government, their introduction to mindless sadism was coming at the convention of the Democratic Party and Johnson administration. In two years, several of them would decide to form the Weather Underground and engage in offensive violence. Tonight they were sprawled on the floor, nursing cuts and bruises, listening to raging officers call them scum and threaten to beat them to death. Fortunately, Newfield, Geoff's brother, Paul Cowan, and Jim Ridgeway, all writers for the *Village Voice,* followed me to police headquarters and, after two hours, bailed me out. When I left the jail, it was three or four in the morning, and with my friends I walked the streets trying to get my bearings. It was no time to be arrested again, and I wondered where I could be safe. As Newfield later recalled that night, "Almost every noise was martial: fire sirens, the squawking of two-way radios, cop cars racing from place to place, the idle chatter of police on duty." I felt naked. I could not be me, not on the streets of Chicago.

As we wandered down the street, several prostitutes approached us, asking if we wanted sex. They were black, well dressed, and wore pink sunglasses and large McCarthy-for-President buttons. "No thanks," I said politely. "I just got out of jail."

"You did?" the lady replied. "So did we."

I grabbed a taxi to the *Ramparts* magazine office, where they published a daily "wall poster" on the convention. They would be up all night, and I could find sanctuary, coffee, a couch, and contemplate a solution to my problem.

Late the next afternoon, Tuesday the twenty-seventh, a new Tom Hayden appeared on the streets. Behind the fake beard, sunglasses, neck beads, and yellow-brimmed hat which I alternated with a football helmet, no one knew me. A friend procured a variety of disguise materials from a stage crafts store, and by dusk I was ready to rejoin people in the streets. My friends didn't know me until they heard my voice. To others, I looked like an undercover cop or random weirdo. I strolled right by the police. Bell and Riggio were hopelessly lost.

That night, the "Unbirthday Party" for LBJ was held in the coliseum, a peaceful sanctuary for bringing together the whole coalition. There were bruised faces and bandaged heads, diehard McCarthy volunteers, the tattered and tired and tenacious listening to Phil Ochs singing "I Ain't Marching Anymore" and "The War Is Over." At the chorus, somebody lit and raised a match in the darkened theater. Somebody else. And another. Ten. Fifty. Five hundred. A candlelight chorus, everyone singing, crying, standing, raising fists, reaching delirium at the words, "Even treason might be worth a try / The country is too young to die."

The reformist spirit of the civil rights movement, withered and repressed, had turned into the hardened rhetoric of the Black Panther Party, whose chairman, Bobby Seale, flew in from Oakland to address the crowd in Lincoln Park the next day. The Panthers were the living incarnation of Frantz Fanon's "revolutionary native" for whom the acceptance of violence was a purifying step toward self-respect. Formed in late 1966, they carried out the call of Malcolm X for armed self-defense. Like Malcolm, they were street people, "brothers off the block," channeling the chaotic rage into armed street patrols, a newspaper that reached 200,000 people weekly, a children's breakfast program, and a support network that enjoyed massive backing in black communities, especially among young people. Their founder, Huey P. Newton, was a mythic figure on the streets of Oakland; he was imprisoned for a gun battle in late October 1967 that left one Oakland policeman dead, another seriously wounded, and Huey shot in the stomach. Yet, because of the Panther presence, Oakland was one of the few black ghettos that never erupted in spontaneous violence in the late sixties. Even two days after the murder of Martin Luther King, when a Panther named "Little Bobby" Hutton was shot and killed while surrendering to Oakland police along with Eldridge Cleaver, the community remained still. Because of this focus on an almost military discipline, the Panthers initially considered the Yippies foolish anarchists and urged their members to stay away from Chicago during the convention. But under the lyrical spell of Eldridge Cleaver, a convicted rapist whose *Soul on Ice* was a nationwide best seller, the Panthers began to reconsider their stand on Chicago, embracing the notion that a cultural rebelliousness among young white people was a necessary prelude to their becoming real revolutionaries.

Seale flew in to endorse the Chicago demonstrations in the middle of the week. While only there a few hours, he gave a speech rich enough in violent metaphors to lead to his indictment a year later. Cleaver was launching a symbolic presidential campaign with the help of the white members of the Peace and Freedom Party, appealing to the Yippie constituency for his white support. Jerry Rubin eagerly endorsed Seale's remarks about "roasting pigs."

It must have been a truly disorienting sight for the undercover agents: a stern Black Panther in beret and black leather jacket boasting of the necessity of "picking up the gun," together with a hairy Yippie dressed, I recall, in love beads and plastic bandolier. It is a measure of the alienation of the times that what seem now to be caricatures of rebellion could have been taken seriously, but they were. The black underclass was connecting with over-privileged whites in a strange and explosive alliance of resentment and guilt. It was deadly serious, especially to Rubin's personal bodyguard, one of several undercover agents posing as Panthers and the Yippies in the crowd.

Though nothing happened after Seale's appearance, it was only a matter of several hours before the nightly ritual of battle resumed. This time a group of ministers held a vigil around a large wooden cross they carried into Lincoln Park. Over a thousand people sang the "Battle Hymn of the Republic," "Onward, Christian Soldiers," and "America the Beautiful" before a huge city truck began gassing them more heavily than the previous night. In addition, our medical stations were overrun and smashed, and numerous reporters were again beaten badly. Again, the nearby streets were choked with running figures, with rocks, bottles, and police batons everywhere in the air. From Lincoln Park, we began trotting in twos and threes southward, over the several bridges on the way to the Loop and Grant Park, where the delegates were returning from the convention. I remember running the several miles, fearing that the police would order the drawbridges lifted to cut us off.

Once outside the Hilton Hotel, we took a dual approach to the returning Democratic delegates. For the most part, we tried chanting "Join us! Join us!" A number of them actually did, especially as the week went on. But for the LBJ-Humphrey delegates, drinking nightly in the bars, filled with alcoholic disgust for hippies, we had another approach. They became the targets of our secret guerrilla-theater unit, a small group with the goal of exposing, surprising, and confronting delegates with the need to take sides. Mainly women. They dressed smartly and strolled through security lines without incident. Kathy Boudin and Cathy Wilkerson used lipstick to scrawl VIETNAMESE ARE DYING on the mirrors in ladies' rooms, and spray painted CIA in huge red letters outside an office we believed to be the agency's local headquarters. Connie Brown and Corinna Fales, another former NCUP staffer, along with Kathy, dropped stink bombs in the Go-Go Lounge of the Palmer House, by dipping facial tissues into butyric acid, a chemical that smelled like rotten eggs. Connie, not a very good criminal, was caught red-handed by a security guard. "I don't know what you're talking about," she protested to the guard. But she couldn't explain the foul-smelling odor coming from her purse. She was hustled away; feeling sorry for her, Corinna and Kathy turned themselves in as well. The three were thrown into cells filled with black lesbians and told by furious Chicago police that they would be jailed for twenty years. Kathy was particularly worried because she was planning to enter law school. Months later, on the advice of her father—noted attorney Leonard Boudin—the three pled guilty to malicious destruction of property and served no time. They became "unindicted co-conspirators" in the Chicago conspiracy trial one year later. Kathy never attended law school; two years later she joined the Weather Underground, and in 1984, she pleaded guilty to second-degree murder and armed robbery and was sentenced to twenty years to life.

FBI MEMORANDUM 9/20/68

******* stated in connection with the apartment where Hayden was staying at 6027 South Kimbark, he noticed photographs in the Chicago newspapers of three young girls who were arrested by the Chicago Police Department for throwing a "stink bomb" in the Conrad Hilton Hotel. He identified these three girls, one he recalled named Brown, prior to her arrest as previously visiting the apartment at 6027 South Kimbark.

    ******* stated he was informed by the janitor of the building that the girl named Brown was a sub-lessee on the apartment at 6027 South Kimbark where Hayden was staying.

(* Material deleted by the FBI)

There were far worse ideas circulating spontaneously. For a friend of mine from the New York Motherfuckers, who threw a sharp-edged ash-tray at the faces of the police, yelling, "Here goes a provocateur action," this was the apocalypse. Another proclaimed to anyone listening, "You're not a free person until the pig has taken your honkie blood!" At one point I even prepared a tape to be played and amplified from inside the Hilton to embarrass the police into thinking I had penetrated their thick lines. The tape ended by calling on the protestors to "join me." Wiser and more cau-tious heads decided to throw the tape away before anyone tried to follow me. It was difficult not to be immersed in a frenzy.

About 2:00 a.m., the police commander curiously announced on a bullhorn that we could stay in Grant Park overnight, provided we were peaceful. A triumphant cheer of relief went up, and the tension was transformed into a more idyllic collective experience. People were lying on the comfortable grass singing protest songs with Peter, Paul, and Mary—the floodlit Hilton in the background. At moments like these, it was perfectly clear how peacefully the protests of convention week might have gone.

But suddenly at 3:00 a.m., the reason for the relaxed police behavior became stunningly apparent. Down Michigan Avenue, in complete battle preparedness, came the first units of the National Guard. Not only did they bear M-1 rifles, mounted machine guns, and gas masks, but they were accompanied by vehicles we'd never seen before, jeeps with giant screens of barbed wire attached to their front bumpers, which we came to call "Daley dozers." They abruptly took positions in front of us, menacing but making no move. A few protestors starting shouting, "Chicago is Prague!"

While the extreme tension continued, many of our people could take it no more and began lying down on the grass or in sleeping bags to rest before the sun came up. I became worried, as did our marshals, that a pre-emptive mass street arrest might be launched by the Guard, sweeping us off these streets as the very day of Humphrey's nomination dawned. I took a bullhorn and told everybody to go home. Then I left quickly to get a few hours' sleep myself before the most critical day of the convention.

That night the police carried their vendetta against the media onto the convention floor, where a security officer slugged Dan Rather. On national television, Rather said, "This is the kind of thing going on outside the hall. This is the first time we've had it happen inside the hall. I'm sorry to be out of breath, but somebody belted me in the stomach." Walter Cronkite added, "I think we've got a bunch of thugs here, Dan."

I was exhausted. I asked Bob Ross, who also lived in the Kimbark building, if he would stay with me in the streets the next night. After being arrested and hunted, I told him that I was worried about what the police might do if they caught me again.

FBI MEMORANDUM 9/20/68

******* learned from other individuals, primarily Rubin and his fellow Yippie Abbie Hoffman, that Hayden had been an active participant in the street disturbances . . . Rubin and Hoffman together with assorted associates were in the habit of discussing events of the previous evening over their morning meals, and it was during these conversations that remarks were made indicative of the fact that Hayden had been one of the few demonstration leaders who actually had taken part in the street action on the occasions previously referred to . . .

In this connection, ******* volunteered the opinion, based on ******* and his observations of Hayden, that Hayden was one of the most likely among their number to deliberately start or create an incident of violence, since Hayden appeared to be one of the few in this leadership who does not mind, or fear, actual participation in disorder . . . it was extremely difficult to remember specific or isolated remarks and incidents . . . Hayden made remarks at various times to the effect that the strength and future of the movement lay in the young people in this country who must be induced to follow the lead of himself and his associates. There was no question that their goal is generally the radical remaking of the structure and form of the United States Government, including its overthrow if necessary. He qualified this comment to the effect, however, that he could furnish no specific quote or remark which in itself would be illustrative of this goal.

(* Material deleted by the FBI)

With little or no rest, our leadership met the next morning—Wednesday, August 28, the day of Hubert Humphrey's ascension to the presidential nomination and the day long anticipated as the showdown between the protestors and official powers.

Dave, Rennie, and I led a meeting in the empty, gray, paper-littered Mobe office. John Froines attended, as did Irv Bock, an undercover agent from the Chicago Police Department posing as the representative of the Chicago Peace Council. Irv was one of the week's marshals, a big, strong fellow who claimed to have time off from his job with American Airlines. He was suspicious since he didn't fit the stereotype of a protestor, but at this point his presence didn't bother us; we had nothing to hide now. Though weary and strained, we had to decide the most crucial questions of the week. Even if the demonstrations were mainly spontaneous, we had the heavy duty of calling the actions, setting the time and place, communicating with the police and press, and making sure that medical and legal help was available.

The dilemmas before us that morning arose from the physical impossibility of achieving our longstanding goal of reaching the amphitheater, about ten miles south of the Loop, at the moment of Humphrey's nomination. We were bottled up in the parks, yet we could not stand by in silence. We did not relish more violence, certainly not after the previous night, but we did want direct moral engagement with the delegates and politicians who we felt were selling out the country.

What, we asked ourselves, were our options? The police were offering the Grant Park Bandshell, near Lake Michigan, about a half mile from the Hilton, for a strictly contrived afternoon rally where we would be allowed to voice our grievances, then be ordered to disperse. This was completely unacceptable from our standpoint. The police wanted our rally to end in the afternoon, while we wanted to demonstrate *during* the nomination proceedings at night. And I suspected that the police were planning to surround us at the bandshell to prevent another night of protest in Grant Park across from the Hilton—the closest thing to demonstrating at the convention site.

We agreed that there should be a rally at the bandshell at noon, to take advantage of the temporary police permit and try to involve those thousands of Chicago citizens who were simply afraid to join us at night. We agreed on music, poetry, and speeches by a cross-section of movement leaders and victims of violence. But there were only two choices for those who intended to remain after the "legal" rally. The first, preferred by Dave, was to organize a nonviolent march toward the faraway Amphitheater. This, of course, would be blocked promptly by the police and probably end in mass arrests without even getting out of the bandshell area. The second notion was to get out of the park by mobile tactics after the rally and regroup in front of the Hilton by the time Humphrey was being nominated. This would avoid the snare of everyone being arrested in the afternoon. If they were going to make a mass arrest anyway, we could try to delay it to the time of the nomination and make them crush us visibly in front of the Hilton rather than in a remote park.

Feeling honest about the alternatives we would lay before the assembled crowd, we made our way to the bandshell about noon. Irv Bock went to a phone booth to inform his superiors of our intentions.

When we arrived, there were about ten thousand people at the bandshell, mostly an outpouring of Chicago citizens. I remember embracing Mickey Flacks, who came with her newborn baby, Mark, trusting, with so many others, that the rally would be a peaceful one. Vivian Rothstein told her she was crazy, but she wanted to be there. We began at 2:25, with people still filing into the park. Phil Ochs started singing. Dave was chairing. A few speakers from draft-resistance organizations and Vietnam Veterans Against the War were heard. I sat toward the rear with a few savvy marshals, trying to assess the large contingent of police who had arrived and stationed themselves in the corner of the bandshell area that was on the most direct route to the Hilton.

They were handing out a leaflet announcing that "in the interests of free speech and assembly, this portion of Grant Park has been set aside for a rally," then going on to warn that "any attempts to conduct or participate in a parade or march will subject each and every participant to arrest." Meanwhile, Vivian and others were distributing a leaflet appealing to the police. While I fully expected the police to continue their brutal behavior, there was nothing wrong with reaching out to their better judgment. Forty-three U.S. Army soldiers at Fort Hood had just been court-martialed for refusing "riot-control" duty in Chicago; why not some of Chicago's finest? The leaflet was poignant in its entreaty to the police:

> Our argument in Chicago is not with you.
>
> We have come to confront the rich men of power who led America into a war she voted against. . . . The men who have brought our country to the point where the police can no longer serve and protect the people—only themselves.
>
> We know you're underpaid.
>
> We know you have to buy your own uniforms.
>
> You often get the blame and rarely get the credit.
>
> Now you're on 12-hour shifts and not being paid overtime.
>
> You should realize we aren't the ones who created the terrible conditions in which you work. This nightmare week was arranged by Richard Daley and Lyndon Johnson, who decided we should not have the right to express ourselves as free people.
>
> As we march, as we stand before the Amphitheater, we will be looking forward to the day when your job is easier, when you can perform your traditional tasks, and no one orders you to deprive your fellow Americans of their rights of free speech and assembly.

By now the convention itself was unraveling from the strain of the week's events. Many of the delegates were joining our nightly protests as they returned to the hotels. Idealistic McCarthy workers, who turned "clean for Gene" from New Hampshire to Chicago, were heartbroken, alienated, radicalized. The effort to nominate their hero was only a matter of going through the motions. On this night, Hubert Humphrey would inevitably be nominated, the wheels of the party machine relentlessly turning regardless of the political consequences. However, a spirited fight would be taking place over the Vietnam platform plank in the afternoon. The Johnson-Humphrey position would prevail numerically, but the size of the peace bloc would measure how far the antiwar movement had reached into the Democratic mainstream.

Suddenly there began a commotion by a flagpole situated between the bandshell and the police line. A shirtless longhair was climbing the pole toward the flag. Nothing seemed to madden the police more than affronts to the American flag, although their hearts never seemed to melt when we sang "America the Beautiful" or "This Land Is Your Land." On this occasion, the teenager on the flagpole intended to turn the Stars and Stripes upside down, an international distress signal, though no one knew his intention at the time. People at the foot of the flagpole were yelling their approval or disapproval. Led by Rennie, our marshals headed over to keep order. A column of police waded in with clubs to make a forcible arrest. A few people threw stones and chunks of dirt at a police car. Dave urged calm over the microphone. The vast majority remained in their seats as Carl Oglesby, the SDS president, was introduced. Carl was an extraordinary orator, and was saying that while we tried to give birth to a new world there were "undertakers in the delivery room" when thick lines of police, clubs in position, began forming in front of the flagpole, facing off against our marshals, who had largely succeeded in calming people down. Rennie later remembered taking the megaphone and telling the police it was under control, we had a permit, and they should pull back to avoid further provocation. "On that last word," Rennie said, "they charged."

The police started forward in unison, then broke ranks, running and clubbing their way through the marshals and into the shocked people sitting on their benches. Human bodies flipped over backward. Others staggered into the benches and fell. Some police stopped to beat again and again on their helpless forms, then moved forward into the screaming, fleeing, stumbling crowd. Tear gas was wafting into the air, and I saw Mickey Flacks running off with her baby's face covered. The police were the Gestapo to her. She approached several of them, screaming, "Here, do you want the baby? Take him, take my baby!" Gaining her control, she began shuttling injured demonstrators to the university hospital on the south side, with the baby asleep in a backseat carrier.

Somebody yelled to me that Rennie was hit and lay bleeding, trampled, and unconscious. Oglesby kept speaking, describing the police state unfolding even as he tried to exercise his freedom of speech and assembly. I was not disguised, so I took my shirt off to change my appearance for the moment. Then I turned over and piled up several park benches to slow the charge of the rioting police. Next I circled around the melee toward the flagpole area to check on Rennie. He was being attended to by our medics and readied for an ambulance. His head was split open and blood was flowing over his face and down his shirt. The man standing over him with a microphone and tape recorder, I later learned, was from Naval Intelligence. Rennie was taken to the hospital by our own medics. Within a short while, the police arrived at the hospital to arrest Rennie, who was beginning to recover from a concussion and abrasions. The hospital staff hid him under a sheet, rolled him on a gurney through the police lines, and placed him in a cab. He was driven to South Kimbark, where he watched the rest of the night's events from the Flacks' couch, his aching head heavily bandaged.

Somehow the insanity subsided after half an hour. The police pulled back to their original position, but now they were reinforced by new units and helicopters from every direction. National Guardsmen were moved into place by the bandshell as well, also taking up visible positions on nearby bridges and the roof of the Chicago Art Institute. Bleeding, gassed, and disoriented, we were now surrounded on all sides. A full force of twelve thousand police, six thousand army troops with bazookas and flame-throwers, and five thousand National Guardsmen with "Daley dozers" stretched from the bandshell back to the Hilton and the Loop.

Surprisingly, the rally went on, with Allen Ginsberg, Dick Gregory, and several other speakers. But eventually it came to a final focus. Dave Dellinger announced that there were options for people: first, joining him in a nonviolent parade attempting to go to the amphitheater; second, staying in the bandshell area; and third, moving out of the park for "actions in the streets." He then introduced someone from the Peace and Freedom Party who made the out-of-place proposal that we go picket with the striking Chicago transit workers. Next came a bizarre Jerry Rubin, with a live pig, which he wanted to enter in nomination for the presidency. A little flustered by these suggestions, Dave reiterated that his proposed nonviolent march would begin in the far corner of the park, and then he introduced me. I was reaching a climax of anger and, curiously, freedom. It didn't matter what happened now. "Rennie has been taken to the hospital, and we have to avenge him," I began, repeating it twice to get people's attention. I pointed out the police, guardsmen, and droning helicopters, and warned that we were now surrounded as twilight approached. I urged people not to get trapped in the park, to find their way out and back toward the Hilton: "This city and the military machine it aims at us won't allow us to protest in an organized fashion. So we must move out of this park in groups throughout the city and turn this overheated military machine against itself. Let us make sure that if our blood flows, it flows all over the city, and if we are gassed that they gas themselves. See you in the streets."

Seconds later, I disappeared from the park with Bob Ross, heading for my Kimbark apartment and a new disguise. A *New York Times* reporter drove with us. I heard on the car radio that the Vietnam peace plank was rejected by the convention by a 1,500–1,000 margin and that a protest rally had begun on the convention floor. In about an hour, I was back at the bandshell with a fake beard and helmet to cover my face. It was late in the day, perhaps five o'clock. Dave's march of over a thousand people was half-sitting, half-standing, blocked by a line of police who would not let them out of the park. Meanwhile, individuals and small groups of demonstrators were headed north along the lakeshore chain of parks looking for a bridge to cross onto Michigan Avenue and access routes to the central downtown area. Each of the crossings was occupied by troops employing mounted machine guns and the "Daley dozers."

By some miracle, our trotting, winding crowd finally came to an open bridge at Jackson Boulevard, north of the Loop, and with a great cry of liberation ran over the short space and into Michigan Avenue, turning left to head the mile back toward the Hilton. There were over five thousand people cheering, running, shaking fists or making V-signs, flowing like a peasants' army toward the castle of the emperors. Seemingly from nowhere, the mule-drawn Poor People's Caravan, which Dr. King had intended to lead before his death, materialized in our ranks with Ralph Abernathy leading it as we headed down Michigan Avenue. It was 7:30, nearly time for Humphrey's nomination. The streets were open, as the police were forced to regroup into the face of our surprising initiative. The Dellinger march disintegrated, and everyone found their way toward the Hilton.

It was nearly dark, the city lights turning on, as we reached the corner of Michigan and Balboa, where all the swirling forces were destined to meet. Lines of blueshirts were in front of us, clubs at the ready. The protest column filled the street and swelled with unity as we moved straight ahead now. The first lines sat down.

As if by magic, hands were suddenly in the evening air, and we began chanting, "The whole world is watching, the world is watching, the whole world is watching."

We saw smoke and heard popping noises a split second before tear gas hit our front lines and began wafting upward into the Hilton and nearby hotels. We stopped, choking, trying to bite into our shirts. Then the blueshirts charged, chopping short strokes into the heads of people, trying to push us back. They knocked down and isolated several people, leaping on them for terrible revenge. One very young longhair was caught in the gutter, four or five police cutting his head open with their clubs. A reporter took a famous picture of him, face bleeding, holding up the V-sign, before he passed out. Medics wearing Red Cross armbands, who tried to get to him and others, were clubbed, choked, and kicked down in the street. Mace was squirted in the face of any others who approached, including the photographers. The mass of people fell back, stunned but orderly, helping the injured, to regroup for another march forward.

Bob and I got through the front lines and around the police to the very wall of the Hilton, where a mixed group of fifty or so McCarthy workers, reporters, protesters, and—for all I knew—plain ordinary citizens, were standing frozen against the wall, between the hotel and the police, who were facing the oncoming marchers. When the marchers fell back, the police turned on our trapped crowd, moving in with a vengeance, clubs and Mace pointed at our faces. We instinctively joined arms. They started pulling off one person at a time, spraying Mace in their eyes, striking their kidneys or ribs with clubs, and tripping them. Their eyes were bulging with hate, and they were screaming with a sound that I had never heard from a human being. Someone started shouting that a woman was having a heart attack. We were so besieged that I couldn't turn around to see what was happening. Then, as people started staggering backward, someone kicked in the window behind us, and we fell through the shattered street-level opening to the Hilton's Haymarket Lounge (named, strangely enough, in memory of Chicago police killed by an anarchist's bomb during a violent confrontation between police and protesters in 1886). The police leaped through the windows, going right by me, turning over tables in the swank lounge, scattering the drinkers, breaking glasses and tables.

Now, the *inside* of the Hilton was a battleground. Trapped demonstrators were trying to sit inconspicuously—in Levi's and ripped shirts—in chairs in the lobby until it was possible to get out safely. Bloody victims were walking about dazed, looking for help, as bellboys and clerks stared in shock. Reporters were rubbing their heads and trying to take notes. The McCarthy forces started bringing the injured to a makeshift "hospital" on the fifteenth floor, where they had headquarters. It had been a very bad night for them. The candidate's wife, Abigail, and children were warned by the Secret Service not to attend the convention; she assumed this was because they could not be protected from the Chicago police.

Upstairs now, the staff members of the defeated presidential candidate were ripping up bed sheets to serve as bandages. Many of the wounded were their own. Some flipped-out political aides were throwing hotel ashtrays at the police down in the street; others were trying to pull them away. Lights all over the McCarthy floors of the Hilton were blinking on and off in solidarity with the protestors in the streets below. Soon, the police cut the phone lines to the McCarthy suites and, in a final orgy of vengeance, stormed the fifteenth floor, dragging sleeping volunteers out of bed and beating them up as well.

At the convention, Humphrey was being nominated, but not without resistance. Senator Abraham Ribicoff, in nominating Senator George McGovern, stated that "with George McGovern, we wouldn't have Gestapo tactics on the streets of Chicago." Mayor Daley, in the first row, was interpreted as screaming, "Fuck you, you Jew son-of-a-bitch, you lousy motherfucker, go home."

After Humphrey's nomination, which took until midnight, the McCarthy contingent vowed to march back to their hotels. About three in the morning, we welcomed them, a funeral column of tie-wearing delegates, each somehow holding a candle against the foul night air. Robert Kennedy had been fond of quoting a Quaker saying in his brief presidential campaign: "Better to light a candle than curse the darkness." Now it had come to this: While I welcomed these candles in the park, I *wanted* to curse the darkness.

I had reached exhaustion; so had the protest. So too had the hopeful movement I had hoped to build only a few years before. Over the course of the next day, the defiance wound down. Dick Gregory led a march halfway to the amphitheater before it was stopped by more arrests, this time of many convention delegates themselves. We heard Eugene McCarthy, with gentle dignity, urge us to "work within the system" to take control of the Democratic Party by 1972. He was harangued embarrassingly by SDS leader Mike Klonsky as a "pig opportunist." Ralph Abernathy spoke from an impromptu stage, an upside-down garbage can, calling it a symbol of Martin Luther King's last cause.

I lay on the grass, pondering the alternatives. Reform seemed bankrupt, revolution far away. We had taught the pro-war Democrats the lesson that business as usual was a formula for political defeat and moral self-destruction. But was anybody listening?

10

Our Identity on Trial

From Trial *(Holt, Rinehart, Winston, 1970)*

These writings still represent my perspectives on Chicago after forty years. As I write, a production of The Chicago Conspiracy Trial *is playing at a community theater in west Los Angeles. This year I attended a student production of the dramatization at Central Michigan University, which played to packed houses five straight nights. Two more productions are planned for 2008: a documentary by Brett Morgan and a feature film written by Aaron Sorkin and directed by Steven Spielberg. Why all the attention?*

Obviously the trial lends itself to theatrical rendition either on stage or screen. But why Chicago instead of Kent State, or Alcatraz Island, or Attica prison? Coming at the end of the sixties, involving a representative selection of defendants, the Chicago trial has become emblematic of the conflicts of the era as a whole. We who went through the experience must turn the privilege of this role to shed permanent light on all the brutal injustices inflicted on so many Americans at the hands of those who preferred war above all.

♦   ♦   ♦

"Our kids don't understand that we don't mean anything when we use the word "nigger" . . . they just look at us like we were a bunch of dinosaurs . . . we've lost our kids to the freaking fag revolution."
—Prosecuting Attorney Thomas Foran in a speech after the trial

OUR CRIME WAS OUR IDENTITY.

Even the sympathetic press misunderstood, billing our case as one of "dissent on trial." So did Bill Kunstler in the beginning, when he spoke of repression of "the spectrum of dissent" and implied that we differed from other Americans only in our political opinions. Although there was a certain amount of obvious truth in this claim, it always seemed superficial to us.

The vague nature of the government's case made us feel we were on trial for something deeper and unspoken. The charges against us made no sense. We spent endless hours trying to comprehend what the case was all about.

Against our common sense the government kept insisting that the trial was not "political," not about the Vietnam War, not about the Black Panther Party, but simply the prosecution of a criminal indictment. It was, for the government, a question of whether we had conspired to cross state lines with the intention of organizing, promoting, or encouraging a riot. To prove its case it relied on evidence from Chicago policemen, undercover and FBI agents, army and navy personnel, two *Chicago Tribune* reporters, and only two civilians with no apparent police connections.

Despite its claims, however, the government presented little evidence of "conspiracy." In fact, government attorney Richard Schultz acknowledged that we never all met together, not even once. Bobby Seale never met any of us until coming to Chicago, and then he met only Jerry Rubin. Evidence of conspiracy in a criminal trial, however, defies the everyday imagination. The government argued that it was necessary only that we "shared a common design." But even if we did, why only the eight of us? Why not several of the other "unindicted co-conspirators" who seemed, from the government's evidence, to have done more in Chicago than had several of us? Why not Dick Gregory, who had announced that the convention would take place "over his dead body" and then, after withdrawing from the planning, returned to lead a march at which more arrests were made than at any other time during convention week? Why not Norman Mailer, whom we invited to speak and who told an angry assembly that we were "at the beginning of a war" and the march immediately afterwards would be one battle in that war?

We became the "conspiracy" not because we did anything together in 1968 but simply because we were indicted together. We became closely knit because of the trial, and perhaps the government was relying on this very process for its proof. By intertwining our names through the testimony (as if the words and evidence reflected the reality of 1968) while we sat together at the defense table for five months, it might begin to appear to a jury that we always had been an interconnected unit. But evidently it never convinced the jury, and it certainly made us feel strange, like survivors of a shipwreck getting to know one another because we shared the same raft.

As for concrete evidence of lawbreaking activity, the government puzzled us further by introducing almost nothing.

David Dellinger, Rennie Davis, Abbie Hoffman: nothing at all. Tom Hayden: one arrest for letting the air out of a police tire, another for spitting at an arresting officer and, in addition, adopting disguises to avoid the police. Jerry Rubin: charged with throwing a sweater at his "tail" and for being in the presence of others who threw a bottle of paint at a police car (and missed). At first we supposed that John Froines and Lee Weiner had been indicted because of heavy evidence of heavy hard acts, but again we had exaggerated the government's case. Froines and Weiner supposedly participated in a discussion, the day after the presidential nomination, in which plans were made to firebomb an underground garage in the Loop. The bombing, according to the government, would "divert" the police from Loop demonstrations. Strangely, however, according to the government's own witnesses, the Mobilization had already ended its convention protests that very morning, and the only demonstrations Weiner was going to "aid" were led by Dick Gregory and convention delegates, who were not indicted. Stranger yet, the indictments charged Weiner with "teaching and demonstrating the use of incendiary devices," but no evidence was given during the entire trial of any such instruction on his part. Strangest of all, the bombing never took place and none of the alleged bombers or any of their materials appeared in city, state, or federal courts.

Froines was further indicted for conspiring to stinkbomb the convention hotels. The truth is that several women, whom some of us knew, carried out some stinkbombing and were arrested, convicted, fined, and placed on probation. None of them was indicted on federal charges (probably because a male-supremacist government does not believe that women are capable of action independent of the knowledge and control of men). John was indicted because he had purchased butyric acid for someone (not any of the women we knew of); and because of his chemistry credentials, the government hoped to make him appear to the jury to be a diabolical scientist. The major stinkbombing evidence consisted only of a 3 a.m. "attack" (drops of the fluid were found on tissues) in the Charade-a-go-go, a nightclub frequented by delegates after their convention responsibilities were discharged. So the jury didn't buy the bomb plot. John and Lee, the only two conspirators charged with concrete lawbreaking activity, were acquitted.

Since the evidence of conspiracy and concrete illegal activity was so weak, the thrust of the government's attack had to be carried out against our "state of mind." As we sat through the months of testimony about our consciousness, we began to realize that the charges against us were really just as *total* as the changes we wanted to make in American society. On the surface there was evidence of conversations, speeches, and plots hatched in the presence of undercover government agents. Many of these were wholly fabricated; others were twisted accounts. The accurate ones—those recorded on tape were never difficult to justify legally. But just below the surface of the testimony there was always the implication that we were dangerous and alien to the America of the jury.

It was not dissent that was on trial, the government maintained. It had no quarrel with those who "oppose" the Vietnam war and racism or those who "favor" new kinds of relationships between people. The government in fact claimed it did not mind if "legitimate" people did many of the very things we were charged with doing. The prosecutor practically bowed and scraped before Representative Julian Bond, for instance, who was not allowed to testify that he too thought of calling the Chicago policemen "pigs"; before Congressman John Conyers, who was arrested on the convention floor; and before Ralph Abernathy, who used the word "pig" for the first time in Chicago and described himself as a Yippie. Benjamin Spock was treated by Judge Hoffman as a respected baby doctor, and Dick Gregory became his favorite comedian. The government had nothing against protest; it was opposed only to the evil that we allegedly injected into legitimate protest activities.

Our crime was that we were beginning to live a new and contagious lifestyle without official authorization. We were tried for being out of control.

First of all, we were internationalists. Not only did we oppose racism; we aligned ourselves with people like Bobby Seale. Not only were we against the war in Vietnam; we aligned ourselves with the Vietnamese people. These were not simply "positions" we took; they were more like the natural reflexes of new human beings trying to be relevant to the world as it is. *The world we see is one in which a decadent and super-rich American empire, with its principles of racial superiority, private property, and armed might, is falling apart. We want to join with the new humanity, not support a dying empire.* We make our judgments according to universal and international principles of social justice, not according to a "national interest." This internationalism leads us to identify with peoples whom the U.S. government defines as enemies. It led Rennie, Dave, and me twice to Vietnam; it led us all to close solidarity with the black-liberation struggle; it led us to place Che's portrait on our defense table on the anniversary of his assassination and to ask Bill Kunstler to speak of Che's spirit in his summation to the jury.

Our most "disruptive" behavior in court, besides attacks on the judge's vanity, seemed to be our support for Bobby. And although we felt we hadn't done enough by merely protesting in court, the judge still saw us as a disgrace to the white race. At the end of the trial he was still asking us if we believed, with Bobby, that George Washington (whose portrait was on the wall) was a slavemaster. At one point Hoffman even threatened to revoke our bail unless we broke our solidarity with Bobby's position. He gave us lunchtime to think it over, but then he mysteriously backed down.

Another example of the internationalism that upset the court was our placing of a National Liberation Front flag on the defense table alongside the American flag during the October Moratorium. For ourselves, it was an affirmation of the belief that our people are not at war with the people of Vietnam. The judge did not comment on the propriety of Dave's trying to read the names of the war dead that day, but he ranted and never forgot about "the flag of an enemy country" appearing in his courtroom. The U.S. marshals not only ripped off this NLF flag: a few minutes later they felt compelled to return for the American one, as if it were disgraced by the likes of us.

It turned out that the presence of an NLF flag was always "proof" in the government's eyes that our marches in Chicago in 1968 were illegitimate. At first we were puzzled as to why the government would introduce as part of its evidence films that showed rather orderly demonstrations. The reason, we finally realized, was the close-up color photographs of NLF flags in the film. In the cross-examinations of Linda Morse and Rennie, the prosecutors were visibly excited by establishing that we favored a revolution by a liberation movement "just like the Vietcong." Foran even thought it was incriminating to get Rennie to admit he believed that the Vietcong were "like some of the early American patriots," and that America was now an "imperial country just like England in the eighteenth century."

Our underlying crime, the evidence of which was revealed every day in the courtroom, was that we were beginning to live a new lifestyle beyond that of capitalist America. Our defense table was a "liberated zone" right in front of the jury's eyes. The room itself was a sterile horror, shaped like a box, the doors smoothly tucked into the walls, neon lighting casting illumination without shadow, as if people did not exist. Paintings of British and American historical figures hung above the bench and just below the Great Seal of the United States. It was a heavy decorum. As many as twenty federal marshals kept "order," instructing spectators that they could not laugh, fall asleep, read, or go to the bathroom without forfeiting their seats. The government's table, nearer the jury, was impeccably clean, the four-member team invariably dressed in gray flannel or, in the case of Foran, sporty gabardine suits. The jury, dressed neatly as well, obeyed their orders to say good morning to the judge but otherwise remained quiet and expressionless throughout the proceedings. The judge, his old man's head attached to his floating robe like a bizarre puppet, called for respect in his gravely, sonorous, vain tone. And there we were, supposedly the victims but somehow the center of everything: our hair growing longer with each passing month; our clothes ranging from hip to shabby; joking, whispering seriously, passing notes, reading newspapers, and ignoring testimony and the rules of the judge; occasionally looking for friendly jurors' faces but eventually giving up and just being ourselves. This behavior was the ultimate defiance of a court system that demands the repression of people into well-behaved clients, advocates, and jurors.

The conflict of lifestyles emerged not simply around our internationalism but perhaps even more around "cultural" and "psychological" issues. For instance, music. When Arlo Guthrie, Judy Collins, Phil Ochs, Country Joe, Pete Seeger, and others tried to sing for the jury, they were admonished that "this is a criminal trial, not a theater." No one, including the press, understood what was going on. From the judge to the most liberal journalist there was a consensus that we were engaged in a put-on, a further "mockery of the court." They seemed incapable of coming to terms with the challenge on any deeper level. The court's concession was that the words to the songs, but not the singing of them, were admissible. But this was a compromise that missed the entire point. The words of "Alice's Restaurant," "I Ain't Marching Any More," "Vietnam Rag," "Where Have All the Flowers Gone," and "Wasn't That a Time" may be moving even when they are spoken, but the words gained their meaning in this generation because they were *sung*. To understand their meaning would be to understand the meaning of music to the new consciousness. From the beginning of rock and roll, there has grown up a generation of young whites with a new, less repressed attitude toward sex and pleasure, and music has been the medium of their liberation. When Phil Ochs sang "I Ain't Marching Any More" in Chicago during the convention, it provoked a pandemonium of emotion, of collective power, that spoken words could not have done. Singing in that courtroom would have jarred its decorum, but that very decorum was oppressing our identity and our legal defense.

Or, for instance, sex. Government attorney Tom Foran's post-trial statement about the "freaking fag revolution" merely confirmed what we could see throughout. Foran represented imperialist, aggressive man, while we, for all our male chauvinist tendencies, represented a gentler, less aggressive type of human being. Schultz kept returning to the phrase "public fornication" as though the words themselves were a crime, since the government introduced no testimony to show that Yippies had acted on this threat (except once in a tree, according to an undercover agent). Allen Ginsberg was cross-examined as to whether he had "intimate" relationships with Abbie and Jerry. Physical affection between the defendants and their friends and witnesses was always noted by either the judge or the prosecution for the record. The scene of Bill Kunstler hugging Ralph Abernathy was particularly offensive to the judge, who declared that he had never seen so much "physical affection in my courtroom."

The conflict of identity on this level was sharpest during Ginsberg's testimony. Most commentators have reduced that episode to Allen's "chanting." The fact is that Allen was allowed to do very little chanting, and even this was as misunderstood as the singing of other witnesses. Actually, Allen was one of the few witnesses to state directly the terms of the conflict that is emerging. He testified that he had favored a Festival of Life in Chicago because

> . . . the planet Earth was endangered by violence, overpopulation, pollution, ecological destruction, brought on by our own greed . . . that it was a planetary crisis that had not been recognized by any government in the world . . . the more selfish older politicians were not thinking in terms of what their children would need in future generations . . . and were continuing to threaten the planet with violence, with war, with mass murder, with germ warfare. . . .

During this part of his testimony, Allen explained and tried to perform the chant that became an "outburst" to the press. The "Hare Krishna" is an Indian mantra chanted to the preserver god, Vishnu, whenever the planet and human life are threatened. Allen later performed the "Om" chant, which is used to prevent crowd panic by reestablishing inner calm in individuals. Although the government wanted its witnesses to recite inflammatory chants (the kind that agitators in the movies are supposed to use), it opposed Allen's introducing and explaining these chants.

The conflict came out into the open during Foran's cross-examination. Instead of questioning Allen about anything he had testified to—such as pre-Convention planning by the Yippies and permit negotiations—Foran asked him to recite and explain three sexual poems apparently selected by the Justice Department agent at the table, a young, bespectacled, high-voiced, short-haired, blue-eyed young man named Cubbage. The first was about a wet dream, the second about a self-conscious young man at a party who discovers that he is eating an asshole sandwich, the third about a fantasy of sleeping between a man and a woman on their wedding night. At Foran's request Allen recited each one calmly and seriously and then tried to answer the prosecutor's sarcastic query about their religious significance. About the third poem Allen stated that he had borrowed an image from Walt Whitman, one of his "spiritual teachers," then explained:

> As part of our nature we have many loves, many of which are suppressed, many of which are denied, many of which we deny to ourselves. He [Whitman] said that the reclaiming of those loves and the becoming aware of those loves was the only way that this nation could save itself and become a democratic and spiritual republic. He said that unless there was an infusion of feeling, of tenderness, of fearlessness, of spirituality, of natural sexuality, of natural delight in each other's bodies, into the hardened, materialistic, cynical, life-denying, clearly competitive, afraid, scared, armored bodies, there would be no chance for spiritual democracy to take root in America. . . .

But the entire trial was structured to crush this vision of Walt Whitman and Allen Ginsberg. The Federal Building itself was once described by the Chicago Art Institute as a building in which "the commitment to order everywhere present is translated into an authoritarian and heroic presence." And the appointed representatives of "the people" in the courtroom itself—the jury—had received instructions from the judge exactly opposite to the exhortations of Whitman and Ginsberg. Our jury was living not in a democracy rooted in a communal and fraternal feeling but in a 1984 Palmer House way of life, totally dependent on government marshals, a life of complete separation from their families and fellow citizens. Above all, they were forbidden any human contact—even questioning—with us, the people whom they were to judge. This process of emotional denial supposedly leads to "rationality," but it is precisely what creates "hardened, materialistic, cynical, life-denying, clearly competitive, afraid, scared, armored bodies."

On redirect examination, we asked Allen to recite "Howl." We were not attempting to introduce "evidence" at this point. Rather, if Foran wanted poetry, then we wanted to hear the original poetic outcry of our times, an outcry which begins "I saw the best minds of my generation destroyed by madness, starving, hysterical, naked . . ." and ends "They saw it all / the wild eyes / the holy yells / they bade farewell / they jumped off the roof to solitude / waving / carrying flowers / down to the river / into the street."

When Allen left the stand we were in tears. Court recessed a few minutes later, and Foran stared at Allen and said, "Damn fag."

A third example of the cultural conflict revolved around language. The government's case was a massive structure of obscene and provocative language attributed to us by police informers, language that the jury was supposed to imagine coming from our mouths as they stared at us across the courtroom. Some of the language was pure invention; most of it was a twisting of words that had once been used by us. Through the testimony over language, we came to the essence of the supposed "communication gap" between the generations.

The language of the Establishment is mutilated by hypocrisy. When "love" is used in advertising, "peace" in foreign policy, "freedom" in private enterprise, then these words have been stolen from their humanist origins, and new words become vital for the identity of people seeking to remake themselves and society. Negroes become "blacks," blacks become "Panthers," the oppressors become "pigs." Often the only words with emotional content are those that cannot be spoken or published in the "legitimate" world: "fuck," "motherfucker," "shit" and other "obscenities." New words are needed to express feelings: "right on," "cool," "outta sight," "freaky." New language becomes a weapon of the Movement because it is mysterious, threatening to conventional power: "We're gonna off the pig"; "we're gonna freak the delegates."

Clearly, some rhetoric of the left is wooden, inflated, irrelevant, crippling to the mind and an obstacle to communication. If we were interested in mild improvements to the system, perhaps we would use the prevailing language of the system. But one of the first tasks of those creating a new society is that of creating a new and distinct identity. This identity cannot be fully conscious at first, but as a movement grows, through years or generations, it contains its own body of experience, its styles and habits, and a common language becomes part of the new identity. The old language is depleted. In order to dream, to invoke anger or love, new language becomes necessary. Music and dance are forms of communication partly because they are directly expressive of feelings for which there is as yet no language.

(Part of the emphasis on "obscenity" was of course created through deliberate courtroom deceit by police witnesses who acted "ashamed" to repeat our words in the presence of the jury. But the deceit may have reflected a reality. Many policemen are vulgar with prostitutes, black prisoners, and fellow officers but "pure" toward their families, priests, and judges. One Chicago psychiatrist told us of several cases in which police wives filed for divorce because their husbands would not even make love with them. Policemen seem to regard women as either virgins or whores. This split life reflects a fear of "permissiveness" that is very much present when the police smash heads. They do it with the terrified excitement of children squashing bugs.)

Filtered through the mind of the police agent, language becomes criminal. The agent is looking for evidence; in fact, he has a vested interest in discovering evidence and begins with the assumption of guilt. Any reference to violence or blood, by an automatic mechanism in the police mind, means an offensive attack on constituted authorities. Our language thus becomes evidence of our criminality because it shows us to be outside the system. Perhaps our language would be acceptable if it were divorced from practice. Obscenity has always been allowed as part of free speech; it is the fact that our language is part of our action that is criminal. A jury of our peers would truly have been necessary for our language to have been judged, or even understood. Or at the very least, our middle-aged jury should have heard the expert testimony of someone who could partly bridge the communication gap.

The conflict of identities always involved the racism of the court toward Bobby. This showdown contained all the same elements—international-ism, culture, sex, language—but in a special framework that Eldridge described in *Soul on Ice*. The judge was the classic Omnipotent Adminis-trator and Bobby his Supermasculine Menial. The sex and violence of the Menial are feared (Foran said Bobby was the only defendant who definitely "wasn't a fag"). But even more threatening is any attempt by the Menial to assert his mind, to achieve power over his own life. The more the Menials assert their ideas, Eldridge says, "the more emphatically [he will] be rejected and scorned by society, and treated as [an] upstart [invasion] of the realm of the Omnipotent Administrator. . . . The struggle of [their] life is for the emancipation of [their] mind[s], to achieve recognition for the products of [their] mind[s], and official recognition of the fact that [they have] mind[s]."

There is no better way to explain why Hoffman continually and emphatically refused to let Bobby represent himself. "The complexity of the case makes self-representation inappropriate," the Administrator intoned.

11.

One Long Sadness: A Vietnam Memoir

"Vietnam Memoir," in Modern Maturity, *2000*

I came to see Vietnam as the latest phase of a longer unrecognized war at the heart of the American experience, beginning with the wars of conquest and continuing through the Balkans and Iraq in the 1990s.

◆   ◆   ◆

I WAS TWENTY-SIX YEARS OLD, sitting in a Hanoi hotel, writing in my journal while entranced with a young waitress named Minh Tinh. She wore a white starched shirt over black pants, and sang teasingly to herself while pouring strong coffee and cleaning tables. She blushed and smiled and glanced over my shoulder at my notebook. She might have been amused at my scribbled question, which was:

If this woman sang for President Johnson, would he really want to kill her?

After all, she was the enemy. For all I knew, she was a communist. She led the self-defense forces at the hotel, whose duties included maintaining the bomb shelter.

I was in Hanoi on a peace mission, to build a bridge to this enemy, a thousand-year-old nation that most Americans had only discovered recently. With scores of others in those years, I was challenging the U.S. government policy of forbidding travel, even by journalists, to North Vietnam. In 1965, Secretary of Defense Robert McNamara was soothing America's conscience by saying that "each target is chosen after a careful review of reconnaissance photographs to ensure that it is isolated and apart from urban populations." This was a deceit, perhaps a McNamara self-deception, because our government was bombing people like Minh Tinh.

I had traveled all the way around the world to learn that the faceless, demonized enemy below the bombs of my country was—a human being. My interest ever since has been to understand why Johnson, McNamara and, unfortunately, a majority of Americans managed to distance themselves from this destabilizing truth.

It is a good thing that many American veterans have gone back to Vietnam for personal reconciliation of sorts. And the forgive-and-forget attitude of many Americans has been more constructive than the McCarthy era of scapegoating after the Korean stalemate. But only a surface normalization has been achieved. Our former enemy is defined by the same stereotypes that rationalized the American intervention in the first place. Senator John McCain still calls them "gooks" in front of reporters (*Nation*, January 3, 2000, p. 15). For most Americans they are inscrutable, shadowy, fanatical. If we are not at peace with our enemies, we may continue to fight their ghosts.

Few American films have addressed Vietnam seriously. There are Rambo-style films that keep alive the John Wayne mythology of reluctant gunslingers standing up against the bad guys. There are sensitive films like *Coming Home, Platoon,* and *Born on the Fourth of July,* which center on the fate of American veterans. *Apocalypse Now* is based on Joseph Conrad's novel *Heart of Darkness,* based on imperialists gone mad in the impenetrable African bush full of exotic natives. *Full Metal Jacket* conveys the message that our technological juggernaut was aimed at a nation of Minh Tinhs. In the final scene, the lone Vietcong sniper who keeps firing, despite the utter destruction of our bombing and shelling, turns out to be a slender young woman. But that is all. She is faceless, nameless, unfathomable.

Looking back, I am not suggesting that the Americans were sinners and the Vietnamese were saints, only that we never knew the Vietnamese "enemy" before, during, or after the war. That ignorance permitted us to view them as Soviet or Chinese agents from the beginning, underestimate their unity and morale during the conflict, and absolve ourselves for the destruction we inflicted. I am suggesting, further, that our ignorance went deeper than some lack of Vietnamese studies, but is the cultural characteristic of a superpower before it declines.

I still have powerful sympathies for the American soldiers used as cannon fodder and doused in Agent Orange by a government that lied to us all, and for the Vietnamese on the U.S. side who were either sent to reeducation centers or wound up on welfare in crowded Orange County apartments. But those who died on "the other side" have received little attention at all. They still suffer from cancer-causing dioxins in defoliants and countless unexploded landmines left behind. Perhaps two million on "the other side" died invisible deaths, but who's counting now that the body counts are over? On my desk are two American fragmentation bombs I once picked up in a Vietnamese village in the Demilitarized Zone. Aside from our veterans, few if any American civilians have ever seen one of these weapons, an avoidance which is important for the protection of our righteousness. These anti-personnel bombs with their tiny skin-ripping pellets—are hard evidence of the intention to inflict extreme and prolonged suffering on the victims. The pellets were designed as jagged shards so that medical treatment would be more difficult. Vietnamese doctors working underground or in tents with few surgical supplies or antibiotics were forced to cut open a victim's flesh to remove fragments the size of a nail head. Perhaps the only American weapon as diabolic was the napalm strengthened with polystyrene to make it burn more adhesively on the victim's skin.

Already most Americans—and certainly American officials—will acknowledge that Vietnam was a "mistake," but they think of it like a no-fault car crash. To believe that it was profoundly wrong, deceitful and a defeat, officials fear, would sink America in a depressing "Vietnam syndrome" and prevent necessary military interventions in the future. The defenders of Vietnam believe the "mistake" was in not bombing them back to the Stone Age at the earliest possible time. This Rambo mentality is based on a failure to acknowledge the extent to which we *did* bomb the Vietnamese back to the Stone Age—and they fought the war from caves and tunnels. America dropped 15 million tons of munitions during the war, twice that dumped on Europe and Asia in World War II, and dumped over 11 million gallons of Agent Orange on one-third of the South. How much more would have done the job?

Healing requires more than acknowledging a "mistake," especially when so many believe the mistake was that we didn't kill enough people. By minimizing public memory of the mass suffering, we only prepare the way for future moral blindness to civilian casualties.

No one knows, for example, how many civilians were killed, or what environmental damage was done, in the 1991 war against Iraq. What mattered to hawkish commentators like Charles Krauthammer, was "not being panicked into demanding further restrictions, Vietnam-style, on the bombing" of Baghdad which, he wrote, was "no cause for guilt."[1]

The latest opportunity to shake off those post-Vietnam pacifist impulses toward civilians came with the U.S. bombing of Yugoslavia in 1999. *New York Times* columnists Anthony Lewis and Thomas Friedman were among many who justified attacks on civilians. Lewis wrote that "the Serbian *people* will suffer, but so they must for the tyranny that have repeatedly endorsed," blithely ignoring that several hundred thousand Serbs had demonstrated against their regime in Belgrade. Friedman, apparently irritated by rock concerts in Belgrade against NATO, added that "we are at war with the Serbian *nation* and anyone hanging around Belgrade needs to understand that."

Soon the old Vietnam euphemism of "collateral damage" was back in style, but the targeting of civilian infrastructure was no accident. The anti-personnel bombs were back in military style as well, turning whole areas of Yugoslavia into a "no man's land" and wounding large numbers of children. The director of Pristina's hospital told the *Los Angeles Times* "he has never done so many amputations as he has since victims of the weapon started coming in."[2]

The debates over the Gulf War and Kosovo are likely to continue for years, but I want here to emphasize policy legacies of Vietnam affecting both wars. First, the policy of avoiding U.S. casualties based on the Vietnam-era belief that Americans only care about American blood and, second, the ethnic demonizing of the enemy in order to justify the mass punishment of civilians. The underlying assumption is that American lives are more precious than any other. The Arabs and Serbs have replaced the Vietnamese in our demonology.

Why do so many Americans—more so than the residents of other industrialized countries—believe we have a national entitlement to military intervention anywhere in the world against faceless inferiors and regardless of massive civilian damage? Where does this comfortable righteousness come from?

The Vietnam War was an eruption of a profound need in our culture to Americanize the world, a need that began long before communism, as long ago as the frontier wars against native people on which the United States was based. While being justifiably proud of the anti-monarchist, pro-democracy spirit of the American Revolution, we tend to sanitize our historical need to demonize and ethnically cleanse the native people of this continent and build our agricultural economy around slavery.

What we did to Indians, African slaves and Mexicans in our country, the French were doing in the Vietnam of Ho Chi Minh's birth. We called it "manifest destiny" while they called it "le mission de civilisateur" (the civilizing mission), and types like Lawrence of Arabia carried out the "white man's burden." In Vietnam, the echo of our Indian wars turned up in titles of U.S. military manuals like *Injun Fighting 1763 – Counter-Insurgency 1963*, and the very names of bombing operations like "Rolling Thunder" and gunships named Cheyennes, Mohawks, and Chinooks. Like Kit Carson toward the Navaho, we deliberately destroyed the Vietnamese food supply and pushed the villagers into "strategic hamlets." General Maxwell Taylor testified to Congress in 1966 that "I have often said it is very hard to plant the corn outside the stockade when the Indians are still around. We have to get the Indians farther away in many of the provinces to make good progress."

During the Indian wars the U.S. government classified the Indian nations as agents of the British or French, just as we labeled Ho Chi Minh as an international agent of the Soviet Comintern. That description allowed us to deny the unsettling reality that we were attacking other nations' rights to self-determination. But American officials knew as early as 1945 that they were intervening against a popular "palm-hut government" throughout Vietnam. In that year, long before we decided to foster an anticommunist South Vietnam, the American journalist Joseph Alsop visited the southernmost Mekong Delta and reported that he "could hardly imagine a Communist government that was also a popular government and almost a democratic government. But this is just the sort of government the palm-hut state actually was while the struggle with the French continued."[3]

The authoritative columnist James Reston wrote ten years later that "even Premier Ky told this reporter today that the Communists were closer to the people's yearnings for social justice and an independent life that his own government."[4] The same premier Ky, incidentally, once said that Adolph Hitler was his greatest hero.

The changes our nation sought to impose on Vietnam reflected an insecure desire to transform others into untroubling, controllable images of ourselves. "Exposure to Western ideas and technology has profoundly changed traditional Vietnamese attitudes," *Fortune* proclaimed in October 1971, "more than highways or ports, these trained people could be the most valuable part of the new infrastructure being left behind in Vietnam by the U.S." Besides the arrogance of turning a different culture into Western "infrastructure," the Americanization quest went to sexual identity itself. Women ranging from from Saigon high-society matrons to street prostitutes underwent surgery during the war to Westernize their eyelids, noses, chins and breasts. One upperclass owner of a plastic surgery clinic, Mrs. Ngo Can Hieu, whose U.S.-trained doctors performed 1,000 operations per month (at bargain prices of $120 for rounded eyes and $480 for inflated breasts), commented that historically "American and Vietnamese conceptions are completely different. Before, Vietnamese didn't place so much importance on the body and people thought a little girl had the ideal form. But . . . particularly during the last ten years the Vietnamese have begun to pay more attention to the body."[5] If America had its way in Vietnam, there would be no more Minh Tinhs, only Barbie dolls.

In my view, then, the primary context for understanding the Vietnam War is that of 500 years of Western Manifest Destiny, not the usual context of the Cold War. That the North Vietnamese were no gentlemen on the battlefield and Stalinist in consolidating power in the South are points I readily and sadly concede. But to blame communism is to forget the long chain of abuses that led to clandestine, hardened communist undergrounds in the twentieth century. Long before communism, Americans were massacring Indians for land, and blaming the victims for savagery.

The point is that Ho Chi Minh should be viewed less like Joseph Stalin and more like Sitting Bull.

The film that became *Coming Home* actually began with the title *Buffalo Ghost*, meant to link the destruction of ancient cultures (and their symbols, the water buffalo and bison) from the Great Plains to the Mekong Delta. It was too difficult to conceive at the time, much less sell to Hollywood. But it is a story we must learn, and it is beginning to be told as many Americans try to reclaim their true history.

If I had lived then, I would have opposed America's Indian wars, as did many now-forgotten Americans. I would have visited the Black Hills to meet and understand the faceless enemy. I would have urged my Irish ancestors, victims of famine and colonialism themselves, to establish co-existence and mutual respect with the Indians, not become Indian killers to prove their patriotism and obtain a plot of land. As an Irish emigrant, I would have tried to stop the cycle of violence, not transfer onto others what British oppression did to us. The only war in which I would have enlisted was the Civil War, on the side of Frederick Douglass.

It is this deeper quest to see Vietnam, not as a mistake in pursuit of the celebrated American Dream, but as an example of the less-explored American Nightmare, that we should undertake. That the Indians and the Vietnamese are forgotten does not mean that they are gone. It only means that we cannot make a proper peace with their memory. Living instead in self-flattering denial amidst a shallow democracy dooms us to battle with their haunting ghosts recycled in the form of new demons. If we confront the tragedies of our history for which we are responsible, if we forsake conformity for real conscience, we can still fight for an America that treats no human being as collateral damage.

NOTES

1. Washington Post Writers Group, February 14, 1991.
2. *Los Angeles Times*, April 28, 1999.
3. *New Yorker*, June 25, 1955.
4. *New York Times*, September 1, 1965.
5. *Los Angeles Times*, February 29, 1972.

Inside Views
Electoral Politics, Public Policy, and the California State Legistlature

12.

From "Make the Future Ours"
Tom Hayden for U.S. Senate Campaign

January–June 1976

After the Vietnam War ended in 1975, about twenty of us who worked together in the antiwar movement held a retreat in Lake Arrowhead, California, to consider what to do with the rest of our lives. We concluded that an opportunity existed to invest ourselves in domestic populism. Some opted for organizing working women, resulting ultimately in SEIU Local 925 and the ascension of lead organizer Karen Nussbaum to a top post in the AFL-CIO. Others committed themselves to what became Citizen Action, a grassroots campaign on economic issues. I ran for the U.S. Senate in order to build a progressive base in California politics. In the final week of the Democratic primary, as I was walking 1,000 miles on the advice of Cesar Chavez, my polling numbers suddenly became competitive with incumbent senator John Tunney. But the insurgency was too sudden, and the whole Democratic establishment started a media campaign attacking me as a "liar" and "worse than Nixon" because I was campaigning against Tunney's retreat on national health insurance. In the end, I was defeated by 63–37 percent, but at least 1.3 million Democrats voted for me. Our ticket carried San Francisco, Berkeley, Arcata, Santa Barbara, and Santa Monica, among other cities. Afterward, we launched the statewide Campaign for Economic Democracy, which lasted five more years, elected many local officials, defeated a nuclear reactor in Sacramento, and led campaigns for toxic controls.

The founders and leaders of CED made a major impact, playing leading roles in ballot initiatives to require labels on cancer-causing products (Proposition 65, in 1986) and tripling tobacco taxes to fund billions for public health and anti-tobacco initiatives (Proposition 99).

Interestingly, one of the prime authors of "Make the Future Ours" was Dick Flacks, my SDS ally who helped draft the Port Huron Statement.

Another was Peter Dreier, who became deputy mayor of Boston and today teaches at Occidental College. Derek Shearer, later Clinton's ambassador to Finland, coined the phrase "economic democracy." Jane Dolan became a five-term supervisor in Butte County. Joan Andersson became a leading progressive attorney, and Cathy Calfo a deputy state treasurer. Bill Zimmerman managed the campaign, and today consults with MoveOn. Bob Mullholland was our veterans' issues coordinator, and today is political director of the California Democratic Party. Andy Spahn, a radical anti-apartheid activist in Berkeley, evolved into staffing the national Democratic Congressional Campaign Committee and, later, top adviser to Steven Spielberg and DreamWorks executives. Dennis Zane became mayor of Santa Monica. Ken Msemaji and Fahari Jeffers built the largest health-care-workers union in California history. Governor Jerry Brown was our closest political ally, especially on issues of nuclear power. Others drifted to the right, like Susan Kennedy, the pro-corporate chief of staff of Governor Arnold Schwarzenegger.

"Make the Future Ours" remains a model for how social movements might engage in successful electoral politics.

◆　◆　◆

GOVERNMENT OF THE CORPORATIONS

The age which is ending is "the American Century," as *Time* called it thirty years ago.

In military terms, it has been an age of Vietnam and Korean wars, smaller interventions elsewhere, and the Cold War philosophy. But, after enormous suffering and destruction, it is now clear that we cannot police the world.

In economic terms, it was an age of American business dominance over the markets, resources and labor of much of the world. It assumed an unlimited supply of cheap resources and American consumption of one-third of the world's energy. The foreign investments of our corporations were thought to ensure unending security and prosperity. We now have very real competitors, however, and Third World countries are reclaiming their resources. Our own multinational corporations have invested so much abroad that we are left with run-away shops, depleted industries, rising unemployment, and higher prices here at home.

Domestically, it was an age which assumed that war and civilian priorities, guns and butter, could both be afforded. The result, we now know, is that we must choose one or the other.

Politically, it was an age of the growth of bureaucratic central government to manage national security in a *bipartisan* foreign policy. But as the Cold War consensus collapsed in Vietnam, the centralized government became a danger to American freedoms.

Philosophically, it was an age in which we knelt before bigness, materialism and profit as ends in themselves.

The new reality is that we live in a world of limits, but live by rules which require an unlimited world. It is the collision of the rules of expansion with the walls of reality which we are now going through, a collision which will require a new philosophy.

DOING WITH LESS SO BIG BUSINESS CAN HAVE MORE

In this new situation, the years ahead will see a worsening conflict between the needs of most Americans and the privileges of the top corporations upon whom we once relied. If we continue to support a system of corporate privilege, excessive profits, status symbols and conspicuous consumption for the few, it will be the majority of Americans who will suffer economic decline. Not just those who have been poor all along, but also the middle Americans who played by the rules and believed in the system, now face an economic crisis.

That this is exactly the future as seen by the privileged economic establishment is clear from an editorial in *Business Week* magazine of October, 1974. Concluding that "it is inevitable that the U.S. economy will grow more slowly than it has," the editorial went on, "some people will obviously have to do with less . . . indeed, cities and states, the home mortgage market, small business and the consumer will all get less than they want.

"Yet it will be a hard pill for many Americans to swallow—the idea of doing with less so that big business can have more. It will be particularly hard to swallow because it is quite obvious that if big business and big banks are the most visible victims of what ails the Debt Economy, they are also in large measure responsible for it."

"Nothing that this nation, or any other nation, has done in modern history," the editorial concludes, "compares in difficulty with the selling job that must now be done to make people accept the new reality."

The giant corporations are not *tightening their belts* for these lean times. Their overall rate of profit may be falling if measured as a long-term percent of investment. Their options for expanded investment may be drying up. But for now, they aren't worrying.

◆　　◆　　◆

As long as the future is made for and by the major banks and corporations, we can expect that our chances for fulfilling personal lives will become less and less. The money and services our cities need will continue to dry up— leading to increased misery for people forced to live in the central cities and a continued upward spiral of fear in our streets. For those who can find work, the work available will not make full use of their training, talents and energies.

This cycle of horrors is what *Business Week* means with the admonition that "cities and states will have to do with less."

Corporate control of our energy future means California will be turned into an energy colony for corporate America. We can expect to see continued reliance on polluting, wasteful forms of energy production as the largest corporations, the energy companies, would be sure to use their great political and economic influence to preserve the present, highly profitable, patterns of energy use, and to resist the development of alternative, decentralized sources over which they would have less control.

Corporate control of our energy future already is underway with the deregulation of the price of natural gas. The monopolies are blackmailing a timid Congress into accepting higher prices which may amount to $110 billion through 1985. Corporate control is the reason utility rates are rising by hundreds of millions to finance Exxon and Atlantic Richfield's search for new energy supplies off Alaska. Corporate control guarantees that if they strike it rich with public financing, the public will receive nothing but first rights to buy at whatever price they can gouge out of us. Corporate control means that consumers are being turned into stockholders without stock. Corporate control means that the Outer Continental Shelf can be leased away by the public to oil companies at scandalously low bids, then sold back at scandalously high prices. Corporate control means that California is being stampeded into accepting, subsidizing and insuring nuclear power plants which are expensive, wasteful and dangerous except to their private investors and government officials. Corporate control will lead to the elimination of the crucial gains made by California's pioneering environmental movement.

Corporate Control of foreign policy will mean continuing the path of the Cold War and Vietnam, modified only slightly by the limits of our power.

It insures that we will not learn the real lessons of the Vietnam War, but instead continue to intervene as we are now doing in Portugal and Angola. It means the threat of nuclear war will continue to hang over the human race. It means the CIA will still carry out secret policies of sabotage and violence without the knowledge or consent of the American people. It means the gap between the have and have-not nations will widen to explosive extremes.

♦   ♦   ♦

Corporate control means having less democracy instead of more. It means more schemes like those of Nixon, Mitchell, Huston and others to create a centralized, computerized police-control apparatus over law-abiding American citizens on "enemies lists." It means police numbers increasing at twice the rate of population growth. It means federal funds for new technological police improvements jumping from $63 million in 1969 to $886 million in 1975, thus diverting technology from more human needs. It means as many as 5,000 personnel in local "red squads," 3,200 FBI agents in "counter-intelligence" programs, unknown numbers of armed forces intelligence personnel and CIA operatives.

It means less freedom for Americans to assemble, to form unions, to enter controversial organizations, to maintain the privacy of their opinions. It means that instead of wider legal forums for debating alternatives to our present problems, opinions will be polarized, labeled and scapegoated. Instead of greater opportunities for peaceful change, it means greater dangers of repression and rebellion.

It means that communities will have less and less control over their own development. It means that the social investments that are needed to ensure health, safety, education and the general well-being of the people will take second place to the drive for profit-oriented capital investment.

It means we will depend on the willingness of these corporations to supply us with the essentials we need to live, with the means of pleasure, relaxation and employment, at prices and on terms that they decide. This not only means an unhealthy dependency, but it is a profound danger as well. When we express discontent at these misplaced priorities, as inevitably we will, we will find the interests of these companies incompatible with democracy itself.

That is not the future we should accept in 1976. We must control the future and make it ours.

GOVERNMENT OF THE PEOPLE

I am not running for the U.S. Senate simply to replace Big Business with Big Government. I do not believe that the way to block corporate power is by trusting the federal government to take care of us. First of all, the history of reform in America tells us that large concentrations of wealth and economic power can stop, distort or take over a process of reform—especially when that process is directed by politicians and experts in Washington. The power of wealth can subvert reform by lobbying incessantly; by using crude and subtle bribes; by controlling the regulatory commissions established to control them; by funding lavish media campaigns that distort the purposed effect of reform; and by waging interminable legal battles to block reforms in the courts. And most fundamentally, the big banks and corporations can defeat reform efforts by slowing down the economic machine—by refusing to invest if they don't like the conditions set on their operations, even though these conditions are legislated by a democratic process and are designed to improve the people's well-being.

But even if it were possible for the reform we need to be legislated at the top, I do not think such reform can and should be relied on to meet our needs. People have every reason to doubt that government bureaucracies and federal investments are going to provide a better future than corporate bureaucracies and Wall Street investments. Neither "Wall Street" nor "Washington" pursue goals that promote the well-being of the people.

TOWARD TRUE SELF GOVERNMENT

The professional politician claims to speak for the people and wants the people to support him. I am running for the U.S. Senate because I want to help people *speak for themselves*, because I want to support people *taking action for themselves*. I am running because I believe the time is ripe for an organized quest for self-government, and that campaigns such as ours can greatly aid this quest. I am running because I believe that *we can use the office of U.S. senator to promote democratic action*. I am running because I think the government can help create the means of self-government rather than destroy them.

I am running because I believe that there is hope for breaking corporate domination over our common life and our future. That hope lies in the possibility that people who don't have the power of wealth behind them will unite and organize to protect their interests and demand their rights.

BUILDING AN ALTERNATIVE

First, campaigns such as ours force those who seek change to develop a positive program based on the shared interests and common sense of the majority. It's no longer enough to be simply against the status quo, for people are rightfully seeking answers beyond protest. It's no longer enough to stand for traditional New Deal–welfare state programs, for people have ceased to trust promises of security that are combined with the centralization of power in corporate and government bureaucracies. There's nothing like a political campaign, where you have to communicate with and persuade the dubious and the indifferent, to force critics and activists to think positively and creatively about social solutions.

What we are presenting here, then, is a contribution to the search for new answers in the years ahead. We have tried to draw on the experience and thinking of many of the groups and individuals in California and around the nation who have been struggling, in their particular areas of concern, for basic reform; in trade unions, farmworker organizing, women's liberation, consumer protection, environmentalism, tenant's rights, health care, tax reform, community self-government, social service, affirmative action, civil liberties, alternative institutions, electoral reform, and the peace movement. We've tried to draw these and other streams of policy and program together—and put them in a framework so they can be heard, tested and discussed by the wider public. Hopefully, through our campaign both the overall need for an alternative to corporate control and the specific policies that might create that alternative can be debated in a wide variety of arenas: in Democratic Party clubs, in unions, churches, community organizations and civic groups, in the media—and by other candidates as well.

Second, in addition to program, the most pressing need of the new political force is for organizational strength. This campaign is dedicated to building a lasting political organization that will go on whether I am elected or not. It will be an organization whose base is in the precincts, workplaces and towns that are reached during the campaign. It will be an organization with thousands of people who have had the experience, as a result of this campaign, of talking not just to themselves (a common failing of reformers) but to anyone willing to listen, and of learning how to operate an efficient grassroots campaign. It will be an organization that hopefully has been able to reach out to the millions of people in this state who no longer believe in the system, but who have turned off to any kind of political action out of a sense of powerlessness or futility. For unless these millions—most of whom are members of the generation born since World War II began—pay attention, register, vote and take political action at every level, then we will have lost our chance to achieve decent lives in the future.

OPENING THE DEMOCRATIC PARTY

Third, the program and organization we are helping to build through this campaign can have a major impact on the Democratic Party in California and nationally. I believe that the Democratic Party is a logical arena for the new populist forces. I believe that the majority of Democratic activists in California will support the kind or program we are presenting. Moreover, the Democratic Party rank and file in California is composed of nearly *six million* people who are suffering most from "business as usual" and who would benefit most from a reinvigoration of democracy. These millions include most industrial workers, most minorities, most public employees, most issue-oriented middle-class people, many small business people. They can be reached by independent candidates and programs.

I don't believe the Democratic Party hierarchy represents this rank and file. The hierarchy tends to be a more exclusive club, dominated by corporate lawyers, and others who have little in common with the rank and file. Nor does the elite have the power to control voters or block independent campaigns like ours. Moreover, the party leadership, like most Americans, is uncertain and divided about the right direction for the country; consequently, despite its relatively elitist cast, many in the leadership are open to pressure from below.

The antiwar movement, minorities and women succeeded considerably in opening the party during the late sixties and early seventies. Today, the same kind of rank-and-file movements for basic economic reform and a new integrity have the potential of *opening the party even further* to new leadership and new program and new, more democratic ways of doing politics. At the same time, those movements must hold fast to their ideas and independence so as not to become simply a respectable opposition limited to the confines of the party.

The antiwar movement did not succeed by giving politicians the leadership. It succeeded by a combined struggle in the streets, in community organizing and electoral politics as well. This independence and variety of action will be crucial to sustain for movements now and in the future.

We face a dangerous situation in 1976. Once element, symbolized by Reagan and Wallace, if elected will attempt a violent counterrevolutionary policy abroad and repression at home. Another element, traditional liberals and moderates, will enact only limited welfare state measures, bringing on more bureaucracy and greater public frustration.

Our movement is the emerging alternative to these traditional reactionary and moderate patterns. The key place to put forth alternatives is the Democratic primary where the voters can make their choice without fear of losing to the Republicans. The Democratic primary is the opportunity to shape something better than "lesser evils." By building organizational strength in the Democratic Party we may be able to check the worst tendencies in American politics, we may be able to change the terms of political debate, we can, at a minimum, veto candidates and policies that we know lead toward disaster. Beyond that, the future decade is hard to predict. The Democratic Party could shift to the right, forcing our movement to create a new vehicle. Or the party could divide from the weight of its internal conflicts. For now, however, we should put forward the vision of a grassroots party in which activists work with their elected officials to struggle both for new programs and to democratize existing ones—a party in which activists are not content to go back to business as usual after an election. A party that is both a movement *and* a major means for maintaining the country's democratic values in the face of entrenched corporate power.

A CAMPAIGN OF EXPRESSION AND INVOLVEMENT

Fourth, this campaign aids the growth of democratic reform by making the vote meaningful as a form of protest and expression. *A vote for Tom*

Hayden for U.S. Senate is a vote against business as usual, a vote for economic justice. For millions of people who find no way of publicly expressing their discontent, who can't take to the streets or speak their minds, voting for a candidate who represents a clear break with the status quo can be effective. The more votes I get, the harder it will be for the professional politicians to ignore the demand for full employment, for adequate health care, for protection of living standards, for real equality and justice.

Fifth, this campaign can help by being an ongoing source of aid for grassroots action. Already, the campaign has supported farmworker organization and other unionization drives; it helped organize consumers to oppose the infamous ARCO deal; it is helping to register voters so that local public-interest candidates can win. By fundraising, by the loan of campaign staff, by the mobilization of campaign workers, and so on, we believe an electoral campaign is a logical and very useful instrument for people to aid causes and struggles that aren't directly affected by the outcome of the election itself. We want to break down the separation that is traditional in American life between "conventional" electoral politics and the "unconventional" politics of the picket line, the protest rally, the boycott and the strike. We think all these forms of action are vital to the process of democratic action, and should be seen as mutually supportive, rather than mutually exclusive.

13.

Hi, L.A., I'm Peter, and I Haven't a Clue

Los Angeles Times, *May 13, 1992*

The failure to "rebuild L.A." was one of the great tragedies in Los Angeles history. After the 1992 riots, a unique effort was launched to privatize economic recovery in the devastated riot zone. The Crips and Bloods declared a peace treaty to end their bloodshed. The promise from L.A. officials was to raise and invest $7 billion in five years to create 57,000 new jobs, but the effort was a disaster. Ten years after the 1992 fires, officials estimated a net loss of 55,000 jobs in South Central.

◆　　◆　　◆

LET'S HOPE UEBERROTH learns much about the inner cities that he seemed deaf to just a few weeks ago.

There has been much discussion of whether Peter Ueberroth, as a white businessman, is best suited to "Rebuild L.A."

Virtually ignored is the question of what policy vision Ueberroth brings to the job. Asked how to rebuild the city, he only speaks generally of bringing the private sector and minority leaders together.

But around what plan?

For an instructive answer, we should turn history back to April 23— one week before the city exploded in flames. That day Ueberroth issued a 107-page, blue-ribbon report on "California's Jobs and Future." Governor Pete Wilson hailed the blueprint of Ueberroth's Council on Competitiveness. The state's media headlined the report at the top of the news.

Less than three weeks old, the Ueberroth report now seems embarrassingly obsolete.

The report makes no mention of an urban agenda. No reference to racism is made, nor do terms like "black" or "inner city" appear at all. The section on small business ignores minority ownership.

There is a lengthy attack on the legal system, not for its treatment of the Rodney Kings, but for its alleged interference in business expansion.

The call for a longer school day is balanced by opposition to any new taxes to pay for it.

And on page 67, there appears the following philosophical assertion: "Getting a job is a necessity, but it is not a right."

Fortunately, copies of the report were not available for review by inner-city youth. If they have no rights as Americans to jobs, what's the point of their participating in the system at all?

Seemingly the only occasion when we educate, train and employ black and brown workers to their fullest potential is during wartime.

So, Mr. Ueberroth, here's an idea: call in Colin Powell and Norman Schwarzkopf. If half of the front-line soldiers in the Persian Gulf were black and brown, why not draft and deploy a similar "multinational force" from the streets of Los Angeles? If we could lay airstrips overnight and rebuild the Emir of Kuwait's palace, why shouldn't we build some transportation and housing overnight here?

The problem is that conventional thinking separates economics from community. According to official doctrine, investment is free to go toward employing a worker, or replacing that worker with technology, or to another country, depending where the reward is greatest.

We need to understand, with economic historian R. H. Tawney, that while "economic ambitions are good servants, they are bad masters." Writing decades ago, Tawney anticipated today's crisis: "Since even quite common men have souls, no increase in material wealth will compensate them for arrangements which insult their self-respect and impair their freedom. A reasonable estimate of economic organization must allow for the fact that, unless industry is to be paralyzed by recurrent revolts on the part of outraged human nature, it must satisfy criteria which are not purely economic."

The issue is not Peter Ueberroth, but old thinking, reinforced by special-interest politics. Ueberroth need not apologize for being a concerned white businessman. We need more of them. But he, and the rest of his co-authors, might apologize for a report that has gone up in smoke.

Such an apology would be refreshing, like a twelve-step program. Think of it: "Hi, my name is Peter, and I don't have a clue." Then we might begin a real recovery.

14

Not a Diversion: Domestic Violence is a Crime
A background paper and legislative proposal by Senator Tom Hayden

July 1994

I found a disturbing double standard on the issues of domestic violence. Hard-line "law and order" advocates tended to exempt men's violence against women from their anti-crime crusades. Liberals were likely to categorize it with such nonviolent crimes such as substance abuse, deserving of an expunged record. Because of the public awareness of the O.J. Simpson trial, I was able to forge a liberal-conservative coalition to recognize domestic violence as a crime the first time it happened to anyone. Governor Pete Wilson signed the bill into law.

◆   ◆   ◆

"When you see your wife commit an offense, don't rush at her with insults and violent blows . . . Scold her sharply, bully and ter-rify her. And if this doesn't work . . . take up a stick and beat her soundly, for it is better to punish the body and correct the soul than to damage the soul and spare the body . . . Then readily beat her, not in rage but out of charity and concern for her soul, so that the beating will redound to your merit and her good."
—Late 15th century, "Rules of Marriage"

➤ Between one-half and two-thirds of all women will experience phys-ical violence in an intimate relationship. —California Alliance Against Domestic Violence

DOMESTIC VIOLENCE STATISTICS

➤ Two to four million women are battered each year in the United States. —California Alliance Against Domestic Violence

➤ Every nine seconds a woman somewhere is being assaulted in her home. —California Alliance Against Domestic Violence

➤ In 1992, 1,431 women were killed by current or former husbands or boyfriends. —Federal Bureau of Investigation

➤ Domestic violence is the second leading cause of injury to women overall, and the leading cause of injury to women aged 15 to 44. —Surgeon General's Office

➤ The United States has three times as many animal shelters as battered women's shelters. —California Alliance Against Domestic Violence

➤ 53 percent of male batterers beat not only their wives or partners, but their children as well. —California Alliance Against Domestic Violence

➤ Each year, domestic violence results in almost 40,000 visits to physicians, almost 30,000 visits to emergency rooms, and almost 100,000 days of hospitalization. —American Medical Association

➤ Nearly one in three female homicide victims in the United States was slain by a current or former intimate. —Federal Bureau of Investigation

➤ Nearly half of abusive husbands batter their wives when they are pregnant, making the women four times more likely to bear low birth-weight babies. —California Alliance Against Domestic Violence

INTRODUCTION

The murders of Nicole Brown Simpson and Ronald Goldman have brought the tragedy of domestic violence to public attention. Although domestic violence is widespread and frequent, California's legal response has been inadequate and often plays a contributing factor in the continuation of the violence. California's domestic violence diversion program is one example of this.

Enacted in 1979, domestic violence diversion programs were intended to offer an alternative to conviction on criminal charges for first-time spousal abuse offenders by allowing them to attend counseling programs.

While rehabilitation is sometimes achieved, there is mounting evidence that these diversion programs fail to change behavior in desired ways. Many advocates have concluded that diversion programs are just that; as presently constituted, they are a diversion from addressing domestic violence as a crime. Instead, they borrow the model of treatment for victimless crimes such as alcohol and drug abuse.

The alternative model that I am proposing is not one that rejects counseling, but that takes domestic violence more seriously as a crime deserving punishment. Simply put, first-time offenders should be convicted, with sentence suspended pending counseling, instead of being diverted to counseling as an alternative to being convicted of an offense.

♦   ♦   ♦

CALIFORNIA'S DOMESTIC VIOLENCE DIVERSION PROGRAM

Since 1979 and the enactment of Penal Code 1000.6, state law has allowed municipal court judges to divert first-time misdemeanor spousal abuse defendants to counseling programs designed to reeducate and rehabilitate batterers rather than prosecute them. If they fail to successfully complete the batterers treatment program or if they assault their spouses again or their cohabitants, they face a mandatory hearing but only possible prosecution on the original charge. If the program is successfully completed, the charges are dismissed and the offense is expunged.

Unlike first-time misdemeanor drug offenses, however, domestic violence is not a victimless crime. In California alone, over 238,895 incidents were reported to the Department of Justice in 1993. It is one of the most severe and pervasive problems in our society, and until we end the consistent denial of its existence, we will be unable to end the abuse. The current laws that govern domestic-violence diversion programs not only undermine the seriousness of domestic violence as a crime, but seek to deny its existence by offering to erase the evidence of abuse.

To be eligible for pretrial diversion, a defendant cannot have any prior arrests for a violent offense in the last ten years, any prior revocation of parole or probation, or any prior domestic-violence diversion in the last ten years. Additionally, diversion is prohibited when the defendant is charged with assault with a deadly weapon, a felony offense or charged with multiple offenses.

Proponents of this program state that it offers an alternative to batterers by allowing them an opportunity to change their violent behavior. Critics argue that it gives batterers a free ride to batter again.

WHY DIVERSION DOES NOT WORK

Nancy Lemon of the California Alliance Against Domestic Violence says that diversion programs are dangerous because they send the wrong message. "Diversion programs communicate to both the batterer and the victim that domestic violence is not a real or serious crime. This is a very dangerous message and until we change that message, we will never end domestic violence. This is particularly inappropriate when other violent offenders are not eligible for similar programs."

Alana Bowman, deputy city attorney of Los Angeles and head of the Domestic Violence Unit agrees. "We don't examine whether or not . . . bank robbers should be tried and sent to prison . . . The traditional belief by many in law enforcement, prosecution and judiciary is that we can't ruin this otherwise good citizen's employment chances or standing in society because he screws up in this one area we really don't consider to be a real crime."

Pretrial diversion is also problematic because the cases are so difficult to prosecute when diversion fails. This often results in charges being dis-

missed. Conversely, immediate sentence impositions, including the threat
of possible jail time, serves as a more powerful deterrent. Commenting on
a study done in Los Angeles regarding diversion programs Bowman states:
"50 percent of domestic violence diversion cases failed outright, and of
these, when they tried to charge the case, 80 percent had to be dropped
because the case was too stale."

STATE AUDITOR GENERAL'S REPORT;
A 50 PERCENT FAILURE RATE

A study released in 1990 by the state auditor general also found diversion
programs to be inadequate. They found in their study of programs in five
counties that probation offices are not regularly monitoring defendants
granted diversion.

According to a study done by the National Institute of Justice, the success of diversion programs requires that there be close monitoring of
divertees by probation departments. The auditor general found that of the
304 cases examined statewide, 54 percent had no evidence of contact for
at least four months. They also found that 48 percent of the programs that
perpetrators were referred to were not batterer treatment programs. And
finally, they found that 27 percent of the 113 cases examined involved a
divertee who was ineligible for the program. In 94 of these cases, the court
granted diversion to defendants charged with assault with a deadly weapon
or felony assault and in 66 of the cases, there were multiple charges.

In 1993, AB 226 (Burton) made efforts to strengthen the administration
of the diversion program by requiring that batterers be referred only to
programs that have been approved and are reviewed annually by local probation offices according to specific standards.

A NEED FOR REFORM

Despite these changes, however, community and legal advocates agree that
the fundamental premise behind diversion, that a batterer should be entitled to avoid prosecution, is false. This perpetuates the common myth

around domestic violence that it is a "private matter" to be resolved behind closed doors. This view has been articulated within the canons of religion, philosophy and law throughout history.

According to British law, for example, men could beat their wives only if the stick was more narrow than their thumbs. This "rule of thumb" standard of British common law embraced this similar right of husbands to forcibly control and discipline their intimate partner for "her own sake" and was adopted by lawmakers in the United States when forefathers were shaping our own policies.

This legacy has changed over the centuries, but slowly. It was not until the 1970's that the women's liberation movement identified, mobilized, and sought policy changes in the laws which govern domestic violence. Much has been gained in the last twenty-five years to protect victims and survivors of domestic violence but much work remains. The domestic-violence diversion program is just one example of lawmaking shaped to condone and perpetuate the battery of women by their husbands, lovers and former lovers, and should be greatly modified or abolished.

RECOMMENDATIONS

Domestic violence is a crime the first time it happens. Diversion programs aimed at reeducating and rehabilitating perpetrators of domestic violence are imperative but should be employed as a condition of conviction and probation rather than as an alternative. The state codes permitting courts to compel perpetrators of domestic violence to counseling or treatment services should limit this authority to a post-conviction only/deferred sentencing model. This model would employ the same program standards under AB 226 but would require that a defendant plead guilty.

15

The Special Interests Still Rule

Los Angeles Times, *November 22, 1994*

During my years in the bowels of government, I observed that the system had become a "Special Interest State." Many have taken up the cause since those days, with little fundamental result beyond the valuable disclosure of campaign funding and lobbyist registration. Now that the new Democrats are matching the Republicans in campaign contributions, I fear that the scandals and rot will increase before another cycle of public outcry. In particular, we need a judiciary that begins to understand how Big Money drowns free speech and therefore deserves no First Amendment protection. It is a fundamental Fourteenth Amendment unequal access issue as well.

◆   ◆   ◆

THE CENTRAL POLITICAL ABUSE that will not be changed by the new Republican Establishment is the ongoing torrent of special-interest money for consultants, commercials and candidates that corrupts the democratic process.

Notably missing from Speaker-elect Newt Gingrich's Republican "contract" is any reform of campaign spending or the sordid skullduggery of the estimated 80,000 lobbyists encamped in Washington.

The new Republican leadership is gearing to stand tall against welfare mothers but can't be found when it comes to confronting contributors seeking handouts. Gingrich declared to political-action-committee representatives in mid-October, "What we've said to all the PACs and, frankly, to their donors is that this is the year." He also warned that "for anybody who's not on board now, it's going to be the two coldest years in Washington."

But the problem now is bipartisan. In all the post-election chatter among Democrats, Republicans and Washington pundits, there has been little reference to reforming a system that obviously disgusts most voters.

Nearly $100 million was spent in the California gubernatorial and U.S. Senate races alone, most of that on clashing commercials aimed at a small percentage of undecided voters. If democracy means a majority vote based on independent information, democracy is being killed by advertising.

Meaningful change is buried as well. Burning issues like the decline of our cities and schools and the inflationary growth of prisons go unaddressed while small but well-heeled farming and mining interests hammer politicians into protecting their century-old, virtually free access to public lands.

Even successful populist efforts of the past, such as Proposition 103, which required an elected insurance commissioner, have been turned upside down by stealth money. The insurance companies elected a pro-industry regulator, Chuck Quackenbush, and were the biggest contributors to Pete Wilson.

Most of the key players in the power game benefit from the current fund-raising rules. The Republicans are not going to surrender the money arsenal that funded their sweep. The Democrats plan to be "comeback kids" in 1996 with funds from interest groups of their own. The consultant industry and the television networks make millions in fees. Only the public withdraws, retching.

If neither party proves capable of breaking its addiction to this treadmill, our situation requires an independent grassroots movement, a legal challenge to the status quo, a statewide initiative in 1996 and perhaps even a third party before the decade is over.

To prevent another 1994 electoral debacle, here are the kinds of reform we need:

> ➤ An educational campaign to reverse the 1975 Supreme Court ruling that the unlimited spending of money in politics is a First Amendment right. It was supported by the ACLU, mistakenly believing that minority views could only be protected by sympathetic millionaires.

It is remarkable that so many politicians attack the courts for being soft on crime and abortion while none have challenged the courts' coddling of wealthy contributors and candidates.

➤ Applying anti-trust doctrine to electoral competition, there must be expenditure limits enacted, with public matching funds for candidates who agree to debates and other fair campaign practices. Contribution limits alone are not enough. Any interest group can arrange for thousands of small contributions in place of one big check.

➤ Regulate or eliminate 30- or 60-second commercials. Paid advertising is a marketing device, not democratic dialogue. It cannot be answered except by those with money. An alternative could be reestablishment of the "fairness doctrine."

➤ Liberate campaigns from Madison Avenue and center them in a multimedia "town square" through interactive video and the free media.

➤ There is no democratic reason to close voter registration 30 days before an election. Nor should elections be limited to 12 hours on a working day when they could be administered on a weekend.

The new Gingrichites, like the incumbents before them, can celebrate the winning of office but it is unlikely that they can govern fairly or efficiently. Their own arrogance leads to policies that are too self-serving to solve the problems of society. The crisis, then, will deepen until their addictive paradigm is shattered.

16

California Cracks its Mortarboards
Written with Connie Rice

The Nation, September 18, 1995

One aspect of the deepening crisis of higher education is that costs are being privatized while affirmative action is being repealed. When I was a student at the University of Michigan, the tuition was $100 per semester. Shifting the cost burden to students and their families results in crushing loan debt and ignores the realities of inequality in America. My studies in California showed that student aid simply never kept pace with escalating costs. These trends were an early sign of a neoliberalism at home, and the decline of the New Deal State under Democrats and Republicans alike. By contrast, other countries under the corporate siege of neoliberalism are struggling to save the right to public higher education. The Sorbonne remains free, and Oxford is a bit over $1,000 per year.

◆   ◆   ◆

ON JULY 20, the University of California regents abolished affirmative action, becoming the first university in the nation to end racial and gender considerations in conducting its business. The regents rejected the minimal diversity standards permitted by the Supreme Court's 1978 *Bakke* decision, and barred U.C. campuses from even considering race and gender in hiring or contracting, as well as admissions.

The decision was bizarre on several counts. The motion to end affirmative action was made by regent Ward Connerly, a black businessman and contributor to Governor Pete Wilson who made his millions as a minority contractor. Connerly's motion was supported by several Latino and Asian regents who, like Connerly, were appointed by Wilson for affirmative-action reasons at the urging of Senate Democrats.

Moreover, the repeal of affirmative action did not apply to the only students who actually *are* unqualified for admission by grade-point average or college test scores, the 1,000-plus "special admits," whose ranks include athletes. Evidently, winning Rose Bowls was important enough to the regents to merit an exception to their strict academic standards.

No alternative to affirmative action was offered. The rationale given was that society has evolved beyond color-consciousness, a strangely unfounded proposition for a university committed to research.

The decision raised troubling questions about university governance. It was imposed against the wishes of the university president, all nine chancellors, the whole academic senate and all campus student governments. Thus the regents, most of them major campaign contributors and political partisans, showed a greater loyalty to Pete Wilson's immediate agenda than to their constitutional public trust. With Wilson running for president, this polarizing of the academy for partisan reasons is likely to be California's latest contribution to American political culture.

The need for affirmative action in higher education remains compelling. The arbitrary abolition of it in California's universities comes at a time when the academic culture still reflects institutionalized barriers to equality. There are nearly twice as many men (25,000) as women (13,000) on the University of California's faculty payroll today. Over the past fifteen years the percentage of black faculty has increased from just 1.8 percent to 2.5 percent, and the absolute number of Native American faculty has dropped from 21 to 19. The regents' act is projected to reduce the fully qualified African-American and Latino students attending the flagship campuses by 50 percent and 15 percent, respectively, bringing their cumulative numbers to less than 10 percent.

At the same time, the attack on affirmative action must be seen in the context of a disastrous downsizing of higher education as a whole, because there is already intense competition among qualified applicants for a dwindling number of seats in its university system. The new policy threatens to create a two-tier segregated campus system. White and Asian students will be isolated in the top-tier schools (U.C.L.A. and Berkeley), while blacks and Latinos will stay in the "bottom" seven, and in sparser numbers. Some campuses will have no black students at all, and there will be no incentive to bring women into the many male-dominated arenas of university life.

Only five years ago, the state legislature and the university reached a consensus to guarantee affordable undergraduate education to all Californians who are qualified applicants. Determined to keep faith with the principles of the state's Master Plan for Higher Education, they called for the addition of three more campuses and 67,000 more students by the year 2005.

Then, faced with a recession, declining revenues and corporate complaints of a "surplus" of college graduates, California embarked on downsizing. In an August 1991 letter, Governor Wilson's administration declared that higher education would undergo "considerable, and permanent," budget reductions. As expansion plans have been tabled, systemwide student fees since 1990 have increased by 134 percent. Student debt has soared to an all-time high. As a result, overall university enrollment has dropped for four consecutive years, by a net of more than 3,000. (Overall, 200,000 students have dropped out of California's public higher education system since 1992.)

According to a RAND Corporation study, California is creating an "access deficit." Further, the study predicts that perpetuation of current budget priorities will probably lead to the end of state funding for the university in twenty years. The regents' decision on affirmative action must be seen in this context. Thousands of students, particularly African Americans and Latinos are already imperiled by skyrocketing fees. Abolishing affirmative action now will only deepen the divide between educational haves and have-nots.

AFFIRMATIVE ACTION IN U.C. ADMISSIONS

This debate is not about admitting unqualified or unprepared minority students. All eligible high school graduates are by definition qualified for admission to the university. They are all among the best and brightest of their high school class, and their grade-point averages are decimal points apart. The University of California is required by the Master Plan to select from the top 12.5 percent of California high school graduates who apply. All students in that top 12.5 percent who complete the required college prep courses and tests are considered fully qualified and guaranteed a place at one of U.C.'s nine campuses. U.C., a public university, is also required by the Master Plan to reflect the vast diversity of California.

Why should arbitrary and narrow distinctions among qualified students bar black and Latino applicants from the flagship campuses? Who would presume to judge that a 3.4 G.P.A. student from a low-income minority area such as Compton is less capable than a 3.7 G.P.A. student from Beverly Hills? Or that a student with an S.A.T. score of 1,400 is less intelligent than a student whose parents spent $3,000 on S.A.T. coaches and emerged with a score of 1500? Should U.C.L.A. and Berkeley be precluded from taking fully qualified black and Latino students because of decimal point differences in G.P.A. and test score gaps that predict nothing of future success or contribution to society? Wouldn't a lottery be fairer?

The regents indulge the fantasy of color-blindness and gender-blindness and ignore the reality that race and gender pose serious systemic barriers that individual adversity does not account for. By exalting test scores and unpredictive differences in G.P.A. above more compelling criteria embodied by race and gender, the regents devalue what many academically qualified minority applicants offer.

The regents stated that preference can still be given to those who can demonstrate individual social or economic hardships. Like guests on *Geraldo,* applicants will have to parade abusive families, "unwholesome influences," economic deprivation, bad neighborhoods or other "dysfunctions" in an effort to be considered for campuses they are fully qualified to attend.

What the regents fail to recognize is that there are no proxies for race and gender. It is a myth that middle-class African Americans and Latinos transcend racism. Just ask white middle-class high school students, who, in one survey, said they would request a million dollars a year as compensation for having to live the rest of their lives as blacks. Countless studies show that women face widespread exclusion from first grade on up that males do not encounter.

The problem with color- and gender-blindness is that people have eyes. Research by the University of California shows that replacing race with socioeconomic status (already a U.C. criterion) in admissions decisions would result in a 40–50 percent reduction in black students and a 5–15 percent reduction in Latino students at the flagship campuses. In practice, the reductions could be worse.

For example, according to U.C.L.A. sources, of 24,000 applicants to that institution, 1,100 apply from the Los Angeles Unified School District's predominantly minority schools, where quality and funding are both grossly inadequate. Two-thirds of these students, despite getting top grades in the toughest courses available and being fully qualified to attend U.C., would rank by test scores in the bottom two academic tiers. They will not be reached by a U.C.L.A. forced to elevate unpredictive test scores and abandon the criteria that best account for many of the systemic barriers.

Moreover, unlike their counterparts at Harvard, University of California admissions officers do not have the means even to interview applicants, never mind minutely evaluate the personal adversity in each of their lives. Without the resources for extensive individual examination, U.C. admissions used race, gender, income, geographic location, etc., not only to achieve diversity but as fair proxies for undeniable systemic inequities.

DIVERSITY IN ACADEME

Diversity is an especially weighty educational value for a public university. It is the test of whether universities are "ultimately concerned with contributing to society," writes Derek Bok in *Beyond the Ivory Tower*. They should seek "students who seem especially likely in later life to use what they learned to benefit their professions and the communities in which they live." In the best of all worlds, U.C. and other schools would choose students who will do the most with their education, enhance the education of fellow students, contribute to the variety of perspectives that enriches the overall learning environment and, most important, contribute to society's well-being. Test scores and grades do not correlate with the "subtler educational goals" of leadership development; interpersonal, political and personal growth; and community reimbursement that all great universities value.

Standardized test scores correlate with first-year college grades but do not predict long-term academic or other success. In fact, one study shows that the L.S.A.T. is an inverse predictor of success in law practice.

A case in point is Dr. Allan Bakke himself. Bakke, the white male graduate of U.C. Davis Medical School who sued to eliminate that institution's sixteen seats for minorities, ended up with a part-time anesthesiology practice in Rochester, Minnesota. Dr. Patrick Chavis, the African-American who allegedly "took Bakke's place" in medical school, has a huge OB/GYN practice providing primary care to poor women in predominantly minority Compton. Bakke's scores were higher, but who made the most of his medical school education? From whom did California taxpayers benefit more?

It is a tragic measure of our national regression on race that today's affirmative action advocates are forced to defend the *Bakke* decision, which only allowed "consideration" of racial factors. In the 1970s, *Bakke* was seen as a setback for civil rights. In the strange logic of the new racism, opponents of affirmative action insist that racism itself has ended, and therefore need not be taken into account. In fact, even to consider racism is to engage in "reverse racism" in Pete Wilson's sanitary new world.

TAXPAYER EQUITY

California taxpayers subsidize U.C. undergraduates who come from families with college-educated parents earning median incomes as high as $66,000 a year. The average taxpayer makes about $16,000 a year and is not college-educated. In Los Angeles, which has a rich/poor gap that ranks third behind Calcutta and Rio de Janeiro, the average black taxpayer makes $12,000 a year. The average Latino taxpayer in Los Angeles earns about $10,000 a year. Neither has a college degree. The children of both attend schools in the Los Angeles Unified School District, and have close to no prospects of attending any college, much less U.C.

Is it fair that black and Latino taxpayers work to subsidize the U.C.L.A. and Berkeley educations of children from relatively wealthy families while the few fully qualified, U.C-eligible children from their communities will not have equal opportunity to attend U.C.'s top two campuses?

California is 27 percent Latino and 7 percent black. Los Angeles County is already 40 percent Latino, 9 percent Asian and 12 percent black. In alarming contrast, the University of California has fewer than 5 percent black and 13 percent Latino undergraduates, numbers that will further decline with downsizing and the end of affirmative action.

Downsizing combined with lack of affirmative action is a poisonous brew, pitting qualified students against each other based on race and gender. The alternative is not to abandon affirmative action but to abandon the pernicious process of downsizing. A retreat from affirmative action combined with a retreat from affordable access to higher education would lead this nation to ruin. Instead of letting Pete Wilson's toxic message spread across America, it is time for an urgent national debate about the sanity of closing the doors of higher education at just the moment when we need to better educate a new multicultural generation of Americans.

17

Ex-Slave Laborers Deserve Far Better

Los Angeles Times, *December 30, 1999*

*Because California regulates its insurance industry, I was able to pass legisla-
tion providing legal remedies for survivors of the Nazi Holocaust and Japanese
slave labor camps (including former American prisoners). In addition, I was
able to force disclosure of documents that insured American slaves as private
property, including the names and partial histories of hundreds of such disappeared people. The eye-opening discovery for me was how contemporary
officials such as the Clinton administration's Stuart Eizenstadt and former
secretary of state Lawrence Eagleburger personally pushed for settlements protecting governments and corporations from onetime slave laborers and state
regulators.*

♦   ♦   ♦

IF AN AMERICAN COURT heard credible testimony that a corporation
had exploited slave laborers to the edge of death, the chances are that the
jury award to survivors would be in the millions.

Under an agreement recently brokered by the U.S. and German governments, however, survivors of slave labor under the Nazis will be
awarded only $790 each for back pay and a lump sum of $7,894 each in
recognition of the fifty-five-year delay. Those who were exploited as
"forced labor," such as Nazi prisoners working in agriculture, will get a
mere $5,000 each. Why is this agreement being hailed by the Clinton
administration as a historic milestone when, in any other context, it would
be dismissed as a slap on the wrist of a bully?

One reason is a public perception that the Holocaust is over, that Jewish survivors have received enough reparation, that anything more would
be a case of the victims becoming greedy. Some Jewish leaders say that the

appearance of greediness might reignite anti-Semitism. "The standard we use is, 'What will the goyim think?'" one said.

This "Holocaust fatigue" syndrome forgets the fact that thousands of slave laborers, many of whom were forced to build roads or make vehicles for the German army, never have been recognized or compensated in the past fifty-five years. Meanwhile, the firms that enriched themselves through slave labor have become respectable and have shrouded their past in glitzy modern commercials.

Famous German firms like Volkswagen, Siemens, Allianz, Daimler Chrysler and BMW will pay only half the total $5.2-billion settlement, the rest coming from the German government and tax breaks. "We don't care how many [survivors] there are or how much they get," one Deutsche Bank official said during the negotiations. "We care only about what we have to pay." Meanwhile, Ford Motor Co. officials are seeking to raise a few hundred million dollars from the 200 American corporations—including General Motors, Kodak, DuPont and General Electric—that participated in the Reich economy.

This is not so much charity as it is buying protection from class-action lawsuits and terrible publicity. The worst proviso of the new agreement preempts slave-labor lawsuits or economic sanctions from states like California, which has a law allowing residents who were slave laborers to sue in state court for compensation. Not only will the companies be spared expensive compensation costs, but they also will be shielded from damaging disclosures in court about their complicity with the Nazis. In addition, European insurance firms that confiscated Jewish assets and Japanese corporations that exploited slave labor during World War II will exploit the agreement to defend themselves from accountability in California.

The California Manufacturers Association lobbied in Sacramento last May on behalf of General Motors and Ford against the legislation, subsequently enacted, allowing compensation suits. GM, through its Opel subsidiary, employed thousands of forced laborers in producing half the trucks and many of the aircraft for the German military. Ironically, in 1967, GM was compensated with $33 million from the U.S. government for the American bombing of its Russelsheim plant.

It sounds perfectly reasonable that the national government, rather than states, should control international negotiations. Yet consider the result. While an American citizen can sue a corporation for millions for making a faulty toaster, a Holocaust survivor will not be able to sue a corporation for being the slave of a regime that put humans in ovens.

The repeated argument of U.S. negotiators is that World War II slave laborers are aging and infirm and deserve closure before they all die. That is true, but it is being politically manipulated to force an inadequate settlement. The U.S. did not make survivor compensation a priority until legislators and lawyers representing survivors began taking action (just as it took official California action to cause economic divestment from apartheid South Africa). For fifty years, the Cold War interests of the American government, which defined Germany as a key anti-Soviet ally, took precedence. Even today, the NATO alliance, including Germany's involvement in the "humanitarian" bombing of Yugoslavia earlier this year, is more strategic to State Department types than achieving full compensation for victims of slavery almost sixty years ago.

Amnesia's cost is hard to calculate. Yet consider this: BMW exploited Dachau inmates and quadrupled its profits during World War II. Is it not dangerous for democracy when corporations can count on consumers without memory?

18

Label Genetically Altered Food
Written with Marc Lappé

Los Angeles Times, *April 9, 2000*

This legislative struggle showed once again how "the market" is suppressed by its corporate promoters when it comes to consumer information and choice. The bill was frustrated in Sacramento's corporate-agriculture-dominated policy committee. A related bill, recognizing a parental right to know if public schools use genetically modified food, went through an education committee but never became law.

◆　　◆　　◆

CORPORATE GIANTS LIKE MONSANTO—which just announced that it has completed a draft of the genetic code of the rice plant—are quick to claim that genetically engineered food will contribute to ending world hunger. Why, then, is there so much industry resistance to labeling their products as genetically modified? All Californians, whether optimist or paranoid, have a right to know whether their food has been genetically engineered.

McDonald's, Burger King and Kentucky Fried Chicken already are eliminating genetically engineered soy and corn ingredients from their menus in Britain, while Americans keep ordering these foods without a clue to their genetic content.

The California Department of Food and Agriculture reviews and comments on hundreds of corporate applications for genetically modified organisms (foods), or GMOs, without even having a single full-time expert working on the issue.

A new report by the National Academy of Sciences claims that genetically modified food is safe, while in the same breath urging research on the

effects on human allergies and whether GMO corn poisons monarch butterflies. This is not a reassuring spin, especially since the leader of the study
left midway to go work for the Biotechnology Industry Organization, and
four researchers received funding from Monsanto, which has a direct economic interest in crops becoming "Roundup ready," i.e., tailored for its
herbicide.

No one can dispute that genetically engineered food differs from its
conventional counterparts. So why not label them to provide consumers
with information and choice? They are detectable. Virtually every gene-
engineered product carries a signature that gives away its ersatz nature. A
simple $5 test can pick out genetically engineered, soy-based products
from their natural peers.

We don't let manufacturers of other products dupe consumers. An
unlabeled, knockoff copy of a CD is a fraud. Even atomically identical, artificial and natural diamonds are allowed to be labeled so the consumer can
make the choice between the engineered version and the real McCoy. People value the "'real thing."

The FDA's bottom-line argument for not labeling is that engineered and
conventional foods are "equivalent." In fact, no one knows if any food
remains identical after it is genetically tampered with. No scientific group,
much less the FDA, has thoroughly examined the actual nutritional
makeup of any genetically engineered foodstuff. What data we do have is
hardly reassuring: the new GMO corn has a toxoid in every kernel. We can
only hope it has no deleterious health effects on human consumers. As a
result of our Freedom of Information Act requests, we know the FDA, our
gatekeeper for food safety, keeps no studies in its files on this corn. There
also is evidence of allergic reactions from novel proteins. When the sleep-
inducing L- tryptophan was genetically boosted a few years ago, several
deaths resulted among unaware consumers.

The fact that no one has noticed that their catsup or spaghetti sauce has
been adulterated with genetically engineered tomatoes some years back
does not give a federal agency the green light to continue this deception.
The FDA already endorses the labeling of irradiated food, organic produce
and processed foods. It allows a kosher symbol on properly prepared items.

None of these foods differs nutritionally in consistent ways from their conventional counterparts. Nor does the label say they do.

Would a label lead to the destruction of the biotechnology industry? We don't see why. The biotech industry need not worry about consumer preference if its products are actually as good as they say they are. Consumers are savvy, smart and ultimately fair. They have won the hard-earned right to choose what they want to eat. Many now choose organic or low-fat foods. Others don't want genetically engineered food. A simple label, now universally recognized in the European Union, that says "contains GMO" should not scare anyone. Mexico's Senate recently has supported an analogous label. Should not shoppers in California and Mexico have the right to fill their baskets with products they can trust are accurately labeled?

Tell the mom or dad looking for baby food that a label is unneeded. Even Gerber has agreed GMOs have no place in its baby foods. Before other manufacturers are forced to eliminate all genetically engineered products, why not give them the option to label?

IV Digging for Root Causes
Ending Gang Violence

19

Be Equally Tough on Causes of Violence

Los Angeles Times, *February 10, 1997*

This piece was the seed of my book Street Wars *(New Press, 2005). Today I serve on a community-based advisory committee on gang violence, reporting to the mayor and city council of Los Angeles. There are presently sixty-one so-called gang intervention workers, whom I call street peacemakers, while the population of out-of-school, out-of-work youth in Los Angeles is 93,000. California competes to lead the world in inmates, most of whom are accused gang members. Politicians still fear the charge of "soft on gangs," the domestic equivalent of "soft on terror." The profitable wars on gangs, drugs and terror derail any serious funding of education, health care or public-service jobs.*

◆   ◆   ◆

JUST AS SOME WERE ASSERTING that our epidemic of violence was in remission, it has returned to Los Angeles with a demoralizing vengeance.

Three murders—Ennis Cosby on a dark freeway offramp, 17-year-old Corrie Williams on a bus, Laurence Austin at his silent-movie theater in the Fairfax area—have attached human faces to the plague of 10,000 homicides in Los Angeles County since 1991.

While supporting the police in their efforts to find the killers, we must also reflect on how to reverse this epidemic. We absolutely need more and better police, more homicide detectives and criminalists. But there will never be enough police to patrol every dark road, every bus, every movie theater where madness may erupt.

There is a public consensus to be tough on crime. But no matter how many anti-crime bills I author or vote for, including three strikes for violent offenders, the feeling grows that violence is out of control. We need a new consensus to be equally tough on the causes of violence.

Most of our public officials, including Mayor Riordan, exhibit little commitment to violence prevention. The city's prevention budget is minuscule. After the slaying of 3-year-old Stephanie Kuhen seventeen months ago, the mayor sought $5 million in federal funding for anti-gang programs. A year later, Los Angeles received $1 million, which is equal to one-fourth of the budget for the city's advertising campaign proclaiming "Together we're the best."

A comprehensive approach to combating the causes of violence would include:

➤ Breaking the cycle of domestic violence. Instead of being hypnotized and numbed by the O.J. Simpson murder trial, we should promote awareness, empower women and toughen penalties.

➤ Reducing the number of school dropouts. Mobilize a service corps of 3,000 local college students, paid through tuition reductions, to work as after-school tutors in public schools.

➤ A living wage. This would lift thousands of families from the grinding poverty that breeds violent frustration. Glossy city brochures promote "unskilled low-wage workers" as a business attraction, and tax subsidies too often go to those who don't need them, like DreamWorks.

➤ Drug treatment. Drug addiction is the most important factor in the cycle of crime, violence, arrests, prison and parole, yet only 1 percent in prison receive comprehensive drug treatment, and many become addicts. We need "drug courts" like those in Oakland and Santa Monica that are dedicated to counseling and treatment.

➤ Rebuild Los Angeles, anyone? The public-private partnership that emerged after the 1992 riots with a goal of 57,000 new inner city jobs has been quietly euthanized. Community leader Father

Gregory Boyle has been saying for years that a job is still the best anti-crime program, so why are hands-on efforts like his so underfunded?

Taking any one of these initiatives is daunting. To sustain them requires a larger vision for restoring urban peace.

Fifty-five years ago, an LAPD memo proposed to take gangs "out of circulation until they realize that the authorities will not tolerate gangsterism." Yet the quagmire deepens.

We need a new approach. If our government can engage in a full-scale peace process in Northern Ireland, why not in South and East Los Angeles?

When the Irish paramilitaries began a cease-fire in 1992, there was a diplomatic flurry, a presidential visit and economic assistance. While those efforts have suffered setbacks recently, violence has been reduced and replaced by a framework for peace. When Crips and Bloods initiated truces the same year, they were ignored as untouchables. But even the LAPD commander for South Central credited the truces for "a real decrease in violence," and warned that "if social conditions and unemployment remain the same, you will have continuing unrest." No one responded.

We need an inclusionary peace process in Los Angeles that reinforces gang truces and follows up with economic incentives. What is needed besides local leadership is a full-time urban peace envoy like George Mitchell, the president's mediator in Belfast, or Dennis Ross in Israel.

What prevents us from committing ourselves to prevention? Some think law and order can be achieved without prevention. One of the mayor's gurus, UCLA professor James Q. Wilson, writes that he "has yet to see a 'root cause' or to encounter a government program that has successfully attacked it."

But psychiatrist James Gilligan, who directed a study of violence at Harvard Medical School, believes that violence is a disease that can be treated. Violence, he believes, arises from an uncontrollable experience of shame.

Too many kids are born into zip codes of shame. They live in a city glutted with guns, drugs and alcohol. They plan more for their funerals than their futures. When shame and dishonor get the better of them, self-destructive violence results.

We need to transform these zip codes of shame to communities of hope. We will pay one way or the other. The cost of holding a kid in the California Youth Authority is $31,000 a year; the cost of educating a child, $4,500. A prison cell costs $100,000.

By contrast, every tax dollar spent on substance abuse treatment programs saves taxpayers $7 by lowering crime and health care costs. RAND Corporation's Peter Greenwood suggests that we invest in parent training and childcare for young, single, poor mothers to break the cycle.

The public should question the irresponsibility of anyone in public office who fosters these breeding grounds of violent shame while leaving the rest of us to reap the lethal consequences on dark roads, on public buses and in silent-movie theaters.

20.

Gato and Alex—No Safe Place

The Nation, *July 10, 2000*

One of my proudest moments was the day a courageous INS judge, Rose Peters, and a courageous U.S. attorney, Alejandro Majorkas, agreed to grant Alex Sanchez amnesty. Today Alex still lives and works the dangerous streets of Pico-Union. Many civil rights and civil liberties organizations, along with individuals like Ethel Kennedy, joined the campaign to free Alex. But since 9/11, it has become much more difficult for even a courageous young man like Alex—and there are many—to receive the benefit of the doubt from public officials.

◆   ◆   ◆

THIS IS THE STORY OF Gato and Alex, two Salvadorans who as children became refugees from America's war in their homeland only to become rivals in America's gang war on the streets of Los Angeles. When these two homeboys finally turned their lives toward peace, there was no safe place for them. They were among the New Untouchables, the supposedly incorrigible "superpredators," whose specter justified the war on gangs that has become the worst police scandal in Los Angeles history.

As a little boy, Gato ("The Cat"), who got his eventual street name because of his feline eyes and agility, saw his father shot in the head by a death squad in his front yard in the San Salvador barrio of Modelo. The shooters came in a car with tinted windows and left no explanation. Gato kept a chain of Our Lady given him by his father, which became his only link to his boyhood, because the war made refugees of his mother, his brother and himself. Along with tens of thousands of Salvadorans in the eighties, Gato landed in the Pico-Union immigrant barrio under the corporate towers of L.A., now one of the densest urban neighborhoods in America.

As a schoolboy in Los Angeles, Gato had an initial distaste for the *cholos*, the gangbangers and dropouts hanging on the corner. He wanted to get a job and fulfill the traditional immigrant aspiration. It was not to be. Someone from a nearby gang called him a *chuntero*—an untranslatable putdown of immigrants—and ripped off the chain of Our Lady. Gato wanted to retrieve his father's chain on his own, but his new friends convinced him he required protection—that he needed to belong to a "neighborhood" with "homies" of his own, who would back him up in his quest for the chain. So he was "jumped into" (hazed and initiated into) the 18th Street Gang, then mainly composed of Mexican immigrants. To assert his own identity, Gato tattooed "El Salvador" in big block letters on his chest, larger than the 18th Street symbols. His Mexican homies objected at first, but 18th Street had started to incorporate large numbers of Salvadorans. The new immigrants claimed turf and identity in a hostile new world, escaping from one war zone in El Salvador to another one in America.

It may be impossible to explain the ensuing phase of Gato's life to anyone safely distant from the cycles of urban violence. The superpredator theory is popular; it attributes violence to the genes, for which there is no cure but the superior violence of the state. To locate gang violence in underlying social factors has been discredited by both Republicans and New Democrats. But neither stern punishment nor exhortations to personal responsibility have prevented the violence.

A better way to look at gang violence is through the mirror, as an underclass mimicry of institutional violence, including state, corporate and entertainment violence. Nation-states, including our own, frequently inflict savage punishment to project power and preserve reputation. Not to do so is thought to invite aggression. We engage in arms races and compete to control resources like oil, while gangs assemble weapons to control the drug underground. We fight over flags. They fight over colors. They are entranced by films about Italian, Jewish and Irish gangsters, and the new gangs emulate those movies in the belief that it is the American way. So there is a certain logic to the madness that Gato began to display.

With his new friends Gato found the homeboy who ripped off the chain of Our Lady. "Remember the *chuntero*?" he asked him, then wounded him with a knife. It was first blood. Not long after, another gang, known as the Crazy Riders, drove into Gato's neighborhood and shot and killed one of his homeboys. Gato shot back, hitting the Crazy Riders in their car. Acting on a human impulse, he pulled the wounded assailants from the vehicle, said they should call 911 and took off running. He was stopped by unsuspecting police and told them to go help the injured. But Gato was identified by a neighborhood resident who had witnessed the shootout and was arrested when he returned to the Pico-Union community weeks later. Convicted of attempted murder, he was sentenced to one of California's toughest prisons, where life was just as dangerous as the street. There his honor was assaulted again. One day Gato found a cellmate masturbating to a photo of Gato's girlfriend, an insult that could not go unpunished. To do nothing would reveal weakness, which would lead to sexual assault or worse. So Gato stabbed him.

Rather than face more time in California's penal colony, Gato took the option of "voluntary departure" and in 1997 was deported to El Salvador. Thus the violence completed its cycle, from Gato's birth in Modelo to his father's execution, forced exodus to Los Angeles, the violent defense of his honor by the code of the street, the brutalizing time in California's prison gulag and the deportation back to his original *chumpa* (shanty).

During the early nineties, Alex Sanchez was also living in Pico-Union. He too was a war refugee from a San Salvador barrio. Unlike Gato, who was fair-skinned and lithe, Alex was dark and powerfully stocky. Alex joined the *mara salvatrucha* (Salvadoran neighborhood) gang, known as MS, the archrival to 18th Street. Alex was the wild, stray child in a family that included a sister, a brother and two parents, all of them naturalized citizens, who anguished over him. If violence is in the blood, as some believe, why was Alex the antithesis of his brother? For whatever reason, he was the angry one, and his gangbanging got him arrested for carjacking and weapons possession. The truth, according to court records, is that Alex had jumped in a convertible with the key in the ignition but jumped out and fled when the owner appeared. Alex's court-appointed attorney pleaded him to carjacking, a felony, which insured that his next offense would be treated as a felony as well. Had Alex been a white teenager, his

offense would have been malicious mischief and the punishment a scold-
ing by his parent. Instead he went to state prison, then took Gato's path of
voluntary deportation. Eventually he returned illegally, pulled by a longing
to be with his tiny newborn son, Alejito. Alex surprised his family by settling down, staying out of sight, working at odd jobs.

In 1996 and 1997, stories in the *Los Angeles Times* and the *New York Times*
sounded the alarm about the rise of Salvadoran gangs. In coverage reminiscent of the anti–zoot suit hysteria of the 1940s, both papers published
graphic photos of tattooed Salvadorans accompanied by vivid stories of
their incorrigible violence. Politicians led by Governor Pete Wilson and
Mayor Richard Riordan called for $18 million in state support for the war
against gangs. State laws were passed making it a crime to "associate" with
gangs, as defined by tattoos, hand signs, the word of paid informants or
undercover police. The LAPD anti-gang units, known as CRASH (Community Resources Against Street Hoodlums), operated with secret budgets,
no civilian oversight and broad public support. As revelations in the Rampart Division scandal would show, they often planted evidence, framed
people, gave beatings and even shot suspected gang members without
cause. More routinely, they "worked up felonies" by issuing tickets for jay-
walking, loitering, riding a bicycle through a stop sign and other petty
citations that were punishable by fines the homies couldn't afford. From
there it was a simple process of arresting them for outstanding citations and
warrants, and sending them to jail.

The targets of this dirty war were the inner-city youths born in the wake
of the civil rights movement, deindustrialization and the U.S.-bankrolled
repression in Central America. They got little sympathy from white liberals. Their nihilistic anger was vocalized only by rap musicians. Their
violence was internalized against one another. Only a few farsighted people like Father Gregory Boyle and Luis Rodriguez, both from East LA,
envisioned the need to transform this self-destructive energy, but they were
isolated.

The lives of Gato and Alex were about to change. There came a new
consciousness that the homies themselves had to stop the madness. Too
much self-hate and self-destruction began to generate a desire for inner

and outer peace. A small group in El Salvador formed a new organization called Homies Unidos, similar in purpose to gang cease-fire efforts in the early nineties by the Crips and Bloods. Working out of an open garage in Gato's barrio of Modelo, Homies Unidos promoted an attitude of *calmado* (calming) on the street, fostered dialogues between 18th Street and MS and started subsistence businesses making organizational buttons, T-shirts and glassware. Most were Salvadorans deported from Los Angeles. They spoke a weird L.A. brand of Spanglish and had L.A. tattoos and tough-guy reps from the mythology of the L.A. streets. In reality, they were trapped between worlds—a living provocation for entrenched gangs and easy targets for revived right-wing death squads.

The center of gravity in Homies Unidos was Magdaleno Rose-Ávila, a massive Mexican-American with a big heart enlarged in the farmworker and Chicano movements in the United States. Magdaleno was living in San Salvador with his wife, Carolina, an international children's advocate, when he started encountering these lost homeboys from L.A. Using his community organizing skills and fundraising contacts, Magdaleno made his living room the birthplace of Homies Unidos. "The key to organizing," he said, was that "we listened to them, to their pain. We offered 'comprehension.' It was dangerous for them, because once they became involved in Homies, as opposed to their old gangs, they became open targets with no one to turn to for safety. But the alternative was more dying."

Gato's mother, who returned to El Salvador in 1993, brought him around to the Homies' little garage, where Magdaleno ran nonviolence workshops, which Gato attended. "It was like therapy sessions for torture victims, like I did for Amnesty International," Magdaleno recalled. "The ability to talk was healing, freeing them from their monsters. Also to talk about your dead homeboy is to honor him, so it was like a ceremony."

I first heard of these homies through an article in the *Nation* by Luis Rodriguez, whom I looked up in Chicago at the 1996 Democratic convention. By then, achieving peace on the streets of America seemed as urgent an issue as stopping the Vietnam War was in the sixties. If our government was promoting peace processes in Northern Ireland and the Middle East, I wondered if it was possible in South Central and East Los Angeles. In 1997

I organized a delegation composed of former L.A. gang members, church workers and community organizers that traveled to El Salvador to explore ways to end the globalized cycle of gang violence. There I first met Gato and heard his life story. He told it calmly, in Spanglish, as he leaned against a wall overlooking a creek that neighborhood women filled with plastic garbage bags. He spoke first of the suffocating cycle of violence that passed as life. "In El Salvador," he said, "the people were terrorized by war, then there was peace, now there is 18th Street and MS killing each other. You never know when you're going to be dead."

One day Gato's comment almost came true. While riding a bus to our meeting place, he was stabbed by a rival MS member. He seemed strangely composed when he showed up in bandages. "I told the guy, 'Man, I don't bang no more. You don't know why you're into that.' And then he told me, 'Fuck you, *puta*,' and claimed his MS "hood." I couldn't understand Gato's new willingness to accept insult and stabbing. "It's hard to forgive somebody when they do bad to you" was all he said when I asked him.

But his defiant spirit had not disappeared. Within the next year, Gato moved with his girlfriend, a younger homegirl known as Spanky, and their new baby, into his old house in Modelo. By now, however, Modelo was claimed as MS territory. Not only was Gato still covered with 18th Street tattoos but, even worse, Spanky was an MS homegirl. This was a homie version of Romeo and Juliet, or like an interracial couple moving into a segregationist neighborhood in the early sixties. But Gato wasn't going anywhere. He was home, assuming his responsibility as a father. "A lot of the MS homeboys don't like me because I'm with my lady," he reflected, "but I don't think anyone should choose for me the woman I'm going to be with for the rest of my life. It would be the same thing for me if I saw a homegirl from 18th Street with a guy from MS."

Thousands of miles north, a similar transformation was occurring with Alex. The double miracle of his own survival and the birth of his son had altered him. When he heard of Homies Unidos he was drawn to the idea of giving something back to the community he had damaged, so he volunteered. In becoming a public organizer, Alex was placing himself in harm's way. But he felt a calling, and soon he learned he had a gift for influencing young people to change their lives. For example, he gradually talked a pregnant, drug-addicted 16-year-old young woman into joining the Homies program. On her birthday, Alex gave her a big party with a cake. But it was raided by the CRASH unit, whose policy was to prevent all "association" among gang members. Alex was shoved against the wall, thrown on the floor, handcuffed. The officers knew Alex was undocumented and enjoyed telling him he could be deported at any time.

Our fledgling peace-process network actively sought to provide safe space for groups like Homies Unidos. In San Salvador we met with the U.S. ambassador, the mayor and the police chief in the capital; in the United States with Doris Meissner, commissioner of the Immigration and Naturalization Service, and Commander Dan Koenig, of LAPD CRASH. We asked that INS provide a special visa for people like Alex to organize without fear of deportation. After all, law enforcement protected informants and undercover agents who were undocumented, so why not a peacemaker? We asked CRASH to stop harassing Homies Unidos members in L.A. Because this was an international problem—fifty Salvadoran gang members are deported weekly from California—we asked them to give us an office at San Salvador International Airport to counsel deportees as they landed and to provide a halfway house, microloans for subsistence businesses and security for Homies in El Salvador. Though the U.S. officials we met in El Salvador and Washington expressed great interest in the project, in the end none were eager to take a risk for peace. They were afraid of being considered soft on gangs.

Last November, Gato was shot six times and killed in front of his house in Modelo, before the eyes of his wife, Spanky, and small son, Vladimir. The shooters were presumably homeboys from MS, but who knows? He was the third member of Homies Unidos to be killed in El Salvador last year. What made Gato take a stand that caused his death? Was it that old code of honor, now displayed nonviolently? Was it the homeboy view of fate itself, "Laugh today, cry tomorrow"? Was it the cycle that began with his father's death before his eyes playing itself out because no one knew how to stop it? For mainstream society it was just another incorrigible superpredator finally dead.

After Gato's murder, Alex kept going. He organized small poetry-writing classes and put on plays, therapeutic channels for Homies Unidos members to wrestle with their inner demons. He traveled to Sacramento to lobby state legislators, prison officials, even the top aides to conservative Democrat Governor Gray Davis. They told him to "think about appealing to the voters in Van Nuys," presumably a tougher version of soccer moms, and to "not seem like a victim." Alex wore a white shirt and tie, and began to describe his mission as reforming lives. Modest gains were achieved, like $3 million in annual funding for neighborhood-based violence-prevention work, but the main impact was that the tattooed homies like Alex were coming in from the cold. Space in the political process was opening to them, when before the only space was the state's prison cells.

But for CRASH officers, the FBI and La Migra (INS), Alex remained the criminal enemy. Once an MS member, they figured, always an MS member. The Rampart CRASH unit singled him out, one day taking him for a three-hour ride in the backseat of a police car. They showed him they knew where his mother lived, drove through enemy gang neighborhoods, told him they could have him deported anytime, then dropped him in the street like a cat drops a mouse. Unfazed, Alex testified at a State Senate hearing in a Pico-Union church, called to investigate police harassment of gang peace efforts. In the church were Rampart CRASH officers threatening young homies who were there to listen or testify. The press was just beginning to explore the Rampart scandal to come.

The Rampart scandal, which is really a CRASH scandal, cannot be understood as simply another case of police brutality against innocent citizens, or even an example of racism in uniform. It is more. It is a case study in what happens when any means are justified in a shadowy war against society's scapegoats. None of the historic commissions on Los Angeles police misconduct, including the 1991 Christopher Commission, addressed the underlying constitutional issues of this dirty war. Now, in response to public and media furor, the LAPD has renamed CRASH as a "special enforcement unit" without the belligerent label, just as it previously changed its original acronym from TRASH (Total Resources Against Street Hoodlums). That the abuses uncovered in the scandal were not the isolated actions of rogue cops is suggested by *Los Angeles Times* stories revealing the direct involvement of the FBI and INS with CRASH. Thus the very immigration officials to whom Alex appealed for asylum have themselves been implicated in covert operations with CRASH.

So it was not surprising when, on January 20 of this year, Alex was arrested by CRASH officers using a year-old immigration warrant, despite a city policy against police collusion with INS sweeps. "You're all going down, Homies is going down," Alex recalls the CRASH officers jeering at him.

The U.S. Attorney for the Los Angeles District, Alejandro Majorkas, proved to be unusually courageous in declining to prosecute Alex for illegal reentry. But that left Alex in the custody of an INS eager to deport him to El Salvador, where, according to an affidavit by the San Salvador police chief, Alex is in danger of being murdered. He has initiated an asylum hearing, and in June a team of civil rights lawyers filed a federal suit on behalf of Alex and Homies Unidos against the LAPD.

Meanwhile, Alex is confined to Terminal Island with hundreds of other immigrants. He has been portrayed sympathetically by the *Los Angeles Times*, CNN and Geraldo Rivera. Federal officials like the INS's Meissner, who has the power to free Alex, allow the hostile INS officers in L.A. to control his fate. Under such conditions, will he grow stronger as a peacemaker? What if another inmate attacks him? What of the gang peace process on the streets? Who will come forward now, seeing the treatment of someone like Alex Sanchez at the hands of police?

These are questions that should concern us all. But do they? The *Times* has been more critical of the Rampart behavior than any local official or candidate for office, including African Americans, Latinos and white liberals. Scapegoating the underclass seems to be a staple of politics these days. This is shortsighted, because the politics of law and order diverts billions from programs that will prevent gang violence more than the police ever will.

Perhaps the chief contribution of individuals like Gato and Alex is that they are living proof, even in death or prison, that so-called incorrigibles can change, that homies are human beings. That should rally Americans to their cause of peace at home. As Gato put it in a last interview, "I hope, you know, someday in the future I see guys from MS and my homeboys really forgiving the past. We are humans, and we are killing each other for nothing."

21

The Myth of the Superpredator

Los Angeles Times, *December 14, 2005*

One year later, I remain in pain over the midnight execution of Stanley Williams. His executioner was Governor Arnold Schwarzenegger, a friend of mine through the Robert Kennedy family, and I wonder if he has any regrets at all. The governor's legal-affairs secretary, Peter Siggens, told me at the time that the order of executions had to be shuffled because they didn't want to kill two black men in a row. Not long after Tookie Williams's execution, a grotesque affair involving failed efforts to find a vein for the lethal injection, the California death penalty was indefinitely suspended for hearings into whether killing with lethal drugs was itself cruel and unusual. If that judicial inquiry had begun a few months earlier, Tookie would be alive today.

◆　　◆　　◆

THE EXECUTION OF Stanley Tookie Williams cannot be allowed to drown out his message: we need to find alternatives to the "embedded sense of self-hate" that propels so many inner-city youth to lash out in killing sprees.

Yet history shows that Los Angeles may not be prepared to listen. In the wake of the 1992 Crips-Bloods truce, which Williams promoted from death row, gang violence in L.A. declined by half. Five years later, the *Times* reported that "police and residents of Watts confirm that gang-on-gang slayings over emotional issues of turf boundaries or gang clothing have virtually disappeared."

But there was no peace dividend, and the truce eventually dwindled, though it never completely died. The plan to privatize urban reconstruction after the 1992 riots—the Rebuild L.A. initiative that promised $6 billion in private investment to create 74,000 new jobs in five years in the riot zone—was a sham that closed down a few years later. The riot zone lost 50,000 jobs in that decade. In the vacuum, youthful rage exploded again in gang warfare.

Around that time, conservatives such as William Bennett and James Q. Wilson began attaching the label of "super-predator" to all the Tookie wannabes. Their notion seemed to be that a fixed percentage of kids were natural-born killers who just couldn't be helped by better schools or jobs—a neo-Darwinian philosophy that fit neatly with the deindustrialization and budget cuts that swept across inner cities like chain saws through old-growth forests.

The superpredator thesis justified the most massive prison expansion in American history, with its epicenter in California, where there were about 150,000 inmates in any given year, two-thirds of them reputed gang members. Prosecutors and politicians pursued the vertical model of the 1920s, going after the alleged godfathers, but in fact the new gangs were replenishing themselves from the outcast underclass. Last year in Los Angeles, there were 93,000 youths between the ages of 18 and 24 who were out of school and out of work. Statewide, the number was 638,000.

How is the city of Los Angeles addressing the gang problem? The city budget reveals that the priority is to suppress and incarcerate, not to turn troubled lives around. Fifty-five million dollars go to LAPD gang suppression efforts, a token $12 million to prevention programs for little kids, and a bare $2 million for intervention programs meant to channel teenagers away from violent paths.

To turn from the treadmill of violence to the path of peace, we must:

▶ Understand that gang members are traumatized veterans of street wars, not Satan's agents or incorrigible psychopaths. There must be a massive expansion of rehabilitation and empowerment programs along the lines of Alcoholics Anonymous, with participation by ex-gang members who command respect. Those who insist on waiting for a sanitized messenger will wait in vain.

➤ Reform of punitive police and prison policies that breed lawlessness on the street. Inner-city youth feel that they are targeted, that humiliation is intended against them and that the criminal-justice system is based on a double standard. This week, it was reported that the L.A. district attorney who led the charge against Williams has not brought a single criminal charge in 442 cases of police shootings since 2001. This—along with the use of untrustworthy police informants such as those who helped convict Williams—can't help but make young people on the streets of South Central L.A. cynical about criminal justice.

➤ Recognize that we have a crisis of exclusion and structural unemployment that renders countless young people hopeless, powerless, helpless, rootless and meaningless, in the analysis of former gang member turned author Luis Rodriguez. Government always has a role to play when the market fails. California taxpayers already contribute $6 billion to the state's prison system—but virtually nothing to jobs in the inner city.

Spectacular executions can divert people's attention from their government's failings and crimes. And it's easier to scapegoat the superpredator than the superpower. But, unlike the white ethnic gang culture of yesterday, for which there is widespread nostalgia in film and on TV, the only doors that are opening for the new generations of street gangs are those of the prison system.

A country that fails to provide living wages for so many of its young is more committed to its present privileges than its future potential. To avoid the message, it thinks it can kill the messenger. But I believe Tookie Williams has eluded his tormenters. His legend and message are understood around the world. Sooner or later, attention will be paid.

V Personal Roots
Thoughts on Ireland

22

The Famine of Feeling

From Irish Hunger: Personal Reflections on the Legacy of the
Famine, *edited by Tom Hayden (Roberts Rinehart, 1997)*

*During the 1990s I became deeply immersed in my Irish identity, tried to stake
out a progressive position in the politics of Irish America, and traveled extensively to Northern Ireland, often as a liaison to President Clinton's commerce
secretary, the late Charles Meissner. On the 150th anniversary of the Irish
Famine, I edited the first collection of reflections between Irish and Irish
American writers on that traumatic experience. This essay became the basis
for a later work,* Irish on the Inside (Verso, 2005).

◆   ◆   ◆

"To be the present of the past. To infer the difference with a terrible stare. But not to feel it. And not to know it."
—Eavan Boland

ALL MY GREAT-GRANDPARENTS were Famine immigrants. Inevitably,
there were other relatives whose names I will never know who died of fever
or starvation. Others wept to the heavens when their children were exiled
to America on the coffin ships. Their mournful keening, Frederick Douglass wrote after a visit to Ireland, reminded him of the "wild notes" of
African mothers during the slave trade.[2]

I am an orphan to this history. My parents never told me of it. Though
they were shaped and influenced by the Famine, I don't know if they themselves were aware of it.

Unlike the horrific experiences of other people, there has been an ocean
of silence over the trauma these millions of Irish suffered. To be sure, there
is a folk awareness that lingers. But there are thousands of unmarked
Famine graves under the green fields of Ireland. Ireland's first Famine

museum opened only a few years ago. Until recently, academic histories and popular literature on the Famine has been sparse. The Famine is neglected in school curriculums too.

When the Famine is recalled at all, it usually is as "the *potato* famine," which seems to imply an unfortunate agricultural accident beyond human control or responsibility. It is not seen as the intentional thinning and removal of a whole rural population considered "surplus" by a foreign power.

A famine repressed, however, breeds an incipient hunger of its own, a hunger to know, to grieve, to hold accountable, to resolve, and to honor. This hunger for memory is stirring. Our stories are being recovered. In William Kennedy's *Very Old Bones,* the character Peter Phelan came to this recognition: "that individuals, families or societies that willfully suppress their history will face a season of reckoning, one certain to arrive obliquely, in a dark place, at a hostile hour, with consequences for the innocent as well as for the conspirators."[3] For the Famine descendants, this is "a season of reckoning."

◆　　◆　　◆

My great grandparents found their way to the farmlands of Wisconsin and Ohio (one was born in Boston just after her parents arrived). According to scant records, my Irish great-grandfather Thomas Emmet Hayden (born 1845) married an Alice Foley (born 1848). Their son Thomas was born in 1868 and died in 1941, his life spanning the successful growth of America as a world power. That Thomas Hayden was a lawyer immersed in Milwaukee ward politics. He married Mary Agnes Ducey, and their child, my father John, was born in Milwaukee in 1906.

My mother's family can be traced to Emmett Owen Garity, who came to Ontario, married Mary Ethel Olwell, and settled in Jefferson County, Wisconsin, with only the barest necessities of life. He was a principled man; during the U.S. Civil War, his farm was a station on the Underground Railroad of escaping slaves.

My grandfather, also Emmett Garity, was killed in a cannery accident in small-town Wisconsin in 1920, leaving my grandmother ("Nannie Ethel") to raise twelve children, including my mother, through the Great Depression. If those times were cruel, no one spoke of it, for crueller times lay in the past, and there was the next generation to look forward to.

The Irish arrived in America impoverished, disoriented, and surrounded by nativist bigotry. From the members of the Know-Nothing Party to an intellectual eminence like Ralph Waldo Emerson, they were scorned as inferior, "a mongrel mass of ignorance and crime and superstition."[5] They competed, often violently, with blacks over the worst, most oppressive jobs. The average emigrant lived only six years.[6] Infants died by the tens of thousands. Insane asylums filled with the Irish. And yet they came, and slowly, painfully, they stayed. And in time, large numbers began to succeed. By the early 1900s, the time of my parents' birth, two-thirds of five million Irish Americans were born in the United States.

The fictional drunkard Studs Lonigan spoke for my parents' generation: "The effects and scars of immigration are upon my life. The past was dragging through my boyhood and adolescence . . . But for an Irish boy born in Chicago in 1904, the past was a tragedy of his people, locked behind 'the silence of history.'"[4]

Why did my parents make a secret of the past? Did they think it best to forget? Or did they themselves not know? I will never know, because when history is not inherited, questions cannot be asked. There was only a present and a future in the existence they provided me.

In my parents' youth, U.S. president Woodrow Wilson had campaigned against "hyphenated Americans" like the Irish. My parents had no desire to be hyphenated. In my entire life, they never mentioned Ireland. Total assimilation was the goal. I was their little pride and joy, the only child, the one who would attend university and succeed. They expected me to become a professional, perhaps a lawyer or doctor. My father was an accountant, my mother a school film librarian. The poets, storytellers, musicians and mystics of the Irish past were being toppled for the ideal of the white collar middle manager. But as my mother noted later, "Tommy always had a nose in his book." It was true, and when I took a college interest in literature and writing, my parents were concerned. When I turned down a job at the

Detroit News to join the civil rights movement, they thought I was throwing my life away. Why work against hunger and discrimination?

◆   ◆   ◆

The threat of historical amnesia due to shame, denial, and the pressures of assimilation has faced the Indians, the African Americans, the Jews, the Armenians, every community that has experienced uprooting, enslavement, or genocide. By comparison, the Irish Famine seems more suppressed in consciousness, not only of the Irish but Americans as a whole. The writer Peter Quinn thinks that people who look back at their Irish origins are particularly subject to criticism and dismissal. He speculates that "maybe people are afraid that if the Irish—the grandparents of all ethnic groups—dissent from the assimilationist myth, the country will fall apart." [7]

What little Irish culture I encountered growing up was distant, trivial, sentimentalized. I have dim childhood memories of St. Patrick's Days where every quaint stereotype of the Irish was repeated and acted out. As late as my fortieth birthday, a close friend held a surprise party complete with Hollywood dwarfs he hired to play leprechauns.

To be cut off from one's past, however, doesn't mean that the past has lost its hold. It only means the ghosts are masked.

> . . . their demonic yells are still ringing in my ears, and their horrible images are still fixed upon my brain.
> —a writer in Cork, 1846 [8]

> . . . the cataclysm stunned many of its victims into traumatized muteness . . .
> —Terry Eagleton [9]

> Starving families boarded themselves into their cabins, so that their deaths might go decently unviewed.
> —Terry Eagleton [10]

How to gain pride from the ditches?
—Seamus Cashman, Dublin publisher and writer

Ireland is pretty *small potatoes* by contrast with the present conflict between the East and West.
—U.S. State Department official, 1949[11]

The struggle of life is between memory and forgetting.
—Milan Kundera[12]

In the Irish past I dwell
Like sound implicit in a bell.
—Seamus Deane, poet[13]

Does trauma and its denial stay with us, only repressed through time?
What is the continuing effect? Or can these matters be wiped from memory, without damage or loss? Is that the meaning of "starting over"?

As the Irish writer John Waters points out, "by blandly insisting that we
'leave the past behind us', we prevent ourselves from doing so."[14] There is
unfinished business with the ghosts.

> *O Hendon, Hayden, OhEideain in Irish* . . . is of frequent occur-
> rence in the Ormond Deeds from the year 1374 . . . the name must
> be regarded primarily as belonging to Co. Carlow . . . one of the
> principal Irish surnames in that county at the time of the 1659
> census . . . Peter *Hayden* of Bolevcarrigan, Co. Wicklow . . . elected
> *captain of the insurgents* in preference to Michael Dwyer, was with
> *35 other prisoners killed . . . in 1798.*
> —Irish genealogy book

Was this Peter Hayden, martyred in the 1798 rising of the United Irishmen, a relation of mine? It seems impossibly fanciful.

But what I need to know, and never will, is whether I am named for
Thomas Emmet, brother and coconspirator of Robert Emmet, who was

considered "the most dangerous man in Ireland" by a British agent, and who was hanged for leading the 1798 rebellion.

Thomas Emmet also was sentenced to death for high treason in 1798, but was banished to America instead, where he became a respected political refugee, a friend of Thomas Jefferson, attorney general of New York, and, according to one text, "a revered link between the frustrated hopes of the Irish Revolution and the opportunities offered by the political freedom of the American Republic." After Emmet's death in 1827 his cause was taken up by many of the Famine generation.

I was named Thomas Emmet Hayden *the fourth*. When I asked my parents about the others I was named after, my mother could only say, merrily, "the first, second, and third." In retrospect, it clearly seems that someone in my family meant to honor and preserve the legacy of Thomas Emmet. Who was that?

One root of my family was from County Monaghan, on the southern border of today's Northern Ireland. When I visit Monaghan, which closely resembles rural Wisconsin, I wander, imagine, and stare at local faces in the city center, trying to understand how history cast us apart. I try tracing my ancestors in the county museum, but am overwhelmed by the task. The archival records from 1849 sound like an account of cattle herds. Careful handwriting records the "Paupers who were admitted into, or discharged from, the Workhouse; and the Number of the Sick, and the number Born, or who died therein, during the week ended Saturday____, day of____." Below this explanation are columns marked "Admitted," "Discharged," "Died," and the count of "Sick and Lunatic Paupers." In June 1849 the workhouse overflowed with 2,000 people.

In 1995, I became gripped with a need to search out the grave sites of this "disappeared" people of Monaghan. With the help of a local historian, Theo McMahon, I drove to the north side of Monaghan city, where the white stucco flats give way to hillside farms. Although Theo knows more than anyone in Monaghan about genealogical records, he never had brought himself to look for Famine graves. We walked up a hill into a field of stones and rubble and, detecting no visible graves, sought the help of an elderly passerby. We learned from him that we were standing on the abandoned site of the Monaghan fever hospital. Soon more neighbors were sharing their folk knowledge and asking questions. The graves were right over there, they said, pointing across several small hills into a little knoll. "And what's being done about it?" they wanted to know. Hundreds of bodies were over there in unmarked graves. The Famine victims were never included in the annual blessing of the graves (and thus, from a strict Catholic viewpoint, could not ascend to heaven). Cows made paths across the field of the dead, dropping dung on Irish ancestors.

My ancestors! Was this all I could know of them? I crossed the long hillside with Theo, following the cattle trails, scanning fields ahead. I was feeling lost when Theo suddenly said, "here they are," and all about us were the overgrown remains of burial mounds. Some had small trees growing from their center. The rest seemed utterly abandoned, from sight, from history, from the simplest reverence. Here wagons had carried them from the fever hospital above, to be dumped in shallow graves, sometimes singly and sometimes together, covered in lime. I had finally traced my "family" history to its resting place in a muddy, degraded and neglected field. I sat down. I knelt. I took a picture. Except for dizziness, I could not feel the emotions I wanted to feel. The history that was buried in the field was too buried inside me to be released.

Monaghan lost nearly forty percent of its population, about 60,000 people, in the Famine decade, suffering the most of any county in traditional Ulster. According to *The Monaghan Story,* an out-of-print history, the local people called the blight "the Blackness."[15] Reading the anecdotes gives a sense of the world of my great-grandparents that the statistics cannot supply. But how can "blackness" be recalled?

Monaghan had four workhouses, the inmates separated from their families and doing hard labor for two meals a day. According to an 1845 Monaghan county record, these institutions were "repulsive to the habits and feelings of a people." The "intolerable overcrowding" was relieved in only two ways: through emigration, or "when death helped to empty the workhouses through fever and disease."

The story of Mary Ann McDermott of Monaghan, who supported her two children by doing chores rather than submitting to the workhouse, reminded me of the fierce, frugal pride of my mother and grand-mother.

> On Friday March 12, 1847, (she) walked from Killeveen to Clones on an errand and she received a cupful of meal which she divided among her children . . . She returned from Clones and got weak and sat down . . . (someone) gave her food but she was unable to eat it. She died on the spot of starvation.[16]

There was callousness bred by hunger, too.

> The fever changed the whole attitude of people to their neighbours. Peter Coogan of Cornamucklagh carried out the beggar, Laurence Daly, first from his own house and then from the house of his cottier, Terry Hughes, and dumped him on the roadside to die. This was a change in Ireland.[17]

The Famine experience is about hidden impacts. I have tried, for example, to identify the print of the Famine experience on my parents. But I wonder now if there was a Famine echo as well. They both hated welfare or dependency of any kind. My mother showed up for work every single day for twenty-seven years. When she died, I found that she had carefully placed a modest $6,000 in life savings in no less than three banks in her small town of Oconomowoc, Wisconsin. Inside the security of the banks, inside their vaults and safety deposit boxes, she still wrapped her money in tinfoil, to protect against a level of catastrophe I could not imagine. A catastrophe like Famine.

My parents believed the world was harsh. "Mourning and weeping in this valley of tears"—the prayers of the Catholic Irish carried this sense of harshness. Not even neighbors or relatives could be trusted, for they would take advantage if they could. Preserving appearances was crucial. My mother often whispered "sshhh" while holding a finger to her lips, even when no one was around. She didn't trust her own sisters. To the end of their lives, she and my father suspected everyone was out to take advantage of me. Deep within both my parents was the post-Famine distrust described by Kerby Miller as a "covert competitiveness which found poisonous expression in . . . incessant gossip and obsessive attention to the most minute indices of comparative status or respectability."[18] "'What will the neighbors think?' became lace-curtain Irish America's secular catechism."[19]

Achieving comparative status or respectability was the end of the rainbow for my parents, what they struggled to obtain. And, "what will the neighbors think?" was a nagging fear. What was the source of this fear of disrespectability? I think it was connected to a horrific immigrant nightmare they still were fleeing. It was flight from respectability's opposite, which is *shame.* But they didn't know what trauma pushed them forward, buried as it was in the dynamics of "making it."

> What we need is not to dominate the Irish but to absorb them . . .
> We want them to become rich, and send their sons to our colleges,
> to share our prosperity and sentiments.
> —*Boston Wasp*, 1887[20]

> . . . the Irish will, before many years are past, be lost in the American . . . there will no longer be an 'Irish question' or an 'Irish vote' . . .
> —editorial, *Atlantic Monthly,* 1896[21]

> In terms of education, income, and occupational achievement, Irish Catholics are the most successful gentile group in American society . . .
> Their college attendance rate . . . is now roughly comparable to that of Episcopalians . . . only the Jews are more likely at the present time to produce publishing academic scholars.[22]

My parents grew up when Irish-Americans were poised to overcome the more blatant and violent prejudice that they had suffered in America. A middle-class life was possible. My mother became a working woman, a secretary, in the Flapper generation of the 1920s. My father was a hotel doorman who attended accounting school at night. They were neither shanty Irish nor the lace-curtain kind. They were ready for the venetian blinds of the suburbs. The American Dream could begin. The experiences of Famine, eviction, banishment, and Fenian nationalism were receding. A twenty-six-county modern Irish state existed across the sea, and an Irish establishment was planted here in America. Normalcy beckoned after decades of trauma. The old Thomas Emmet could be forgotten. The Hibernians were putting American flags in every parochial school class-room. By 1900, the nationalist hymn "A Nation Once Again" was being eclipsed by the new ballad, "When Irish Eyes Are Smiling" (a sad song of total denial, which begins "There's a tear in your eye / And I'm wondering why / For it never should be there at all . . .")

My parents moved from Milwaukee to Detroit and my father became an accountant at Chrysler Corporation. I was born in 1939. Our household bliss was disrupted by World War II, when my father was drafted into the marines. But he remained stateside, and we lived with him in San Diego until the war ended. After World War II, we moved to a new suburb of Detroit, Royal Oak, which symbolized this transition.

Then, at the beginning of the Golden Age of the 1950s, my parents divorced.

> . . . romanticism seems to have been pretty well crushed out by the famines and the Penal Laws . . . Since the Great Famine, it would seem, both Irish and Irish-American women and men have had a much harder time in being affectionate than they used to.[23]

Neither of them ever tried to explain what happened. It was something after the war. My father took over a year to return from the coast. My mother said he was hitchhiking across the country. When he came home, I recall him spending night after night at the American Legion hall, a kind of pub for veterans. From my bedroom, I would hear him stumbling up the staircase.

One night I heard my father yelling and my mother crying. While I lay silently under my sheets, he was fifteen feet away, smashing a hammer against their bedroom door, which was locked. Though our whole house was shaking with their pain and violence, the incident was never mentioned. Then came a night when my father opened the door, sat down on my bed, and told me he was leaving in the morning. He kissed me on the cheek for the last time.

They were good parents, I thought then, and I think so today. After the divorce, we ate dinner together every weekend, and my parents remained amicable in front of me. I took summer vacations with my father and lived with my mother year round. But the silence never lifted from what had happened between them. Feelings were not expressed, and I don't know if we were in touch with any. I assumed that such silent family failures were normal, internal setbacks on the path to external success.

I thought being drunk was normal too; it was strongly approved of in the circles I grew up in, despite the destructive effects of alcohol on my father that I could see as a child. My father's Legion drinking buddies were like the "bachelor boys" of post-Famine Ireland, young men dispossessed from traditional roles and reassembled around the ideal of being a "hard drinker." Obviously the Famine can't be blamed for every disorder in life. But what else but the disintegration of their cultures makes Native Americans and Irish Americans have the highest percentages of alcoholism? Why else do the Irish have the highest rates of mental illness in the world, and why the massive rates of alcoholism and schizophrenia among Irish-Americans? It is thought that the Irish drink for escape, for denial, that numbness might conquer an ancient depression.[18]

There was other family denial too, some that took me fifty years to uncover. I have a child's image, for example, of an "Uncle Bill," my father's younger brother. In an off moment of candor while I was growing up, my mother smiled and, with her finger over her lips, hinted that Uncle Bill was not well. I took this to mean he was in an insane asylum, never to be seen or mentioned again. Recently, however, I learned that Bill was a gay fireman who lost his job and lived alone in Milwaukee all his life. Without telling anyone, my father sent Bill a check every month. In his mind, support for a "queer" brother had to be kept secret.

◆   ◆   ◆

> . . . the intense level of religious devotion characteristic of the Irish on both sides of the Atlantic is a rather recent phenomenon, dating to the time of the Great Famine.[25]

> The cataclysm of the Great Famine convinced most peasants not only that their old beliefs were ineffectual in staving off disaster, but that God had punished them for their wicked resistance to the Church's teaching.[26]

While their Irishness was bleached away by this time, my parents still were motivated by their inherited Catholicism. Though there was little or no talk of spiritual matters around the house, it was extremely important to my parents that I have a Catholic education.

In the 1920s, when Royal Oak was a virulent anti-Catholic center of the Ku Klux Klan, the Church sent a crusading young priest to establish our parish. His name was Father Charles Coughlin, an Irishman from Canada who spoke in a fearless brogue. He became the most powerful priest in America in the 1930s, a populist with an audience of several million radio listeners.

What I remember as a small boy was Father Coughlin's ability to paint a picture of heaven and especially hell that was more vivid and dramatic than my own picture of life on earth. His was an Augustinian/Puritan theology that viewed sin as our sickness and obedience as the cure. Life was brief, the fires of hell eternal. Obedience was the key, and when any of us forgot this lesson, the priests were waiting with rulers and rods to lash our hands while we knelt, arms outstretched, on painfully hard floors. The good news was that devout Catholics could reach heaven; but as for Protestants and Jews, that was another matter.

My parents told me nothing of the earthly political controversies surrounding Father Coughlin. He was more powerful than any other priest or teacher in my life, and completely a mystery.

Coughlin embodied key contradictions of the Irish assimilation. On the one hand, he preached of social justice for the dispossessed, the small businessmen, farmers and workers of Depression America. They were, in the Catholic view, whole human beings with souls, not cogs in the industrial machine. Receiving as many as 400,000 letters per week after his Sunday radio sermons, he was a powerful advocate for the kinds of relief that eventually constituted the New Deal.

On the other hand, he violently opposed secular movements for socialism and industrial unionism, and he demonized the Jews at the time of Nazi ascent in Germany. The communists and the Jews were enemies of the Christian God, unlike Nazism which professed a Christian root. Ironically, while castigating the "international Jewish bankers," Father Coughlin speculated in the silver market himself. His own secretary held 500,000 ounces of silver, making her the largest owner in Michigan. Finally in 1939, after Coughlin's personal emissary met with Count Von Ribbentrop in Berlin, our pastor was instructed to end his political activities by the Vatican, under U.S. government pressure.

I knew none of this until researching a book twenty years later. But the Irish-Americans knew. The "radio priest" had tens of millions of listeners every Sunday afternoon. The "Studs Lonigan" Irish not only knew, they approved of this "Father Moylan," as James T. Farrell fictionalized Father Coughlin.

> "Well, I know what we ought to do. Put all the foreigners we got taking jobs away from Americans, *pack them in boats,* and say to them, 'Now see here, America belongs to Americans.'"
>
> "It's only right, America is America, and it should be for Americans," Studs said.
>
> "You're damn right it should be. And you know who's going to wake Americans up? It's men like Father Moylan who speaks on the radio every Sunday. He tells 'em and he talks straight."
>
> "And he's a Catholic, too," Studs said proudly.[27]

In supporting Father Coughlin, many Irish were following the immigrant path from a culture of inferiority to its opposite extreme: superpatriotism.

[Catholic] societies seemed merely Irish Catholic replicas of native Protestant institutions, proclaiming American patriotism . . . the Ancient Order of Hibernians (AOH) by providing American flags for every parochial schoolroom in the country . . . the Knights of Columbanus by being conspicuously patriotic in wartime. [28]

In 1960 the Irish immigrant success story culminated in the election of a Roman Catholic, John Fitzgerald Kennedy, to the presidency. It was the first time in my life that I actually heard the subject of Irish Catholics being discussed in public, as if one's heritage was an issue. I did have a dim memory of hearing my mother express disappointment about the defeat of Al Smith in 1928. Kennedy was a redemption for that earlier wrong. But since by 1960 I was so assimilated, I simply dismissed the attacks on Kennedy's religion as obsolete, irrelevant echoes from a past that no longer mattered. I was so Americanized that I did not feel any ethnic heartbeat. My primary connection with John F. Kennedy was generational, not an Irish one.

When I went away to university, to be swept up in the civil rights and antiwar movements of my time, my parents' world was turned upside down. Instead of assimilating, I was seceding. Instead of conforming, I was defying. I was causing shame and destroying the respectability they did everything to build.

My father blamed the world for what had gone wrong. "I don't know who influenced him when he went away, but it's not the way he was raised," he told a reporter. A tight-lipped man to begin with, he simply stopped talking to me for fifteen years, even after he remarried and raised a new daughter. As for my mother, she never broke our connection but neither did she ever stop reminding me how I had embarrassed and nearly ruined her life. Secretly, I thought she liked my friends and even became drawn to the controversies I was always in. She just didn't want the neighbors to know, and prayed I would grow out of it.

At the time, I was unaware of any Irish dimension to my radical discontent. As I would discover later, the Irish tradition is filled with poets and political leaders supportive of progressive, often radical, causes. They were heavily involved in American labor radicalism, producing such personalities as Mother Jones and Helen Gurley Flynn. They were stalwart supporters of the New Deal, which wouldn't have happened without the support of the Irish political machines. But during the new movements of the Sixties, I mainly thought of Irish-Americans as propping up the status quo, their politics mired in traditional ethnic machines, out of step with the modern currents of change I was experiencing. I didn't know it, but such assimilationist politics had been the great fear of Irish nationalists like Jeremiah Donovan Rossa, who condemned those "whose shamrocks blossomed like diamonds," and James Connolly, who called Irish-American politicians "descendants of the serpents St. Patrick banished from Ireland."[29]

The most famous of the Irish machines was that of Major Richard Daley of Chicago, described by Father Greeley as "an Irish chieftain governing through a complex system of clan loyalty."[30] He was born and lived all his life in the Chicago neighborhood of Bridgeport, originally the site of a canal built by Irish labor. This was the ethnic neighborhood culture of Studs Lonigan, and the source of Finley Peter Dunne's stories of "Mr. Dooley," the bachelor philosopher from County Roscommon. Daley's Chicago was home to America's most durable political machine, until a fateful clash of destinies in 1968.

From New York to San Francisco, the political machine was a gift of the Famine Irish to American culture. In Famine Ireland, the Irish had no vote, no government of their own to represent and defend their interests. On a political level, they were beggars. Seán O'Faoláin's biography of their leader, Daniel O'Connell, was entitled *King of the Beggars*. In the new land, they would beg no more.

"Living in a new country, in the aftermath of the Famine, the Irish employed political power as a buckler of community solidarity . . . a means with which to shield themselves . . . and a sword with which to fight back."[31] Perhaps there was a moment after the Famine when Irish-American politics could have mixed militant Irish nationalism with social radicalism in the new homeland. I can imagine myself working for the banished Fenian Rossa, for example, in his 1870 campaign for the New

York State Senate. Rossa apparently defeated Boss Tweed himself, only to have his election stolen by fraud. After that, the Democratic Party gradually became the vehicle of assimilation, not a broader vision of change.

According to Kerby Miller, "Irish-Americans henceforth voted with their stomachs . . . repeatedly rejecting nationalist pleas to desert and punish the Democratic Party for its indifference or hostility to Irish freedom."[32] Who could blame them? Faced with destitution and prejudice, the Irish needed whatever protection the Democratic Party ultimately offered. Ethnic politics was a protective reaction against a world in which true justice was impossible, but additional injustice was preventable. If there was no hope for the redistribution of wealth, the saying went, at least the Irish could redistribute the graft.

There were heavy costs for this Irish assimilation via the patronage system. For one, while the Irish didn't bring racism to America, they learned it here. From the first, Irish labor was pitted against blacks in brutal competition. Irish maids took the jobs of black women in the North. While Irish nationalists like O'Connell preached passionately against slavery, others defended the Confederacy which kept blacks from competing for jobs as freemen. While 100,000 Irishmen fought on the Northern side, the Irish also sparked mass riots against the draft, including attacks on black New Yorkers. The same Democratic Party which opened its doors to Irish immigrants was pro-slavery at the time. While many Irish today prefer to believe that the Irish-black conflict was only economic in nature, the Famine suggests a sadder dynamic as well: the Irish-Americans transferred to black people the very racial stereotypes long used against the Irish. Having been stigmatized as chimpanzees, wild animals and bog-creatures, the Irish chose whiteness when the chance came along. They wounded the heart of Frederick Douglass.[33]

A second cost of striving to assimilate after the Famine, I believe, was the exaggerated patriotism and super-loyalty summarized in the philosophy of so many former immigrants: "America, right or wrong." It was not enough for the Irish to change their accents or names. For most, it seemed necessary to conform culturally, for one's Americanism to exist beyond question. The quest for respectability ended with the defense of conservative law-and-order. The Cold War against communism was also a religious war against atheism, a chance to assert a new Irish Americanism in the form of McCarthyism.

The tragic outcome of such politics was Vietnam, where American military involvement from 1954 to 1964 was shaped by a newly powerful Catholic lobby. Several hundred thousand Catholics streamed out of the communist North in 1954 at the urging of Catholic missionaries (and the American CIA), only to become the doomed and loyal base of the Catholic dictatorship of Ngo Dinh Diem in Saigon. The rest is history. The irony was that the war left millions of dead, wounded and uprooted refugees on a level as devastating as the Irish Famine a century before. To the extent that Irish Americans supported U.S. policies, it was a replay of what the Irish had been through themselves. But the mirror was broken.

Looking back I see the Irish Catholic conservatism that surrounded my growing up as an unconscious but ongoing response to the Famine. The immigrants brought with them a religious Jansenism, a stern doctrine of shame that very nearly blamed the Irish for their own starvation. In the wake of Famine horror, the Church promoted an "otherworldly fatalism," in Oscar Handlin's phrase. The Irish Americans formed intensely tribal political associations based in their parishes. They translated their shame into silence, and fiercely forgot the Famine as the possibilities of a better life materialized before them.

But by its very nature, this repressive drive for a secure assimilation ultimately brought about its own demise in the 1960s. For one thing, the Irish achieved a level of success in America that permitted a relaxation of the old ways. For another, the rigid conformity demanded by the post-Famine church and political machines conflicted with an underlying Irish soul. At a mystical moment in the early 1960s, the authoritarian ice began to thaw. Pope John XXIII's *Pacem in Terris* found its way into the Port Huron Statement, the founding manifesto of Students for a Democratic Society. The hardline doctrines of Cardinal Spellman were challenged by priests like the Berrigans and politicians like the Kennedys. The burning of Vietnamese villages was met with the burning of American draft cards, the first by David Miller, a Catholic Worker. Finally, the Irish law-and-order machine of Mayor Daley was to confront new rebels like myself on the streets of Chicago.

It was almost an Irish civil war within the larger divisions of the decade. By the end of the 1960s, Father Coughlin even came out of retirement to attack priests like the Berrigans as "swingers" and "loud-mouthed clerical advocates of arson, riot and draft card burning." He added "that he tremendously admires the youth of today, even the Chicago Seven, one of whom, Tom Hayden, had attended the Shrine of the Little Flower. On the other hand . . . Father Coughlin said that the man he admires the most on the contemporary scene is Judge Julius Hoffman, the presiding judge in the Chicago Seven trial."[34]

◆　　◆　　◆

The 1960s made me Irish. Partly it was an identification with Robert Kennedy. His older brother, President Kennedy, seemed to be an icon of assimilation, while Robert Kennedy became a raw Celtic spirit. It is interesting, however, that President Kennedy decided to make his 1963 visit to Ireland against the advice of his Boston Irish advisers who saw "no political or diplomatic advantages to be gained by such a *sentimental excursion*."[35] The president was moved by visiting the cottage of his great-grandfather, Patrick Kennedy, an 1848 Famine emigrant from Dunganstown. Upon his leaving, the President quoted a poem of an exile's pain:

> 'Tis the Shannon's brightly glancing stream,
> Brightly gleaming, silent in the morning beam
> Oh! the sight entrancing.
> Thus return from travels long, years of exile,
> Years of pain
> To see old Shannon's face again,
> O'er the waters glancing.

After his brother's assassination, Robert Kennedy became identified with an Irish persona I had not known before. It was not a crusty, conservative and old-fashioned Catholicism. This Bobby Kennedy had long since evolved from his days as legal counsel to Joseph McCarthy. He could hold the traditional Irish vote, but there was also a wild Irishman in Bobby Kennedy, who identified with nonconformists, resisters, farmworkers, ghetto dwellers, the Sioux on their desperate reservations. For the first time I felt there was such a thing as an Irish soul.

Robert Kennedy spoke of the Famine experience in the first speech he gave after his brother's murder to the Friendly Sons of St. Patrick, in Scranton, Pennsylvania. "There was," he recalled,

> that black day in February 1847 when it was announced in the House of Commons that fifteen thousand people a day were dying of starvation in Ireland . . . So the Irish left Ireland. Many of them came here to the United States. Many left behind hearts and fields and a nation yearning to be free. It is no wonder that James Joyce described the Atlantic as a bowl of bitter tears.

Reminding his audience of times when no Irish could vote, he said that

> there are Americans, who—as the Irish did—still face discrimination in employment . . . There are walls of silent conspiracy that block the progress of others because of race or creed without regard to ability. *It is toward concern for these issues—and vigorous participation on the side of freedom that our Irish heritage must impel us. If we are true to this heritage, we cannot stand aside.*[36]

Bobby Kennedy was the last national political leader who bridged the gap between white ethnics like Irish Americans and the disaffected minorities of the ghettos and fields.

On the night that his body was flown back to New York, I wandered into St. Patrick's Cathedral for the first time. The largest cathedral in the United States, St. Patrick's was built by the Famine generation, completed in 1879. Its famous Archbishop John Hughes was the most powerful leader of the Irish in New York City, providing famine relief, battling the Know-Nothings, and holding "firm in his belief that the Irish-Americans should be concerned first and foremost with the affairs of their adopted country."[37] Having started as the spiritual fortress of the immigrant Irish, St. Patrick's now was the symbol of their success and power.

But now another Kennedy lay in wait for eulogy. It was late, the end of a dark night. I sat in a back pew, staring at the small wooden coffin in the centre of this vast historical space, and began to cry. America was not what my parents promised it would be. Even the symbols of Irish success were dead.

♦　　♦　　♦

The identity which I received from my parents continued to unravel during 1968, finally ending on the streets of Chicago. Assimilation led to emptiness. All around me others were realizing new identities for themselves, as liberated women, black or Chicano nationalists, even gay people. They were leaving the melting pot to regain their roots. But who was I?

History tells of a "hidden Ireland," of a native character behind the Anglicized facade. I was beginning to understand that there was a hidden Irish America too. There was not only Cardinal Spellman but Bobby Kennedy; not only Charles Coughlin, but the Berrigan brothers; not only George Meany, but Elizabeth Gurley Flynn. The figures in American life who most repelled and most attracted me, who warred for my soul, seemed all to be Irish.

Then a "hidden Ireland" across the sea came alive. Precisely at the peak of the protests in Chicago, on 24 August 1968, several thousand civil rights marchers took to the streets in Northern Ireland, singing "We Shall Overcome" for the first time. On 5 October, in a scene that resembled Chicago, 400 marchers were blocked from protesting in Derry, beaten into the ground with batons, hosed with water cannons, and began street battles in the Bogside. While the whole world may have been watching in Chicago, now I was watching, for the first time in my life, *these Irish who seemed and looked so much like me.*

Now I knew I was Irish too. But what did it mean, how to describe it?

Being "Irish American" sounded a bit too settled and middle class. I wasn't just "Irish." Maybe I was an exiled Irishman, an *Éireannach Éigin*. A recovering Irishman? After almost thirty years, I still am not sure. But the recognition that arose in 1968 continued to grow and surprise me.

In 1969, a friend of mine from the Bobby Kennedy campaign arrived in Los Angeles from Belfast, where he spent the year after the murder of his hero. He regaled me with stories of republican activists, tapes of Bernadette Devlin speeches, books of nationalist history, recordings of rebel songs, which I consumed with Irish whisky. The romantic phase of my Irish identification was underway.

FEDERAL BUREAU OF INVESTIGATION

DEC. 15, 1971

URGENT

TO: DIRECTOR FROM: LOS ANGELES

THOMAS EMMET HAYDEN

SOURCE ADVISED DECEMBER FIFTEEN INSTANT. THOMAS EMMET HAYDEN DEPARTED LOS ANGELES EVENING OF DECEMBER FOURTEEN LAST, FOR NEW YORK CITY, ULTIMATE DESTINATION, IRELAND.

SOURCE STATED HAYDEN PLANS ON GOING TO NORTHERN IRELAND THROUGH SOUTHERN IRELAND AND ANTICIPATES TAKING PART IN PRESENT REVOLUTION.

ROUTE OF TRAVEL FROM LOS ANGELES TO NEW YORK UNKNOWN BY SOURCE. SOURCE STATED HAYDEN MAY BE UTILIZING THE NAME EMMET GARITY, MAIDEN NAME OF MOTHER.

In 1971, I decided to experience Ireland for the first time. Instead of the emigrant's return, however, I was banished.

The Irish authorities acted on U.S. and British intelligence cables warning that I was a dangerous radical on a subversive mission to Belfast. All I wanted to do was experience the island of my ancestors. After twenty-four hours of fruitless argument in Shannon airport, I was placed on a plane, my romantic desire for roots abruptly terminated.

The emigration official who stamped my expulsion papers from Shannon was named Garity, my mother's name. For all I knew, he was a relative of mine, part of the family tree I was trying to explore. When my son was born eighteen months later, Jane Fonda and I decided to name him Troy O'Donovan Garity, for his grandmother and for Ireland. For expulsion and return.

Five years later, the Irish authorities finally admitted me, and I took my 2-year-old son to Ireland. Where my parents had erased Ireland from my past, I wanted it to be my son's earliest possible memory. That it was. In Belfast, he experienced camouflaged British soldiers sticking automatic weapons into his father's face at checkpoints. In Dublin, while happening to walk by the General Post Office, Troy started pointing at people and asking, "are those my ancestors?"

Each of us carries a legacy of the past that stretches back far before our parents' time. While most therapists or biographers focus only on our parents' effects on us, we also carry the legacies, spirits, traumas, and qualities of our invisible and even unknown ancestors. While this "hidden Ireland" within is largely lost, we can create an image of the life of our ancestors before they were uprooted. At the very least, we can honor the memory of those Famine relatives who died in ditches or were cast from coffin ships. We can complete the journey they began. And in gaining access to the texture, the *feeling*, of this past, it may be possible to discover the sources of scars in ourselves that we need to open and heal.

If there could be an archaeology of the past self, you might find below the comfortable hillside home of an Irish-American today a single-family suburban one, and below that an inner-city apartment, and below that a cellar in New York, and before that a cargo hold, and finally, the burned decaying ruins of a stone cottage in an Irish field of shallow graves. Those ruins, those graves, are deep in ourselves. We cannot go home again, but we will never be at home in our present lives until our memories can return to the places from which we have been severed. Through this process I have begun to end the famine of my feelings.

The Irish-Canadian novelist Jane Urquhart ends her novel *Away* with the universal consciousness that is the gift of knowing one's particular self: "Then she saw the world's great leavetakings, invasions and migrations, landscapes torn from beneath the feet of tribes, the Danae pushed out by the Celts, the Celts eventually smothered by the English, warriors in the night depopulating villages, boatloads of groaning African slaves. Lost forests. The children of the mountain on the plain, the children of the plain adrift on the sea. And all the mourning for abandoned geographies."[38]

In 1996, Irish president Mary Robinson, who has led the Irish national effort to commemorate the Famine, was kind enough to welcome me home to the Ireland my family had forgotten. She took special care to show me the permanent light in her window for all the Irish who are away.

I am coming to realize that the Famine experience has not ended, and will not end until forgotten ghosts of our past are finally at rest in our reverence, until the world's children are safe from famine today, until we live in a world where all of us are truly home, and none of us feel away.

NOTES

1. Eavan Boland, "The Dolls' Museum," from *In a Time of Violence* (Manchester: Carcanet Press Limited, 1994).
2. Ronald Takaki, *A Different Mirror: A History of Multi-Cultural America,* (New York: Little Brown, 1993), p.139.
3. William Kennedy, *Very Old Bones* (London: Penguin Books, 1993).
4. James T. Farrell, *Studs Lonigan* (University of Illinois, 1993, 1932), p.iv.
5. Kerby Miller and Paul Wagner, *Out of Ireland, The* Story *of Irish Emigrants to America* (Washington D.C.: Elliott and Clark, 1994), p.54.
6. Ibid., p.41.
7. Personal correspondence.
8. Cited in Helen Litton, *The Irish Famine, An Illustrated History* (Dublin: Wolfhound Press, 1994), p.52.
9. *Terry Eagleson, Heathcliff and the Great Hunger, Studies in Irish Culture* (London: Verso, 1994) p.13.
10. Ibid., p.8.
11. Cited in Sean Cronin, *Washington's Irish Policy, Independence, Partition, Neutrality* (Dublin: Anvil Press, 1987), p.243.
12. Milan Kundera, *The Unbearable Lightness of Being,* (New York: Harper & Row, 1984).
13. Seamus Deane, "Return," from *Selected Poems* (Gallery Books, 1988).
14. John Waters, "We Cannot Escape Our History No Matter How Hard We Try," in *Irish Times,* October 12, 1995.
15. Peadar Livingstone, *The Monaghan Stork; A Documented History of the County Monaghan from the Earliest Times to 1976* (Enniskillen: Clogher Historical Society, 1980), pp.211–222.
16. Ibid., p.218.
17. Ibid., p 217.

18. Kerby Miller, *Emigrants and Exiles, Ireland and the Irish Exodus to North America* (New York and Oxford, 1985), p.414.

19. Ibid., p.498.

20. Ibid., p.497.

21. Ibid., p.497.

22. Andrew Greeley, *The Irish Americans: The Rise to Money and Power* (New York: Harper & Row, 1981), p.2.

23. Ibid., p.122.

24. On Irish and alcoholism, see Niall O'Dowd, "The Myth and the Reality," *Irish America*, October 1988. O'Dowd reports a National Institute of Mental Health study showing 36 percent of Irish men drink "nearly every day," twice the figure for WASPs and Jews. Also, according to the World Health Organization, the Irish in Ireland have the highest rate of mental illness in the world, and Irish Americans have the highest hospital admission rate from alcoholism and schizophrenia of all ethnic groups in the U.S. Monica McGoldrick has written in *Irish Families* that "more than other ethnic groups, the Irish struggle with their sense of sin and guilt. Irish schizophrenics, for example, are commonly obsessed with guilt for sins that they might not even have committed."

25. Greeley, *The Irish Americans*, op cit., p.144.

26. Miller and Wagner, *Out of Ireland*, op cit., p.101.

27. James T. Farrell, *Judgement Day*, op cit., p.735.

28. Miller, *Emigrants and Exiles*, op cit., p.534.

29. Ibid., pp.536, 544.

30. Greeley, *The Irish Americans*, op cit., p.155.

31. Peter Quinn, Introduction to William L. Riordan, *Plunkitt of Tammany Hall*, (New York: Penguin, 1995), p.xvi.

32. Miller, *Emigrants and Exiles*, op cit., p.537.

33. On Frederick Douglass's speaking tour in Cork, Belfast and elsewhere in Ireland, see William S. McFeely, *Frederick Douglass*, (New York: Touchstone, 1991), p.126, 318. Douglass, traveling during the Famine, "saw what his anti-slavery hosts seemed blind to . . . The anti-slavery people stepped around these Irish poor as they made their way into Douglass's lectures about mistreated Africans in America." But Douglass recorded in his diary that "I see much here to remind me of my former condition . . ." Later, in America, he spoke against British tyranny in Ireland, comparing it to slavery, in a powerful image: "We want no black Ireland in America!" Nevertheless, most Irish immigrants entered the pro-slavery Democratic Party, fearing that freed former slaves would take back the menial jobs which they had taken from blacks in the North. Douglass noted in 1853 that "every hour sees us elbowed out of some employment to make room for some newly-arrived emigrant from the Emerald Isle, whose hunger and color entitle him to special favor. These white men are becoming house-servants, cooks, stewards, waiters and flunkies . . . If they cannot rise to the dignity of white men, they show that they can fall to the degradation of black men . . ." See Noel Ignatiev, *How the Irish Became White*, (London: Routledge, 1995), p.111. Meanwhile, although Daniel O'Connell continued to denounce American slavery in the 1840s, many Irish nationalists, including the Revered John Mitchel, supported the slave-holding Confederacy, to Douglass's great sadness.

34. Sheldon Marcus, *Father Coughlin, The Tumultuous Life of the Priest of the Little Flower* (New York: Little Brown, 1973), p.223.

35. Kenneth O'Donnell and David Powers, with Joe McCarthy, *"Johnny We Hardly Knew Ye": Memories of John Fitzgerald Kennedy* (New York: Little Brown, 1972), p.358.

36. Edwin Guthman and Richard Allen, *Robert F. Kennedy Collected Speeches* (New York: Viking, 1993), pp.107–08.
37. John A. Barnes, *Irish American Landmarks, A Traveler's Guide* (Detroit: Visible Ink Press, 1995), p.107.
38. Jane Urquhart, *Away* (New York: Viking, 1994), p.128.

23

Drumcree 1998 Is Mississippi 1963

San Francisco Chronicle, *July 21, 1998*

The Northern Ireland crisis has been "sorted out," as the Irish like to say, thanks to the decision by Sinn Fein and the Irish Republican Army (IRA) to shift from armed struggle to political organizing after operations against the British occupation reached a stalemate. The IRA also recognized that the loyalists had to be accommodated, while the British and loyalists were forced to accept the notion of "parity of esteem" for the nationalist and Catholic population. I made over twenty trips to Northern Ireland leading up to the peace agreement, serving at times as an advisor to the Clinton administration's commerce official, the late Charles Meissner.

◆　　◆　　◆

IMAGINE 3,000 ANNUAL MARCHES by the robed Ku Klux Klan, backed by sympathetic troops, through black ghettos in the United States, and you have an idea of what it's like to be a nationalist/Catholic during marching season in Northern Ireland.

"When I was a little boy, they scared me to death, marching along and chanting about drinking Fenian blood," recalled one journalist at the scene. The militant Orange leader at Drumcree, Joel Patton, declared that "to allow marches to be re-routed is to surrender a piece of the United Kingdom to the enemy."

This year the Orange Order was trying to march back to the past, in opposition to the April peace agreement that creates a state which, if not green, is no longer exclusively orange. The so-called Good Friday Agreement promises an equalization of nationalist and unionist. These confrontations, at Portadown's Drumcree church and later on Belfast's Lower Ormeau Road, were the Orangemen's last stand.

The Orange Order had managed to drum up a 29 percent "no" vote against the Good Friday Agreement and then, in June, elected nearly enough anti-agreement candidates like the Rev. Ian Paisley to wreck the new Assembly. At Drumcree, they were planning to mobilize 50,000 Orangemen to overrun the fixed line of security forces and march down Garvaghy Road in an apocalyptic counterrevolution.

To understand such seemingly anachronistic fanaticism, one only need compare Portadown loyalists with the staunch segregationists in America's South in the 1960s, or today's right-wing militias resisting a government they denounce as "multicultural." Rather than being irrelevant, such opponents of modern multiethnic democracy pose a challenge throughout the world.

Portadown, in northern Armagh, was the founding site in 1795 of the Orange Order, an anti-Catholic secret society created to divide and destroy the United Irishmen, a nationalist movement whose banner was to unite Catholic, Protestant and Dissenter. Today, Portadown is like rural Mississippi in 1960, a lawless killing zone resistant to the outer world.

This year, however, sharp differences emerged between the fundamentalist and individual Orange leaders.

David Trimble, who previously polished his Orange credentials by standing with Wright and Paisley in past Drumcree confrontations, is now the "first minister" of the new Northern Assembly. At first he demanded a march down Garvaghy Road, but soon was denouncing the Orangemen who now wanted his head on a pole, at least politically.

British Prime Minister Tony Blair and Northern Ireland Secretary "Mo" Mowlam had infuriated nationalists in 1997 by allowing an Orange march. Leaked British documents showed that Blair and Mowlam had already approved "Orange feet on Garvaghy Road" while professing to be neutral mediators.

This year, however, Blair and Mowlam were confronted with a conspiracy to overthrow the peace agreement and the new government itself. Faced with a crisis of state, they could only react by attempting to hold the line, as President John Kennedy was forced to do in the Deep South in the 1960s.

The fundamentalists' plans to "bring Northern Ireland to a standstill" might have succeeded, since the British government did nothing to prevent or disperse the buildup of thousands of Orangemen at the Drumcree line on Sunday, July 11. It was the arson murder of three small children of the Quinn family in Balleymoney, so reminiscent of the 1965 killing of four black children in Birmingham, that drained the homicidal energy from the gathering Orangemen.

The crisis has subsided temporarily, with a political victory for nationalists, a discrediting of the Orangemen and, most important, a preservation of the Good Friday Agreement.

But Drumcree is an awful reminder of how great the resistance will be to the equality provisions of the pact. The fact is, Orange supremacy remains institutional in Northern Ireland's economy. Cease-fires are not enough: the root causes of violence in discrimination and unemployment must be confronted. Continued support for reform from the Clinton administration is critical. The U.S. government must be willing to pressure the British on equal rights for nationalists, and American investment must create jobs in Irish ghettos. The Irish peace process can be a model for U.S. foreign policy—and perhaps for addressing the tinderbox in our own inner cities.

VI Personal Life

24.

Jane

From Reunion: A Memoir *(Random House, 1988)*

Our marriage lasted until 1989. In the years following the Vietnam War, our lives normalized, the differences between us became more open, and our relationship became more difficult to sustain. In August, 2007, Jane and I joyously celebrated the marriage of our son Troy, then 34, to Simone Bent, she of Brooklyn by way of Jamaican and Costa Rican families. Love is confused, but love endures. Seven-year old Liam, my child with Barbara, is the brother of Troy and Vanessa and uncle to Vanessa's two children who are Liam's age. The family tree is a bush with roots.

◆   ◆   ◆

SHE CAME FROM THE ORBITS of fame, power, and success. A popular actress and the daughter of Henry Fonda, she burst like a dislocated star onto the movement scene in 1970 but came only slowly and haltingly into my life. In February 1971, I was in Ann Arbor, speaking about Vietnam at an event promoting May Day protests, when I met Jane on the stage. Beginning with visits to the Indians occupying Alcatraz, and accelerating after Kent State, she was constantly crisscrossing the country at the time, followed by cameramen and FBI agents, as she supported students, feminists, Black Panthers, Indians, and especially GIs being prepared for assignment to Vietnam. For several months she had been encouraging and recruiting veterans who had told her of atrocities in Vietnam to testify at the Winter Soldier Investigation being organized in Detroit (which was founded on Tom Paine's distinction between phony sunshine patriots and truly committed winter soldiers). On the stage in Ann Arbor that night, she showed the tensions of the constant motion. She was skinny and taut, her long fingers playing nervously with the purple shirt that was pulled over her jeans. There was something shrill and perhaps memorized in her brief, impassioned call to "stop the government unless it stops the war," but her urgency was real and the audience was moved.

FBI MEMORANDUM   6-25-70

TO: SAC, LOS ANGELES

FROM: DIRECTOR, FBI

You are authorized to prepare a letter and mail to Army Archerd, the Hollywood "gossip" columnist. Insure that mailing cannot be traced to the Bureau.

NOTE: Los Angeles proposed that a letter from a fictitious person be sent to Hollywood "gossip" columnist of the "Daily Variety" in connection with the column on 6/11/70 indicating Jane Fonda, noted film actress, would attend a Black Panther Party fundraising function on 6/13/70. The proposed letter states the writer attended the function and was searched upon entering, urged to contribute funds for jailed Panther leaders, and to buy guns for the "coming revolution." Also, that Jane and one of the Panthers led a refrain, "We will kill Richard Nixon, and any other M . . . F . . . who stands in our way." It can be expected that Fonda's involvement with the BPP cause could distract from her status with the general public if reported in a Hollywood "gossip" column.

I called her at a Howard Johnson's in Detroit the next morning. We met in the coffee shop, where Jane was sitting alongside a French woman, a writer who wanted to talk about American radicals. I was disappointed that she wasn't alone.

It wasn't love at first sight; in fact, to this day, Jane cannot remember what we talked about. She admired my writing and thinking, and she does remember my letting her know that I was "in a relationship" with someone; she was "in a relationship" herself, with Donald Sutherland. She remembers that when she couldn't understand what I was talking about, she would nod her head, or say, "That's interesting." We discussed the trend in the movement toward collective groups, and she spoke of possibly giving up her movie-star status to find a new role in some sort of political film collective. She had already spent months living in a Detroit household filled with veterans, attorney Mark Lane, and some of the staff of the Winter Soldier Investigation. I remember cautioning her against giving up acting, knowing from experience how collectives could confuse professionalism with privilege. I could imagine the Red Family¹ demanding that she work underground to shed her bourgeois leanings. All in all, however, it was a casual conversation. Nothing clicked.

The next day, however, in a carload of people dropping me at Detroit Metro Airport for my flight to the coast, we had a better time. I was sitting in the backseat, and Jane was in the front. Suddenly I put my Irish cap on Jane's head. She turned, and our eyes locked. Both of us finally noticing each other as human beings, we found ourselves laughing absurdly in the middle of a war crimes discussion.

I didn't see or call Jane for a year. We seemed destined not to connect. A few months after the uneventful Howard Johnson tryst, she came to Berkeley to film *Steelyard Blues*. Asking my whereabouts, she was told that I had left the commune; no reason was given by the tight-lipped cadre. Mystified but trusting, Jane moved into the neighborhood and left her two-year-old daughter, Vanessa, at the Blue Fairyland day-care center, under the care of Bruce Gilbert, a twenty-one-year-old Beverly Hills High School graduate who had occasionally dreamed of being a Hollywood producer before joining the revolution.

FBI MEMORANDUM   8/18/71
TO: SAC, SAN FRANCISCO
FROM:

**** stated that this nursery school seems to be operated by various radicals who reside on Bateman Street. She further advised that Jane Fonda has been observed by her on Bateman Street during the past week when Fonda was filming some kind of a picture with the residents of Bateman Street. **** stated that it is her understanding that Vanessa Fonda is attending the Blue Fairyland Nursery school and that her mother, Jane Fonda, will return for her in the near future.

FBI MEMORANDUM   12/28/71

****advised on 11/21/71 that he recently was made aware of the fact that a child care center being operated at 3031 Batemen Street, Berkeley, California, was operating without having previously obtained a state or local license. **** has noted approximately one dozen children on the premises and paraphernalia indicating that a school of some sort was being conducted.

(*Material deleted by the FBI.)

I had seen *Barbarella* in Berkeley with Anne Scheer, my partner then, and both of us were properly critical of its political shortcomings. In those times, there was a "correct line" even on movies, especially regarding sexism. To be entertained (which I was) was not a valid reason for seeing a film. Sexual arousal (which I experienced) was to be sublimated and, if possible, denied. Earlier, I had been very moved by *They Shoot Horses, Don't They?*, which Jane shot in 1968. About the Depression, it could as well have been about the spiritual exhaustion induced by Vietnam.

It was with intense curiosity that I went to watch this suddenly serious woman in *Klute* in 1971. I did not expect to be as affected as I was. Jane brought tremendous life to Bree Daniels, an independent, aspiring actress whose unashamed ethics justified making a living as a high-class call girl and becoming the "invalidation of all the official virtues," as Simone de Beauvoir once described the prostitute. The movie was about the sexual exploitation of women, following Bree down a slope of loneliness that, on the one hand, avoided genuine love as too threatening to personal freedom, but also left her vulnerable to sadistic violence in the unregulated shadow world beyond the law.

There were several improvised scenes in which Bree talked with a therapist about her emotional dilemmas; in these I felt it was really Jane talking to a camera about herself. I could see nothing but her face and hands, and I felt unavoidably pierced by the sense that she was having an intimate conversation with me. Describing her life alone, before she fell in love with the detective who protected and saved her (Donald Sutherland, as John Klute), she says, "I don't really give a damn. What I would really like to do is be faceless and bodiless and be left alone." At a later point, after becoming aware of unexpected intimacy and the beginnings of love toward Klute, she reacts by saying,

> I just wish I could let things happen and enjoy it for what it is . . . and while it lasts, and . . . relax about it. But all the time, all the time I keep feeling the need to destroy it, to break it off, to go back to the *comfort of being numb* again. . . . I keep hoping it's going to end because, I mean, *I had more control* before when I was with tricks . . . I set everything up.
>
> Now I . . . that's what's so strange, I'm not setting anything up . . . It's a new thing and it's so strange, the sensation that *something that is flowing from me naturally to someone else without its being all prettied up* . . . he's seen me horrible, he's seen me ugly, he's seen me mean . . . and it doesn't seem to matter and he seems to accept me . . . I guess having sex with somebody and feeling those sorts of feelings toward them is very new to me and *I wish I didn't keep wanting to destroy it* [emphasis added].

Jane Fonda as Bree Daniels (or was it Bree Daniels as Jane Fonda?) touched me sharply at a moment when I was painfully open. I too seemed to prefer the "comfort of being numb," if that meant I could "set everything up" and keep a self-protective control over my relationships; the choice of intimacy, or losing control to another, had always seemed in my life to fail and transform itself into anguished loss. Such intimacy had been fleeting at best with my parents, my friends, my lovers. My history was one of broken connections. However, despite my powerful feelings of attraction toward the Bree/Jane character, or perhaps because of them, I had no conscious thought of seeing Jane Fonda again. How the conscious self deceives.

By the beginning of 1972, my Indochina classes[2] involved nearly one hundred students in busy workshops producing pamphlets, slides, and—most impressively—a portable poster display that could transform an entire room into a museum of Indochina. It was not the conventional political art with peace doves, clenched fists, and slogans, but instead an art designed to upset assumptions and leave individuals to reorder reality for themselves. There were floor-to-ceiling panels of repeated photo-silkscreen images of land, people, and war. Flanking these images would be panels of cryptic quotations by U.S. officials or poetry by eighteenth-century Vietnamese writers. The whole exhibit could be folded into a large suitcase. With these tools, it was possible to bring the human reality of the war anywhere in the country, as a multimedia teach-in. I began taking the program on the road, enjoying the experience of teaching again. I started writing a book on the same subject and creating a version for public television.

On the distant horizon, the barricades began to beckon. The Republicans planned their 1972 national convention in San Diego, and I joined a group of southern Californians considering a massive demonstration. This was a time, still unknown to the public, of intense counterintelligence activity by the White House plumbers unit. Illegal operations were intensified against the antiwar movement after Kent State. On July 23, 1970, Nixon approved what *Newsweek* called a "blueprint for a super secret police," under the direction of such individuals as Tom Charles Huston, Charles Colson, and E. Howard Hunt, whose hatred for the New Left went back to their roles as leaders of Young Americans for Freedom in the early 1960s. After targeting and burglarizing Daniel Ellsberg in 1971, one of their next major projects was to counter any demonstrations at the upcoming San Diego convention. They had some contact with a paramilitary extremist group in San Diego, the Secret Army Organization (SAO). According to later Watergate testimony, G. Gordon Liddy proposed the kidnapping of myself and other demonstration leaders and our abduction to Mexico during the convention. On January 6, 1972, a bullet was fired through the window of the San Diego house where Bruce Gilbert participated in a meeting about the convention plans. The bullet missed Bruce's head by less than a foot and shattered the wrist of an activist named Paula Tharp. The shot was fired by an SAO member from a parked car; an FBI informant was sitting next to him. Fortunately, in the end, the Republican convention site was shifted to Miami, without the administration's admitting the embarrassing fact that they had been "forced out by the threat of antiwar demonstrators," as White House official Jeb Magruder later wrote. The subsequent arrests of White House operatives in June 1972 at the Watergate complex in Washington subdued the repressive visions in the White House basement.

During this period, Jane was engaged in an effort of consciousness raising among GIs, called the FTA show (leaving the audience to guess whether the initials meant Free the Army or Fuck the Army). With a troupe of talented people including Donald Sutherland, she was providing antiwar theater for GIs at bases in the United States, Okinawa, and the Philippines (they were denied permission to perform in South Vietnam). An alternative to the usual Bob Hope fare, the FTA was drawing large crowds and making the Pentagon extremely nervous. So, early in 1972, when I heard Jane was making a speech and slide presentation at the Embassy Theater in Los Angeles, it was natural for me to attend.

There we met for keeps.

By now she was an accomplished speaker, effectively sublimating the nerves that showed the year before and making a persuasive presentation to a sympathetic audience. I noticed that her approach was more "political" than mine, using slides primarily to show the results of U.S. bombings, heroic NLF guerrillas dashing forward, and the Seven-Point Peace Plan being offered by the other side. It was effective, but primarily for the well informed or converted. I went backstage to say hello and ask if we might cooperate somehow in creating these educational resources. I must have been a strange sight. Deeply immersed in researching native American parallels to Vietnam, I had let my hair grow long, pulled back by a headband. We spoke for only a minute and agreed to meet soon. Jane claims that I touched her knee, and at that moment she *knew* we were going to fall in love. All I sensed was a gleam of friendliness from her; I was still self-absorbed in my inquiry into identity. Besides, I was also with Joan Andersson, although she was going to Cuba for a few weeks. Jane had separated from Donald Sutherland and was "seeing" (in the technical phrase of the time) any number of men, including Anne Scheer's ex-husband, Bob Scheer, whom she met while Vanessa was in the Blue Fairyland. Complicated relationships would not go away.

Something was happening to me, because, not long afterward, I went to Jane's Laurel Canyon house to show her my Indochina materials. We sat on her living-room floor in front of the fireplace, and I flashed slide after slide on the opposite wall. Reflecting my emphasis on culture and people, the slides went through the unknown history of Vietnam, the village culture, the importance of land, their cultural modesty. Then it switched to the "Honda culture" of Saigon, the impoverished refugees, the brothels and bars full of teenage prostitutes.

Jane was starting to cry. I kept flipping slides of grotesque young Saigon women, talking about the breast and eye operations performed to turn them into round-eyed, round-bodied Westernized women, transforming them body and soul into creatures of our culture. Suddenly I understood why she was weeping: I was talking about the image of superficial sexiness she once promoted and was now trying to shake. I looked at her in a new way. Maybe I could love someone like this.

Jane was right. We did fall in love soon after. I was 32, she 34; both of us were starting over.

The passion of our common involvement no doubt caused our involvement in passion for each other. Being able to fight the same hazardous battles daily, and to do so *together* rather than in loneliness, was a powerful basis for this love. Work now took on a sheer enjoyment for the first time in years. Inner sources of love between two people cannot be fully analyzed; they are private and full of mystery. But it was important that Jane was a woman who could not be eclipsed or diminished in my shadow, and I was a man who was not threatened by her greater fame and power. She was fatigued by men who either pursued her as a notch on their belt or were rattled by being in her shadow. In addition, each of us reassured the other in fundamental ways: She wondered if she could be taken seriously, genuinely, as a committed person or whether she was a shallow late-comer to a decade-long movement; I wondered if there was any way to assert a public leadership role without damaging my personal relationships. We helped each other overcome these doubts.

Of course, there were differences too. She had missed the early years of the sixties, which were so important to my vision, patience, and organizing approach. She had entered the movement at its most overheated state, when everyone and everything had hardened. In a very deep way I was still participating in the experience of youth, an outsider with no possessions or responsibilities, living by wits and ideals on the economic margin. She had dropped out of Vassar, gone straight into a successful career, become a mother, and amassed significant income, which was spent on her material desires. I could keep my clothes in one large drawer; she needed extensive closets and domestic help. I was a famous radical who was morally and politically skeptical about fame; she was an actress whose career itself depended on public acclaim. We must have appeared like a remake of *Beauty and the Beast,* but these differences were more amusing than stressful as we happily came to know each other that summer. Not least of the pleasures was getting to know Vanessa, then three, who was born at the time of Chicago 1968 and had lived in the Blue Fairyland just after I left Berkeley; we had been just missing each other at these key moments in our lives. The first night that Jane and I made love, Vanessa marched out of her bedroom, a 3-year-old inspector, and stared at me. I stared back, smiling; here I was starting over in yet another relationship with a young child not my own. Her father, Roger Vadim, seemed to be a loving and supportive parent, with children from several marriages scattered from Los Angeles to Paris, so I didn't worry much about Vanessa finding her own way in life. Besides, after a shattered relationship with Christopher Scheer, I was *very* tentative about committing myself to someone else's child.[3]

Then, on a spring day in a New York hotel room, fresh from Vietnam, where she had seen women having children in the face of death, Jane was moved to create life as her answer to numb alienation. With a slight sigh, she stood behind me, naked, and whispered, "I want to have a child with you." With a tearful smile, I said yes.

My answer was immediate, even though my feelings toward having a family had oscillated between extremes. The breakup of my parents after my father returned from the marines had been an utter shock. When I married Casey, the threat of war became my excuse to forswear having children. For several years the concept of children had simply been erased, or repressed, from my desires; in the same way, I had separated myself from all conventions of society. At one point in the mid-1960s, when an important woman in my life became pregnant, we immediately decided on an abortion, without emotion or debate, as if there were no other real choice. Then, as the polarization of society deepened, only survival seemed to matter. What I didn't realize until living with Christopher in Berkeley brought it home, was that I had smothered a longing that was volcanic. Jane's simple words caused it to erupt.

This new infatuation with life seemed to embolden us toward a new commitment to ending the incessant war. In fact, rather than withdrawing into personal happiness, or sharply dividing private from public life, we decided that the only meaningful course was to hurl our personal relationship into the center of public life and resume antiwar work as a team, pregnant and all.

In a few months, we created an ambitious plan to barnstorm America against the war. We decided to organize an educational speaking tour of vast proportions, a campaign against the numbness that had set into people's thinking after a decade of Vietnam body counts, with three goals in mind: First and foremost, it was to revive public attention to Nixon's war at a time when the media interest was waning; to urge people, especially young people, to register to vote against Nixon in November; and to move the antiwar forces out of their growing isolation and into the mainstream. It was an effort to repair the painful gap between generations, between radicals and Middle Americans. We rapidly assembled a national network which we called the Indochina Peace Campaign (IPC), mostly composed of sixties veterans like myself who yearned to work again in the mainstream. In fact, the personal dimension of the project was akin to a rebirth for many, a return of exiles.

I remember the excitement, for instance, of Shari Whitehead Lawson, the middle-class daughter of a military family who had become a typical Berkeley revolutionary. IPC offered many like her a path out of the mounting debris of the movement. As a sign of our return to the mainstream, I gave her an American flag pin to wear on her jacket, which she happily did, as she orchestrated the first IPC tour event at, of all places, the Ohio State Fair.

We were worried at what the reception would be in the American heartland, and we were delighted at what we found. On a rainy September night, we spoke to three hundred people gathered under a tent. We watched a high school theater group perform a program about the generation gap, which was called *They're Killing Us with Words*. That same night we were welcomed at another fair in Dayton, ending with a midnight presentation in a downtown theater. We called the experience the Ohio miracle. We were "coming home."

FBI MEMORANDUM   9/13/72
RE: INDOCHINA PEACE CAMPAIGN

On September 4, 1972, a first confidential source, who has furnished reliable information in the past, advised that an organizational meeting was held at the Wesley Foundation, 82 East 16th Avenue, Columbus, Ohio. The purpose of the meeting was to organize the programs of the Indochina Peace Campaign for Ohio and the Midwest region. Among those present and representing the National Headquarters of the IPC were Jane Fonda, movie actress, Tom Hayden, Holly Near and Ruby Ellyn.

The sheer magnitude of the speaking tour was unique. Jane and I, along with singer Holly Near and former POW George Smith, spoke several times a day in ninety cities that fall, a more grueling schedule in many respects than a presidential campaign. The Indochina class multimedia exhibition was shown all over the country, from city halls to art museums. The slide show was reproduced in two hundred sets and sent to local organizers across the country, who showed it two thousand times in those two months. We hawked 100,000 copies of the Pentagon Papers digest. But the centerpiece of our educational kit was a four-page leaflet designed by Fred Branfman, a pioneering researcher on casualties in Indochina. On the front page was a photo of Richard Nixon's smiling face lifted from the Committee to Re-Elect the President (CREEP). It was entitled *Six Million Victims: The Human Cost of the Indochina War under President Nixon*. Inside, the human costs were documented in credible and detailed statistics and charts. Newspapers reprinted much of the material, and George McGovern began referring to "six million victims" in his antiwar speeches. We distributed two and a half million copies.

There was some hostility, especially to Jane over her recent trip to North Vietnam. I was amazed, and still am, at the hatred and controversy her trip generated. She was accused, but never charged, with having made seditious broadcasts to American GIs. She met several POWs and believed them when they indicated that they were not tortured. She was photographed wearing a helmet and looking at an antiaircraft gun. Unlike her critics, I listened to her interviews on Hanoi radio and heard her talk of bombed villages in the same way she talked at home. If anything, these were acts of naïveté, not acts of treason. More important, the international publicity surrounding her trip may have helped prevent U.S. plans for bombing the dikes of North Vietnam. She was deeply troubled by the Pentagon Papers memo recommending shallow flooding of the rice to threaten widespread starvation and traveled to Hanoi principally to protest any such American plan. But the hostility she triggered was shocking. Forgotten were her years of work with American GIs; now she was attacked as the enemy. Was it because she was a woman? a sex symbol turned into an accuser of macho men? a successful American rejecting the system that rewarded her? Why the hate? I wondered. What if a famous American actress had visited the Indians fighting the U.S. Cavalry a century before? Would history still define her act as scandalous today? What were these groups of narrow-minded patriots showing up at our rallies really angry about?

We had some minor violence in Morristown, New Jersey, at a Methodist church, where a right-wing group cut the electrical wires and threw cherry bombs into the audience. There were hostile pickets in many places, and frequent bomb threats. But what was most amazing was the open interest of most of the people we met around the country. In Muskegon, Michigan, where George Wallace won the Democratic presidential primary and the local press was merciless toward us, two thousand citizens turned out at the local auditorium and stayed late. We were proudly introduced there by an 80-year-old man who said he opposed the Vietnam War in the 1950s. He made Holly Near cry as she sang that night. In Detroit, we spoke at the state fair, with my mother in the audience, and at a community college where my old high school coach was the president. We saw many people change before our eyes. In Philadelphia, as a Vietnamese student friend of ours spoke movingly about her homeland, I saw a young Nixon campaign worker remove his button. In Chicago, we met a veteran who said he was the security guard who kept Jane off an air force base the previous year; he handed her his badge this time.

Holly was a wonderful, rapid writer, and one day I asked if she could put these transforming experiences into a song. She said she would try, starting with her memory of the 80-year-old man in Muskegon. In a few days, she did it. The song was called "Oh, America," and its chorus was always interrupted by applause and often brought hopeful tears to long-time antiwar activists.

> *Oh, America,*
> *I now can say your name,*
> *Without feeling bitter,*
> *Without feeling shame.*
> *Because I've traveled 'cross the country,*
> *To your cities and your towns,*
> *And I've seen some friendly people*
> *Who turned my head around.*

Jane was a tremendous trouper and almost always won over skeptical members of the audience. If people expected to hear how she intended to change society, they left with more of an understanding of how people like themselves, "ordinary Americans," had changed her. She described an empty life in the sixties ("I didn't think women could change anything, except sheets"). Then she told of meeting Vietnam veterans when she lived in Paris, men who recounted stories of war crimes she didn't want to believe. Then she saw the Chicago demonstrations in America over television, amazed at their scale and intensity. So she stopped being Barbarella, floating in space, and came home. After telling her story to the audience, Jane usually ended by raging against the forces that had made people like herself feel helpless and numb for so many years. Far from being a glitzy and remote movie star, she connected on a personal level.

On November 1, the Seventh Circuit U.S. Court of Appeals reversed the Chicago conspiracy convictions. The appellate decision cited the "demeanor of the judge and prosecutors," as well as numerous judicial errors, in a lengthy and historic opinion. The government prosecutors announced they would not retry the case. A few months earlier, the same federal court had reversed Judge Hoffman on the contempt-of-court charges and ordered a new hearing, before a new judge. (It was remarkable that during those several years of political trials on conspiracy charges, the federal government failed to win against *any* of the sixty-five conspiracy defendants. Such defendants as the Harrisburg Seven, the Camden Seventeen, and the Gainesville Eight always managed to win, either before juries or appeals courts, a dramatic difference from the McCarthy era, only fifteen years before.)

I was delighted to have my paranoia proven wrong, and the long burden of a five-year sentence at last lifted. There was something miraculous as well. Not only was the threat of imprisonment removed, but I was going to have the child that prison would have denied me. At about the same time as the court reversal of the Chicago convictions, Jane became pregnant. We think it happened in an upper berth of a van between speeches in upstate New York.

Back in Santa Monica, I bought my first house for $45,000. I was finally settling down. It was a two-story, wood-shingle dwelling in a small, charming, unconventional neighborhood one block from the ocean. To say the least, Jane was accustomed to more luxurious surroundings than I was. My tastes had not changed much since college; I liked old, sagging, wood-frame houses. She yielded, and found ways (like sandblasting the walls) to give it at least a rustic elegance.

I called my mother with the news that she was going to be a grand-mother. At first she hadn't believed that her son's relationship with a movie star would last. Now the thought of having a grandchild caught her completely by surprise. Instead of being delighted, I could tell she was worried by something.

"What's the matter, Mom?" I wanted to know.

"You're not getting married?"

"So?" The thought of marriage hadn't much occurred to me, and Jane didn't bring it up either.

"Don't you understand what people are going to think? Don't you have enough causes already?"

Despite my happy embrace of the mainstream, I had all but forgotten that people out there still got married and still wagged their heads at those with children out of wedlock. Under the influence of Simone de Beauvoir, the sixties culture suspected marriage of being a hoax that killed natural love and eroticism and created a form of servitude for most women. In addition, our own experience was negative: our parents were divorced, we had gone through failed marriages, and I only knew two or three couples whose marriages had survived the 1960s.

I talked it over with Jane. Did we want to fight the war, fight Nixon, and fight marriage? A good question, she agreed. That's how our consideration of marriage began. But as we talked, over and over, we realized there was a deeper problem we were starting to face: commitment.

To have a child meant wanting to have a future together. That commitment seemed so profound that, like a pair of walking wounded, we took it one day at a time. But the more we talked, the more we understood that a future was what we missed and wanted in our lives. So with Jane three months pregnant, we were married at her home on January 19, 1973. About forty friends, from Vietnamese students to Vietnam veterans, Irish priests, and balladeers, gathered 'round to see us through the vows. Henry and Shirlee Fonda, who were always supportive, sat by the fireplace with

Vanessa on their laps. Peter Fonda sang sweet songs with Holly Near. My mother watched with a smile and pride from a corner. The only one missing was my father. We invited him, but heard nothing back.

It wasn't exactly Norman Rockwell, but we made a family.

NOTES

1. The Red Family was a Berkeley commune in which I lived with a dozen people from 1969 to 1971.
2. I was teaching courses—on the history of Indochina—at Immaculate Heart College, Pitzer College, and UCLA Adult Extension.
3. In Berkeley in the late sixties I was in a relationship with Anne Weills Scheer and took responsibility for her infant son Christopher half time. We joined the Red Family commune, but our relationship deteriorated and I was drummed out of the family.

25

Your Son Became a Defendant Instead of a Lawyer

Modern Maturity, *January/February 1996*

◆   ◆   ◆

DEAR MOM AND DAD,

God, I can't believe it's been just over a decade since your deaths. The kids are the age I was when the movement began. Troy is 22, my age when I joined the civil rights movement. That's when you thought I was throwing away the college education you'd worked so hard to provide me. Vanessa, at 27, is the age I was in Chicago when you thought I'd had my mind snatched by mad revolutionaries. They are both greatly disturbed by the corruption and privilege they see here and everywhere, but the tragic state of the world has not seeped like poison into their souls, as it has for so many. They know the alienation we all went through, and don't want to recycle it.

Dad, it still hurts that we could not talk for fifteen years. I'm overjoyed that we finally reconciled, but the loss of those years is permanent, a hole in the center of the sixties. Mom, thank you for sticking with me through an era you just couldn't understand. I'm sorry I couldn't explain the damned war more clearly (you kept calling it "Indonesia" instead of "Indochina").

We were supposed to get the American Dream on the installment plan, but nothing turned out that way, did it? You and Dad got divorced after he came home from his war. Your son became a defendant instead of a lawyer. In your twilight, as I became a parent as well as a son, we finally honored each other. Seeing a reflection of ourselves in each other was more powerful than the blinding stereotypes to which we so nearly retreated.

What did it all mean? For you, World War II meant making sacrifices to protect democracy against foreign threats. For me, the 1960s meant making sacrifices to save democracy from the establishment here at home. What you thought was un-American I believed was the American thing to do.

For you, becoming a success in America meant leaving our Irish Catholic origins behind. So I grew up thinking nothing was worth salvaging from the past. I never was told seven of my eight great-grandparents were starved out of Ireland during the Great Famine. Did you know? What happens when we lose memory of our ancestors' holocaust? Who benefits from amnesia?

So where are we? Wondering how to meld our new diversity into a democratic and pluralistic richness instead of new forms of paranoiac separation. Realizing our economic security can no longer come from ripping off the planet. Searching for a new spirituality to resist the creeping corruption of institutions. In the sixties we shook off apathy, ended Southern segregation, expanded voting rights, stopped the Vietnam War, defied an imperial presidency, empowered the powerless, and became aware of the worst environmental crisis in our history. There's now an all-out effort to treat the sixties as if it were all a video that could be edited and deleted, or a building that could be dynamited into oblivion by patriotic militias. Believe me, dear parents, even you would not approve of this current backlash against the world your son tried to build.

I believe this raging storm will pass, just as it did between us. The sixties cannot be erased. But neither have the sixties been resolved. We need to make peace and move on. Our antagonisms, yours and mine, were born in love and reconciled in our children. I hope it will be the same for our country.

26

Eulogy for Patrick Lippert

July 14, 1993

◆　　◆　　◆

WE ARE HERE TO CELEBRATE the life and mourn the death of our friend Patrick Lippert, and to bury him in the memory of our love.

Thank you for coming. In the next hour, we will hear from Patrick's mother and father, from his sister and a number of his friends. There will be an opportunity for any of you to express your feelings too. Afterwards the family invites you to the Border Grill.

We will leave as the sun goes down. And we will know that the dawn always is breaking somewhere new.

The Gospel says, "Unless a grain of corn fall into the ground and die, it abideth alone. But if it die, it brings forth much life."

And Henry Thoreau wrote, "Though I do not believe that a plant will spring up where no seed has been, I have great faith in a seed. Convince me that you have a seed there, and I am prepared to expect wonders."

Patrick lived in this spirit. He was a dreamer during a dreadful decade. He was compassionate when greed was the gospel. He had the wonderment of a child when everyone around him was becoming prematurely adult. He was an organizational magician when few around us thought they could make a personal difference.

Patrick left his native St. Paul to chase his dream to Los Angeles in 1981. Ronald Reagan had just become president, and a decade of war, injustice, and AIDS was about to begin.

Patrick was literally a face in the crowd when Jane and I met him. He heard us speaking on pesticides and toxics outside a movie premiere in Century City, and volunteered to help.

He was a trusted activist and treasurer in my campaign for the Assembly in 1982. Soon after, he joined the staff of the Hayden Committee to organize fund-raising events.

By 1986, we had the idea of trying to organize a new generation of Hollywood activists, and Patrick was the coordinator. He played a key role in Proposition 65, the campaign to "get tough on toxics," managed then by Tom Epstein, who is here tonight for the president.

In 1988, Patrick went on to coordinate a flock of actors and actresses for the Democratic Party and the Dukakis campaign.

Patrick originated the bus caravans we saw used so successfully by Bill Clinton last year. There was the "Clean Water Caravan" for Prop 65 in 1986, and the "Star-Spangled Caravan" for voter registration all the way to the Canadian border in 1988.

By 1990 Patrick was working on anti-apartheid, pro-choice and environmental issues for the Hollywood Policy Center. He also found time to support Central American refugees.

In 1992 Patrick took over "Rock the Vote," and the rest is history. They registered thousands of voters, produced award-winning specials on television, helped elect Bill Clinton, and became a driving force in passage of the first voter registration reform bill in years. In May, Patrick and his parents stood in the Rose Garden at President Clinton's side when the bill was signed.

And he did all of this while coping with AIDS.

Patrick did more than anyone else of his time to organize a new generation of Hollywood to social responsibility. He did more than anyone of his generation to spur those artists to awaken young Americans to the importance of voting. He made a big difference in the election of a new American president only ten years after volunteering for his first political act.

Perhaps because he was gay, Patrick never felt fully accepted or at home in our society. We cannot imagine what Patrick would have been if he felt totally free to express himself. But we know why he could empathize with the pain of so many underdogs, and why he always was sensitive to making everyone feel comfortable with themselves.

And the last year, Patrick discovered a greater secret than any secret he kept in his life. All the closet doors opened, and he found that he was loved for who he was, not for what he managed to achieve.

So let us pray that we can bring ourselves close to Patrick's spirit now. Close your eyes and imagine him with all your heart. See the sparkle of his eyes. Feel his pain and hurt. Think of him on the phone. Remember the last time you saw him. Remember now what he meant to you and others.

As Wendell Berry once wrote, "If this memory hurts, if there is a wound, it is because you are opening a grave for him in your heart. Your grief receives him now. But the grief is a gift. The wound, like a grave in the earth, will heal over, keeping the spirit force of Patrick alive for as long as memory overcomes forgetting and creativity survives decay."

From it, the seed of Patrick will grow in the seasons of our hardships when we will need him more than ever.

Heaven is not out somewhere in the sky. We on earth already are out somewhere in the Milky Way. Patrick's body will be returned to this good earth, to regenerate life. And whenever we truly love Patrick, his soul will be in the only heaven he really wanted.

Much will be said here tonight about Patrick organizing the artists, but we also ought to remember that Patrick's life was a work of art as well.

There is a song that creativity sings, that is the song of every special spirit. There is a dance that creativity dances, that is in their footsteps too. There is a painting that creativity paints, though the painter has no brush. Patrick was a vessel and a mask for life creating further life.

Now we must leave. Now we are what we have lost. Now we all are Patrick's remains. We breath now the breath he left behind. As each of you leaves, please remember to take Patrick home with you.

VII Protecting the Environment

27

Rainforest Journal

From The Rolling Stone Environmental Reader *(Island Press, 1992)*

I chaired the California Senate Committee on Natural Resources for several years, an experience that plunged me into constant fights to save endangered species and ecosystems. It was this highly personal struggle to prevent extinctions that opened me to a deeper understanding of the broken connection between politics and spirituality. As an adviser to the United Nations Environmental Programme headed by Noel Brown, I traveled through the Amazon in 1999.

◆   ◆   ◆

MANAUS, BRAZIL, JANUARY 1, 1999

> To read or listen to most accounts of Amazonas is to conclude that only a maniac would ever set foot out of doors.
> —Peter Matthiessen, *The Cloud Forest, 1961*

I believe the environment has to become more than just another issue. We are living through a period of the greatest ecocide, the greatest era of species extinction, since the dinosaurs 65 million years ago. Environmental consciousness needs to be more central in our lives, an ethic about which we are passionate. But how?

Maybe the wilderness has an answer. I don't. And it's lonely.

Thankfully, I am traveling with Troy, my seventeen-year-old son; it's a male initiation ritual Robert Bly would appreciate. Even though I live with Troy, I'm shocked that he's so tall now, six feet two inches, and 165 pounds of muscle. He's a student at Santa Monica High, with a keen curiosity, a sense of humor and a tight gang of friends who tend toward baseball, Nintendo and rebellion, the kind who play "Fight the Power" while going to the prom in their tuxedos. The kid within him expects this trip to be a wild adventure, an Amazon safari, and equipped with camera, he's planning a class report. But I'm becoming aware of the man evolving in him, too, the person who'll be leaving the nest for college this year. We may not be together quite like this again.

Troy is reading Joseph Conrad's *Heart of Darkness*, the classic novel about a white adventurer who becomes mad from tampering too deeply with the truths of the tropical jungle.

This journey also has its formal agenda. There is a Smithsonian-Brazilian research project in the rain forest where I will learn more about the critical need for research on threatened species. And Dr. Noel Brown, the head of the United Nations environmental program in North America, has encouraged me to visit a cooperative where local people are trying to find American markets for rain-forest products like Brazil nuts.

Manaus was built on one of the many fantastic dreams that brought explorers to Amazonia, that of rubber production. Until the English stole seedlings from the rubber tree, replanted them in Malaysia and ruined the Brazilian rubber boom, Manaus was a city where men lit their cigars with dollar bills, where electric trolleys were running before Boston had them and where one of the world's largest opera houses was built in order to replant the culture of Europe.

The dream of European opera has faded, but the population of Manaus has doubled since 1960 as impoverished Brazilians have moved here to work in a free-trade zone, assembling electronics products. Middle-class Brazilians travel here to shop, take a day trip on the Amazon and return home, where they sell the VCRs they have bought in Manaus to pay for their plane tickets.

We slept five hours in a local hotel, long enough for me to imagine a green and yellow parrot with six-foot wings, before the phone rang and the jeeps were ready to leave.

We bounced along a red clay road north toward what has been called the largest experiment in the history of ecology. Its name is at least the most unlikely: the Minimum Critical Size of Ecosystems Project or, alternatively, the Biological Dynamics of Forest Fragments Project. Although a joint project of the Smithsonian and the Brazilian environmental agency, this venture is mostly associated with Dr. Thomas Lovejoy, a biologist who began observing and banding birds in Amazonia as a graduate student twenty-six years ago. After years at the World Wildlife Fund, he now serves as assistant secretary for external affairs of the Smithsonian. Yale educated, accessible, a scientist who can speak plain English and the creator of the *Nature* series on public television, he is the main rain-forest guru for everyone from U.S. senators to Hollywood environmentalists. His creative solution to the rain-forest crisis, already adopted by several nations, is exchanges of debt for nature, in which debtor countries, instead of destroying forests to pay international banks, qualify for debt reduction by setting forest lands aside.

The Critical Size project studies isolated patches of forest for the impact of logging or slash-and-burn practices. The question is, how much room does an insect, a jaguar or a creeping vine need to survive and prosper? The answer, Lovejoy's researchers have found, is far more than we realize. A simple colony of army ants needs seventy-five acres; a viable jaguar family may require as much as 1,900 square miles of running room. With tropical forests being destroyed at a minimum rate of fifty-seven acres per minute, Lovejoy's message carries urgency.

We careened along toward Camp 41, eighty-one kilometers north toward Venezuela, then turned left into the forest on an eroded, soggy, boulder-covered, one-lane road until, after four hours, the drivers suddenly stopped, and we continued on foot.

Everything was a green blur—quiet, shadowy, moist. A shriek from somewhere above. Thick vines spiraling up 100 feet toward sunlight. Palms that alone would fill most living rooms. I tried to focus my eyes and feet on the path, while Troy started looking for the giant snakes—bushmasters—that either kill you or provide the source of great stories.

Accounts of the Amazon had forewarned me of this "apparent emptiness," the "green stillness" of camouflage concealing its life, but I was still losing my balance when after five minutes we came to a tiny clearing.

I recognized Tom Lovejoy, who was smiling and walking toward us. And with him, here in the most remote place I had ever been, was Tom Brokaw.

At Robert Redford's Sundance Institute one year before, Tom and his wife, Meredith, had pledged to visit and film the Amazon rain forest. And true to their word, here they were, returned from a morning of bird-watching. (Another big question: how much do North American songbirds depend on wintering in tropical rain forests?)

We will spend two days here, "touring" the forest. I am fascinated by the guides—two British graduate students affiliated with Brazil's National Institute for Amazon Research. One of them, Andrew Whittaker, is a self-educated, talking encyclopedia of bird lore. He seems to hop through the forest, while the other guide, Nigel Sizer, glides invisibly. Nigel is slender, with large red sores that suggest AIDS or leprosy but come from leishmaniasis, which erupts about a month after one is bitten by an infected sand fly. He shrugs them off, the inevitable wounds of his quest to understand this forest.

Nigel speaks softly of environmental apocalypse. "The dinosaurs had time to evolve into birds," he remarks. "But we don't have the time." It's the 200th anniversary of Mozart's death, he says cryptically. Nigel has been here two years.

We spent the afternoon in the forest, and I still could not adjust to the orgy of life. In an area of four square miles, there are 1,500 varieties of flowering plants and 750 species of trees; by contrast, all of North America has 400 tree species. Meredith and I watched a blue butterfly with giant wings. A pack of capuchin monkeys leaped after fruit growing in the green canopy above us. Troy photographed a column of leafcutter ants that have more muscle, relatively, than we do. He's still an urban child, but I detect a growing fascination with this place. Meanwhile, I stared at a strangler fig, which is born in bird shit and somehow grows to curl around a tree until absorbing and destroying it.

Later we came across a seven-foot boa constrictor. Andrew delightedly grasped it behind the head and draped it over my shoulders. Brokaw looked away for a second, and the snake tried to attack him at the waist. With the snake menacing, Brokaw filmed a New Year's greeting to David Letterman.

I wondered if the bats we saw at dusk were vampires, if the mosquitoes carried yellow fever, malaria or elephantiasis and if Santa Monica doctors could cure leishmaniasis. At first, Troy wouldn't even cool off in the campside stream because he had read about the candiru, a wormlike catfish that slips into bodily crevices and stabs its pointed fin upward. All Amazon travelers have chronicled their phobias. But it's not what the forest might do to us that is so troubling. It's what we have done to it.

At least 50 percent of all living things—some say more—exist in rain forests, the gardens of Eden where our amphibian ancestors perhaps first crawled upon land. There might be 30 million species, but we are only guessing because less than 10 percent of such life, the genetic base of all we are, has been thoroughly identified. At least five species, plant or animal, become extinct every day. According to Lovejoy, we are destroying species before we discover them.

A scientist like Lovejoy is inspired by more than pragmatic arguments. I am interested in the deeper emotions and motives that drive someone like him. "The rain forest has become more than the rain forest—it's awakening us to the environment," Lovejoy says. "We're disrupting the planetary ecology in ways we can't even understand."

"It's really been about two and a half years since I started getting truly upset," Lovejoy continues, "when the global-warming data was coming in, when you could no longer think of it except as a truly major problem. I think we need a real revolution."

As a biologist, Lovejoy comprehends more than I the importance of the forest as a genetic laboratory; at least 50 percent of the gene pool of the whole world is here in Amazonia. He points out that one mouse chromosome contains as much information as is stored in all the editions of the *Encyclopedia Britannica* ever printed. We would be outraged if someone tried to burn books in the Library of Congress, but Amazon fires routinely burn species to extinction. The less diversity of species, he notes calmly, the greater the threat to our species. For example, if the peregrine falcon had not been around to die of DDT poisoning, the pesticide would have imperiled us far more than it did. "When we overshoot," Lovejoy says, "there will be all kinds of natural disasters and diseases."

Nigel was treating his leishmaniasis with an ointment as we talked by candlelight. "The problem is short-term thinking," he said. "We cut down the forests for so-called development today but threaten all life tomorrow." He muttered again about its being Mozart's anniversary, and I realized it was because Nigel believes that life should be ordered like a Mozart symphony, a perfect reflection of the universe, and not according to the interests of politicians and generals.

RIO NEGRO—JANUARY 6

We traveled up the Rio Negro, the Amazon's largest tributary, to a wild archipelago of countless forested islands; I couldn't be sure where the banks of the river were. The river supports 800 species of fish, 200 more than are found in the United States.

The most famous of these is the wicked piranha, which Troy wanted to catch for a cheap thrill. He and I took a small boat and, with hand-held lines and bamboo poles, hooked up bloody scraps of meat and gradually caught a bucketful. No species gives the Amazon its forbidding image more than this eight-inch fish, which looks like a bluegill with fangs.

Our guide for this leg of our trip is a good-natured man named Nonato, who belittled the danger and urged us to swim. We refused. I caught a "vegetarian" piranha, one that feasts on fruit droppings from the forest above. But the rest of our catch was carnivorous, and one bit off the flesh on the end of Nonato's little finger. Whatever was rotting in its mouth infected the bleeding finger. Hours later, Nonato said his fingertip felt like someone was pounding it with a sledgehammer.

Later that night, Troy started singing the theme song *of Happy Days* while beating the bed with both fists. "I need a little civilization to balance this," he cracked. Later, while reading *Heart of Darkness*, he looked up and said, "Maybe this is the civilized world, and we live in an uncivilized society."

RIO NEGRO—JANUARY 7

The world's rain forests are being destroyed by lumber companies, cattle ranchers and governments that dream of selling teak to Japan and hamburgers to America and Europe or paying off debts to the world's biggest banks. Brazil's debt is $113 billion. Since most desirable land in a developing country is owned by a wealthy 1 percent of the population, a government like Brazil's historically channels its country's exploding population toward the unsettled forests. The result, writes author Norman Myers, is that "the number one factor in disruption and destruction of tropical forests is the small-scale farmer," an "unwitting instrument," just like a soldier in war. Compared with the poverty and unemployment found in the cities, a plot of land in the jungle is appealing to farmers like Odair Lopes Ferreira.

We met Lopes Ferreira by pulling up to his floating dock, about two hours from Manaus, and introducing ourselves as curious North Americans. His view was breathtaking—"the sort of place you can put a $2 million home someday," Troy observed—but for now it was a tiny homestead perhaps like those that dotted our own frontier 200 years ago.

Lopes Ferreira, who welcomed our chance arrival as if he'd been waiting for us, was a short, powerfully built man of perhaps forty years, wearing only ripped shorts on his deeply brown body. He had obtained his plot through a government resettlement program, had constructed two buildings and had hacked out ten acres or so of forest for his crops.

He and his wife like subsistence farming much better than life in Manaus, where, he said with anger, "the rich billionaires get richer. It's going to stay that way, and I'm tired of fighting it." Here, he simply chopped down some rain forest, burned it and planted his manioc, cashews, pineapples and vegetables. He felt free to chop his way to the next river. And if more and more people moved from Manaus, he planned to open a little store on the riverbank.

"We have a lot of problems with environmentalists," Lopes Ferreira complained. "I don't agree with them. I am using the land productively. The real problems are the big cattle ranchers and developers. It's hard work, but I'd rather work hard on this land myself than in a factory in Manaus. This way I can be self-sufficient and live and work for myself alone."

We parted after ninety minutes, Lopes Ferreira waving cheerfully as we headed down the river to Manaus. Perhaps, I thought, the poverty of the soil and the hardship of forest clearing will limit his expansion, but then what? Will he find a way to use and sell products from the forest—Brazil nuts, fruit, vines for baskets and brooms in Manaus—instead of cutting it down? Will he just keep cutting and moving on until the forest is gone and the soil is dead?

RIO BRANCO—JANUARY 9

"And outside, the silent wilderness surrounding this cleared speck of the earth struck me as something great and invincible, like evil or truth, waiting patiently for the passing away of this fantastic invasion."
—Joseph Conrad, *Heart of Darkness*

We are flying three hours westward to Rio Branco, crossing over what my contacts have called the "road that killed Chico Mendes." (Mendes was the organizer of a rubber-tappers union that made common cause with environmentalists trying to protect the forests; he was shot and killed by local cattle ranchers in 1988. Between 1985 and 1989, there were 539 assassinations due to Amazon land conflicts. Two of Mendes's killers were convicted in a Rio Branco courtroom in late 1990.) BR-364, as the highway is known, was hacked through the jungle to bring the landless to Amazonia, and between 1970 and 1985 they came, the state growing in population from 100,000 to 730,000. With them came cattle ranchers, deforestation and the 1987 fires whose smoke, in NASA satellite photos, seemed to cover the earth.

Such destructive policies are being slowed, I am told. Mendes's struggle influenced the development banks to reconsider the backing of reckless road-construction projects, and the Brazilian government has cut tax subsidies to cattle ranchers and placed the renowned environmentalist José Lutzenberger in charge of the country's ecological policies.

Mendes's key idea was to create "extractive reserves" in Amazonia, where rubber tappers, subsistence farmers and Indians could live by harvesting products from the forest for commercial sale instead of burning it down, an idea the new Brazilian government now endorses.

From Rio Branco, a helicopter will take us to Mapia, at the center of a one-million-acre reserve. The Mapia community has a $200,000 loan from the Inter-American Development Bank for Brazil-nut extracting, is seeking a joint venture with Goodyear for rubber and is being watched by the UN as an experiment in balancing economic growth with rain-forest protection. Mapia's leader is a man whose formal signature is Paulo Roberto Silva e Souza but whom everyone calls Paulo Roberto.

The wilderness around Mapia stretches north and west to Bolivia and, at the base of the Andes, Peru. It is where the Incas fled the Spanish 500 years ago and where, in the sixties, Che Guevara launched his guerrilla campaign for continental liberation.

Leaving Rio Branco, we fly low over the stunning canopy of the untouched forest until, after an hour, we drop into a clearing of perhaps 300 acres. We land in a pasture surrounded by a few dozen cabins, administrative buildings and a large circular structure that seems to be a church. It has a large cross on top but with an upturned crescent and two horizontal bars. Staring at us are the curious, friendly faces of some fifty people, mostly kids, a dog angry at the helicopter and several very spooked head of cattle. I'm not ready for this abrupt entry, but the alternative is to spend four days in a canoe plagued by flies whose bite can give you river blindness.

I focus on a slender man with friendly, riveting eyes, a slight mustache, a baseball cap and a rain-forest T-shirt, knowing instinctively he is Paulo Roberto. He steps forward, grips my hand at length and introduces us to a second Paulo, an earnest, bespectacled administrator of the project. Circled by friendly stares, we are taken to Paulo Roberto's house a few yards away.

On the outside, it looks like an unfinished, unpainted two-story barn. Inside, it has the open feel of a communal dwelling in northern California or Vermont. There is a spacious living room, a dining area and kitchen, and a staircase that leads to bedrooms upstairs.

On the wall are large portraits of Saint Sebastian, the Virgin Mary and a black woman walking on water (I am told she is an African goddess of the river). There are smaller pictures of Christ and a book on Amazonia by Jacques Cousteau. There are two photos of an elderly man with a flowing beard. There are no electric lights, and the windows are simply open apertures that can be closed by sliding panels.

Paulo Roberto's wife, Nonata, and several friends are waiting with water and coffee. Physically, Nonata reminds me of Nigel; her very languid body seemed to fit right in with the forest environment. Her hair is long and as black as her eyes. Later, I learn she suffers continually from malaria.

Paulo Roberto and Paulo the administrator, I realize, are too middle class to be rubber tappers, and I ask about their background. Paulo Roberto, now 41, was a Rio de Janeiro therapist interested in "bio-energy," the removal of emotional blockages, who began a "spiritual quest" that took him to Rio Branco a decade ago [1981]. There he met Nonata, joined this fledgling community and moved to the jungle. The other Paulo was originally Paulo Roberto's patient in Rio, where he now stays to write grants, administer the project's budget and deal with government agencies and media.

"Our goal is to be a model by 1992," says Paulo Roberto, referring to the UN conference. The problem of Amazonia, he says, is that forest dwellers have faced a "false dilemma" between rain-forest preservation and economic development.

"When we got here in 1982," Paulo Roberto says, "we saw the paradox that we lived in the richest region in the world yet we were the poorest people. Deforestation was coming at the rate of one football field per minute. And we came to a solution on three levels: ecological, social and economic."

By next year (1992), he says, they will have the Brazil-nut production fully operating; at present they can export sixty-eight tons yearly ("not much," he says, "but we'll reach 200 tons"). Brazil's president, Fernando Collor, will attend the ribbon-cutting ceremony for the co-op's school for

100 children this year. The talks with Goodyear over a rubber contract are promising, and the rubber tappers are coming up with new ways to reduce the costs of extraction. There are forty more products the community can develop, including eighteen types of vegetable oils, medicinal plants, fruits, seeds, straw, soaps, buttons. And they are cooperating with Indian tribes to the north and south: "We can process their nuts," Paulo Roberto says, "and do research on medicinal plants—they know 1,200 medicinal plants."

I ask how he chose this site. Paulo Roberto points to the portrait of the man with the flowing beard and smiles. "He did, that man. He was our spiritual leader, Padrino Sebastian. He died last year. I am his son-in-law."

MAPIA—JANUARY 10

"Tell me, pray," said I, "who is this Mr. Kurtz?" "The chief of the Inner Station."
—Joseph Conrad, *Heart of Darkness*

We spent yesterday afternoon walking around the settlement. The food is good: meat, fish, manioc, vegetables and rice, all produced here. The buildings are constructed out of twenty-seven varieties of trees. The typical dwelling is a spacious hut with a thatch roof, usually out in the forest where the tappers work all week, coming into the community only on the weekend. Troy and I now enjoy the verdant flora that we wouldn't have noticed a week ago: here, in a few square feet, are a cashew tree, an avocado tree, a coffee plant and something called an *inhame* that has giant green leaves and roots—the extract of which is good for the blood. There is an urucum tree whose red flowers yield spice, skin oil and facial paint for Indian ceremonies.

"Before this," Troy told me, "nature was just there, something out the window. I never saw its power." He finally made himself jump in the cold, deep-running creek nearby to cool off. We washed ourselves with soap from the copaiba tree while standing on a log in the current. Troy exercised his upper back by swimming against the current until, exhausted, he floated back to the log. "I still don't trust jumping in here," he admitted. "It's not like falling back into a friend's arms."

Afterward we walked on, coming to a low-frame building next to five earthen vats, perhaps six feet deep, hollowed in the ground. "That's where we prepare the daime for our rituals," Paulo Roberto stated matter-of-factly. Daime? Rituals? He explained that daime is the community's "plant of wisdom" and a drink, created from the yagé vine and the rainha leaf, that has been used since before the time of the Incas for "self-revelation." The ingredients are pounded and flattened, then boiled in water in the vats. "There will be a ceremony tomorrow you can attend," Paulo Roberto said, "and we will discuss it again later."

"Is this some kind of weird drug cult?" Troy whispered to me. I felt unprepared for the new information but shrugged and said: "Who knows? I doubt it. They just believe in sacraments and ceremonies, like the Indians." I felt more curiosity than worry. But then again, a voice in my head warned that most crazy cults look normal until it's too late.

In the evening we sat on Paulo Roberto's floor for after-dinner conversation among flickering candles that created an atmosphere of expectation. I decided that Paulo, when fully animated, looked like a bird with jointed wings, short beak, incisor eyes and a wide pelican mouth. He told some scary stories about a local man attacked by a jaguar ("The most frightening is the smell of its breath on you") and the time when anacondas surfaced in the stream where we had been swimming ("You know when they come because the water is shaking everywhere, and you can tell there is death in it"). Troy was spellbound.

During one of the long silences that punctuate conversations in the dark forest, I quietly asked Paulo Roberto if he would return to his earlier comments about a spiritual quest and the daime ritual. I knew that he was waiting to do so and that this was the heart of whatever Mapia is.

"The *seringueiros* [rubber tappers] were, how would you say, compromised as human beings by the rubber barons," Paulo began to explain. "They were treated as nothing. So we decided to found the community on a spiritual basis. Padrino Sebastiano"—he looked at his father-in-law's picture—"drew spiritual knowledge, and self-knowledge, from a very old tradition in the Amazon."

"When the Spanish conquerors came," he continued, "one Inca prince,

Atahualpa, got on his knees, offered them gold and was killed. The other, Huascar, went to Machu Picchu [the Incan retreat atop the Peruvian Andes, 11,000 feet above sea level], then came here by the Purus River. He made a big impression on Indian tribes.

"Then the rubber tappers came here in the last century, by the river from the northeast, bringing with them faith in a cosmos, and their own rituals of self-knowledge," Paulo Roberto said. "One of them, Raimundo Irineu Serra, met forest people who knew the ritual, and created our church, whose teachings he passed on to Padrino Sebastiano.

"We need an identity to replace slavery," he continued, "a freedom to know who we are here at this time. The main thing for us is to get this kind of self-knowledge and identity."

I looked up from taking notes, already sensing that my entire journey was coming down to the next question. And, already knowing the answer, I asked, "What is that identity?"

"*To be friends of the earth. We have a right to live in harmony with our great Mother.*"

And how is the identity achieved?

"The big challenge is knowing your inner self and its relationship to your community and to the cosmos," Paulo Roberto said. "For us to live here in harmony with each other and with the environment is a big challenge. It is difficult to describe; it comes from an altered state of consciousness, from the daime."

The daime, I began to sense, was more than a drug that induced an altered state; it was a plant that contained an essence considered sacred. Paulo refused to call it a drug. In fact, he claimed that daime cures addictions to alcohol and cocaine, that it never creates "bad trips" but comes from a healing tradition. It is taken mainly in ceremonies, usually once or twice a month. It is nonaddictive, purifies the system and is self-regulating, making one throw up if too much is taken. "If it's a drug, it's one that makes you encounter yourself, not run away," he said, "and if not for the daime, people would be drunk on *cachaca* [the white lightning of Brazil]."

(Later, in the United States, I learned that daime is made from *Banisteriopsis caapi* and *Psychotria viridis*. Dr. Andrew Weil, at the University of

Arizona, confirmed most of Paulo Roberto's claims. He described daime as a powerful hallucinogen belonging to the family of indoles, which are widely found in nature. "Besides being present in the seeds of many legumes and mushrooms," Weil said, "there is a hormone produced in the pineal gland of our brain with the same structure, interesting because it suggests a commonality of all life." He said that daime is used by Peruvian tribes—who call it *ayahuasca*—for male coming-of-age rituals. He stressed, however, that daime has its desired effects in a ritual or religious context with positive expectations; taken by itself, the drug can set off adverse reactions.)

I asked Paulo Roberto if this was a cult we were visiting. With a laugh, he answered no, as if the question were frequently raised. Of the seven communities in the extractive reserve, only Mapia uses daime and, he said, "we are people you can count on. We get up with the sun and work until it goes down, and then we come here to pray. The sacred knowledge is freely taken. You have to seek it yourself. What is important is the program of action: economic, social and environmental.

"The forest is basic to our values," he continued. "If it is destroyed, we are destroyed. There was a time before man was a hunter when he was a kind of 'ecological man' who didn't interfere in the environment but lived in total harmony."

"What happened over a million years was an Oedipal problem between people and the Earth," Paulo Roberto said. "There was a splitting, as when a boy grows up from the parent. Since they couldn't have the father, who is God, they killed the father, then tried to possess the mother, who is Earth. So there was no longer a way of guiding people in how to live in nature. In the collective unconsciousness, there exists the memory of total harmony with nature, which the daime helps us discover."

I asked him if he was saying one needs the plant to really understand what he was saying.

"You can do it by yourself without the plant," Paulo Roberto replied, "but plants are better. God created them for our health, our bodies, but also for our souls. You need something to go inside yourself—it's like the deep sea; you cannot swim there by yourself."

Troy and I were exhausted. This was too much to think about. We agreed that we instinctively liked Paulo and the people and would let this adventure take its course. We went upstairs to a room we shared with a nest of bats. Troy quickly passed out, stretched diagonally in his hammock and covered by a sheet and mosquito netting. I looked out the window and was jolted by the sky. From horizon to horizon it seemed to be a thick glowing forest, a sky forest, of stars as densely packed as the trees below. When I closed my eyes, my mind expanded until I experienced the whole arc of sky and forest within me, and thought: "The universe in all its mystery may be centered here."

MAPIA—JANUARY 11

Today we went looking for pink dolphins—that's right—in the Purus River and talked with visiting officials of the Brazilian environmental agency, one of whom wore a T-shirt saying "We are all entitled to make a mistake." The government representative led a meeting on how better to use the clearing, warning that beans take a lot of nutrients out of the soil. It was a relief to hear such familiar and practical discussion. But I can't get the talks with Paulo out of my mind.

Tomorrow will be the ceremony.

MAPIA—JANUARY 12

The ceremony began like a country Sunday service anywhere. About 200 people came flocking in, the men mostly dressed in white jackets and pants, the women in white dresses with a green overlay, like vines, on their shoulders. It was the ninety-first or ninety-second birthday of Padrino Sebastiano, whose remains lay in a small white crypt by the church. I decided I would follow Paulo Roberto to the service, which he joined after some morning errands, while Troy continued sleeping (the bats had kept him up). I could hear a rhythmic chanting from the church several hundred yards away.

"How long will this be going on?" Troy had asked the night before. "All day, eight or nine hours," we had been told, which deepened the mystery.

In the center of the church was an altar of wood, a trinity-shaped star within a Star of David. The sun, the moon and the stars were represented as the trinity of nature, interwoven with Christian symbols and linked by the root of daime. I noted one thing truly weird, or funny: one of those battery-powered dancing flowers you pick up at airports. It was making the same movement as the people around me. The men (the sun) and women (the moon) were rotating round the altar in a shuffling two-step, singing hymns that contained the religious teachings. A high energy was maintained by stringed instruments and the shaking of cans filled with pebbles.

> I will call the star of water
> To come and illuminate me
> Give me strength, give me love
> Allow me to enter
> The depths of the sea
> The depths of the sea
> The force is the daime
> The daime is the Light
> He is the Messenger
> On the way of Jesus
> For ever I must love
> The sun, the moon, the stars,
> The forest, the wind, the sea . . .

On two tables were urns of daime, which Paulo motioned me to drink if I chose. The matter was not simple. Since we live in an age of drug confessions, here's mine: I had never done any hard drugs, even though chemicals seemed to be exploding all around me in the sixties. I rejected the notion that inner change could happen by reliance on external substances, and I was afraid of losing control. I covered this anxiety with the belief that one should reach inspirational breakthroughs in a "natural" state (though I didn't mind the chemical of alcohol).

So why start in the nineties? If someone asked me to take daime in the

Broadway Deli, I wouldn't be interested. But this seemed to be an opportunity that would come only once, to share an ancient ritual, in a tribal setting, in the wildest environment in the world. I was less afraid of ego loss at this point in my life than of missing this experience. To say no would have been like being among the Oglala Sioux too years ago and refusing a peace pipe on the grounds that I didn't use tobacco. Troy could make his own choice.

I reached for the daime, telling Paulo with a laugh that I wanted to be able to keep taking notes. "One glass then," Paulo said. "That will open the doors and be enough. Two, three glasses"—he waved his hand—"and you will go somewhere else."

The drink was bitter. After downing it quickly, I sat with Paulo Roberto off to the side of the service. "Breathe in and stay with the vibration of the music," he said. I remembered a question: why would the service take eight hours or more? "Because," he said deeply, "self-purification is a long process, you have to reach your limits—physical, emotional, mental, every-thing—before you can transcend them."

What was Paulo Roberto's dark side, I wondered. Why would an educated shrink from Rio believe in the divine power of a plant—unless it gave him power over people? I didn't have an answer but somehow chose to trust him in this situation.

After a few minutes, Troy arrived, freshly washed. He looked at me suspiciously, with a slight grin. "Did you take any? How much?" he asked. When I told him, he asked whether he should. Paulo said a little would be all right, and so Troy took two or three swallows. Father-son bonding for real, I joked. He sat down next to me, taking pictures of the dance.

The doors opened slowly. After about an hour, I felt myself becoming more serene, floating calmly.

I looked at my son. He seemed centered, watchful, quiet. Smiling, I asked him how he was feeling. "Nothing at first," he said. "But now the dancers are starting to spin." A while later he turned with widening eyes. "My legs just went *vooom* from under me. I can't tell if you're hearing me or if my voice is only in my head." He muttered something and laughed. I told him to just close his eyes and tell me what he saw. "I see the forest everywhere," he said. After these two weeks it was not unknown, fearful or claustrophobic anymore.

I looked at Troy and realized that I had been fearing a disconnection with his leaving home. Was it the same disconnection that develops between nature, the source of our life, and the human species it gives birth to? Can that cycle be restored?

I kept taking notes while one after the other the symbols of the universe flashed through my mind. The music lofted me. Then I surrendered myself to the power of the nature concentrated there, and the forest around us became a holy cathedral, full of song.

LOS ANGELES—JANUARY 15

> "I found myself back in the sepulchral city resenting the sight of people hurrying through the streets to filch a little money from each other. . . "
> —Joseph Conrad, *Heart of Darkness*

I'm back in L.A., waiting for the Persian Gulf war to begin on television.

Here's a good question: Are we ultimately more dependent on rain-forest resources than on Middle Eastern oil? Does anyone care?

Dr. Noel Brown at the UN cares. He called to discuss the possible Goodyear contract for the Mapia community. By 1992, 700 tappers there might produce and ship 1,000 tons of rubber here. More investments will follow, hopefully, from big medical and pharmaceutical firms. In the last two years [since 1989], twenty-one firms have begun importing rain-forest products, including Ben & Jerry's (Rainforest Crunch), Patagonia (buttons) and the Body Shop (ingredients for cosmetics). Negotiations are going on with ninety-two others, including some *Fortune* 500 companies. Between Sting fans and Greenpeace members, there is a growing green market.

I've called Tom Lovejoy and spoken with University of California officials about new research ventures in the Amazon, and the response has been good.

Troy feels changed by his experience. It felt like we were two brothers living together, he said, not like a dad and kid. As for the daime, he thinks it would make one feel "totally paranoid around here" and strongly believes it should remain in the forest. I agree.

But could the spirituality, the inner journey and the environmental wisdom of the forest people be transplanted to this society of asphalt, lead, asbestos, oil and chemicals? Is harmony with nature an outdated idea in a world of industry and war?

The question, and the Amazon experience, create in me a vulnerability, a palpable pain, in response to nature's agony in the modern world. I can choose between the pain becoming unbearable or numbing myself enough to work on reform. Small steps are all one can take every day, I know, and an optimist would note that global concern for the rain forest has increased significantly this decade. But fifty acres a minute is no longer an abstraction to me. I see nightmare visions of it every day. I would not wish these visions on anyone.

The age of species extinction will not be ended soon and not by mere tinkering with industrial consumer society. It also means a new vision—Lovejoy's "real revolution," Incan wisdom, the rediscovery of nature in our innermost selves, environmental spirituality, call it what you will—that finally sees the evolving earth as our only living parent and deepens the vital connection as we did, father and son, in Amazonia.

28.

The Politics of Nature

From The Soul of Nature: Visions of a Living Earth
(Continuum, 1994)

My old friend Al Gore has helped propel the environmental movement to unprecedented global levels, but too many environmental advocates tend to work within antiquated institutions, pray to own a Toyota Prius, and count on alternative resources to become cost-effective despite the distortions of the market model due to Big Oil. The American people, especially younger folk, seem more ready to engage more deeply with issues interconnecting environmentalism, spirituality, and politics than most of our elected representatives. The themes in this essay are explored further in my Lost Gospel of the Earth *(Sierra Club, 1997).*

◆　　◆　　◆

THE MACHINERY OF POLITICS is based on a heartless and hidden debasement of nature. Political scientists speak of the function of politics as the allocation of resources, assuming that nature's bounty is destined to become a Gross National Product for distribution to the powerful. In this way, the dominant politics of growth rests blindly on the death of nature.

Can all this change? Can politics represent ecosystems instead of special interests? Restoration instead of taking? Or does environmentalism have to reject and somehow replace the present political system for its inherent role in causing pollution?

These are questions I ask myself everyday as a state senator. Until recently, not many political thinkers have addressed them. Now, as the environmental crisis begins to overwhelm our past assumptions, it is time for a theory and practice of politics based on restoration and sustainability.

In my lifetime, world population has doubled and natural resources have been cut in half, creating a collision course between industrial growth and the natural world. California is a microcosm, with the fastest-growing population in the U.S. pressing down on a land the first European explorers called "terrestrial paradise."

For example, the development of California has resulted in the loss of all but five percent of the state's original redwood forests. California forestry law promotes "maximum timber productivity" as an official policy goal. That means that a grove of ancient trees, which sheltered our ancestors for thousands of years, which preserved and promoted a living forest for millions of years, is valued only for the price it brings as the deck of a condominium.

U.S. Justice William O. Douglas argued fifty years ago that such trees should have standing in courts of law "to sue for their own preservation." His prophetic opinion has been ignored, and yet corporations, which are utterly artificial entities, are accorded such rights in perpetuity.

This devaluing of ecosystems is reinforced in the case of forests by the vast power of timber interests which, despite their relatively small voter base, can rent the services of willing politicians under a campaign-finance system based on unlimited contributions. Corporate contributions are a form of "free expression" astonishingly protected under the First Amendment, at least as presently interpreted by the courts. By contrast, the standing of ecosystems in industrial society is similar to that of the Native Americans or African slaves: a wilderness to be destroyed or domesticated for economic use.

The major strides in environmental law since 1970 must be seen in this context which overwhelmingly favors the utilitarian exploitation of nature. The Endangered Species Act, for example, cannot be triggered until an isolated species is on the edge of extinction. Even then, the dying species must survive for years until bureaucrats and interest groups determine its final fate.

To place a value on nature beyond its immediate use to human society requires a transformation of religious and cultural assumptions that ultimately must be reflected in politics and economics. In this "new paradigm," political economy will no longer be viewed in terms of the machine metaphor of the old industrial order, but in terms of the organic image of a sustainable human community living integrally with nature.

The difficulty of achieving this changed perception cannot be overstated and yet the deepening environmental crisis will compel more and more people to creative adaptation and a rethinking of values. My faith is that the human survival instinct, which forces us to examine our place in the world, is stronger ultimately than the addictive need to cling to obsolete dogmas.

We are entering a transitional era with only two possible endings: either a downward spiral of violent human conflict over diminishing resources, or a spiritual redirection of twenty-first-century humanity toward harmony and reciprocity toward each other and the earth. Each of us matters in this unpredictable journey.

Politics is a reflection of preexisting assumptions about the universe and the role of human beings within it. In technological society, all politics is Newtonian. In his epic *Principia*, the philosopher asserted that "every body continues in its state of rest . . . unless it is compelled to change that state by forces impressed on it . . . and to every action, there is always opposed an equal reaction."

This mechanistic law of the universe was translated into the dialectical materialism of Karl Marx, the atomistic marketplace of Adam Smith, and the theory of checks-and-balances in pluralistic democracies. As James Madison wrote in Federalist Paper 51, "ambition must be made to counter ambition." According to historian Clinton Rossiter, the new American leaders believed that God "had set the grand machine of nature in motion" according to laws "as certain and imperative as those which controlled the movement of the universe." God was, in Rossiter's image, "the great Legislator" of all nature.

In all such theories, political economy was seen as a machinery that rested atop nature, drawing on the environment for raw materials and depositing waste back into that same environment. Such a model externalized nature as somehow "outside" and "below" society, a vast storehouse of resources and debris. In an agrarian society, the model was meant literally too, as in this passage from the letters of George Logan: "By political economy is to be understood, that natural order appointed by the Creator of the universe, for the purpose of promoting the happiness of men in united society. This science is *supported by the physical order of cultivation, calculated to render the soil the most productive possible.*"

The mechanistic worldview blended with the Genesis mandate into a powerful rationale for subduing the new American continent and its inhabitants; the "savage wilderness" teeming with "savage Indians," as Governor John Winthrop starkly described what lay ahead. The legal argument for taking and exploiting the new lands rested on the Lockean premise that undeveloped land was "waste" or, as Adam Smith described America, "rude" and "barren." Since the Indians had not subdued this *vacuum domicilium* into productive private property, they had forfeited all rights to ownership. The land itself was given value through cultivation by agriculture and mining by industry (for Marx, the "labor theory of value" made the same assumption of nature as only raw material). On a seemingly endless frontier, particularly in comparison with the settlers' densely enclosed European homelands, this vision became our manifest destiny.

The American dream of individual materialist prosperity suppressed a broader dream of the continent. For at least 10,000 years the Native people had developed culture, religion, and political economy in reciprocity with their natural world. Unlike the Puritans or Locke, they revered a Great Spirit present throughout the earth community on which their lives depended. Instead of exploitation, they practiced reciprocity toward species around them, from the tiniest flower to the greatest bison. While they sometimes self-destructed or exceeded the carrying capacity of their surroundings, the Native people were on the whole, in the words of a Smithsonian historian, our "first ecologists."

The European conquerors, from Christopher Columbus in the Caribbean to Sir Francis Drake on the California coast, at first observed this intelligent respect for nature in the Natives they encountered. A religious worship of God above and gold below, however, smothered the possibility of an America based on sharing and coexistence between human communities and nature. But if we seek an alternative politics based on sustainability, we must return to our lost continental dream.

The tribes, particularly the Iroquois, believed in a mechanistic governing theory of their own, one of counterbalancing powers, expressed in
their structure of confederation. But they also held a view of power as
more than the capacity to bend other people or ecosystems to one's will.
Power was a creative expression of human energy achieved through an
understanding of connectedness with a Great Spirit present in nature. This
power was known as *medicine*, a word which itself implies healing. This
power was obtained through meditation, ritual, and practice, and was
available not only to an individual shaman but to a whole tribe. In many
tribes, following the power of a certain chief was a voluntary act, not one
of submission and obedience.

Tom Paine encountered this dream around the Iroquois Council fires
where the elders discussed their Great Law of Peace. Paine, who was flu-
ent in the Iroquois language, noted in his diaries that "there is not, in that
state, any of the spectacles of human misery which want and poverty present to our eyes in all the towns and streets of Europe." Benjamin Franklin
and Thomas Jefferson were influenced similarly, the latter describing himself to European courts as "a savage from the mountains of America."
Franklin wrote that Indian government was based on a "Council of the
Sages, those with powerful medicine," and that there was "no Force; no
prisons, no officers to compel Obedience, or inflict Punishment." Jefferson, whose Monticello living room still contains a vast buffalo hide
inscribed with a Sioux creation story, pondered the fact that the native
Americans never "submitted themselves . . . to any coercive power (or)
shadow of government."

These American founders borrowed the Iroquois design of the Albany
Plan and the Articles of Confederation. But tragically, they failed to pursue
the Indian dream in its community and ecological dimensions. Perhaps it
reminded the new Americans too much of their own tribal roots, such as
the clans of ancient Ireland, which had been weakened or replaced by the
modern nation-state. More likely it was speculative fever that kept the
colonists from adopting the Native attitude towards possessions. As Sitting Bull once observed, "the love of possession (was) a disease with them,"
and thus the early American revolutionaries succumbed to the politics of

expanding frontiers. Captive of their times, they perhaps rationalized their choice with the thought that there would always be enough westward American frontier for the preservation of Indian culture and wilderness alike.

The American founders settled on a model of government which was more like the Roman Empire than a tribal confederation. The viability of their project rested on a national psychology of the conquering frontiersman and the availability of unlimited frontiers, symbolized in the nineteenth-century spirit of General George Armstrong Custer. The subject of more paintings than any other general in American history, Custer caused settlers and railroads to invade the great buffalo plains of the Sioux with his fevered reports that the Black Hills were filled with gold. He died "breaking down the gates of Hell" according to one history of the Battle of Little Big Horn. The unrestrained lust for frontier would be a more candid explanation.

In making the fateful choice to be a frontier nation, America's founders consistently rejected the alternative vision of living within limits in sustainable, community-based decentralized governing structures. In the Madisonian/Federalist view, an "extensive Republic" was necessary to provide an outlet for the inherent tendency to factionalism in human nature. Thinkers like Montesquieu, the anonymous anti-Federalist "Brutus" and, in his later life, Jefferson, all believed that democracy could flourish only in a human-scale and sustainable setting. As Robert Louis Stevenson eloquently wrote during the frontier era, "We cannot hope to escape the great law of compensation which exacts some loss for every gain." But the founders' doubts were swept aside in the inevitability of the conquest of the frontier once before them. "Indian society may be best," Jefferson once reflected, "but it is not possible for large numbers of people."

This historic debate remains at the core of political and environmental philosophy three centuries later. The dominant view among Americans and world political leaders is that expanding markets and environmental exploitation are basic to growth and progress, and that environmental mitigation can only be financed from the dividends of such growth. What has changed in our time, however, is the relationship of population to frontier. Where there was a certain logic to boundless expansion in 1775, pursuit of the same logic today is a dangerous and senseless addiction leading ever closer to human ecological destruction.

A new political theory for the ecological era is needed, one which should restore and modernize the older beliefs in decentralization, community-scale institutions, and environmental sustainability which were the dreams of our indigenous ancestors on the continent.

The foundations of an American environmental politics can be recovered from the nineteenth-century Romantics, Ralph Waldo Emerson and particularly Henry David Thoreau, whose visions ultimately animated John Muir toward founding the Sierra Club in 1892. Like the Native Americans, they believed in revelation and transcendence through a spirit within nature. These nature mystics and transcendentalists worshipped the forests and mountains as great cathedrals, not as resources to be felled or mined. They were reacting to the first ravages of commerce created by the railroads and settlers' axes. Some like Thoreau identified with the victims of expansion, the Native people, Mexicans, and African slaves. All of them wanted to preserve wilderness for its own sake, but also because they recognized in wilderness the essence of the human spirit. In wilderness was the preservation of the world. In place of the machine model of expansionary bureaucracy, they identified with the tradition of the New England town meeting—a model of grassroots, participatory democracy.

29

California Salmon on the Verge of Extinction

On February 14, 1996, I delivered the following opening statement as chair of the California Senate Natural Resources and Wildlife Committee hearing on saving salmon through strengthening the California Endangered Species Act.

◆　　◆　　◆

FIFTY YEARS AGO Governor Earl Warren exclaimed that California "should not relax" until we "put into operation a statewide program that will put every drop of water to work." At the same water conference, a Unitarian minister named Everett Pesonen replied that California should listen to "the voice of the salmon," whose survival would be threatened by those who only see water as a "sterile inanimate liquid." On the contrary, he said, the existence of salmon showed that water "is a medium in which life occurs," and planning of water use "must be expanded to include all the life-supporting values of water." We are here today to examine whether our greed to use water to the last drop has been restrained enough to protect the California salmon, or whether we have threatened the extinction of salmon with our thirst for irrigation and overdevelopment.

The decline of salmon is not only a California phenomenon, but is occurring at alarming rates on the Pacific and Atlantic coasts. On March 7, 1994, a scary article appeared in the *New York Times*, "U.S. Fishing Fleet Trawling Coastal Water Without Fish." The article reported that the salmon decline is "catastrophic—threatening to wipe out not only whole industries but culture and communities." Just this month, new research indicated that remaining salmon are becoming smaller in 45 of 47 runs from California to Japan. The number of eggs per female is also continuing to shrink. According to a July 1995 AP report, "Biologists tend to blame human action, mainly the overgrazing of the ocean by billions of hatchery fish and fishing techniques that skim off big fish."

Officially, both state legislation (SB 2261, 1988) and the federal Central Valley Project Improvement Act state a goal of doubling the numbers of naturally spawning California salmon by 2000 and 2002, respectively.

But nowhere in public policy is there a greater gap between words and deeds than in the flouting of these mandates of the law.

Far from being doubled in numbers by the year 2000, the California salmon may well be doomed.

The statistics of decline are chilling. In 1969 there were 100,000 winter-run chinook counted in the Sacramento River. Between 1982 and 1988, counts averaged 2,334 adult fish annually, a 97 percent decline. The fish were "nearing extinction" according to studies published by the University of California in 1991, because of "conscious management decisions that demonstrated a lack of concern for the needs of the species."

Other runs of chinook and coho are declining as well. Coho salmon have been petitioned for listing under the ESA. Studies in 1991 indicated that the spring chinook were "seriously depleted from historic levels and fast approaching the need for protection under the Endangered Species Act." UC expert Professor Peter Moyle now states that, from a biological standpoint, listing the spring- and late-fall runs on the Sacramento River as endangered is clearly justified, and that the fall run is in decline.

For a more vivid example, one should visit the Steinhart Aquarium in San Francisco where 261 chinook salmon circle in a large holding tank. A placard tells the public that the Aquarium is attempting "to preserve the genetic material of this imperiled salmon. We are only buying time until the (Sacramento) river improves. Like the condor, the last of this race will disappear in captivity unless we save their habitat."

A world without salmon would be a diminished world for humans. Not only would thousands of jobs and billions of dollars be lost in California's oldest industry, as a 1998 report by Meyer Resources, Inc. has pointed out. But the loss of salmon also would mean the loss of wild rivers and rich forests that salmon depend on.

Gone too would be the genetic intelligence that has allowed salmon to undertake an odyssey from their freshwater spawning grounds to the vast ocean and back again to the same spot, to spawn again and die. A world without salmon would diminish the human imagination.

Salmon have been a source of inspiration for poetry and nature writing for centuries, and they are considered sacred in many cultures. In Irish tradition, they originally were a god of wisdom.

The Yurok people considered the joining of the Klamath and Trinity Rivers as Qu'-nek, the center of the world. Among all coastal tribes from California to Alaska the seasonal cycle of the salmon was regarded with reverence.

Recently state and federal officials held a press conference in Sacramento to celebrate the Bay-Delta Agreement which, among other promises, claimed to provide more fresh water for several runs of salmon. With the press conference, the signatories claimed an "end to California's water wars."

This hearing will raise serious questions about whether salmon are indeed safe and the water wars are over. Announcement of the Bay-Delta Agreement was not accompanied by any scientific information on which its claims were based. There is nothing in the plan to achieve the goal of doubling the numbers of naturally spawning fish by 2000–2002. The water promised in dry years is 400,000 acre-feet short of what the State Water Board itself recommended in its 1988 draft salinity standards, which were dropped because of political pressure.

Many environmentalists and commercial salmon fishermen were unrepresented in the negotiations. The handful of environmentalists who did sign this unenforceable "statement of principles" have no guarantees that it will keep the Delta from going the way of Mono Lake.

This hearing also will examine whether the Endangered Species Act should be invoked to save California salmon. Currently only the winter-run salmon in the Sacramento River are listed as endangered, and that decision came only after years of public pressure and outcry.

When salmon are facing a threat of extinction it is no time to be thinking of weakening the Endangered Species Act. As Zeke Grader and Glen

Spain of the Pacific Coast Federation of Fishermen's Associations have argued, "the ESA is the key to the watershed restoration and salmon protection throughout the region. It is also the only hope for putting a stop to onshore practices which destroy fishermen's livelihoods."

But weakening the ESA is clearly the agenda of our new leaders in Congress and a major priority of Governor Wilson as well. According to internal documents, the governor plans to use executive orders as well as legislation to weaken the protections that the Endangered Species Act provides to salmon and other species. For example, the governor would exclude consideration of "habitat modification" from definitions of illegal "taking" of species that are threatened or endangered. But clearly salmon are doomed if their water is exported to southern California, if streams are silted by erosion, and if the delta is filled with pesticide runoff.

Does Governor Wilson want to be known in history as the governor who presided over the extinction of the California salmon? That is just the legacy his policies are risking unless there is serious reconsideration of the state's priorities.

As a first step, the governor needs to give a clear signal to his fish and wildlife officials to disregard special-interest pressures and do their jobs as independent professionals. It is widely believed, as the fish and game wardens' own association has charged, that "political pressure from adversaries of the salmon upon the governor and the legislature cause the Department to discourage field personnel from enforcing the law."

I have asked Charles Warren, the distinguished former head of the President's Council on Environmental Quality, and former member of this legislature, to serve as special consultant to our committee on the Endangered Species Act. We will hold three to five public hearings on the Act to examine all grievances from all parties and find ways that the Act may achieve its intended goals more effectively.

After twenty-five years of study, it is time to question whether we are studying the salmon to death. In 1970 a citizen's advisory committee was formed to study salmon and steelhead declines. In 1971, the committee issued a report called "An Environmental Tragedy," calling for habitat restoration. In 1972, there was a second report, "A Conservation Opportunity." In 1975, the report was titled "The Time Is Now." In 1982, a new committee was formed. They published five more reports, including "The Tragedy Continues." After the 1988 report, the state adopted the doubling of the population of salmon and steelhead by the year 2000 as an official goal. Twice the State Water Resources Board issued draft standards, in 1988 and 1993, but both times the draft plans were dropped because of pressure by water exploiters.

It is perhaps the last chance to face this issue now, before the streams and rivers of California are turned from spawning grounds to burial grounds of the last of the salmon.

30

Earth Day Sermon

University Synagogue, Los Angeles
April 21, 1995

In 1994 I formed an ad hoc committee of religious people called Clergy for All Creation in order to defend the idea that saving species was a spiritual responsibility. My friend Rabbi Allen Freehling welcomed me to present this sermon to challenge his congregation. I gave similar talks across California, trying to introduce spirituality—or at least the notion of intrinsic value—into the environmental conversation in California politics.

◆   ◆   ◆

ON THIS SABBATH EVE of Earth Day, I want to share with you my deepest feelings about religion's obligation to defend the whole earth.

Since the first Earth Day twenty-five years ago, there has been definite progress in confronting our environmental crisis and changing human consciousness across the world.

That progress now is threatened by the backlash contained in the "Contract for America" which intends to erase the major environmental laws which were established after the first Earth Day.

The fact that the "Contract" fears to mention the word "environment" reveals the good news that most Americans desire a continuing commitment to environmental restoration.

But the "Contract" also reflects a deepening angst among a few that leads to a nihilistic assault on nature to preserve their current standards of consumption and production.

These attitudes, described as "rescuing Western civilization," come from an alienation from the earth and the universe itself. Removing environmental obstacles to our greed will only intensify our crisis.

Let us remember the magnitude of the crisis before us. For all the progress we have made in twenty-five years, the global context is rapidly worsening.

POPULATION: There are eight new Calcuttas born yearly. I say Calcutta because the growth is in areas already desperately poor, where thousands die from hunger every day. Two hundred million children have perished from malnutrition and polluted drinking water since the late 1960s.

SPECIES EXTINCTION: From invisible microorganisms to vast rain forests, we are experiencing a biological holocaust unparalleled in millions of years.

TOXIC THREATS: Three to five toxic chemicals are introduced daily, a total of 65,000 since World War II.

OVERCONSUMPTION: With 5 percent of the world's population, we continue to consume 30 percent of its resources. Advertising, the drug that stimulates consumption, has doubled since 1960. The average kid sees 360,000 commercials before high school graduation.

Why is this happening? Because our thinking, our habits, our values have not changed as rapidly as the state of the world has. We are the first generation to experience the collapse of our own life-support systems. We are the transitional generation to either a sustainable planet or one filled with violent conflict over diminishing opportunity.

I concluded several years ago that this is a religious and spiritual issue. We need the guidance and inspiration that comes from our sacred traditions. In fact, I began my explorations in Rabbi Freehling's study in this very synagogue, reading David Jeremy Silver's *History of Judaism*.

The key problem is that a strictly utilitarian criterion has come to rule our environmental decisions. The environment is seen as a vast storehouse of raw materials for our consumption. The earth and even the vast universe are defined as lifeless matter that we are privileged to live upon.

For example, the general policy of the State of California is set forth in Section 1600 of the Fish and Game Code: "Fish and wildlife are the property of the people and provide a major contribution to the economy of the state as well as providing a significant part of the people's food supply and therefore their conservation is a proper responsibility of the state." These species have no value except as they benefit our economic needs.

California forestry policy has as its goal that the "maximum sustained production of high-quality timber products must be achieved." Under this doctrine, the last stands of our ancient redwood are nothing but economic raw materials to be exploited by corporate raiders.

A bill now in the legislature would mandate that we itemize each endangered species we want to save, put a price tag on the creature, and include the cost in our annual budget. How to put a price tag on a bald eagle? What about the forest it nests in? The smaller invisible creatures it feeds upon? Even if we could price an eagle, we could never debate the cost of each one of the 200 plants, animals and marine species that already are endangered in California. This is a plan to accelerate their extinction.

By contrast, we all agree that human beings have an inherent worth beyond any utilitarian price tag. Yes, it is true that we do not live up to this standard. We have treated whole communities of people as subhuman, as objects, to be exploited, discarded, even destroyed. But we have worked toward a common ideal that all human beings have an inherent right to live, an ideal whose ultimate roots are religious.

To save the very environment we depend upon, we need to reexperience a spiritual covenant, a sense of reverence and kinship, toward the inherent worth of the natural world.

I say *reexperience* because our oldest religious traditions shared a spiritual bond with the environment.

The Chumash who inhabited this very place for thousands of years celebrated an earth goddess, whose name was Hutash, during their acorn harvests. They believed she was married to the Milky Way. The Chumash believed they originated on idyllic Santa Cruz island, which was made by the goddess with seeds of a magic plant. The Chumash crossed to our mainland on a bridge the goddess made from a rainbow. When a few looked down and fell into the ocean, she turned them into dolphins.

According to a Chumash narrative, "this world is a single congregation, the noble principles of the soul are the same."

In our Biblical tradition, Adam and Eve were purged from Eden for their original sin. The Chumash lived in Eden until expulsion by conquest in the name of the Bible.

The old world of the Chumash is nearly gone, replaced by a growth on the land misnamed the City of Angels. Fourteen million of us use Santa Monica Bay as a toilet bowl for everything from toxic chemicals to plastic cups. Cement flood channels have buried the once-mighty Los Angeles River. We draw electricity from the nation's largest nuclear and coal plants, in Arizona. We generate 50,000 tons of garbage daily (25 percent of it grass and tree trimmings), and haul it to gaping landfills torn out of the desert. Two-thirds of the city is paved to meet the needs of the automobile. Our "air" is "conditioned."

We cannot return to the world of the Chumash, but we can return to their dream of nature. In fact, it is a universal dream that appears throughout our faith traditions.

"The Earth is the Eternal One's and the fullness thereof," say the Psalms (24:1). Not the timber industry's, not the chemical companies', not the developers', none of us owns the earth, for we are all "sojourners" and "strangers resident" upon it. It is not our mission to dominate and exploit but "to till and to tend."

As the Christian tradition has its Saint Francis and Hildegard of Bingen, so the Jewish tradition has its nature philosophers and mystics too. In his *The Guide for the Perplexed*, we find Maimonides defending the inherent worth of all creatures, saying that "it should not be believed that all things exist for the sake of the existence of humanity. On the contrary, all the other beings too have been intended for their own sakes, and not for the sake of something else."

Far from a lifeless universe, it is taught that God placed "sparks of holiness" throughout all of creation.

God is not present to clean up after us. As Ecclesiastes Rabbah states, "God showed the first people the beauty of the world and then instructed them: do not destroy or corrupt my world, for if you do, there is no one to set it right after you."

Far from indifference to the fate of species, Nachmanides wrote that "scripture (Deuteronomy) will not permit a destructive act that will cause the extinction of a species even when it has permitted the use of that species for food." Preserving species is preserving God's creation. The Tur of Maimonides says that "trees are more important for the settling of the world than buildings."

And let us not forget the original significance of the Sabbath we celebrate here. As my friend and teacher, Rabbi Dan Swartz, has written, the Sabbath is the time when "we put aside all our attempts at gain . . . the Sabbath reasserts the essential harmony of life, the balance between work and rest, between striving and acceptance, between the momentary and the eternal . . . the Sabbath becomes for time what wilderness preservation is for space." If we followed these maxims, the human community would be in balance with the earth. We would see the earth as alive, as numinous with the energy of God.

It is no criticism of anyone here, or any particular faith, to observe that we have failed to follow these teachings of scripture.

Most religion has become human-centered instead of creation-centered. The covenant we most often worry about is between God and human society, not the rainbow covenant between God and all living things declared in the story of Noah.

Until recently, the environmental crisis has been low on the agenda of our major religious institutions. For example, during the twelve years I have served in Sacramento I have never seen a representative of a religious community testify on environmental legislation.

As chairman of the Senate Natural Resources Committee, I intend to change that spiritual void this year. Rabbi Allan Freehling, no stranger to path-breaking initiatives, will join other religious leaders in supporting the Endangered Species Act against attack.

What we need is an awakening to the environmental challenge in *all* our religious traditions.

When the fabric of our spiritual culture changes, our secular culture and institutions will change as well.

Martin Buber left us with the ethical question this generation must answer. In *I-Thou*, a great book that focused on treating each other like subjects rather than objects, Buber briefly raised the question whether we can have an I-Thou relation with a tree. "Of that I have no experience," he admitted, but offered a tentative conclusion: "It can come about, if I have both will and grace, that in considering the tree I become bound up in relation to it. The tree is no longer 'it.'"

We must stop treating nature as *it*, and begin treating nature as *us*.

In psychology, we treat mental health separately from the environment. We are under the spell of Freud who wrote that "the principle task of civilization, its actual raison d'etre, is to defend us against nature." We must heal this split of the self from nature, and understand that a healthy environment produces healthy people.

In education, environmental literacy is seen as only an elective, not a requirement. There are too many textbooks with passages such as this, from a physics primer: "The earth is our cradle and has served us very well. But cradles, however comfortable, are soon outgrown." We need to understand, with John Dewey, that "the intelligent activity of man is not something brought to bear upon nature from without, it is nature realizing its own potentialities . . ."

In the media, the main environmental news is the weather report. What if there was a real *Daily Planet*? What if the cancer rate from pollution received as much daily attention as O. J. Simpson's murder trial? In 1980, U.S. president Jimmy Carter was discredited because television announced every night how many days our hostages had been held in Iran. We should demand that the news media report how many acres of rain forest are destroyed daily while politicians sleep.

In economics, we treat the environment separately, as a so-called externality, in our academic charts of production and consumption. The Gross National Project measures progress by the rate at which we turn the natural environment into goods and services. If we run out of resources, so what? Newt Gingrich has said "the moon is an enormous natural resource." We must change to an economics that invests in restoring the environment to create sustainable work.

In politics, we still define government as a reflection of the lifeless Newtonian universe, a Machiavellian machine which allocates the GNP to placate the immediate needs of avaricious interest groups.

I am not advocating spiritual withdrawal. What I am saying is that pragmatic politics alone will not suffice. The political system will be of limited value until the moral and cultural assumptions driving the system are challenged.

We need what I call a politics of the spirit opposed to the politics of the machine. As Václav Havel, the brave president of the Czech Republic, has argued, when we pollute the air we not only harm our health but we "soil the heavens." We create a metaphysical crime against nature. "Having recognized that we are but a tiny speck in the grand physical design of things," he writes, "we must eventually recognize that we are but a speck in the metaphysical structure of things as well."

The Dalai Lama has gone further. The exiled Tibetan leader declares that "the entire Tibetan plateau should become a free refuge where humanity and nature can live in peace and harmonious balance."

In our own country, Vice President Gore calls the environmental crisis "an outer manifestation of an inner crisis that is, for lack of a better word, spiritual."

This means abandoning any notion that we are lords of the universe for the humbler realization that we are all part of a great mystery. This does not mean falling into superstition or abandoning our reason. In fact, the more we inquire into the universe, the less we seem to know. How can this be? Because science is quantitative and deductive, and creation is infinite and shapeless. We can make progress in understanding the world but never be closer to the ultimate nature of things than we already are.

We know how to write and count, but not what consciousness is. We can see the heavens through a lens but not notice that we are in them already. We know when we were born, but not how old the universe is. Science should lead us to higher levels of informed humility, not greater depths of arrogance.

How can we claim to conquer, control and manage what we cannot finally understand? The modern state attempts to transcend, dominate and borrow from nature. But the effort is in vain.

No state can be greater or more sophisticated than the state of nature. No government can usurp the invisible governance of the universe. No legislators can repeal the laws of nature's making. Modern politics and statecraft, in its drive for control and mastery, is idolatrous and sinful.

We need a politics grounded in our relationship with the eternal, with the spirit of the creator of universe. A politics that is in harmony with the environment, that sees nature as a source of life and not merely a resource to be exploited for selfish ends. A politics that is accountable to the inherent worth of living things, that follows Maimonides instead of Machiavelli. A politics that sees the agony of endangered species not as a mark of progress but a prophetic warning to ourselves.

So on this Earth Day Sabbath let us offer a prayer for the earth and all its inhabitants. Each of us is unique, and also related. None of us will pass this way again. It has taken billions of years for the creator to give us the universe, for the universe to give us the earth, for the earth to become home for the human, for the soil, the air, the water to make life possible for us now.

As we reflect on this miracle, let us try to feel ourselves as the forms the Great Spirit of the universe has created to reflect on itself in conscious self-awareness. Let us reject the arrogant claim that we are masters of the universe for the ancient and wiser understanding that we are miracles of God.

VIII

Lessons Learned
Progressive Politics and Foreign Policy

31.

The Mission of UCLA's Hunger Strike

Los Angeles Daily News, *June 14, 1993*

In response to urgent phone calls, I drove to UCLA as the hunger strike for Chicano studies began. It would last two weeks, and I was chosen by the students to sign the final agreement as a guarantor. These students had learned from the United Farm Workers of America to be effectively nonviolent, so it was fittingly named the César Chávez Department of Chicano Studies and remains an important campus institution as the city evolves into the most important Latino metropolis in North America.

◆   ◆   ◆

THE FIRST HUNGER STRIKE in student history has ended on a redemptive note for UCLA and for a city increasingly lost in its search for racial peace.

Chancellor Charles Young is insensitive to say "their hunger strike accomplished nothing." In fact, the chancellor's negotiators made constructive concessions in response to the hunger strike. A César Chávez Center was created instead of a lower-status Chicano studies program.

They committed full-time faculty and representation for community and student representatives in creating the center. And instead of prosecuting the students as criminals, the issues of restitution for damages will move to a conflict-resolution process.

By creating the César Chávez Center, UCLA will be a beacon for all of Los Angeles, not simply West L.A., especially to the majority of public school students who are Chicano.

The hunger strikers were deeply conscious of their familial and community roots. At an emotional turning point in the negotiations in Murphy Hall, hunger striker Jorge Mancillas spoke of his 6-year-old son.

331

"He's afraid, and that weighs so much on me. He says, 'Daddy, don't die, you have more to teach me.' I don't want him to grow up without a daddy. But I don't want him to grow up in a city torn apart by hate and violence either."

There are many, however, who viewed the strike and ethnic studies in general as divisive, promoting a Balkanizing of campus and community. Some people were even leafleting UCLA to promote "white studies."

But there is a more positive possibility, a new "e pluribus, unum" that can come from embracing diversity instead of burying it. Truth and reality are mosaics, not monoliths. It is essential to being a whole person to understand that native and Mexican cultures were suppressed when California was created.

In 1851, Governor Peter Burnett endorsed a "war of extermination" against native people in his inaugural message to the very first session of the California Legislature. As I sit in the Senate chamber today, I wonder if any of the one million visitors to the Capitol have the slightest idea of that ominous beginning.

Discovering the buried history of another people can make all of us see ourselves anew. My own consciousness of Irish roots, for example, was awakened first by hearing Malcolm X, not by jokes about leprechauns or cheering for Notre Dame.

My empathy for the UCLA hunger strikers is deepened by my knowing survivors of Catholic hunger strikes in West Belfast. My struggle to comprehend slavery is aided by knowing about my Irish ancestors coming to America as indentured servants in shiploads of squalor and starvation.

I am proud that Notre Dame is beginning an Irish studies center under the leadership of the distinguished Irish literary historian Seamus Deane. It would not have happened without the wider cry for multiculturalism.

Multiculturalism is often criticized as if it means the replacement of European culture on campus by enclaves of fanatics chanting in tents. Such fears are extreme. The real danger is that many of us live in denial of our own nature because we are willfully ignorant of each other.

Multiculturalism doesn't go far enough. I do not mean we need more separatism; we still are in a stage of discovering and respecting our diversity. The next stage will be to reidentify the common themes by which we recognize the universal in each other. Humanity is diverse, but it also is one, as is the planet.

Naming Chicano studies after César Chávez is a step toward recognizing both diversity and a universal humanity. Many college buildings are named after donors representing personal wealth, not humanity's needs. But César Chávez was both a Chicano leader and a universal human being.

He never went to college, but educated us all. He worked with his hands, but opened our hearts and minds. He revered the earth instead of poisoning it. Now, just when many were saying his ideals were obsolete, a new generation of strikers has created a center of learning in his name.

This is a deserved recognition of Chicano identity, but also an honoring of the humanity and earth we all share in common.

32

"We Will Not Be Ashamed to Say We Are Czech"

Los Angeles Times, *January 8, 1990*

This brief description of the 1968 Prague Spring, glimpsed by a close friend, reveals the exuberant hopefulness of those times. Soviet tanks arrived there that August and, on a much tinier scale, U.S. troops arrived in Chicago, where some protesters held up signs proclaiming "Chicago Is Prague." Spirited Czech resistance kept the Soviet occupiers at bay for a time, leaving a slender hope for peaceful reform of the communist system. Though the repression was severe, only five Czechs died in the 1968–69 mass protests. In January 1969, a student named Jan Palach immolated himself to demand democratic reform. Over 100,000 attended Palach's funeral in a silent protest. Then in April 1969, the communist reformer Alexander Dubcek was replaced by the pro-Soviet Gustav Husak, and the next twenty years were characterized by "resignation, cynicism, emigration, escape into the private sphere and outward collaboration with the regime, which was neo-Stalinist, repressive and primitive and transformed the country into a cultural wasteland." (from an unpublished manuscript by Jan Pauer, 2007). It was in this "museum of communism" that my friend Anna was forced to spend the best years of her life. Those wasted years never could be regained, but she was fortunate to experience a second moment of liberation, once in 1968 and again in the peaceful revolution that swept across the Western communist world in the 1990s.

◆   ◆   ◆

I met Anna in Prague on the eve of 1968, when all things seemed possible. She was an angelic student working in a youth hostel. I was a passing tourist. She led me through the gray facade of the communist state to a magic counterculture of students, artists, seekers of freedom. We were infatuated with each other and with the times.

Shortly after, the Soviets and their Warsaw Pact allies invaded Czechoslovakia to put down the Prague Spring. Anna, who was in England studying, decided to return home. I never heard from her again. Years later, I found a scrap of paper with her Prague address and kept it out of sentiment.

In December, when the streets of Prague filled with students, launching the revolution that would bring that sixties counterculture to power, I sent a telegram of congratulations to Anna's 1968 address. Ten days later I received this letter, dated December 18:

Dear Tom:

It is just fantastic that I've got a wire from you. You cannot imagine what pleasure it is to hear from the people who share the same feeling of hope and happiness with us. But, to be honest, congratulations don't belong to us—I mean our generation. It belongs to the students and young people—well, in fact, to our children.

We were silent more than anything else for 20 years and we were afraid, having had such bad experiences and a sort of common memory stretching back to 1968. That is no excuse, that is reality. Even now I am afraid in some moments.

If I speak about our silence I mean it symbolically, because we kept doing something—celebrating various sad anniversaries and being repeatedly caught by police and some of us beaten; organizing funny political jogging events; writing and signing petitions and after that, being called to the police and even being threatened that they would take our children from us (this happened to me)—in a word, we were left in fear.

All this was a great advantage for young people because they didn't worry much about our fear, they didn't share our memory. The result was they had courage.

They were terribly beaten on November 17 and even now we

do not know whether, or how many, dead students there are. But that was the last drop. Since the next morning all Prague was marching through the streets bringing flowers and candles to those places and crying when we saw blood on the pavement and on the walls of houses.

There were moments we were extremely frightened when the police appeared and we were shouting various slogans to encourage ourselves. I remember the moment we were crossing the bridge (and) seeing the police troops coming across neighboring bridges. People couldn't stand the fear and started running. We thickened and thickened while rhythmically running and shouting, "Stop being afraid"—and we were very afraid.

Now we are full of hope and we know it is our best chance. We have to win, otherwise I think I could not have survived it any more. There was too much disappointment after 1968.

I'm sorry you cannot see it—so much enthusiasm, happiness, there is also very much fun and a lot of practical jokes. Prague is all papered and labeled with both serious and funny slogans. Students work on it days and nights. They do a lot of work and we all must succeed. Keep your fingers crossed for us, please, we will still need it.

I do not live at that address any longer, but I was lucky to get your wire. I got married and changed my name to Cerna. I gave birth to two daughters, Teresa and Katerina, I got divorced and now I live with my daughters and a dog.

I told my girls how enthusiastic you were when I met you here, and how kind you were to help me to get to England . . . You may not know that I didn't stay there long because of that Russian invasion. I left England immediately, never to come back, not even as a tourist. That was the time I realized that I wasn't ever able to leave my country, however stupid and bad and cowardly, and . . . and . . . it was. But now we hope everything will change and we will not be ashamed to say we are Czech.

I will always be very happy to hear from you again, or to see you again. I'm afraid it is too far, but you would like our revolution, which is given attributes like "kind," "calm," and "velvet." In a way, I am sorry that you live so happily not to have any revolutions.

Love, Anna

33

As a Father, I Cannot Stand It

From a speech delivered in Los Angeles, January 12, 1991

◆   ◆   ◆

WHAT IS HAPPENING reminds me of the final hours of the Cuban missile crisis in 1961, when so many Americans felt so very vulnerable as the deadline neared, and we knew not whether the gods above had decided on war or compromise. Now it is more vivid, because we see the faces of those who will die, the villages that will be crushed, the desert that will be a cemetery. This killing is so very scheduled, which is what entrances us, horrifies us, can make us feel so helpless.

And that is why protest now is so important. It is literally now or never, time to speak out, time to reach down deep inside ourselves to find out who we really are.

I'll tell you something of who I am. Twenty-five years ago I opposed the Vietnam War, and in the process lost the understanding and support of my Marine Corps father. Like so many, our family was torn and divided by that war.

And so when I think if this coming war, the personal dynamic is reversed. I think today as a father myself, a father of a young man only six months from being old enough to die in the Persian Gulf. Like those young Americans there already, he has dreams and a future to live for. This war is not about my life but his, and his is a more important life than my own. I imagine him in that sea of earnest faces in the Gulf, and I cannot stand it.

We can do what our parents' generation did not always do for us, stand in the way of this war to save our own sons and daughters.

I cannot stand it because I thought we had learned as a nation never to be in this place again, ready to shed such innocent blood for a cause not innocent at all.

We are being stampeded to war by an administration that cannot tell us the real reason. In fact, the White House has conducted private opinion surveys to decide what reasons "work" in arousing Americans to the necessary emotion.

To anyone who believes this policy makes sense, I ask them to simply review its zig-zagging madness. We supported Saddam Hussein in his war with Iran. We were silent when Saddam Hussein gassed the Kurdish people. When told by Saddam Hussein that he was thinking of action against Kuwait, our ambassador suggested we would not complain too loudly. When he invaded, we rallied the world to economic sanctions. Then we declared them ineffective. Where is the logic in this lurching towards war?

If the purpose is to deter further Iraqi aggression, we do not need to start an offensive war. If we want to stop Saddam's nuclear bomb, our experts say we have years, perhaps a decade, before that threat becomes a reality. If we want to stop megalomaniacs from projecting their power, why are there so many evils we silently accept? If economic sanctions worked against South African and Poland, why won't these more stringent sanctions work against Iraq?

The lack of answers will foster the suspicion that we are risking these innocent lives not for sacred principle but to support two monarchies, Saudi Arabia and Kuwait, who don't believe in democracy, who don't believe in a free press, who don't believe in women's rights, but do believe in gouging us at the gas pump whenever possible, and who want American soldiers to shed blood to keep their profits flowing.

And who benefits here at home? Let's start at the top. It is scandalous that the American media has said not a word about President Bush's own oil company having built Kuwait's offshore wells.

This same president does nothing about our shameful waste of energy. Our automobile fleet gets nineteen miles per gallon on the average today. If we increased that to twenty two, it would eliminate our country's need for George Bush's oil wells in Kuwait and Iraq as well. If we raised the standard to thirty, we could do without Persian Gulf oil altogether. But the president is more willing to commit 400,000 Americans to risk their lives for the petroleum status quo than to fight for serious energy conservation and end the power of anyone to use oil as a political weapon.

So let us say that to ask why, to be willing to wait, are not signs of weakness but of wisdom.

And let us wish that someday the bravery of our troops can be channeled to a greater cause. Many Americans are ready to sacrifice for our children, for a better world, for democratic principles, for an end to energy dependency. But that this administration would spill the blood we gave our children to protect America's right to gas-guzzling cars is an abomination we cannot suffer, do not deserve, and must not allow in silence.

34

An Exiled Son of Santiago

The Nation *Web site, April 4, 2005*

Not long after I wrote this essay, the people of Chile fittingly chose Michelle Bachelet as their president, a democratic rebuke to decades of U.S.-supported dictatorship. The lessons of exile grow more important in our globalized world.

◆　　◆　　◆

"Everywhere, begin the remembering."
—from a mural by Francisco Letelier, Venice, California

AT A BACKYARD PARTY in the counterculture community of Venice, California, a few years ago I met a young artist named Francisco Letelier. He had the long black hair of a warrior or musician, a classic Roman face and the muscular physique of a bodybuilder. His name, however, is what inevitably defines him, and what drew me to the event. Francisco—whose friends called him Pancho—is the son of Orlando Letelier, the Chilean diplomat murdered along with his assistant, Ronni Karpen, in Washington, D.C., in 1976 by agents of Augusto Pinochet's dictatorship. The lives of then-17-year-old Francisco, his mother Isabel and his three teenage brothers were ruptured permanently when anti-Castro Cubans, dispatched by the Chilean secret police, detonated a bomb attached to Letelier's family car.

Though at the time I was immersed in California politics, the bombing jolted me viscerally, as it did thousands of opponents of Pinochet worldwide. The killings had taken place on Embassy Row, not a faraway Third World capital. Letelier, his assistant, and her husband, Michael Moffitt, who alone survived the blast, worked at the D.C.-based Institute for Policy Studies, a respected center that served thousands of civil rights and peace activists. The terrorist killings by agents of the Chilean directorate of national intelligence (DINA) sent the message that no one in progressive movements was safe.

Now, years later, in Francisco's backyard, I wondered how he had coped. For any teenager, the father is God. When that God dies at the hands of sinister powers, how does one build an identity faithful to that fallen God yet also grow to independence on one's own terms?

In this country, the parallels are with the children of the assassinated Kennedy brothers and the descendants of Martin Luther King Jr. and Malcolm X. The transition is turbulent, never ending. Orlando Letelier himself was a complex person, a man called to politics whose soul was that of a poet and musician. Francisco Letelier, while called to politics by his father's death, has his father's cultural sensibility, choosing art and poetry to process the tragedy, from political murals to poetic works that universalize suffering, beauty and indigenous cultures. At the same time, he represents his father's name at rallies, in persuasive op-ed articles for the *Los Angeles Times*, by yearly vigils at the site of his father's murder and by human rights solidarity work. The nature of Francisco's art and politics arises from the exile condition as well as from what it means to be his father's son.

Like many multicultural Americans, Francisco's exile status is personally present on a daily basis while invisible to the mainstream Americans around him. He must learn to live in a country whose political culture forgets and forgives the crimes of a U.S.-backed dictatorship that killed his father. As one of some one million Chileans who left their country during the Pinochet regime (one-tenth of the population at the time) he is a member of what some call "the harvest of empire" or "the fruits of war," an immigrant populace that is changing the complexion and future of America. It is a question whether such exiles—trapped between memory and amnesia, between psychic integration and a splitting of the self—will be assimilated into the superpower ethos that distances so many Americans from the world or whether they will become a binational force of conscience and human rights.

In pursuing these questions, I recently visited Francisco in Santiago when he was visiting his mother, Isabel Morel de Letelier, and his Congressman-brother, Juan Pablo Letelier. Together we met with human rights advocates and journalists who have been investigating the Pinochet case for three decades.

Chile itself has changed, at least on the surface, since the dictatorship was rejected by popular referendum in 1989. It is considered a modern country, which means much of its citizenry enjoys the perks of a consumer culture while the society itself downplays its bitter past. But most of the population has relatives who disappeared, were tortured and killed or managed to survive imprisonment. A majority strongly backs the civilian democratic process, but about one-third remains pro-Pinochet or in denial of the past. Strong pressures are exerted against punitive tribunals for fear of reopening divisions beneath the surface. A Socialist Party candidate, Michelle Bachelet, could be elected president this spring on a platform reflecting this surface reconciliation. Chileans know that her father was tortured and died in a Pinochet prison and that she herself was jailed, tortured and exiled, but Bachelet says little of her experience. She served as Chile's defense minister in 2002, becoming a symbol of stable reconciliation. Her presidency would be more moderate than those of her neighbors in Brazil, Argentina and Uruguay. But first she must win the endorsement of the center-left majority coalition, then defeat a right-wing, pro-Pinochet candidate in the general election.

Yet the trauma of the 1976 murders on Embassy Row is far from over for the political generation of the Leteliers, and the case itself continues to erupt in surprising ways. The week before I arrived, for example, the former head of Pinochet's secret police, Gen. Manuel Contreras, was imprisoned a second time for his role in political assassinations. Only a few years before, human rights lawyers in Europe and Chile miraculously pierced Pinochet's immunity as a former head of state, leaving him trapped in a permanent web of criminal investigations. What began as a utopian quest has established new precedents in global human rights jurisprudence, with the Letelier-Karpen murders as the touchstone.

The U.S. government is silent these days about the terrorist acts committed not far from the White House in 1976. With pressure from the families and public opinion, the Justice Department successfully pursued the case against five anti-Castro agents in 1978 but three Chilean DINA agents who were indicted were never extradited to face trail. The Clinton administration later disclosed previously classified official documents that shed new light on American collaboration with Pinochet and Operation Condor, a Pinochet-inspired collaboration of secret police units from Chile, Brazil, Argentina, Bolivia, Uruguay and Paraguay. Today the Letelier-Karpen case is technically "open" at the Justice Department, but not actively pursued.

Perhaps the fact that George H. W. Bush happened to be CIA director during the period of the Letelier-Moffitt murders and the Condor conspiracy, and Donald Rumsfeld secretary of defense has something to do with the present administration's inactivity. Immediately after the Letelier-Moffitt assassinations, Bush (senior) authorized a CIA disinformation campaign planting stories that blamed the killings on left-wing radicals seeking to make a martyr of Letelier. In addition, the U.S. government has attempted to both deny and distance itself from the Condor project, but memos classified for twenty-five years suggest a greater CIA involvement than previously acknowledged. For example, as early as 1974 the CIA knew that Condor assassins were killing nonviolent political opponents. More documents remain under wraps at the Justice Department, on the pretext that they would have value to the prosecution in any future case against Pinochet.

Also having reason to worry might be America's new spy chief, John Negroponte, who served in the State Department in Vietnam during Operation Phoenix, the assassination program targeting Vietcong and Vietcong sympathizers, and as ambassador to Honduras during the notorious death-squad period of the 1980s. In other words, the Pinochet papers, when and if fully disclosed, may illuminate links in a thirty-year policy of tolerating, even promoting, torture and "renditions" as a matter of U.S. policy, not the excessive behavior of a few "bad apples."

While their feelings are bittersweet, the Letelier family can claim some satisfaction as the case continues to unfold. At dinner in Santiago with

Francisco, his brother Juan Pablo and his mother, Isabel, the family was firm in its desire that Pinochet "play the piano," as Juan Pablo put it, using an expression for fingerprinting. For the historical record, Juan Pablo said, it is crucial that Pinochet be convicted as both a "dictator and a thief." Ironically, Juan Pablo, an official in his father's Socialist Party and a four-term congressman, plays an overseeing role in a new investigation of Pinochet's secret deposits of million of dollars in the Washington, D.C.-based Riggs Bank.

The Riggs scandal was uncovered by U.S. Senate investigators using the money-laundering provision of the Patriot Act, added by Democratic Senators Paul Sarbane and Carl Levin, which requires enhanced due diligence and criminalizes the hiding of stolen money in American bank accounts. The Pinochet investigation thus may become a case study of hidden linkages in U.S. policy between militarism and economic privatization. It was not dictatorial megalomania alone that drove Pinochet, but violent opposition to the socialist policies of the elected government of Salvador Allende.

If Francisco manifests the artistic side of his father's personality, Juan Pablo has managed to follow in Orlando's political footsteps, becoming a key leader and strategist in his father's party. It has been a painful journey for Juan Pablo, who, like Francisco, wears his hair at shoulder length. The brothers are very close and, in fact, Francisco was in Chile partly to join Juan Pablo in a wilderness expedition in Chile's south. I learned more about Juan Pablo in an interview with the journalist Monica Gonzales, who consented to see me at the suggestion of Francisco. Gonzales is a torture victim and one of the few journalists to pursue the Pinochet investigation since the coup on Chile's September 11, in 1973.

Gonzales's emotions and tears cascaded freely across her face as she discussed the experience of evil in her small, crowded office at the weekly journal *Siete + 7*. I noticed during our discussion that Francisco was quiet. This was the first occasion they had met, and it appeared that Monica and he shared a bond across time and space, perhaps a familiarity grown from common grief. Monica said "it's finally time to talk about the people who are still alive, the living dead who never recover from torture but walk the streets, and the numbed children who never speak." She had contacted Juan Pablo when he returned to Chile in 1982 after graduate training in East Berlin and Mexico. Francisco would return one year later. The dictatorship was in power, but faltering. "I contacted Juan Pablo," Monica said, "because I wanted to find out what had happened to the sons of all those murdered fathers." They unexpectedly talked for six hours. Juan Pablo told her of sitting on a bench in Europe at Christmastime, shortly after his father's death. He was watching families celebrate the season inside their happy homes. He had hit bottom, could not speak. When he told Monica of this experience, she said, he cried, "enough for all his brothers. We both cried about the silenced crying of those years."

Francisco and his brothers were exiled three days after his birth in 1959. Orlando was fired from a research position in the copper industry for supporting Salvador Allende's unsuccessful campaign for the presidency. The Letelier family retreated to friendly Venezuela, and from there, Orlando made his way to the Inter-American Development Bank and American University in Washington, D.C.. Letelier was an intellectual, a singer, an artist and, only reluctantly, a politician and diplomat. The revolutionary times dictated his destiny. Maurice Zeitlin, now a UCLA sociology professor who in 1965 was a Ford Foundation researcher in Chile, recalls the fervor as Chileans excitedly experienced the rise of "a genuine, mass-based revolutionary left." Zeitlin recalls that "Allende was always the unifier, and he never wavered from the idea of a peaceful transition to socialism." The streets seemed perpetually filled with militant hope.

Like Luiz Inácio Lula da Silva in Brazil a generation later, Allende ran four times before being elected in 1970 with a 36.2 percent plurality, including 75 percent of the working-class vote, and was confirmed as president by the Chilean Parliament. Zeitlin, whose daughter happened to date Francisco in his exile years, remembers passionate arguments in the 1960s over Chilean coffee in Santiago about the prospects of the "peaceful road." The Chileans he knew, many of whom became national leaders later, insisted that their country was "the England of Latin America," peaceful and constitutional. "They thought they were special," he recalls, even though there was the chilling example of the 1967 CIA-supported military coup in Greece, another nation claiming a democratic heritage. The deposed Greek leader Andreas Papandreou, Allende's counterpart, "wrote in his memoir that he had understood the possibility of a coup in his own country intellectually, but not emotionally," says Zeitlin. "In Greece, there were no safe houses, no contingencies to protect the leaders, and it was the same in Chile."

Orlando Letelier, a committed member of Allende's Popular Unity coalition, flew from Washington to Santiago after Allende's 1970 election, and offered his services. Orlando had unique leadership qualities, among them a sophisticated grasp of the complexities of American politics that was rare among Latin American revolutionaries. President Allende therefore sent Letelier back to Washington as Chile's new ambassador, where Isabel and the boys (Christian, 18, Jose, 17, Francisco, 17, and Juan Pablo, 16) adjusted to embassy life. Sheridan Circle, where Orlando soon would be killed, was their backyard. Francisco and Juan Pablo opened their first savings accounts at Riggs Bank. Their schoolmates included Donald Rumsfeld's daughter, Marcy, and James Baker's daughter Patricia. Even today, Francisco has a memento of an Easter egg hunt at the White House, signed "with warmest regards, Pat Nixon." The daughter of another Chilean official, Pascal Bonnefoy, who attended parties with Francisco, remembers the time as one when she lost the Spanish language "and almost was a gringa." Instead, Pascal would return eventually to Chile to become one of its most respected human rights investigators.

But beneath the diplomatic veneer, the wheels of destruction were turning. Declassified White House documents expose President Nixon ranting that he wanted to "smash that son of a bitch Allende" by a military coup or by "making the economy scream" or both. The International Telephone and Telegraph (ITT) company was scheming with the CIA and White House to overthrow Allende. The Nixon government poured millions into *El Mercurio*, a savagely anti-Allende newspaper. Weapons and funds were passed by the CIA to plotters who eventually killed Defense Minister General Rene Schneider, who was pledged to protect the legally elected Allende government.

As the crisis intensified, in 1972 Orlando Letelier was called back by the beleaguered Allende to serve, it turned out briefly, as minister of foreign relations, then defense. In the latter role, he supervised Augusto Pinochet, then head of the army. The young Francisco, back again in Santiago, was just finishing eighth grade. He vividly recalls Pinochet standing "in my father's study, the Andes visible in the windows behind him. I remember that he looked strangely disconcerted."

When the tanks, troops and bombs were finally unleashed against Allende's offices on September 11, 1973 (a day that one U.S. military adviser called "our D-Day" and Chile's "day of destiny"), Orlando Letelier was arrested at his own defense ministry. With others, he was immediately dispatched to Dawson Island, a frozen enclave hundreds of miles off the southern Chilean coast. A light poncho was his protection from the cold. While Francisco and his brother had "adolescent nightmares" about their father who never came home, Isabel made daily rounds to ministries to advocate for her husband's release. She even met Pinochet, and remembers him suddenly exploding in rage during her brief appeal for Orlando's return.

At the time of his father's deportation, Francisco was living in the shadow of Huelen Hill, the spot where the city of Santiago was founded. Eight times the Mapuche Indians destroyed the Spanish foothold at the site, and though never conquered, they were driven back across the Bio-Bio River. As a boy Francisco would climb the hill and imagine the Mapuche warriors and the mixed-blood Chileans who came after them. Orlando and Isabel once sat near that hill and imagined having their children. After the coup Francisco continued to wander the old fortifications and try to "imagine my nation." Years later he wrote a poetic vision of a new gathering on Huelen Hill, a reverse colonization in which all the far-flung exiles of the Americas would come home to

Take the streets
Help the lost children
Hidden on corners
Hold the children
Make the world
Everywhere begin the remembering
Of places we will make our monuments.

While his father was missing, Francisco remembers watching Chilean bodies floating in Santiago's central river and experiencing the impact of the military takeover in his school. Eventually, without telling his mother, he stopped attending classes. "For her, it was 'well, at least the kids are still going to school.' That thought still gave her some peace of mind. So I would stay home when she was out or just go over to my grandmother's. It was a little easier for us than it was for our mother because we were still discovering the world for ourselves at this point. Our mother's world, though, had been completely destroyed."

After one year of this surreal existence, vigorous Venezuelan diplomacy resulted in the sudden release of Letelier from Dawson Island on the condition that he immediately leave Chile. The family once again began resettling in Caracas, but then Orlando Letelier decided to head for Washington, at the proposal of an American writer, Saul Landau. In 1975 Letelier took a position with the Institute for Policy Studies (IPS), where Landau worked at the time, and plunged into writing, speaking and lobbying the U.S. Congress and European governments against the Pinochet regime. He soon became the leading voice of the Chilean resistance. According to John Dinges, who has been following the case for thirty years, Orlando "was on the short list of possible presidents in a post-dictatorial Chile."

On June 8, 1976, Henry Kissinger met with Pinochet in Santiago and, according to a declassified document, told the Chilean dictator that "we are sympathetic with what you are trying to do here. I think that the previous government was headed toward communism. We wish your government well." While Kissinger gingerly expressed hope that Pinochet would take cosmetic steps to deflect congressional pressures over human rights violations, he reinforced Pinochet's paranoia, telling him that "my evaluation is that you are victim of all left-wing groups around the world." Pinochet's director of secret police, General Contreras, would give formal orders that very month to prepare Orlando Letelier's assassination. Now, over tea with Kissinger, the dictator probed twice about Letelier, complaining that Letelier was providing "false information" all over Washington. Kissinger said nothing in defense of Letelier, and offered general support for the dictator's government. "In my opinion, Kissinger at least unwittingly gave Pinochet the green light to kill Orlando Letelier," says Landau, now a professor in Southern California.

Three months later, on September 18, Michael Townley planted a plastic explosive on the underside of the car in the Letelier driveway in Bethesda, Maryland. Francisco was asleep just a few feet away. "Everyone in my family used the car. I had driven it to my school prom. . . . Any one of us could have turned the key."

On that morning, Landau's wife, Rebecca, who worked for several representatives on human rights issues, was among the first to witness the wreckage as she drove to work along Embassy Row. As Landau remembers, "She called me and said she'd just witnessed the most horrible accident in her life, pieces of clothes, blood, car parts everywhere in the street. A minute later we learned it was Orlando. There was hysteria at the IPS." Landau, then 40 years old, was left in charge while IPS founders Marcus Raskin and the late Richard Barnet went to the hospital with Isabel. There they learned that Ronni Karpen was injured as well, bleeding from a severed carotid artery. Landau says he "had no idea what to do, so I said, 'Lock the doors'" (to the IPS building). The FBI, which at the time was being sued for harassment and surveillance of the IPS, soon arrived, accompanied by dogs. When the agents asked who was responsible and were told "DINA," they responded, "Could you spell that name?" Landau remembers seeing Francisco and one of his brothers that day, "glazed teenagers, no idea what had happened, so incredibly traumatized, between grief and incomprehension."

Landau suggested Raskin and Barnet call a news conference to announce that Isabel would take Orlando's place. They agreed. She would remain at IPS working on the Letelier-Moffitt case and human rights issues until the early 1990s, when she finally returned to Santiago.

How does a mother of four sons heal her family after such a catastrophe? Isabel told me at her home in Santiago that her philosophy of parenting was threefold: first, to have "cool hands" to relieve fevers and make nightmares go away; second, a "burning heart" to love one's children "no matter what because they are immigrants who come to your heart;" and third, "open arms to release them." She soldiered on, pursuing

Pinochet and Condor, raising her sons admirably by all accounts. When one of the DINA conspirators in her husband's assassination pleaded guilty in a Washington proceeding, he asked Isabel if he might be forgiven. She did so spontaneously, she said, since he had acknowledged his role and was accepting punishment. It was a revealing Catholic act on her part, leading a surprised Marcus Raskin to comment that he "always knew you were a Buddhist." When I asked the Leteliers at dinner about their approach to forgiveness, Francisco offered only that "thirty years of action has made forgiveness more possible."

Shortly after his father's murder. Francisco began painting murals with the Orlando Letelier Muralist Brigade, formed with solidarity committees around the United States. He enrolled at the California College of Arts and Crafts, then at the University of California, Berkeley, and concentrated in ethnic studies. He traveled as a muralist to Nicaragua in 1980.

Then he returned to Chile in 1983, living with his brother Juan Pablo. They participated in clandestine demonstrations that were repressed by the police. An exhibit of Francisco's artistic work on the disappeared, sponsored by the French Institute, was shut down. Then he became very sick with hepatitis and decided to return to the U.S. for health reasons and graduate school. The years 1985 to 1988 found him in the fine arts program at UCLA, traveling to Nicaragua with muralists, doing the art for Jackson Browne's *World in Motion* album and working on murals with incarcerated youth in L.A. County.

Then his exile's inner life took a strange turn. He married and had a son with a woman whose background shadowed his own. Monica Mercedes Pérez Jiménez was the beautiful daughter of Marita Lorenz, a former lover of Fidel Castro at the beginning of the Cuban revolution, who later turned into a CIA agent. Several years after the affair with Fidel ended, the agency sent Marita back to Havana to seduce the Cuban leader and murder him. As the story is passed down, Fidel willingly met his old flame, looked directly at her and said, "So they've sent you here to kill me." Whether the line reawakened Marita's passion is unclear, but it terminated the assassination plot. That was only the mother's side of Monica's world. Her father was the dictator of Venezuela, Marcos Pérez Jiménez. Whatever was pulling

Francisco, whose father was killed by anti-Castro Cubans under Chilean direction, toward this daughter of a dictator's CIA wife with a love/hate relationship with Fidel Castro, it finally waned. But not before the couple birthed a child, Matias Orlando, in 1991, on the very same day that Francisco was inaugurating a mural, coincidentally called *Inheritance*, with incarcerated gang members in L.A. County.

In the following decade Francisco continued with murals, ranging from a 1997 showing in Santiago's contemporary art museum to a giant "ring of peace" done with artists from Belfast's divided East and West neighborhoods. Two attempts to move back to Chile were bogged down by unresolved custody issues over Matias. In 1997 Francisco became a permanent resident of Venice, working on murals and beginning to write articles for the *Los Angeles Times* and elsewhere after Pinochet's arrest in London in 1998. His American roots were deepened by the birth of a second son, Salvador Nahuel, with Kayren Pace in Santa Monica. By my personal observation, both the sons are lively, handsome inheritors of the Letelier heritage.

Francisco lives today on the same property as his brother Christian, "the most First World of my sons," says Isabel. Christian is a marine biologist with an intenational law degree, a handsome Hollywood extra and a volunteer with Heal the Bay. Another brother, Jose—"a good student, very political," says Isabel—lives on remote Easter Island, engaged in ecotourism. Juan Pablo, with a wife and three children, remains in Chile.

Judy Baca, the famed Chicano artist and director of an art center in Venice, has observed the arc of Francisco's work since the 1980s. In her first memory, he was very politicized, but she adds, "Candidly, I thought Francisco was kind of torn" about the artistic direction he wanted to take, perhaps fatigued by the permanent need to be Orlando's son. He became "all buffed out, turning everybody's head," but also more deeply spiritual and indigenous. Her agency sponsored Francisco's mural on the bakery wall in Venice. Last year, Baca noticed, Francisco was producing, in her estimation, his "most impressive, remarkable" pieces, including an exhibit featuring the poncho his father wore on Dawson Island combined with declassified documents damning George H. W. Bush as CIA director.

Faviola Letelier, Orlando's sister, is lovingly seen by her nephews as the most militant member of the family. Now in her early 70s, for decades she has been a dogged human rights lawyer on behalf of her brother and other victims of Pinochet. Her erect carriage, piercing eyes and long, narrow face carry suggestions of nobility, and of what Orlando might have looked like as a grandfather. After a two-hour bus ride to the coast, I found her in a small getaway cottage near a beach that resembled Venice, California, circa the 1930s. As we strolled along the shore, her keen mind downloaded endless findings in her thirty-year campaign against Pinochet. She has been sorting the evidence, for example, that "their first idea was to kill Orlando and others with sarin gas," a chemical project pursued by Chile's army in the 1970s.

I have come, however, to ask her about exiles, her broadest passion. Affidavit by affidavit, she has been filing class-action suits demanding that the Chilean government offer reparations for the "loss of identity" and "psychological rupture" inflicted by forced emigration. She hopes that the Inter-American Commission on Human Rights will soon recognize exile as a human rights violation deserving compensation.

As we looked across the ocean at our feet, she said mournfully that "exile violates the project of life. The Greeks and Romans said it was worse than death."

Two days later, suddenly back on Venice Beach, alongside the same Pacific currents, I stopped for a closer look at Francisco's nearby mural. It features a tall, beautiful sea goddess whose umbilical cord circles the earth. The mural is beginning to decay, however, because the building is slated for removal as part of Venice's ongoing gentrification. The city may not preserve the mural for another reason, since Francisco's work is associated with the local neighborhood council, which, according to an internal City Hall memo, has "gone rouge." I have to recover the faded verses from Francisco, who e-mails them from Santiago where he has finished climbing a mountain peak in the wilds of Punto Arenas with Juan Pablo. The poem is called "Santiago Son, Becoming the Circle."

> *Look at us*
> *So fine and wild.*

Rare and undiscovered tribe,
Later on they'll talk about the way we moved,
They will.
And we will be examples of a way
So others may create a safe place within the heart
We leave behind.
Let us make a place
Where children become the mystic travelers.

35

Things Come 'Round in Mideast

Common Dreams, *July 21, 2006*

This apology was not enough, but I had to give it. I've yet to hear a word of criticism, or of surprise or praise, from my many friends in L.A.'s Jewish community.

◆   ◆   ◆

TWENTY-FIVE YEARS AGO I stared into the eyes of Michael Berman, chief operative for his congressman-brother, Howard Berman. I was a neophyte running for the California Assembly in a district that the Bermans claimed belonged to them.

"I represent the Israeli defense forces," Michael said. I thought he was joking. He wasn't. Michael seemed to imagine himself the gatekeeper protecting the Los Angeles Westside for Israel's political interests, and those of the famous Berman-Waxman machine. Since Jews represented one-third of the Democratic district's primary voters, Berman held a balance of power.

All that year I tried to navigate the district's Jewish politics. The solid historical liberalism of the Westside was a favorable factor, as was the strong support of many Jewish community leaders. But the community was moving in a more conservative direction. Some were infuriated at my sponsorship of Santa Monica's tough rent-control ordinance. Many in the organized community were suspicious of the New Left for becoming Palestinian sympathizers after the Six-Day War; they would become today's neoconservatives.

I had traveled to Israel in a generally supportive capacity, meeting officials from all parties, studying energy projects, befriending peace advocates like the writer Amos Oz. I also met with Palestinians and commented favorably on the works of Edward Said. As a result, a Berman ally prepared an anti-Hayden dossier in an attempt to discredit my candidacy with the Democratic leadership in the California state capital.

This led to the deli lunch with Michael Berman. He and his brother were privately leaning toward an upcoming young prosecutor named Adam Schiff, who later became the congressman from Pasadena. But they calculated that Schiff couldn't win without name recognition, so they were considering "renting" me the Assembly seat, Berman said. But there was one condition: that I always be a "good friend of Israel."

This wasn't a particular problem at the time. Since the 1970s I had favored some sort of two-state solution. I felt close to the local Jewish activists who descended from the labor movement and participated in the civil rights and anti–Vietnam War movements. I wanted to take up the cause of the aging Holocaust survivors against the global insurance companies that had plundered their assets.

While I believed the Palestinians had a right to self-determination, I didn't share the animus of some on the American left who questioned Israel's very legitimacy. I was more inclined toward the politics of Israel's Peace Now and those Palestinian nationalists and human rights activists who accepted Israel's pre-1967 borders as a reality to accommodate. I disliked the apocalyptic visions of the Israeli settlers I had met, and thought that even hard-line Palestinians would grudgingly accept a genuine peace initiative.

I can offer my real-life experience to the present discussion about the existence and power of an "Israel lobby." It is not as monolithic as some argue, but it is far more than just another interest group in a pluralist political world. In recognizing its diversity, distinctions must be drawn between voters and elites, between Reform and Orthodox tendencies, between the less observant and the more observant. During my ultimate 18 years in office, I received most of my Jewish support from the ranks of the liberal and less observant voters. But I also received support from conservative Jews who saw themselves as excluded by a Jewish (and Democratic) establishment.

However, all these rank-and-file constituencies were attuned to the question of Israel, even in local and state elections, and would never vote for a candidate perceived as anti-Israel or pro-Palestinian. I had to be certified "kosher," not once but over and over again.

The certifiers were the elites, beginning with rabbis and heads of the multiple mainstream Jewish organizations, especially each city's Jewish Federation. An important vetting role was held as well by the American-Israel Political Action Committee (AIPAC), a group closely associated with official parties in Israel. When necessary, Israeli ambassadors, counsels general and other officials would intervene with statements declaring someone a "friend of Israel."

In my case, a key to the "friendship issue" was the Los Angeles-based counsel general Benjamin Navon. Though politics drew us together, our personal friendship was genuine enough. I think that Benny, as he was called, wanted to pull me and my then-wife Jane Fonda into a pro-Israel stance, but he himself was an old-school labor/social democrat who personally believed in a negotiated political settlement. We enjoyed personal and intellectual time together, and I still keep on my bookshelf a wooden sculpture by his wife, of an anguished victim of violence.

The de facto Israeli endorsement would be communicated indirectly, in compliance with laws that prohibit foreign interference in an American election. We would be seen and photographed together in public. Benny would make positive public statements that could be quoted in campaign mailings. As a result, I was being declared "kosher" by the ultimate source, the region's representative of the state of Israel.

Nevertheless, throughout the spring 1982 campaign I was accused of being a left-wing madman allied to terrorism and communism. The national Democratic leader Walter Mondale commented jokingly during a local visit that I was being described as worse than Lenin. It was a wild ride.

I won the hard-fought primary by 51 percent to 45 percent. The Bermans stayed neutral. Willie Brown, Richard Alatorre and the rest of the California Democratic establishment were quietly supportive. I easily won the general election in November.

But that summer I made the mistake of my political career. The Israel Defense Forces invaded Lebanon, and Benny Navon wanted Jane and me to be supportive. It happened that I had visited the contested border in the past, witnessed the shelling of civilian Israeli homes, and interviewed Israeli and Lebanese zealots—crazies, I thought, who were preaching preventive war. I opposed cross-border rocket attacks and naively favored a demilitarized zone.

Ever curious, and aware of my district's politics, I decided we should go to the Middle East—but only as long as the Israeli "incursion," as it was delicately called, was limited to the ten-kilometer space near the Lebanese border, as a cushion against rocket fire. Benny Navon assured me that the "incursion" was limited, and would be followed by negotiations and a solution. I also made clear our opposition to the use of any fragmentation bombs in the area, and my ultimate political identification with what Israeli Peace Now would say.

There followed a descent into moral ambiguity and realpolitik that still haunts me today. When we arrived at the Israeli-Lebanon border, the game plan promised by Benny Navon had changed utterly. Instead of a localized border conflict, Israel was invading and occupying all of Lebanon—with us in tow. Its purpose was to destroy militarily the Palestinian Liberation Organization (PLO) haven in Lebanon. This had been General Ariel Sharon's secret plan all along, and I never will know with certainty whether Benny Navon had been deceived along with everyone else.

For the next few weeks, I found myself defending Israel's "right" to self-defense on its border, only to realize privately how foolish I was becoming. In the meantime, Israel's invasion was continuing, with ardent Jewish support in America.

Finally, a close friend and political advisor of mine, Ralph Brave, took me for a walk, looked into my eyes and said: "Tom, you can't do this. You have to stop." He was right, and I did. In the California Legislature, I went to work on Holocaust survivor issues while withdrawing from the bind of Israeli-Palestinian politics. When the first Palestinian intifada began, I sensed from experience that the balance of forces had changed, and that the Israeli occupation was finished. Frictions developed between me and some of my Israeli and Jewish friends when I suggested that Israel must make a peace deal immediately or accept a worse deal later.

It is still painful and embarrassing to describe these events of nearly twenty-five years ago, but with Israel today again bombing Lebanon and Israeli officials bragging about "rolling back the clock by twenty years" and reconfiguring the Middle East, I feel obliged to speak out against history repeating.

How do I read today's news through the lens of the past?

What I fear is that the "Israeli lobby" is working overtime to influence American public opinion on behalf of Israel's military effort to "roll back the clock" and "change the map" of the region, going far beyond issues like prisoner exchange.

What I fear is that the progress of the American peace movement against the Iraq war will be diverted and undermined, at least for now, by the entry of Israel from the sidelines into the center of the equation.

What I fear is the rehabilitation of the discredited U.S. neoconservative agenda to ignite a larger war against Hamas, Hezbollah, Syria and Iran. The neoconservatives' 1996 "Clean Break" memo advocated that Israel "roll back" Lebanon and destabilize Syria in addition to overthrowing Saddam Hussein. An intellectual dean of the neoconservatives, Bernard Lewis, has long advocated the "Lebanonization" of the Middle East, meaning the disintegration of nation states into "a chaos of squabbling, feuding, fighting sects, tribes, regions and parties."

This divide-and-conquer strategy, a brainchild of the region's British colonizers, is already taking effect in Iraq, where the United States overthrew a secular state, installed a Shiite majority and its militias in power and now portrays itself as the only protection for Sunnis against those same Shiites. The resulting quagmire has become a justification for American troops to remain.

What I fear is trepidation and confusion among rank-and-file voters and activists, and the paralysis of politicians, especially Democrats, who last week were moving gradually toward setting a deadline for U.S. withdrawal from Iraq. The politics of the present crisis favor the Republicans and the White House in the short run. How many politicians will favor withdrawing U.S. troops from Iraq under present conditions? Isn't this Karl Rove's game plan for the November elections?

What I know is that I will not make the same mistake again. I hope that my story deepens the resolve of all those whose feelings are torn, conflicted or confused in the present. It is not being a "friend of Israel" to turn a blind eye to its never-ending occupation.

One might argue, and many Americans today might agree, that Hezbollah and Hamas started this round of war with their provocative kidnappings of Israeli soldiers. Lost in the headlines, however, is the fact that the Israelis have 9,000 Palestinian prisoners, and have negotiated prisoner swaps before. Others will blame the Islamists for incessant rocket attacks on Israel. But the roots of this virulent spiral of vengeance lie in the permanent occupation of Palestinian territories by the overconfident Israelis. As it did in 1982, Israel now admits that the war is not about prisoner exchanges or cease-fires; it is about eradicating Hezbollah and Hamas altogether, if necessary by an escalation against Syria or even Iran. It should be clear by now that the present Israeli government will never accept an independent Palestinian state, but rather harbors a colonial ambition to decide which Palestinian leaders are acceptable.

In 1982, Israel said the same thing about eliminating PLO sanctuaries in Lebanon. It was after that 1982 Israeli invasion that Hezbollah was born. I remember Israeli national security experts even taking credit for fostering Hamas and Islamic fundamentalism as safe, reclusive alternatives to Palestinian secular nationalism. I remember watching Israeli soldiers blow up Palestinian houses and carry out collective punishment because, they told me matter-of-factly, punishment is the only language that Arabs understand. Israelis are inflicting collective punishment on Lebanese civilians for the same reason today.

It is clear that apocalyptic forces, openly green-lighted by President Bush, are gambling on the impossible. They are trying to snatch victory from the jaws of defeat in Iraq through escalation in Lebanon and beyond. This is yet another faith-based initiative.

If the American people do not see through the headlines; if the Democrats turn hawkish; if the international community fails to intervene immediately, the peace movement may be sidelined to a prophetic and marginal role for the moment. But we can say the following for now: militarism and occupation cannot extinguish the force of Islamic or Arab nationalism. Billions in American tax dollars are funding the Israeli troops and bombs.

There needs to be an exit strategy. The absence of any such exit plan is the weakest element of the U.S.-Israeli campaign. Just as the White House says it plans to deploy 50,000 troops on permanent bases in an occupied Iraq, so the Israelis speak of permanently eliminating their enemies, from Gaza to Tehran. The result will be further occupation, resistance and deeper quagmire.

The immediate conflict should not become a pretext for continuing the U.S. military occupation of Iraq. American soldiers should not be stuck waist-deep in a sectarian quagmire. Congressional insistence on denying funds for permanent military bases is a vital first step. Otherwise we will witness a tacit alliance between Israel and the United States to dominate the Middle East militarily.

Most important, Americans must not be timid in speaking up, as I was twenty-five years ago. Silence is consent to occupation.

36

A Top Cuban Leader Thinks Out Loud

Truthdig, August 29, 2006

We will never know, unfortunately, what might have happened if our government followed a policy toward the Cuban Revolution rooted in Franklin Roosevelt's Good Neighbor policies that pledged nonintervention, withdrew American occupation forces from the Caribbean, and accepted the nationalization of U.S. oil companies in Mexico and Bolivia. Instead, Cuba has become the focal point of the longest-running U.S. embargo in the entire fifty years of my writings. I first visited the island in January 1968 and was privileged to speak with Fidel Castro. Perhaps because of Che Guevara's recent capture and assassination, he was deeply concerned about black revolutionaries inside the United States and thought they should organize a united front instead of adopting a Third World model of guerrilla war. I didn't return to Cuba for twenty-five years, visiting again in 2000 and 2006. After all they have gone through, I think of the Cubans as having the greatest wealth of experience of all those countries combating Yanqui imperialism over the years, and believe it to be an absolute tragedy that Cuban views are rarely heard in the U.S. debate over Latin America. In addition to the embargo on trade and travel to Cuba, there is another embargo, one that prevents Americans from learning from or about the Cuban experience. One of Cuba's most important political leaders, Ricardo Alarcon, is trying to adapt Marxism to Cuba's current set of circumstances. He seems to be inching toward resurrecting a social-democratic model, and a defense of reformism, so ridiculed by Leninist parties of old. I was particularly struck by Alarcon's disagreement with the orthodox revolutionary notion that capitalism cannot be reformed. One wonders if the U.S. government could tolerate such a peaceful evolution in the Cuban future. Judging from the U.S. posture toward the elected pro-socialist government in Venezuela, coexistence still may be a long time coming.

◆   ◆   ◆

"LET'S TRY TO IMAGINE what Karl Marx would be doing today." It was Sunday, May 21, and my host posing the question was Ricardo Alarcon, president of the Cuban National Assembly. It was Alarcon's sixty-ninth birthday, and I was having difficulty understanding why he had pressed me to fly down for a visit. The purpose was nothing more than "two old guys talking," according to his daughter Maggie, a thirty-something single mom and formidable interpreter of Cuba to many North Americans.

Looking back today, I don't know whether or not Alarcon already knew that his longtime comrade Fidel was diagnosed as needing serious surgery. The question would become a "state secret," at Castro's wish. Alarcon is third in line to succeed Fidel after Raul Castro, although it is more likely Alarcon will blend into a collective transitional team.

The prospect of three days' conversation with Ricardo Alarcon reflecting on his long revolutionary experience was too important to put off, and our interviews may be of greater value during the current rampant and reckless speculation over Fidel's status. Few individuals alive have the range of Alarcon's experience, from being a Havana student leader during the Cuban Revolution to Cuba's United Nations ambassador (1965–78 and 1990–92) to foreign minister (1992–93) and National Assembly president since 1993. And so we sat at a seaside restaurant on his birthday with daughter Maggie and his advisor, Miguel Alvarez. A Venezuelan cargo ship passed just offshore.

"I think Marx would be asking what are we doing about all the millions today who are protesting for peace and justice," said Alarcon in answer to his question. In a recent essay on "Marx after Marxism" he argued that Marxists should begin to see the world anew. Scoffing at neoconservatives who embrace the end of Marxism (and the end of history itself), Alarcon also emphasizes the need for "self-critical reflection on our side as well." In effect, he is proposing a return to the original spirit of Marx before the twentieth-century revolutions in his name. That original Marx organized an early transnational labor movement, with the central demand the eight-hour day, and wrote more theoretical works on nineteenth-century capitalism. According to Alarcon, that earlier Marx never meant a science-based, inevitable march to socialism based on some objective truth revealed through communist parties. That Marx was a practical revolutionary who himself famously declared "with all naturalness," Alarcon points out, "I am not a Marxist."

For Alarcon and the Cubans, history always has been contingent, subject to human will and unexpected developments, rather than an unfolding of the inevitable. After Cuba's decades of dependency on the Soviet Union during the Cold War, which caused a degree of "subordination" to Soviet interests and "reinforced dogmatism," Alarcon calls for active exploration of new trends in global capitalism and its oppositional movements. "Old dogmatists are incapable of appreciating new possibilities in the revolutionary movement," he says.

All the talk of the United States becoming a sole superpower "falls to pieces with its bogging down in Iraq" and the derailment of its neoliberal agenda for Latin America, Alarcon believes.

He identifies new obstacles facing capitalist growth. Every twenty-five years a population equivalent to the whole planet's numbers in Marx's time is born. Alarcon believes climate changes are irreversible, forests are being transformed into deserts, cities becoming uninhabitable and, as a result, an environmental challenge to capitalism has arisen which requires rethinking of Marxist political economy.

Alarcon revises the Marxist (and Leninist) conceptions of the nineteenth-century proletariat accordingly. Today there are growing numbers of those from different stations of life "who do not conform, are unsatisfied and rebel." "For the first time, anti-capitalist malaise is manifested, simultaneously and everywhere, in advanced countries and those left behind, and is not limited to the proletariat and other exploited sectors." And so "a diverse group, multicolored, in which there is no shortage of contradictions and paradoxes, grows in front of the dominant system."

"It is not yet the rainbow that announces the end of the storm," Alarcon says, warning that the diverse movements lack a common theory, are marked by spontaneity more often than organization, and need to develop further without either sectarian factionalism or becoming carried away.

He pauses, points an index finger for emphasis, and tells me "the most important task for the Latin American left" is to reelect President Luiz Inácio Lula da Silva in Brazil. Having met with leftists highly critical of fiscal moderation in power, Alarcon says that "notwithstanding his faults, if Lula is defeated, all of Latin America will be worse off." This advice may not sit well with some radical advocates of Latin American revolution, but Alarcon takes a longer view. The recent nationalist electoral wave in Latin America—Brazil, Argentina, Venezuela, Uruguay, Chile, and a near success in Mexico—inevitably brings dilemmas of governance to the forefront. But for Alarcon and Cuba, the overall changes in Latin America further a benign result, the full integration of Cuba into Latin America after decades of Cold War antagonisms. The permanent embargo by the United States makes the Cubans especially wary of any reversals in the continental process, as the defeat of Lula in the October 1 election would represent.

Alarcon is pragmatic. He believes in the Cuban philosophy that "the duty of the revolutionary is to make the revolution," that it must be a "heroic creation." But he is aware, perhaps painfully, that revolutions cannot be "imprinted or copied" and that the "mandates" of mass movements like those that have elected Lula must be respected. "There is no alternative in Brazil. The guys who were mad at me for saying this went to meet with the landless movement representatives in Brazil, and they told them the same thing."

Continuing at a dinner conversation, Alarcon opined that there should be "many forms of socialism," depending on the needs of different countries and movements. Even the social-democratic parties, the historical rivals of the European communist parties, have an important role to play today, he said. "I hope they go through the same sort of introspection we have," Alarcon said, referring to the tendency of the moderate socialist parties to cut social programs and "tail" after U.S. military and economic policies. "I would go further," he said. "I don't believe that capitalism cannot be reformed. The Great Society in your country is an example."

Alarcon seems to be hinting at a role for revolutionaries in shaping a clear alternative to global neoliberalism, one pushed in the streets by social movements and eventually resulting in a reform of capitalism like the New Deal on a global basis. Differing with some earlier views of Third World liberation, he sees a crucial role for activists and movements inside the North American colossus itself. Whereas earlier Marxists argued that unionized workers were a "privileged aristocracy" benefiting from the exploitation of the Third World, he says, "they are not any longer an aristocracy. If you go to North American workers and tell them they are an aristocracy, they will say you are crazy." He points to the 1999 Seattle protests against the World Trade Organization, in which labor called for "workers of the world to unite." Marx, he says, would be "very interested in North American workers losing jobs to India" and what that means for workers' movements.

His point is that "the Third World [now] penetrates the First, as dramatically illustrated by the current immigration controversies, rooted as they are in the historic patterns of capitalism needing cheap labor and resources and impoverished workers needing jobs. The Empire harvests its own internal opposition from the May Day 2006 immigrant marches inside the U.S. to the growth of Islamic rage inside the ghettos of East London or housing projects on the edge of Paris.

"To free the immigrants from their exploitation becomes essential to the emancipation of the workers in the developed countries," those who are undermined by cheap immigrant labor. "One must help these two [groups of workers] to converge," both to avoid an upsurge of racism and forge the basis of majority coalitions favoring reforms like a global living wage as the alternative to neoliberalism's notorious "race to the bottom."

What is interesting about these words of a top Cuban leader, spoken freely and without reserve, is how far they diverge from the stereotypes of Cuba as a gray, thought-controlled Marxist dictatorship. Cuba is not a free society by measurements like multiple parties, but Cuba's people, from Alarcon to the neighborhoods, are more conversant about trends in the United States than Americans are about Cuba. The ever-tightening U.S. embargo has boomeranged into a dangerous narrowing of American thinking, demonstrated in recent weeks by one hallucination after another. For example, Senator Mel Martinez, a Florida Republican, was seen on television several weeks ago opining that Fidel was already dead. The streets of Miami filled with cheering Cuban exiles with no way to influence the island. According to the July 6, 2006 edition of the *Los Angeles Times*, the "most obvious interest [in Castro's passing] comes from the gambling and tourist industries," which were run off the island in 1960. One Florida-based developer's master plan envisions "moving out all Cubans currently living in Havana" and replacing them with Miami exiles. The U.S. government is constantly updating its official "transition plan" to restore both free markets and the Miami exiles, with the emphasis on "disruption of an orderly succession strategy," according to the Congressional Research Service (August 23, 2005). Eighty million U.S. dollars was recently budgeted to support Cuba's opposition groups. On August 2, 2006 the *Miami Herald* reported, "There are no plans to reach out," declared White House spokesman Tony Snow after Fidel was hospitalized.

The notion of opening a dialogue with an accomplished diplomat like Ricardo Alarcon is completely out of the question. The Helms-Burton Act forbids any negotiation or loosening of the embargo if Raul Castro remains in power after Fidel.

Voices of realism like the head of the Organization of American States (OAS), Jose Miguel Insulza, say "there's no transition, and it's not your country" to prepare a transition for (Reuters, May 23, 2006). "It just drives the Bush people crazy," says one former diplomat, referring to the fact that Cuba hasn't collapsed in accord with neoconservative wishful thinking.

The fact is that Cubans will not rise up to welcome a mass influx of mostly white, revenge-oriented exiles from Miami backed by U.S. arms. The neocon analogy with the so-called "captive nations" of Eastern Europe doesn't fit. Despite all the Cuban people's legitimate criticisms of their government, it remains their government and they will not trade it for a U.S.-installed one. However they complain, Cubans have become more socialist in everyday life than many of them realize, as seen in their common acts of solidarity, their response to the Elian Gonzales showdown, their educational achievements, their health care and their social safety nets. They hardly lack for world support and, in Venezuela, have found a solid source of oil and a continental opportunity for their legions of doctors and teachers. ("In the 1960s, we only had a revolutionary ideology to export, but now we have valuable human capital," one Cuban intellectual told me.)

A persistent interest of mine is why Cuba seems to be the only country in the world without street gangs. There certainly is a black market in contraband goods, but nothing like the *pandilleras* found everywhere else in the Americas. Part of the reason is an extraordinary network of 28,000 social workers who persistently act on the belief that "some morality remains in everyone," as opposed to the "superpredator" theories popular among the neoconservatives.

It seems evident that the Cuban people want reform of their socialist state if and when Fidel passes on, and obviously not the "regime change" anticipated by the Miami Cubans and their Washington, D.C., patrons. They want a peaceful process controlled by Cubans, not by foreign powers. Who wouldn't? The question is whether the U.S. government has an interest in normalizing relations with a better, more democratic, more open but still socialist Cuba. Sadly, it is doubtful, because such a Cuba would be a triumphant example to Latin America and the world. And so the United States, along with Miami's Cubans—the armed and aggressive state within a state on American soil—hold out against the 182 nations of the world who condemn the embargo at the United Nations. In fact, our government is holding out against the desires of many of its own capitalists who hunger to invest in Cuba; even the *Wall Street Journal*, on August 2, 2006, editorialized for repeal of the 1996 Helms-Burton Act. A walk through Old Havana reveals some twenty new hotels and sixty-five restaurants, none with American investors.

Meanwhile, Ricardo Alarcon waits. He has negotiated with the United States before, in secret, during the Clinton era. He managed the Elian Gonzales crisis with aplomb. He is overseeing the case of the Cuban Five—men imprisoned in the U.S. for surveilling Miami-based exiles trying to bomb and sabotage Cuba. Alarcon is an experienced man of this world, one who could facilitate a normalization deal with the United States if ever one was on offer.

Instead, he sits for hours with the likes of me discussing the state of the revolution which he helped start over fifty years ago. He takes care of an invalid wife. He plays with his grandchild, Ricardito. He goes to dinner with a never-ending stream of visitors. He patiently answers reporters. He runs the domestic affairs of the National Assembly. He flies to international conferences.

He even finds time to read the *Port Huron Statement* line for line in English, with an updated foreword titled "The Way We Were" (in Spanish, he says, *"como eramos"*). He also reads a book of mine on religion and the environment, *The Lost Gospel of the Earth*. He did so, apparently, to prepare himself for a documentary interview for Cuba's historical archives. When the morning of the interview arrives, he is perfectly ready to ask questions comparing Vietnam with Iraq, Chicago 1968 versus Seattle 1999, or issues of environmental spirituality, without stumbling once in English. When the interview is complete, our several days together have ended as well. "Sorry, but I have to go back to government business," he apologizes, and with a *hasta luego* returns to his daily rounds. I miss him as he drives off. Maybe he knew of Fidel's diagnosis that day, maybe not.

I flew back to Los Angeles that afternoon, carrying the strange feeling that America has embargoed itself from a Cuba that it refuses to recognize. In the weeks following Fidel's surgery, according to friends who spent ten days on the island, Cuba remains quiet, stable and alert. A transition definitely seems underway, but U.S. officials may be the last to know of it.

Reflections on the 1960s

37.

The Way We Were
The Future of the Port Huron Statement

From The Port Huron Statement: The Visionary Call of the 1960s
Revolution *(Thunder's Mouth, 2005)*

◆ ◆ ◆

OUTSIDE OF PORT HURON, MICHIGAN, where a dense thicket meets the
lapping shores of Lake Huron, the careful explorer will come across rusty
and timeworn pipes and a few collapsed foundations, the last traces of the
labor camp where sixty young people finalized the *Port Huron Statement*—
the seminal "agenda for a generation" in 1962.

Some hope that our legacy will be washed out with the refuse in those
pipes. Out of sight, out of mind. For the conservative icon Robert Bork,
the *Port Huron Statement (PHS)* was considered "a document of ominous
mood and aspiration," because of his fixed certainty that, by misreading
human nature, utopian movements turn out badly. David Horowitz, a former sixties radical who turned to the hardcore right, dismisses the *PHS* as
a "self-conscious effort to rescue the communist project from its Soviet
fate." Another ex-leftist, Christopher Hitchens, sees in its pages a conservative reaction to "bigness and anonymity and urbanization," even linking
its vision to the Unabomber.[1] More progressive writers, such as Garry
Wills, E. J. Dionne, and Paul Berman, see the *PHS* as a bright moment of
reformist vision that withered due to the impatience and extremism of the
young. Excerpts of the *PHS* have been published in countless textbooks,
and an Internet search returns numerous references to "participatory
democracy," its central philosophic theme. Grassroots movements in
Argentina and Venezuela today use "participatory democracy" to describe
their popular assemblies and factory takeovers. The historian Thomas
Cahill writes that the Greek *ekklesia* was "the world's first participatory

373

democracy" and the model for the early Catholic Church, which "permitted no restrictions on participation: no citizens and non-citizens, no Greeks and non-Greeks, no patriarchs and submissive females."[2] In modern popular culture, authorship of the *PHS* has been claimed by the stoned hippie character played by Jeff Bridges in *The Big Lebowski*.

The story of the 1962 Port Huron convention has been told many times by participants and later researchers, and I will describe it here only briefly so as to focus more on the meaning of the statement itself.[3] The sixty or so young people who met in Port Huron were typically active in the fledgling civil rights, campus reform, and peace movements of the era. Some, like myself, were campus journalists, while others were active in student governments. Some walked picket lines in solidarity with the southern student sit-in movement. More than a few were moved by their religious traditions. My adolescent ambition was to become a foreign correspondent, which was a metaphor for breaking out of the suffocating apathy of the times. Instead, I found myself interviewing and reflecting on southern black dispossessed sharecroppers; students who were willing to go to jail, even die, for their cause; civil rights leader Dr. Martin Luther King Jr. as he marched outside my first Democratic convention; and candidate John Kennedy, giving his speech proposing the Peace Corps on a rainy night in Ann Arbor. I was thrilled by the times in which I lived, and I chose to help build a new student organization, the Students for a Democratic Society, rather than pursue journalism. My parents were stunned.

SDS was the fragile brainchild of Alan Haber, an Ann Arbor graduate student whose father had been a labor official during the last progressive American administration, that of President Franklin Delano Roosevelt. Al was a living link with the fading legacy of the radical left movements that had built the labor movement and the New Deal. He sensed a new spirit among students in 1960 and recruited me to become a "field secretary," which meant moving to Atlanta with my wife Casey who had been a leader of the campus sit-ins in Austin, Texas. While participating in the direct-action movement and mobilizing national support by writing and speaking on campuses, I learned that passionate advocacy, arising from personal experience, could be a powerful weapon.

Haber and other student leaders across the United States became increasingly aware of a need to connect all the issues that weighed on our generation—apathy, *in loco parentis,* civil rights, the Cold War, the atomic bomb. And so, in December 1961, at twenty-two years of age and fresh from jail as a Freedom Rider in Albany, Georgia, I was asked to begin drafting a document that would express the vision underlying our action. It was to be a short manifesto, a recruiting tool, perhaps five or ten single-spaced pages. Instead it mushroomed into a fifty-page, single-spaced draft prepared for the Port Huron convention in May 1962. That version was debated and rewritten, section by section, by those who attended the five-day Port Huron meeting and was then returned to me for final polishing. Twenty thousand copies were mimeographed and sold for thirty-five cents each.

The vision grew from a concrete generational experience. Rarely, if ever, had students thought of themselves as a force in history or, as we phrased it, an "agency of social change." We were rebelling against the experience of apathy, not against a single specific oppression. We were moved by the heroic example of the black youth in the South, whose rebellion taught us the fundamental importance of race. We were treated legally as wards under our universities' paternal care and could not vote, but as young men we could be conscripted to fight in places we dimly understood, such as Vietnam and Laos. The nation's priorities were frozen by the Cold War: a permanent nuclear arms race benefiting what President Eisenhower had called "the military-industrial complex," whose appetite absorbed the resources we believed were necessary to address the crises of civil rights and poverty, or what John Kenneth Galbraith termed "squalor in the midst of affluence."

Apathy, we came to suspect, was what the administrators and power technicians actually desired. Apathy was not our fault, not an accident, but rather the result of social engineering by those who ran the institutions that taught us, employed us, entertained us, drafted us, bored us, controlled us, wanted us to accept the absolute impossibility of another way of being. It was for this reason that our rhetoric emphasized "ordinary people" developing "out of apathy" (the term was C. Wright Mills's) in order to "make history."[4] Since many of us had emerged from apathetic lives (neither of my parents were political in any sense, and I had attended conservative Catholic schools), we began with the realization that we had to relate to, not denounce, the everyday lives of students and communities around us in order to replicate the journey out of apathy on a massive scale.

We chose to put "values" forward as the first priority in challenging the conditions of apathy and forging a new politics. Embracing values meant making choices as morally autonomous human beings against a world that advertised in every possible way that there were no choices, that the present was just a warm-up for the future.

THE LASTING LEGACY OF PARTICIPATORY DEMOCRACY

The idea of participatory democracy, therefore, should be understood in its psychic, liberatory dimension, not simply as an alternative concept of government organization. Cynics such as Paul Berman acknowledge that the concept of participatory democracy "survived" the demise of the New Left because it "articulated *the existential drama of moral activism*" (italics added).[5] The notion (and phrase) was transmitted by a philosophy professor in Ann Arbor, Arnold Kaufman, who attended the Port Huron convention. Its roots were as deep and distant as the Native American tribal traditions of consensus.[6] It arose among the tumultuous rebels of western Massachusetts who drove out the British and established self-governing committees in the prelude to the American Revolution. It was common practice among the Society of Friends and in New England's town meetings. It appeared in Thomas Paine's *Rights of Man* in passages exalting "the mass of sense lying in a dormant state" in oppressed humanity, which could be awakened and "excited to action" through revolution.[7] It was extolled (if not always implemented) by Thomas Jefferson, who wrote that every person should believe himself or herself to be "a participator in the government of affairs, not merely at an election one day in the year, but every day."[8] Perhaps the most compelling advocate of participatory democracy, however, was Henry David Thoreau, the nineteenth-century author of *Civil Disobedience,* who opposed taxation for either slavery or war, and who called on Americans to vote "not with a mere strip of paper but *with your whole life."* Thoreau's words were often repeated in the early days of the sixties civil rights and antiwar movements.

This heritage of participatory democracy also was transmitted to SDS through the works of the revered philosopher John Dewey, who was leader of the League for Industrial Democracy (LID), the parent organization of SDS, from 1939 to the early 1950s. Dewey believed that "democracy is more than a form of government; it is primarily a mode of associated living, of conjoint community experience." It meant participation in all social institutions, not simply going through the motions of elections, and, notably, "the participation of every mature human being in the formation of the values that regulate the living of men together."⁹

Then came the rebel sociologist C. Wright Mills, a descendant of Dewey and prophet of the New Left, who died of a heart attack shortly before the Port Huron Statement was produced. Mills had a profound effect in describing a new strata of radical democratic intellectuals around the world, weary of the stultifying effects of bureaucracy in both the United States and the Soviet Union. His descriptions of the power elite, the mass society, the "democracy without publics," the apathy that turned so many into "cheerful robots," seemed to explain perfectly the need for democracy from the bottom up. The representative democratic system seemed of limited value as long as so many Americans were disenfranchised structurally and alienated culturally. We in the SDS believed, based on our own experience, that participation in direct action was a method of psychic empowerment, a fulfillment of human potential, a means of curing alienation, as well as an effective means of mass protest. We believed that "ordinary people should have a voice in the decisions that affect their lives" because it was necessary for their dignity, not simply a blueprint for greater accountability.

Some of the Port Huron language appears to be plagiarized from the Vatican's *Pacem in Terris*—Peace on Earth.¹⁰ That would be not entirely accidental, because a spirit of peace and justice was flowing through the most traditional of institutions, including Southern black Protestant churches, and soon would flourish as Catholic "liberation theology," a direct form of participatory democracy in Third World peasant communities. This "movement spirit" was everywhere present, not only in religion but in music and the arts. We studied the lyrics of Bob Dylan more than the texts of Marx and Lenin. Dylan even attended an SDS meeting or two. He had hitchhiked east in search of Woody Guthrie, after all. Though never an activist, he expressed our sensibility exactly when he described "mainstream culture as lame as hell and a big trick" in which "there was nobody to check with," and folk music as a "guide into some altered consciousness of reality, some different republic, some liberated republic."[11]

The experience of middle-class alienation drew us to Mills's *White Collar*, Albert Camus' *The Stranger*, or Paul Goodman's *Growing Up Absurd*. Our heady sense of the student movement was validated in Mills's "Letter to the New Left" or "Listen, Yankee!" The experience of confronting structural unemployment in the "other America" was illuminated by Michael Harrington and the tradition of Marxism. Liberation theology reinforced the concept of living among the poor. The reawakening of women's consciousness was hinted at in Doris Lessing's *The Golden Notebook* (which some of us read back to back with Clancy Sigal's *Going Away*), or Simone de Beauvoir's *The Second Sex*. The participatory ethic of direct action, of ending segregation, for example, by actually integrating lunch counters, drew from traditions of anarchism as well. (At a small SDS planning meeting in 1960, Dwight Macdonald gave a keynote speech on "The Relevance of Anarchism."[12]) The ethos of direct action leaped from romantic revolutionary novels like Ignacio Silone's *Bread and Wine*, whose hero, a revolutionary masked as a priest, said that it "would be a waste of time to show a people of intimidated slaves a different manner of speaking . . . but perhaps it would be worthwhile to show them a different way of living."[13]

The idea was to challenge elite authority by direct example and to draw "ordinary people," whether apathetic students, sharecroppers or office workers, into a dawning belief in their own right to participate in decisions. This was the method—call it consciousness-raising—of the Student Nonviolent Coordinating Committee, a method that influenced SDS, the early women's liberation groups, farmworkers' house meetings and

Catholic base communities before eventually spreading to Vietnam veterans' rap groups and so on. Participatory democracy was a tactic of movement building as well as an end itself. And by an insistence on listening to "the people" as a basic ethic of participatory democracy, the early movement was able to guarantee its roots in American culture and traditions while avoiding the imported ideologies that infected many elements of the earlier left.

Through participatory democracy we could theorize a concrete, egalitarian transformation of the workplaces of great corporations, urban neighborhoods, the classrooms of college campuses, religious congregations, and the structures of political democracy itself. We believed that representative democracy, while an advance over the divine right of kings or bureaucratic dictatorships, should be replaced or reformed by a greater emphasis on decentralized decision-making, remaking our world from the bottom up.

Some of our pronouncements were absurd or embarrassing, like the notion of "cheap" nuclear power becoming a decentralized source of community-based energy, the declaration that "the International Geophysical Year is a model for continuous further cooperation" and the unquestioned utilization of grating sexist terminology ("men" instead of "human beings") in sweeping affirmations about dignity and equality. We could not completely transcend the times, or even predict the near future: the rise of the women's and environmental movements, the war in Vietnam, the political assassinations. The gay community was closeted invisibly among us.[14] The Beat poets like Jack Kerouac and Allen Ginsberg had stirred us, but the full-blown counterculture, psychedelic drugs and the Beatles were two years away.

Yet through many ups and downs, participatory democracy has spread as an ethic throughout everyday life, and become a persistent challenge to top-down institutions, all over the world. It has surfaced in campaigns of the global justice movement, in struggles for workplace and neighborhood empowerment, resistance to the Vietnam War draft, in Paulo Freire's *Pedagogy of the Oppressed*, in political platforms from Green parties to the Zapatistas, in the independent media, and in grassroots Internet cam-

paigns including that of Howard Dean in 2004. Belief in the new participatory norm has resulted in major, if incomplete, policy triumphs
mandating everything from Freedom of Information Act disclosures to
citizen participation requirements in multiple realms of official decision-
making. It remains a powerful threat to those in established bureaucracies
who fear and suppress what they call "an excess of democracy."[15]

THE PORT HURON STRATEGY OF RADICAL REFORM

If the vision of participatory democracy has continuing relevance, so too
does the strategic analysis of radical reform at the heart of the *Port Huron
Statement*. Our critique of the Cold War, and liberals who became anticommunist Cold Warriors, bears close resemblance to the contemporary
war on terror and its liberal Democratic defenders. The Cold War, like
today's war on terror, was the organized framework of dominance over
our lives. This world was bipolar, divided into good and evil, allies and enemies. The U.S.-led Cold War alliance included any dictators, mafias or
thieving politicians in the world who declared themselves anticommunist.
The Cold War alliance scorned the seventy-plus nonaligned nations as
being too soft on communism. The United States and its allies engaged in
violence or subversion against any governments that included communist
or "pro-communist" participation, even if they were democratically
elected, like Guatemala (1954) and Chile (1970). Domestically, the American communists who had helped build the industrial unions, the Congress
of Industrial Organizations, the defense of the Scottsboro Boys and the
racial integration of major league baseball, who had joined the war against
Hitler, suddenly found themselves purged or blacklisted as "un-American"
for the very pro-Soviet sympathies that had been popular during World
War II. [16]

The parallels between Washington's Cold War alliances and today's war-
on-terror coalition (including unstable dictatorships like Pakistan) and
between the McCarthy-era witch hunts and today's USA PATRIOT Act
roundups of suspicious Muslims are eerie. Then, it was a ubiquitous
"atomic spy ring"; today, the ubiquitous Al Qaeda. The externalizing of the

feared, ubiquitous, secretive, religiously alien and foreign "communist" or "terrorist" enemy, the drumbeat of fear issuing from "terror alerts" and mass-media sensationalism, the dominance of military spending over any other priority, and the ever-increasing growth of a National Security State, all these themes of the Cold War have been revived in our country's newest crusade.

Of course the "threat" of violence is not imaginary. Raging militants have attacked innocent Americans and are likely to do so again. Our government's $30-billion intelligence budget failed to stop them. But those who question the current military priorities or dare to speak of root causes—addressing the abject misery and poverty of billions of people that contributed to the growth of communism in the past or Islamic militancy today—are dismissed too often as enemy sympathizers or softheaded pacifists who cannot be trusted with questions of national security. ("Sentimentalists, the utopians, the wailers," historian Arthur Schlesinger called them during the Cold War.[17] Today they are accused of "blaming America first" by critics ranging from neoconservative Jeane Kirkpatrick to onetime SDS leader Todd Gitlin.[18]) During the Cold War the CIA routinely funded a covert class of liberal anticommunists everywhere, from the American Committee for Cultural Freedom to the AFL-CIO to the U.S. National Student Association.[19] There is a direct line, even a genealogical one, from the leaders of those groupings, such as Irving Kristol and Norman Podhoretz, to their neoconservative descendants like William Kristol, editor of the *Weekly Standard*, and John Podhoretz, from the 1940s celebration of "the American Century" to today's neoconservative project the Committee on the New American Century. As for the definition of "the enemy," during the Cold War it was a conspiracy centralized in Moscow and operated through a myriad of puppet regimes and parties; today it is Al Qaeda, an invisible network consolidated and controlled by Osama bin Laden and a handful of conspirators.

The *Port Huron Statement* properly dissociated itself from the Soviet Union and communist ideology, just as antiwar critics today are critical of Al Qaeda's religious fundamentalism and terror against civilians. But the

PHS broke all taboos by identifying the Cold War itself as the framework that blocked our aspirations.[20] As a result, SDS was accused of being insufficiently "anti-communist" by some of its patrons in the older liberal-left who had been deeply devoted to the liberal anticommunist crusade.[21]

The truth lay in contrasting generational experiences: we were inspired by the civil rights movement, by the hope of ending poverty, with the gap between democratic promise and inequality as reality. The Cold War focused our nation's attention and its budget priorities outward on enemies abroad rather than the enemies in our face at home. The nuclear arms race and permanent war economy drained any resources that could be devoted to ending poverty or hunger, either at home or among the wretched of the Earth. Most, not all, of the liberal establishment, the people we had looked up to, left behind their idealistic roots and became allied with the military-industrial complex. Today a similar transition has occurred within the Democratic Party's establishment. Despite their roots in civil rights and anti-poverty programs, members of that establishment have become devotees of a corporate agenda, promoting the privatization of public assets from Latin America to the Middle East, creating the undemocratic World Trade Organization, whose rules taken literally would define the New Deal as a "restraint on trade."[22] With the attacks of September 11, 2001, many of the same liberals have abandoned their pasts in the anti–Vietnam War movement or the McCarthy, Kennedy and McGovern campaigns, to help pass the USA PATRIOT Act, invade Afghanistan and Iraq, justify the use of torture and detention without trial and expand the Big Brother national security apparatus, while leaving the United States at the bottom among industrialized countries in its contributions to UN programs to combat hunger, illiteracy and drinking water pollution.[23] Consistent with the Cold War era, any politician who questions these priorities, even a decorated war veteran, will be castigated as soft on terrorism and effectively threatened with political defeat.[24]

The *Port Huron Statement* called for a coalescing of social movements: civil rights, peace, labor, liberals and students. It was an original formulation at the time, departing from the centrality of organized labor, or the working class, that had governed the left for decades, and again causing some of our elders to grind their teeth. The statement reaffirmed that labor was crucial to any movement for social change, while chastising the labor "movement" for having become "stale." The Port Huron vision was far more populist, more middle class, more quality-of-life in orientation than the customary platforms of the left. The election of an Irish Catholic president in 1960 symbolized the assumed assimilation of the white ethnics into the middle class, and offered hope that people of color would follow in turn. The goal of racial integration was little questioned. Women had not begun to challenge patriarchy. Environmentalism had yet to assault the metaphysic of "growth." And so we could envision unifying nearly everyone around fulfillment of the New Deal dream. The *Port Huron Statement* connected issues not like a menu, not as gestures to diverse identity movements, but more seamlessly, by declaring that the civil rights, anti-poverty and peace movements could realize their dreams by refocusing America's attention on an unfulfilled domestic agenda instead of the Cold War.

The document contained an explicit electoral strategy as well, envisioning the "realignment" of the Democratic Party into a progressive instrument. The strategy was to undermine the racist "Dixiecrat" element of the party through the Southern civil rights movement and its national support network. The Dixiecrats dominated not only the segregationist political economy of the South but the crucial committees on military spending in Congress. The racists also were the hawks. By undermining the Southern segregationists, we could weaken the institutional supports for greater military spending and violent anticommunism. The party thus would "realign" as white Southerners defected to the Republicans, black Southerners registered as Democrats and the national party retained its New Deal liberal leanings. Through realignment, some of us dreamed, a radical-liberal governing coalition could achieve political power in America—in our lifetime, through our work.

This is the challenge that SDS took on: to argue against "unreasoning anticommunism," to demand steps toward arms reductions and disarmament, to channel the trillions spent on weapons toward ending poverty in the world and at home. It was the kind of inspired thinking of which the young are most often capable, but it also was relevant to the times. After Port Huron, Haber and I traveled to the White House to brief Arthur Schlesinger on our work, hoping to spark a dialogue about the new movements. There was a handful of liberal White House staffers like Harris Wofford and Richard Goodwin who seemed to take an interest. Also, we had funds from—and the goodwill of—Walter Reuther, president of the United Auto Workers (whose top assistant, Mildred Jeffrey, happened to be the mother of Sharon Jeffrey, an Ann Arbor–based SDS activist).

History has completely ignored, or forgotten, how close we came to implementing this main vision of the *Port Huron Statement*. President John Kennedy and his counterparts in Moscow were considering a historic turn away from the Cold War arms race, sentiments the president would express quite boldly just before he was killed. At a time when his generals sought a first-strike policy, Kennedy promoted a nuclear test ban treaty and offered a vision beyond the Cold War in August 1963, three months before the assassination. At the same time, Kennedy's positions on civil rights and poverty were rapidly evolving as well. At first the Kennedys had been taken aback by the Freedom Riders, with Attorney General Robert Kennedy wondering aloud whether we had "the best interest of the country at heart" or were providing "good propaganda for America's enemies."[25] President Kennedy is heard on White House tapes calling the Student Nonviolent Coordinating Committee (SNCC) and its chairman, future U.S. Rep. John Lewis,[26] "sons of bitches."[27] "The problem with you people," he once snapped, [is that] you want too much too fast."[28] In this sense, the Kennedys were reflecting, not shaping, the mood of the country. Sixty-three percent of Americans opposed the Freedom Rides that preceded Port Huron. The *New York Times* opined that "nonviolence that deliberately provokes violence is a logical contradiction."[29] President Kennedy, who at first opposed the March on Washington as too provocative politically, finally changed his mind and welcomed the civil rights leadership to the White House.[30] By the time of his assassination, he and his brother Bobby almost were becoming "brothers" in the eyes of the civil rights leadership. In addition to their joint destiny with the civil rights cause, President Kennedy was sparking a public interest in attacking poverty, having read and recommended Mike Harrington's *The Other America*. One of the original plans for the "war on poverty," according to a biography of Sargent Shriver, was "empowering the poor to agitate against the local political structure for institutional reform," which would have aligned the administration closely, perhaps too closely, with SNCC and SDS community organizers.[31]

For Kennedy truly to address poverty and racism in a second term would have required a turn away from the nuclear arms race and the budding U.S. counterinsurgency war in Vietnam. Robert Kennedy suggested as much in a 1964 interview: "For the first few years . . . [JFK] had to concentrate all his energies . . . on foreign affairs. He thought that a good deal more needed to be done domestically. The major issue was the question of civil rights. . . . Secondly, he thought that we really had to begin to make a major effort to deal with unemployment and the poor in the United States."[32] Despite efforts by today's neoconservatives to portray Kennedy as a Cold War hawk, the preponderance of evidence is that he intended to withdraw all American troops from Vietnam by 1965. Two days before his murder, for example, his administration announced plans to withdraw 1,000 to 1,300 troops from South Vietnam. But two days after his death, on Nov. 24, a covert plan was adopted in National Security Memorandum 273, which authorized secret operations, "graduated in intensity," against North Vietnam.[33]

The assassination of President John F. Kennedy was the first of several catastrophic murders that changed all our lives, and the trajectory of events imagined at Port Huron. The dates must be kept in mind: most of us who assembled were about 21 years old in June 1962. An idealistic social movement was exploding, winning attention from a new administration. Just as we hoped, the March on Washington made race and poverty the central moral issues facing the country and the peace movement would hear a president pledging to end the Cold War—and then a murder derailed the new national direction. I was about to turn 24 when Kennedy was killed. The experience will forever shadow the meaning of the sixties. The very concept of a presidential assassination was completely outside my youthful expectations for the future. No matter what history may reveal about the murder, the feeling was chillingly inescapable that the sequence of the president's actions on the Cold War and racism led shortly to his death. The subsequent assassinations of the Rev. Martin Luther King Jr. and Sen. Robert Kennedy in 1968 permanently derailed what remained of the hopes that were born at Port Huron. Whether one thinks the murders were conspiracies or isolated accidents, the effect was to destroy the progressive political potential of the sixties and leave us all as "might-have-beens," in the phrase of the late Jack Newfield.

Hope died slowly and painfully. There still was hope in the year following President Kennedy's murder—for example, in the form of the Mississippi Freedom Democratic Party, the most important organized embodiment of the Port Huron hope for political realignment. Organized by SNCC in 1963–64, the MFDP was a grassroots Democratic Party led by Mississippi's dispossessed blacks, seeking recognition from the national Democratic Party at its 1964 convention in Atlantic City. The MFDP originated in November 1963, the very month of the Kennedy assassination, when 90,000 blacks in Mississippi risked their lives to set up a "freedom vote" to protest their exclusion from the political process. Then came Freedom Summer 1964, which included the kidnapping and murders of James Cheney, Andrew Goodman and Mickey Schwerner. FBI Director J. Edgar Hoover at first suggested that the missing activists had staged their own disappearance to inflame tensions, or that perhaps "these three might have gotten rather fresh."[34]

Next, just before the Democratic convention, on August 2, the United States fabricated a provocation in the Gulf of Tonkin that expanded the Vietnam War along the lines suggested in NSM 273 ("a very delicate subject," according to Pentagon chief Robert McNamara).[35] President Lyndon B. Johnson drafted his war declaration on August 4, the same day the brutalized bodies of the three civil rights workers were found in a Mississippi swamp. On August 9, at a memorial service in a burned-out church, SNCC leaders questioned why the U.S. government was declaring war on Vietnam but not on racism at home. On August 20, Johnson announced the official "war on poverty" with an appropriation of less than one billion dollars while signing a military appropriation 50 times greater.[36] The war on poverty, the core of the Port Huron generation's demand for new priorities, was dead on arrival. The theory, held by historian William Appleman Williams among others, that foreign policy crises were exploited to deflect America's priorities away from racial and class tensions, seemed to be vindicated before our eyes.

Johnson was plotting to use the party's leading liberals, many of them sympathetic to the fledgling SDS, to undermine the civil rights challenge from the Mississippi Freedom Democrats three weeks after the Tonkin Gulf incident. Hubert Humphrey was assigned the task, apparently to test his loyalty to Johnson before being offered the vice-presidential slot. He lectured the arriving Freedom delegation that the president would "not allow that illiterate woman [MFDP leader Fannie Lou Hamer] to speak from the floor of the convention."[37] Worse, the activists were battered by one of their foremost icons, the UAW's Walter Reuther, who was flown by private jet to quell the freedom challenge; he told Humphrey and others that "we can reduce the opposition to this to a microscopic fraction so they'll be completely unimportant."[38] White House tapes show clearly that Johnson thought the Freedom Democrats would succeed if the matter was put to a convention vote.

This became a turning point between those who tried bringing their morality to politics, not politics to their morality, said Bob Moses, then a central figure for both SNCC and SDS. It was so intense that Humphrey broke down and cried. At one point, LBJ stole off to bed in the afternoon, vowing for twenty-four hours to quit the presidency.[39] The Mississippi Freedom Democrats and the hopes of the early sixties were crushed once again, this time not by the clubs of Southern police but the hypocrisy of liberalism. If Johnson had incorporated the Mississippi Freedom delegation, we believed, he still could have defeated Barry Goldwater that November and hastened the political realignment we stood for. But the possibility of transformation evaporated. In the resulting vacuum, the first Black Panther Party for Self-Defense was born in Lowndes County, Alabama, in response to the rejection of the MFDP. Only days after the convention, while Johnson was mouthing the words "no wider war," his national security advisor, McGeorge Bundy, was suggesting that "substantial armed forces" would be sent.[40]

That fall, the Port Huron generation of SDS met in New York to ponder the options. Just two years before, the war in Vietnam seemed so remote that it barely was noted in the PHS. Some of us, following the SNCC model and convinced that realignment was underway, had moved to inner cities to begin organizing a broad coalition of the poor, under the name Economic Research and Action Project (ERAP). Others were excited about the Berkeley Free Speech Movement and prospects for campus rebellion. Still others were planning protests if the Vietnam War should escalate. Amid great apprehension, the SDS national council adopted the slogan, "Part of the Way With LBJ." While the president vowed never to send America's young men to fight a land war in Southeast Asia, even on election day the White House was nevertheless drafting plans for expanding the war.[41] By springtime, 150,000 young American men were dispatched to war. In May, SDS led the largest antiwar protest in decades in Washington, D.C. But it was too late to stop the machine. Having learned that assassinations could change history, our generation now began to learn that official lies were packaged as campaign promises.

The utopian period of Port Huron was over, less than three years after the statement was issued. The vision would flicker on but never recover amid the time of radicalization and polarization ahead. Since the Democratic Party had failed the MFDP and launched the Vietnam War, those favoring an electoral strategy were frustrated and marginalized. Resistance grew in the form of urban insurrections, GI mutinies, draft-card burnings, building takeovers and bombings. Renewed efforts at reforming the system, like the 1967–68 Eugene McCarthy presidential campaign, helped to unseat LBJ but failed to capture the Democratic nomination. RFK was the last politician who rekindled the hopes of realizing the vision of Port Huron, not only with interest in anti-poverty programs and his gradual questioning of Vietnam, but most eloquently with his 1967 speech challenging the worth of the gross national product (GNP) as a measure of well-being. I supported his candidacy, attended his funeral, and finally embraced the death of hope and the birth of rage. After Richard Nixon's election, I was convicted with the so-called Chicago Eight of inciting a riot at the 1968 Democratic convention, a judicial process that ended in acquittal in 1972. By then, the long-awaited political realignment was partly underway, starting with Senator George McGovern's presidential 1972 campaign, then leading to the ascension of Southern liberals like Jimmy Carter, Bill Clinton, Al Gore, Andrew Young and John Lewis to national power. But by that time it was too late to keep white Southern voters in the Democratic Party with populist economic promises. The threat to their Southern white traditions drove them into the Republican Party. It was Nixon's strategy of realignment that prevailed.[42]

The importance of the mid-1960s turning points, however, is missed by most historians of the era, who tend to blame SDS for "choosing" to become more radical, sectarian, dogmatic and violent, as if there was no context for the evolution of our behavior. Garry Wills, whose book *Nixon Agonistes* extolled the *Port Huron Statement*,[43] later accused the young radicals of having prolonged the Vietnam War.[44] In his view, the movement should have practiced constructive nonviolence like Dr. King's, an approach that aimed at gaining national acceptance. This analysis ignores the fact that Dr. King himself was becoming radicalized by 1966, and starting to despair of nonviolence. Liberal bastions like the *New York Times* editorially blasted him for speaking out against the Vietnam War in 1967. His murder and that of Robert Kennedy stoked violent passions among many of the young. Wills also writes that it was easier to unite Americans against the manifest evil of racism than against the Vietnam War, in which, he believes, "the establishment was not so manifestly evil."[45] But for our generation, the fact of the U.S. government dropping more bombs on Vietnam than it did everywhere during World War II, while lying to those it was conscripting, was a manifest evil. Wills writes that the police simply "lost their heads" in Chicago, as if the beating and gassing of more than sixty journalists was somehow "provoked." Wills complains too that his classes at Johns Hopkins were interrupted by student bomb threats, not an easy disruption to accept, but not different from the 1960 lunch-counter sit-ins that disrupted the normalcy of innocent (white) people. Wills laments that "civil disobedience had degenerated into terrorism,"[46] without acknowledging the causes or the fact that violent rebellions were taking place in both the armed forces and American ghettos and barrios at an unprecedented rate. Were the student radicals to blame for this turn toward confrontation, or was it explainable by the failure of an older generation to complete the reforms begun in the early sixties instead of invading Vietnam? As Wills himself wrote in his 1969 book, "the generation gap is largely caused by elders who believe they have escaped it."[47]

Similarly, some still believe that the election of Hubert Humphrey in 1968 would have ended the Vietnam War and restored liberalism as a majority coalition. Who is to say? Humphrey remains an icon for an older generation of liberals to this day. For the Port Huron generation of SDS and SNCC, however, he remains the symbol of how liberalism, driven by opportunism, chose Vietnam over the Mississippi Freedom Democrats. Whichever of these views is chosen, the forgotten fact is that Humphrey probably would have won the 1968 election if he had taken an independent antiwar stand. In late October, Nixon led 44 percent to 36 percent in voter surveys. With the election one week away, the U.S. ordered a bombing halt and offered talks. On November 2, both the Gallup and Harris polls showed Nixon's lead shaved to 42 percent–40 percent. According to historian Theodore White, "had peace become quite clear, in the last three days of the election of 1968, Hubert Humphrey would have won the election."[48] The final result was Nixon 43.4 percent, Humphrey 42.7 percent, a margin of 0.7. Would Humphrey have ended the war? Perhaps; perhaps not. But there is no single factor that causes a loss by less than one percentage point. Anyone who magnifies the blame directed against one group or another is indulging in self-interested scapegoating.[49]

There is no doubt that many of us, myself certainly included, evolved from nonviolent direct action to acceptance of self-defense or street fighting against the police and authorities by the decade's end. On the day the Chicago defendants were convicted, for example, there were several hundred riots in youth communities and on college campuses across the country, including the burning of a Bank of America by university students in Isla Vista, California. No one could have ordered this behavior; it was the spontaneous response of hundreds of thousands of young people to the perceived lack of effectiveness of either politics or nonviolence. A Gallup poll in the late sixties showed one million university students identifying themselves as "revolutionary."[50] What many fail to ask is where it all began, where the responsibility lay for causing this massive alienation among college students, inner-city residents and grunts in the U.S. military. It was convenient to accuse the teenagers and twentysomethings in the 1960s of "losing their heads," unlike the heavily armed and professionally trained Chicago police, who knew their "riot" would be approved by their mayor. "Vietnam undid the New Left," Wills writes, because it "blurred the original aims" of the SDS.[51] One wishes in this case that Wills had dwelt on how Vietnam undid America.

When the period we know as "the sixties" finally ended—from exhaustion, infighting, FBI counterintelligence programs and, most of all, from success in ending the Vietnam War and pushing open doors to the mainstream[52]—I turned my energies increasingly toward electoral politics, eventually serving eighteen years in the California legislature, chairing policy committees on labor, higher education, and the environment. This was not so much a "zigzag" as an effort to act as an outsider on the inside.[53] It was consistent with the original vision of Port Huron, but played itself out during a time of movement decline or exhaustion. The lessons for me were contradictory. On the one hand, there was much greater space to serve movement goals on the inside than I had imagined in 1962; one could hold press conferences, hire activist staff, call watchdog hearings with subpoena power, and occasionally pass far-reaching legislation (divestment from South Africa, anti-sweatshop guidelines, endangered-species laws, billions for conservation, etc.). Perhaps the most potent opportunities were insurgent political campaigns themselves, raising new issues in the public arena and politicizing thousands of new activists in each cycle. On the other hand, there was something impenetrable about the system of power as a whole. The state had permanent, neo-Machiavellian interests of its own, deflecting or absorbing any democratic pressures that became too threatening. The state served and brokered a wider constellation of private corporate and professional interests that expected profitable investment opportunities and law and order, when needed, against dissidents, radicals or the angry underclass. These undemocratic interests could reward or punish politicians through their monopoly of campaign contributions, media campaigns and, ultimately, capital flight. The absence of a multi-party system with solidly progressive electoral districts was another factor in producing compromised and centrist outcomes. I think of those two decades in elected office as an honorable interlude, carrying forward or protecting the gains of one movement while waiting for others to begin, as happened with the anti-sweatshop and anti-WTO campaigns in the late 1990s.

ACHIEVEMENTS OF THE SIXTIES

SDS could not survive the sixties as an organization. In part, the very ethos of participatory democracy conflicted with the goal, shared by some at Port Huron, of building a permanent New Left organization. Not only was there a yearly turnover of the campus population, but SDS activists were committed in principle to leave the organization in two or three years to make room for new leadership. Meanwhile, it seemed that new radical movements were exploding everywhere, straining the capacity of any single organization like SDS to define, much less coordinate, the whole. Administrators, police and intelligence agencies alternated among strategies of co-optation, counterintelligence and coercion. SDS disintegrated into rival Marxist sects that had been unimaginable to us in 1962, and those groups devoured the host organization by 1969. (I would argue that one of them, the Weather Underground, was an authentic descendent of the Port Huron generation, rebelling against the failure of our perceived reformism.)

But it would be a fundamental mistake to judge the participatory sixties through any organizational history. SDS, following SNCC, was a catalytic organization, not a bureaucratic one. The two groups catalyzed more social change in their seven-year life spans than many respectable and well-funded nongovernmental organizations accomplish in decades.[54] If anything, the sixties were a triumph for the notions of decentralized democratic movements championed in the *Port Huron Statement*. Slogans like "Let the people decide" were heartfelt. The powerful dynamics of the sixties could not have been "harnessed" by any single structure; instead the heartbeat was expressed through countless innovative grassroots networks that rose or fell based on voluntary initiative. The result was a vast change in public attitudes as the sixties became mainstreamed.

In this perspective, the movement outlived its organized forms, like SDS. Once any organizational process became dysfunctional (national SDS meetings began drawing 3,000 participants, for example), the movement energy flowed around the structural blockages, leaving the organizational shell for the squabbling factions. For example, in the very year that SDS collapsed, there were millions in the streets for the Vietnam Moratorium and the first Earth Day. In the first six months of 1969, based on information from only 232 of America's 2,000 campuses, over 200,000 students were involved in protests, 3,652 had been arrested, and 956 suspended or expelled. In 1969–70, according to the FBI, 313 building occupations took place. In Vietnam, there were 209 "fraggings" (attacks on superiors) by soldiers in 1970 alone. Public opinion had shifted from 61 percent supporting the Vietnam War in 1965 to 61 percent declaring the war was wrong in 1971.[55] The goals of the early SDS were receiving majority support while the organization was becoming too fragmented to benefit.

When a movement declines, no organization can resuscitate it. This is not to reject the crucial importance of organizing, or the organizer's mentality, or the construction of a "civil society" of countless networks. But it is to suggest a key difference between movements and institutions. The measure of an era is not taken in membership cards or election results alone, but in the changes in consciousness, in the changing norms of everyday life, and in the public policies that result from movement impacts on the mainstream. Much of what we take for granted—voting by renters, a five-day workweek, clean drinking water, the First Amendment, collective bargaining, interracial relationships—is the result of bitter struggles by radical movements of yesteryear to legitimate what previously was considered antisocial or criminal. In this sense, the effects of movements envisioned at Port Huron, and the backlash against them, are deep, ongoing and still contested.

First of all, American democracy *indeed became more participatory* as a result of the 1960s. More constituencies gained a voice and a public role than ever before. The political process became more open. Repressive mechanisms were exposed and curbed. The culture as a whole became more tolerant.

Second, there were structural or institutional *changes that redistributed political access and power.* Jim Crow segregation was ended in the South, and as a result of the civil rights movement, about 20 million black people in the United States began voting. The 18-year-old vote enfranchised an additional 10 million young people. Affirmative action for women and people of color broadened opportunities in education, the political process and the workplace. The opening of presidential primaries empowered millions of voters to choose their candidates. New checks and balances were imposed on an imperial presidency. Two presidents, Lyndon Johnson and Richard Nixon, were forced from office.

Third, *new issues and constituencies were recognized in public policy*: voting rights acts, the clean air and water acts, endangered-species laws, the Environmental Protection Agency establishment, occupational health and safety acts, consumer-safety laws, non-discrimination and affirmative action initiatives, the disability rights movement, and others. A rainbow of identity movements, including the American Indian Movement (AIM), the Black Panther Party and the Young Lords Party, staked out independent identities and broadened the public discourse.

Fourth, *the Vietnam War was ended and the Cold War model was challenged.* Under public pressure, Congress eliminated military funding for South Vietnam and Cambodia. The Watergate scandal, which arose from Nixon's repression of antiwar voices, led to a presidential resignation. The U.S. ended the military draft. The Carter administration provided amnesty for Vietnam-era deserters. Beginning with Vietnam and Chile, human rights was established as an integral part of national security policy. Relations with Vietnam were normalized under the leadership of President Bill Clinton, a former McCarthy and McGovern activist, and Senator John Kerry, a former leader of Vietnam Veterans Against the War.[56]

Fifth, *the sixties consciousness gave birth to new technologies*, including the personal computer. I remember seeing my first computer as a graduate student at the University of Michigan in 1963; it seemed as large as a room, and my faculty adviser, himself a campus radical, promised that all our communications would become radically decentralized with computers the size of my hand. "It is not a coincidence," writes an industry analyst, "that, during the 60's and early 70's, at the height of the protest against the war in Vietnam, the civil rights movement and widespread experimentation with psychedelic drugs, personal computing emerged from a handful of government- and corporate-funded laboratories, as well as from the work of a small group . . . [who] were fans of LSD, draft resisters, commune sympathizers and, to put it bluntly, long-haired hippie freaks."[57] While it is fair to say the dream of technology failed, there is no doubt that the Internet has propelled communication and solidarity among global protest movements as never before, resulting in a more participatory, decentralized democratic process.

The sixties, however, are far from over. Coinciding with their progressive impacts has been a constant and rising backlash to limit, if not roll back, the social, racial, environmental and political reforms of the era. Former President Clinton, an astute observer of our political culture, says that the sixties remain the basic fault line running through American politics to this day, and the best measure of whether one is a Democrat or a Republican. It is important to note that the sixties revolt was a global phenomenon, producing a lasting "generation of '68," sharing power in many countries including Germany, France, Mexico, Brazil, Argentina, Uruguay, Northern Ireland, South Africa and South Korea, to name only a few.

Social movements begin and end in memory. The fact that we called ourselves a "new" left meant that our radical roots largely had been severed, by McCarthyism and the Cold War, so that the project of building an alternative was commencing all over again. Social movements shift from the mysterious margins to the mainstream, become majorities, then are subject to crucial arguments over memory. The 1960s are still contested terrain in schools, the media and politics, precisely because the recovery of their meaning is important to social movements of the future and the suppression or distortion of that memory is vital to the conservative agenda. We are nearing the fiftieth anniversary of every significant development of the 1960s, including the *Port Huron Statement*. The final stage of the sixties, the stage of memory and museums, is underway.

STUDENTS, THE UNIVERSITIES AND THE
POSTMODERN LEGACY

Of all the contributions of the *Port Huron Statement*, perhaps the most important was the insight that university communities had a role in social change. Universities had become as indispensable to economics in what we called the automation age as factories were in the age of industrial development. Robert McNamara, after all, was trained at the University of Michigan. In a few years, University of California President Clark Kerr would invent the label "multiversity" to explain the importance of knowledge to power.

Clearly, the CIA understood the importance of universities; as early as 1961, as the *Port Huron Statement* was being conceived, its chief of covert action wrote that books were "the most important weapon of strategic propaganda."[58]

We saw the possibilities, therefore, in challenging or disrupting the role of the universities in the knowledge economy. More important, however, was the alienation that the impersonal mass universities bred among idealistic youth searching for "relevance," as described in some of the most eloquent passages of the *Port Huron Statement*. We wanted participatory education in our participatory democracy, truth from the bottom up, access for the historically excluded to the colleges and universities. Gradually, this led to a fundamental rejection of the narratives we had been taught, the myths of the American melting pot, the privileged superiority of (white) Western civilization, and inevitably to the quest for inclusion of "the other"—the contributions of women, people of color and all those marginalized by the march of power. The result of this subversion of traditional authority became known as multiculturalism, deconstruction and postmodernism. In his perceptive 1968 study, *Young Radicals: Notes on Committed Youth*, Harvard researcher Kenneth Kenniston was the first to conclude that our "approach to the world—fluid, personalistic, anti-technological, and non-violent—suggests the emergence of what I will call the post-modern style."[59] It could also be called the Port Huron style, the endless improvising, the techniques of dialogue and participation, learning through direct action, the rejection of dogma while searching for theory. It was typical of the style that the *Port Huron Statement* was offered as a "living document," not a set of marching orders.

When I first met Howard Zinn, he was a professor at a black women's college in Atlanta, where both of us were immersed in the early civil rights movement. He was one of the few engaged intellectuals I had ever met. While witnessing and participating in the civil rights movement, he was discovering a "story" far different than the conventional one he knew as a trained historian. His work was published as *A People's History of the United States, 1492–Present*, and has sold over a million copies to date (2008).

Thanks to Zinn and numerous subsequent writers, the "disappeared" of history were suddenly appearing in new narratives and publications developed in ethnic studies, women's studies, African-American studies, Chicano studies, queer studies, environmental studies. Films like *Roots*, *The Color Purple* and *Taxi Driver* expanded and deepened this discovery process. Conservatives like Lynne Cheney, wife of Vice President Dick Cheney, were distressed that more young people knew of Harriet Tubman than the name of the commandeer of the American revolutionary army, George Washington.[60]

Cheney has been working since the Reagan era to undercut the sixties cultural revolution, but the effort is not simply Republican. Among the corporate Democrats, Larry Summers, former Treasury secretary and now president of Harvard, is devoted to "eradicating the influence of the 1960s," according to a recent biography.[61]

The unexpected student revolt that produced the *Port Huron Statement* was the kind of moment described by the French philosopher of deconstruction Jacques Derrida who took the side of the French students at the barricades in 1968. In his words, Derrida tried to "distinguish between what one calls the future and *l'avenir*." There's a future that is predictable, programmed, scheduled, foreseeable. But there is a future, *l'avenir* (to come), which refers to someone who comes whose arrival is totally unexpected. For me, that is the real future. That which is totally unpredictable. The Other who comes without my being able to anticipate its arrival. So if there is a real future beyond this other known future, it's *l'avenir* in that it's the coming of the Other when I am completely unable to foresee its arrival."[62]

The *Port Huron Statement* announced such an unexpected arrival, with a simple introductory sentence: "We are people of this generation, bred in at least modest comfort, housed now in universities, looking uncomfortably at the world we inherit." Now as that same Port Huron generation enters into its senior years, it's worth asking whether we are uncomfortable about the world we are passing on as inheritance, and what may still be done. For me, the experience of the sixties will always hold a bittersweet quality, and I remain haunted by another question raised by Ignazio Silone in *Bread and Wine*: "What would happen if men remained loyal to the ideals of their youth?"[63]

Now that deconstruction has succeeded, is it time for reconstruction again? The postmodern cannot be an end state, only a transition to the unexpected future. Transition to what? Not an empire, not a fundamentalist retreat from modernity, for they are no answers to the world crisis. As the *Port Huron Statement* said, "The world is in transition. But America is not." New global movements, symbolized by the 1999 Seattle protests against the World Trade Organization, declare that "another world is possible," echoing the Zapatista call for "one world in which many worlds fit." The demands of these new rebels are transitional too, toward a new inclusive narrative in addition to the many narratives of multiculturalism. Perhaps the work begun at Port Huron will be taken up again, this time around the world, for the globalization of power and capital and empire surely will globalize the stirrings of conscience and resistance. While the powers that be debate whether the world is dominated by a single superpower (the U.S. position) or is multipolar (the position of the French, the Chinese and others), there is an alternative vision appearing among the millions involved in global justice, peace, human rights and environmental movements—the vision of a future created through participatory democracy.

NOTES

1. *New York Times Book Review*, December 19, 2004.
2. *New York Times*, April 5, 2005.
3. See Tom Hayden and Richard Flacks, "The Port Huron Statement at 40," *The Nation*, Aug. 5/12, 2002; Hayden, *Rebel: A Personal History of the Sixties*, Red Hen, 2003; Todd Gitlin, *The Sixties: Years of Hope, Days of Rage*, Bantam 1987; Richard Flacks, *Making History: The American Left and the American Mind*, Columbia, 1988; James Miller, *Democracy Is In the Streets: From Port Huron to the Siege of Chicago*, Simon and Schuster, 1987, 1994; and Kirkpatrick Sale, *SDS*, Random House, 1973.
4. These distinctions are discussed elegantly in Flacks, *Making History*.
5. Paul Berman, *A Tale of Two Utopias: The Political Journey of the Generation of 1968*, Norton, 1996, p. 54.
6. At various times, Benjamin Franklin, Thomas Paine and Thomas Jefferson wrote approvingly of Indian political customs. As one historian described Iroquois culture, there were "no laws or ordinances, sheriffs and constables, judges and juries, or courts or jails." These idyllic themes evolved into the 1960s communes, organic gardening and medicine, environmentalist lifestyles, and other practices. See Howard Zinn, *A People's History of the United States*, Harper Collins, 2003, pp. 1–23. John Adams wrote in 1787 that "to collect together the legislation of the Indians would take up much room but would be well worth pains," as cited in an excellent collection by Oren Lyons, John Mohawk, Vine Deloria, Laurence Hauptman, Howard Berman, Donald Grinde, Curtis Berkey and Robert Venables, *Exiled in the Land of the Free*, Clear Light, 1992, p. 109. The 1778 Articles of Confederation Congress actually proposed an Indian state headed by the Delaware nation, p. 113.
7. Thomas Paine, *Rights of Man*, Penguin, 1984, p. 70, 176.
8. In a Jefferson letter dated February 2, 1816, cited by Berman, p. 51.
9. Berman, *A Tale of Two Utopias*, p. 53
10. Retreating both from Enlightenment beliefs in "infinite perfectibility" and negative beliefs in "original sin," the *Port Huron Statement* asserted that human beings are "infinitely precious" and possessed of "unfulfilled capacities for reason, freedom and love." The wording was provided by a Mexican-American Catholic activist, Maria Varela, who quoted from the copy of a Church encyclical she happened to carry. Casey Hayden spoke of those years as a "holy time."
11. Bob Dylan, *Chronicles, Volume One*, Simon and Schuster, 2004, pp. 34–35.
12. Sale, *SDS*, p. 27
13. Ignazio Silone, *Bread and Wine*, 1936, Signet, 1986; see also James Miller, *Democracy Is In the Streets*, p. 53.
14. For example, the late Carl Wittman, who joined SDS shortly after Port Huron and worked with me as a community organizer in the Newark project, eventually came out of the closet to write "A Gay Manifesto," a defining document of the gay liberation movement, six years after Port Huron. See David Carter, *Stonewall: The Riots That Sparked the Gay Revolution*, St. Martins, 2004, pp. 118–119.
15. The phrase is that of Harvard professor Samuel Huntington, in a speech to the elite Trilateral Commission in 1976, during the bicentennial of the Declaration of Independence. Huntington noted that "the 1960s witnessed a dramatic upsurge of democratic fervor in America," a trend that he diagnosed as a "distemper" that threatened both governability and national security. Huntington proposed there be "limits to the extension of political democracy." See account in Zinn, *A People's History of the United States*, pp. 558–560.

16. The sudden reframing of America's relationship with the Soviet Union was described by Cyrus Sulzberger in the *New York Times* thusly: "The momentum of pro-Soviet feeling worked up during the war to support the Grand Alliance had continued too heavily after the armistice. This made it difficult for the Administration to carry out the stiffer diplomatic policy required now. For this reason . . . a campaign was worked up to obtain a better balance of public opinion to permit the government to adopt a harder line" (March 21, 1946). Instead of seeking coexistence with the Soviet Union, the U.S. began talk of a "cold war," an "iron curtain," and an "iron fist" instead of "babying the Soviets"; the Republican Party campaigned in 1946 on a platform of "Republicanism versus Communism," and the U.S. Chamber of Commerce collaborated with the FBI in distributing anticommunist materials, all before the Chinese communist revolution or Soviet testing of an atomic bomb. See Virginia Carmichael, *Framing History: The Rosenberg Story and the Cold War*, University of Minnesota, 1993, pp. 32–33.

17. See Paul Buhle, "How Sweet It Wasn't: The Scholars and the CIA," in John McMillian and Paul Buhle, *The New Left Revisited*, Temple, 2003, p. 263.

18. See Todd Gitlin, *Letters to a Young Activist*, Basic Books, 2003. Gitlin has not moved to the conservative camp but has identified himself with "progressive patriotism," including use of military means to quell terrorism and denunciations of street demonstrators at places like the 2004 Republican convention. Oddly, his advice to the new radicals in *Letters* omits taking a position on the wars in Afghanistan and Iraq.

19. Buhle, "How Sweet it Wasn't," on the Committee on Cultural Freedom. In 1967, *Ramparts* magazine exposed the longtime CIA funding of the U.S. National Student Association. The CIA and the State Departments have long provided funding for international AFL-CIO projects designed to subvert radical labor movements in Latin America and elsewhere. According to Senate hearings held by Sen. Frank Church, the CIA funded several hundred academics on more than 200 campuses to "write books and other material to be used for propaganda purposes." See Zinn, *A People's History of the United States*, 2003, pp. 555–556.

20. Drafted in part by Michael Vester of the German SDS, then a student at Bowdoin College, the section on the Cold War foreshadowed the later movements to demilitarize Europe.

21. For my own account, see Tom Hayden, *Rebel*, p. 79–84; or Gitlin, 113–126.

22. See Lori Wallach and Patrick Woodall, *Whose Trade Organization? A Comprehensive Guide to the WTO*, New Press, 2004.

23. The portion of America's gross national income given in foreign aid has declined by nearly 90 percent since the time of the *Port Huron Statement*, from 0.54 percent in 1962 to 0.16 percent in 2004, ranking the U.S. government behind twenty other nations (*New York Times*, April 18, 2005).

24. Recent victims of the "soft on terrorism" charge were U.S. Senator Max Cleland, a paraplegic Vietnam veteran, in 2002, and of course U.S. Senator and decorated Vietnam War hero, John Kerry, in the 2004 presidential race.

25. Taylor Branch, *Pillar of Fire*, 1998, pp. 475–476

26. At the time, Lewis was the chairman of the Student Nonviolent Coordinating Committee, the most radical and front-line civil rights organization. Attempts were made to edit and dilute his speech given at the March on Washington, which asked a good question, "Where is our party?" Later Lewis became an elected Atlanta congressman and prime sponsor of the Smithsonian's African-American Museum, near the spot where the 1963 march took place.

27. Jonathan Rosenberg and Zachary Karabell, *Kennedy, Johnson, and the Quest for Justice, The Civil Rights Tapes*, Norton, 2003, p. 172.

28. Ibid., p. 31.

29. "The Sixty Three Percent Disapproval of Freedom Rides," in Taylor Branch, *Parting the Waters:*

America in the King Years, 1956–63, Simon and Shuster, 1988, p. 478. *New York Times* editorial, Branch, p. 478 as well.

30. Rosenberg and Karabell, p. 130

31. Scott Stossel, Sarge, *The Life and Times of Sargent Shriver*, Smithsonian, 2004, p. 476

32. Edwin Guthman and Jeffrey Shulman, *Robert Kennedy in his Own Words*, Bantam, 1988, p. 300

33. Richard Parker, *John Kenneth Galbraith: His Life, His Economics, His Politics*, Farrar, Straus, Giroux, 2005, p. 405. James K. Galbraith, "Exit Strategy," *New York Review of Books*, October/November 1963. Robert McNamara confirmed Kennedy's plan for a complete withdrawal by 1965 in a speech at the LBJ Library on May 1, 1995, based on White House tapes. On October 4, 1963, a memorandum from General Maxwell Taylor stated that "all planning will be directed towards preparing RVN forces for the withdrawal of all US special assistance units and personnel by the end of calendar year 1965."

    In a conversation with Daniel Ellsberg, Robert Kennedy stated that "we wanted to win if we could, but my brother was determined never to send ground troops to Vietnam. . . . I do know what he intended. All I can say is that he was absolutely determined not to send ground units. . . . We would have fuzzed it up. We would have gotten a government that asked us out or that would have negotiated with the other side. We would have handled it like Laos." Daniel Ellsberg, *Secrets: A Memoir of Vietnam and the Pentagon Papers*, Viking, 2002, p. 195.

    In an earlier, more ambiguous interview in 1964, while he was mulling his own thoughts about Vietnam, RFK gave noncommittal answers to John Barlow Martin:

    "Q: There was never any consideration given to pulling out?

    A: No.

    Q: But at the same time, no disposition to go in—

    A: No. . . . Everybody, including Gen. MacArthur, felt that land conflict between our troops—white troops and Asian—would only end disaster." Robert F. Kennedy in his own words, *The Unpublished Recollections of the Kennedy Years*, Bantam, 1988, p. 395. On these issues, I disagree with Noam Chomsky and numerous others who have claimed that LBJ's escalation of the war was simply a "continuation of Kennedy's policy," to quote Stanley Karnow as cited in Galbraith.

34. Michael R. Beschloss, *Taking Charge: The Johnson White House Tapes, 1963–64*, Simon and Schuster, 1997, p. 439.

35. Ibid., p. 508.

36. Ibid., p. 455.

37. According to SNCC participants in the meeting.

38. Beschloss, *Taking Charge*, p. 534.

39. Ibid., p. 532–33

40. Beschloss, p. 546.

41. According to Daniel Ellsberg, then at the Pentagon, an interagency task was set up by the president the day before the Nov. 3 election to make plans for escalation. "It hadn't started a week earlier because its focus might have leaked to the voters. . . . Moreover, we didn't start the work a day or week later, after the votes were cast, because there was no time to waste. . . . It didn't matter that much to us what the public thought." Daniel Ellsberg, *Secrets: A Memoir of Vietnam and the Pentagon Papers*, pp. 50–51.

42. See Kevin Phillips, *The Emerging Republican Majority*, Arlington House, 1969.

43. Garry Wills, *Nixon Agonistes*, Signet, 1969, pp. 327–333.

44. Garry Wills, *A Necessary Evil: A History of American Distrust of Government*, Simon and Schuster, 1999, pp. 289–298.

45. Ibid., p. 293.

46. Ibid., p. 293.

47. Garry Wills, "Nixon Agonistes," p. 301.

48. Tom Hayden, *Rebel*, p. 299.

49. In 2000, by comparison, I campaigned for Al Gore over the third-party campaign of Ralph Nader.

50. Sale, *SDS*.

51. Wills, *A Necessary Evil*, p. 294

52. Many of us were targeted for "neutralization" by the FBI. See Tom Hayden, *Rebel*, for FBI documents. For declassified FBI counterintelligence documents against dissenters over the years, see Ward Churchill, Jim Vander Wall, *The Cointelpro Papers*, South End, 1990, 2002.

53. The "zigzag" accusation is from Berman, p. 109.

54. One exemption to this rule is the National Organization for Women (NOW), which has managed to balance the catalytic and bureaucratic poles since its inception in 1965. Another is the Sierra Club. In both cases, the grassroots membership plays a key role in the energy flow through the organizational machinery.

55. All figures in Zinn, *A People's History of the United States*, 2003, pp. 490–492.

56. The then-secret Pentagon Papers quote administration advisers in 1968 as saying "this growing disaffection accompanied as it certainly will be by increased defiance of the draft and growing unrest in the cities because of the belief that we are neglecting domestic problems, runs great risks of provoking a domestic crisis of unprecedented proportions." In his memoirs, President Nixon wrote that "although publicly I continued to ignore the raging antiwar controversy . . . I knew, however, that after all the protests and the Moratorium, American public opinion would be seriously divided by the war." Note that these concerns were based purely on cost/benefit calculations, not on moral or public policy grounds. In Zinn, Ibid., pp. 500, 501.

57. John Markoff, *What the Dormouse Said: How the Sixties Counterculture Shaped the Personal Computer Industry*, Viking, 2005. See *New York Times* review, May 7, 2005.

58. From Senate hearings, in Zinn, *A People's History of the United States*, 2003, p. 557. At the time, in 1961, I was writing a pamphlet on the civil rights movement for the U.S. National Student Association, for international distribution. Without my knowledge, CIA funds were paying for it, presumably to show an idealistic image at international youth forums.

59. Kenneth Kenniston, *Young Radicals: Notes on Committed Youth*, Harcourt Brace, 1968, p. 235.

60. Lynne V. Cheney, *Telling the Truth*, Touchstone, 1996, p. 33.

61. Richard Bradley, *Harvard Rules*, HarperCollins, 2005; quoted in *New York Times* review, March 27, 2005.

62. Kirby Dick and Amy Kofman, *Derrida*, Routledge 2005, p. 62.

63. Ignazio Silone, *Bread and Wine*, Signet, 1986, p. 146.

38

Conspiracy in the Streets

Afterword from Conspiracy In the Streets: The Extraordinary Trial
of the Chicago Eight, *edited by Jon Weiner (New Press, 2006)*

*Looking back after four decades, things in the rearview mirror may be closer
than they appear.*

◆　　◆　　◆

NONE OF US WERE RAISED as conspirators. We grew up in the fifties
void, when McCarthyism seemed to have eradicated any trace of subversion from American culture. We were radicalized when our youthful
dreams of reform encountered a systemic pattern of violent response. In
the Chicago Conspiracy trial, McCarthyism was resurrected once again,
this time to fail. Times had changed.

I was a student editor of the campus newspaper at the University of
Michigan when I began writing about the nonviolent direct-action campaign against racial segregation by Southern black students. Nonconformist
by nature, I lacked any concrete political beliefs beyond an understanding
that America's democratic promise was for everyone. As a reporter I had
been arrested, beaten, jailed, and run out of Southern counties by a chain-
swinging mob by the time I was 21. When I met with Justice Department
officials to plead for protection, I was told that civil rights workers in Mississippi couldn't be defended by their own federal government. Later I was
arrested as a Freedom Rider for complying with federal law in southwest
Georgia. And so it continued in Newark from 1964 to 1967, when I witnessed firsthand a culture of police brutality and investigated twenty-six
deaths in the July 1967 riots, including that of a 19-year-old with forty-two
shots to the head and upper torso, and in North Vietnam, where I interviewed peasants, women, and children wounded forever by U.S.
fragmentation bombs. As idealism waned, a violent resentment filled my

heart. As Albert Camus wrote of his experience in the French resistance, "seeing beloved friends and relatives killed is not a schooling in generosity. The temptation of hatred had to be overcome."

We were on our own. My father stopped talking to me, my mother couldn't understand me. She confused Indochina with Indonesia. To protest the war meant breaking their hearts. While my parents and the Catholic Church raised me to conform, I was antiauthority on some primal and instinctive level. At first there were editorials, then petitioning, then community organizing, then marching, then civil disobedience. Innocent blood kept spilling to achieve reforms long overdue, like equal treatment at a Woolworth's lunch counter, or voting-rights legislation in 1965 after the deaths in Mississippi and the bloody Selma march. Yet Vietnam continued, claiming hundreds of American lives every week by 1968—and who knew how many Vietnamese, Cambodians, or Laotians? We who could be drafted could not vote for or against the politicians who sent us to Vietnam.

I was 28 years old during the August 1968 Chicago protests, 29 when the conspiracy trial began. I felt that my life would be taken away, either by ten years behind bars, as our lawyers advised, or taken more literally. I considered going underground. Something enabled me to believe that if we could convince one good juror to vote for our acquittal—in legal terms, to nullify the prosecution—we could be vindicated by the kind of civil disobedience within the court system that we carried out by marching in the streets despite the unjust suspension of permits in Chicago 1968. In the end, we narrowly failed, because four jurors who thought we were completely innocent nevertheless compromised under pressure from the prosecution, finding five of us guilty of one felony count each. Bobby Seale had been found in contempt by the judge, and the remaining two were found innocent of all charges.

There was much talk at the time, even among blue-ribbon commissions, about a "youth crisis." Looking back, I believe it was more a "crisis of the elders" that was responsible for the trial and the events of the sixties. I also believe that the parents and grandparents of today, who came of age in the 1960s, must remain faithful today to the way we were and not repeat the shortcomings of our own parents. Without elders, the past has no form.

There always was an Other America, whose heritage the "Chicago Conspiracy" rescued from oblivion. (Remember that Howard Zinn's *A People's History of the United States, 1492–Present,* which reclaimed the radical tradition, was first published ten years after the conspiracy trial, in 1980.) Before Bobby Seale and the Black Panther Party there were Nat Turner, Denmark Vesey, Harriet Tubman, Sojourner Truth, and the Underground Railroad. Before the Weather Underground (which exploded during the trial) there were the Haymarket anarchists, the Wobblies, the Mollie Maguires, and John Brown. Before Dave Dellinger there were the Quakers of New England and nonviolent saints like Dorothy Day and Rosa Parks. Before Rennie Davis, Lee Weiner, and John Froines there were the abolitionists, Henry David Thoreau, and the American populists and progressives. Before the Yippies there were the Diggers and Levellers, and Thomas Morton's revelers at Merry Mount, praised by Nathaniel Hawthorne and arrested by Captain Miles Standish.[1] I personally took heart from the lonely life of Thomas Paine. And, of course, our main lawyers, William Kunstler and Leonard Weinglass, stood in the tradition of lawyers like Clarence Darrow. As the historian Staughton Lynd tried to testify at the trial (he was rejected by the prosecution), the Chicago Eight were similar to the rebels at the 1770 Boston Massacre, described by none other than John Adams, lawyer for the British soldiers, as "a motley rabble of saucy boys, negroes, and molattoes, Irish taigs and outlandish jack tarrs."[2] Abbie Hoffman went even deeper into historical identity during the trial, for example, when he testified that he resided in "the Woodstock Nation," which he described as a "state of mind" like that of an Indian tribe. At trial's end, Abbie told the judge that he knew the patriots whose pictures hung on the courtroom wall: "I played with Sam Adams on the Concord Bridge. I was there when Paul Revere rode right up on his motorcycle and said, 'The pigs are coming, the pigs are coming.'"

This Other America, never triumphal but never defeated, once again rose in the 1960s. Millions of young people, and some (but not many) of our parents, were on the march. They were riveted by the Chicago demonstrations and subsequent trial—a larger "jury," if you will, whose verdict of rage was delivered in the streets on the day we were convicted, when there were dozens of riots, and one bank-burning in sunny Santa Barbara. Chicago not only radicalized many Americans, it also awakened a liberal conscience in response to the perceived outrages of the Nixon years.

The lesson for me was that some of us gave up on America prematurely. The Chicago defendants were acquitted on appeal, four years after the trial. Many outsiders of 1968 became Democratic Party insiders by 1972. The law-and-order Republicans of the Nixon era were impeached or imprisoned just five years later. The Vietnam War, which Congress almost unanimously authorized in 1964, ended when Congress cut off funding ten years later. Heading into a downward spiral of chaos, the system stabilized itself by a surge of reforms: ending the draft, enfranchising 18-year-olds, reforming the presidential primaries, passing the War Powers Act and environmental laws, and the rest. The 1969 Woodstock Festival and the great Vietnam Moratorium both occurred at the very time that the Chicago trial was meant to chill dissent. It wasn't the revolution we imagined, nor was it the repression we feared. It was both real reform and a return to pacified stability.

But the human losses outweighed the gains. Two million Vietnamese, Cambodians, and Laotians were estimated dead, millions more wounded or displaced. Fifty-eight thousand dead Americans, many more wounded, disabled by Agent Orange, emotionally drained. Hundreds of billions of dollars wasted that could have been invested in ghettos, barrios, schools, and habitat preservation. Wars came and went to dispel the "Vietnam syndrome" and replace it once again with what Robert J. Lifton has called a Superpower Syndrome. Conservative cultural counteroffensives were launched to launder the stains of the sixties from the robes of reproclaimed innocence. The 1960s are fifty years old and still contested.

There are important reverberations of the 1960s today in the recent movements against the Iraq War, corporate globalization, and curtailing of civil liberties. Back in the day, Attorney General John Mitchell declared, "We are going to take this country so far to the right you won't even recognize it." Instead of putting protesters in detention camps (the idea of his assistant, Richard Kleindienst), Mitchell went to jail himself amidst the Watergate scandal that terminated the conservatives' dream of repelling the sixties legacy. It would take three decades, culture wars, Contra wars, an (arguably) stolen election, and suicide attacks on New York and Washington before their opportunity to push rightward returned with the invasion of Iraq and passage of the Patriot Act.

The new cycle of radical protest began even before the Iraq War, with the "battle of Seattle" in 1999, which, like the opening of the 1960s, caught the authorities and the media entirely by surprise. I was in the California state senate at the time, concerned about the threat of the World Trade Organization to California's laws on clean water, clean air, endangered species, and minority-owned and women-owned business preferences, all subject to challenge as "barriers" to the free-trade doctrines of the multi-national corporations. But I was unaware of the rising intensity of resistance to the WTO among a new generation of young people. I received a call from a Yale student, Terra Lawson Remer, the daughter of sixties friends of mine, urging me not to miss Seattle. Then calls came from Michael Dolan, the Public Citizen coordinator, wanting me to speak as an "old-timer" at a kickoff rally. "Seattle," like "Chicago," became a single-word summary of a new historic event. It had happened before, in the general strike of the 1930s, the Wobbly campaigns before then, all the way back to the naming of the city for Chief Seattle, there had been repeated cycles of action and apathy, meaning and forgetting.

Comparisons between Seattle 1999 and Chicago 1968 are useful. The Seattle protest was not only larger than Chicago by tenfold but was based on an alliance between street radicals, environmentalists, and organized labor never achieved in the sixties. Seattle actually *shut down* the secret and undemocratic WTO ministerial meeting, going beyond the resistance actions of the sixties. The spirit was the same. More women were involved in leadership. The affinity groups, born of necessity in Chicago, were far more sophisticated in Seattle, augmented by cell phones, mountain-climbing gear, and couriers on high-speed bikes.

One major difference was that Seattle exploded unexpectedly out of a context of a surface calm, while Chicago seemed to be the culmination of a near-decade of escalating resistance on many fronts. The word on Seattle among cynics and administration defenders was that it was "isolated."

But it seems to me that *the Seattle phenomenon has been a slow-moving Chicago.* Far from isolated, Seattle-type events keep occurring in places as diverse as Quebec City, Genoa, Cancún, Porto Alegre, and eventually at the gates of American political conventions. There was another parallel, too: as the sixties movements began in the segregated South and vaulted into the campus and antiwar movements, so these new movements began in the global "South" and grew into a broad resistance movement against economic and military empire. And even before the events of September 11, 2001, "Seattle" had become the pretext for a new politics of law and order instead of an occasion for America's elders to rethink their system of power.

In 2000 in Los Angeles, in a scenario quite like Chicago, the FBI, the police, the Secret Service, and the mayor warned that up to 70,000 "anarchists" representing "another Seattle" would descend on the Democratic national convention. In 1968, the same federal agencies, plus the Chicago police, issued warnings of black uprisings, hippie anarchy, free-love festivals, and LSD in the city water supply, all designed to frighten the public, discredit the antiwar protests, and justify preemptive measures like the denial of routine permits for marches, concerts, and sleeping in public parks. A side benefit was the opportunity for a bonanza in public funds for law enforcement to stockpile rubber bullets, pepper-spray launchers, and surveillance equipment in the event of future urban "disorders." In addition, going beyond Chicago, the Los Angeles authorities began constructing fenced-in "protest zones," topped with concertina wire, pens that were suited to their cramped vision of free expression.

Of course the projections always were wildly inflated. Instead of 70,000 anarchists in Los Angeles, there were some five to ten thousand homegrown activists, approximately the same number who turned up at the height of Chicago. There was virtually no disruption by protesters, except briefly on the first night when police forcibly shut down a fenced-in concert by Rage Against the Machine, firing rubber bullets and gas grenades into the crowd after two or three black-clad anarchists started scaling a fence hundreds of yards from the convention site. My son Troy, then 28 (the same age I was during Chicago), was shot and wounded on the wrist by one of the hundreds of "less than lethal" bullets fired that night. It could have blinded or killed him, as we shall see.

The same pattern has played itself out periodically during the past five years, with police making inflated and irresponsible predictions prior to official events such as Republican and Democratic conventions (2000, 2004), a WTO ministerial in Cancún (2002), and the Free Trade Agreement of the Americas meeting in Miami (2003); imposing severe restrictions on the First Amendment; raiding apartments without warrants; infiltrating undercover provocateurs and spies into peaceful protest groups; and doctoring their own videos to suppress evidence, while all the time collecting tens of millions in public funds for high-tech weaponry.

Police behavior at the conventions of 2004 far surpassed or equaled the 1968 Chicago police tactics, but with one exception: the police had learned not to beat young people bloody on television as they did in 1968. While there were exceptions—police overkill in Oakland on April 7, 2003, and New York City on April 27 of the same year, gassing was a constant, some beatings were administered in Seattle, a protestor was run over and killed in Genoa—the police had devised forms of control less shocking to the eye. For instance, fishnets were routinely used to scoop up scores of flailing protestors (and unlucky pedestrians) in New York, instead of vivid scenes of club-swinging police wading into crowds to make arrests. Though fewer skulls were cracked on camera, the main policy change was in public relations. Violence was rendered less visible. Plastic flexicuffs still could bind ankles to wrists; demonstrators could be held in special buses for twelve or eighteen hours, blinded with pepper spray, denied toilets, food, and water.[3]

From Seattle 1999 to New York 2004, another lesson of the Chicago conspiracy trial was adopted by the authorities: while useful to magnify the anarchist threat before the official event, there should be no federal conspiracy trials afterward. There was a partial exception in the case of John Sellers, Ruckus Society coordinator, during the 2000 Republican convention in Philadelphia, but charges were dropped. The government has learned to avoid public spectacles like the Chicago trial if at all possible. Protesters have turned the tables with successful litigation against the police in Oakland and New York City over the 2003 incidents. The exceptions are important, however. The never-ending drug war, largely a continued backlash against the sixties counterculture, proceeds to incarcerate millions, despite public support for decriminalization and medical marijuana. Second, the sweeps and prosecutions against alleged Muslim terrorists are publicized to feed the public's anxiety, but even these cases have received critical responses at home and abroad. Managing the perception of terror, which would seem easier than the earlier task of repressing antiwar activists, proved too much for Attorney General John Ashcroft. Alongside its fear of hidden terrorists, the public still maintains a suspicion of government prosecutors rooted in the 1960s and revived by the intelligence scandals over weapons of mass destruction.

Instead of imposing conspiracy charges after an event, a new approach is to preempt or chill mass demonstrations by silently deploying FBI agents to interrogate, even subpoena, political activists in their hometowns before they decide to attend events like political conventions. In 2002, the homeland security agency issued an all-points bulletin to investigate anyone with an "expressed dislike of attitudes and decisions of the U.S. government," and warn them that withholding information about civil disobedience is punishable.[4] In 2003, federal prosecutors subpoenaed Drake University for information on organizers of a peace forum.[5] In the same year, the FBI circulated a memo to all police departments to investigate and report suspicious activities.[6] In response to a lawsuit, the government revealed that it had over 3,500 pages of documents on the ACLU and Greenpeace combined, and inside memos on the 2004 Republican convention protests.[7] Then, during hearings on the appointment of John Bolton to the United Nations, the National Security Agency revealed that it supplied government agencies with names of some 10,000 Americans on whom it had eavesdropped between January 2004 and May 2005.[8] Under the pretext of preventing another Seattle or 9/11, this was the revival of the sixties' counterintelligence programs all over again, if indeed they were ever terminated.

For months leading up to the Republican convention of 2004 in New York City, the police claimed as usual to have "secret" intelligence about subversive plots, none of which materialized. A massive law-enforcement buildup thus was justified, including a huge mechanical contraption said to emit a shrieking sound so piercing that demonstrators all around would collapse in quaking disorientation. The machine was aimed directly at demonstrators but not turned on, thus legitimized as a deterrent without a murmur of official concern. As in Chicago, routine permits were denied for mass rallies, even one many miles from the convention in the Great Lawn in Central Park. It was said that the grass would be disturbed by marching feet. Three times as many protesters were arrested in New York City—1,821—than during Chicago, the largest number ever at an American political convention. As of this writing, almost all the cases have been dropped for lack of evidence or resulted in acquittals. The New York security forces pocketed approximately $100 million for their security expenses. They escaped with little public embarrassment, except the convention-eve handcuffing of eighty-six-year-old Mike Wallace for doubleparking and being "overly assertive."[9] Like a few others of us, Wallace had covered the 1968 Chicago convention, where he was punched on the chin and threatened with arrest on the convention floor.[10] Further documents and forensic analysis were released in December 2005, showing that New York undercover officers had instigated one of the week's only violent disruptions, as well as having arrested Rosario Dawson, who was filming a movie during the demonstrations.[11]

In Boston at the 2004 Democratic convention, there were virtually no demonstrators at all despite the usual predictions of chaos. The police still received more than $20 million in federal funds for a protest cage, surveillance cameras that they installed permanently in the ghetto, and the usual allotment of rubber bullets, pepper spray, and launchers. A few months later they used their new weaponry on college students partying the night of the Red Sox's World Series victory, killing a twenty-one-year-old woman, Victoria Snelgrove, with a direct shot in the eye from a pepper-spray pellet gun. Commenting on the Red Sox riots for the *New York Times,* the Seattle police chief said the aggressive new crowd-control techniques began with the 1999 Seattle demonstrations, which "really woke up the police."[12]

The ghost of John Mitchell must be smiling up from its undisclosed location. Despite the revival of vigorous democratic protest, the machinery of preemptive arrest and detention is being used on an experimental basis under the pretext of deterring terrorists. If and when there is another terrorist incident here—and the experts who are paid to protect us say that it's inevitable—one wonders what new limitations on freedom are prepared already.

Seattle symbolized the beginning of a new global movement for peace and justice not seen since 1968. The system is more flexible and cushioned than forty years ago. What was confined to the outside now is permitted on the inside. The media, as stenographers to the powerful, underplay or ignore those in the streets. But this new cycle of protest is not over, and—who knows—the new movements may come to far exceed those of my generation. I consider it a personal blessing to have experienced such movements twice in a lifetime.

NOTES

1. Peter Lamborn Wilson, "Caliban's Masque: Spiritual Anarchy and The Wild Man in Colonial America", in Ron Sakolsky and James Koehnline, *Gone to Croatan: Origins of North American Dropout Culture*, Autonomedia, 1993, p. 95.
2. Howard Zinn, *A People's History of the United States*, 2003, p. 67.
3. See National Lawyers Guild summary, "The Assault on Free Speech, Public Assembly and Dissent," August 2003; Lewis Lapham, "Crowd Control," *Harpers*, October 2004.
4. Lapham, Ibid.
5. Ibid.
6. *New York Times*, Aug. 16, 2004.
7. Ibid.
8. *New York Times*, July 17, 2005.
9. In *Newsweek*, cited in *New York Times*, Aug. 10, 2005.
10. Daniel Walker, *Rights in Conflict*, Dutton, 1968, p. 327. Lest anyone be mistaken in thinking that Mike Wallace was a liberal sympathizer, he met with me a few weeks after the convention to propose that I support Richard Nixon. "Tom, believe me, he's a 'new Nixon,'" Wallace confided. I passed.
11. *New York Times*, Nov. 1, 2004.
12. Ibid.

39

Image and Reality
The Vietnam Years

Los Angeles Times, *June 22, 1986*

The current U.S. war and occupation of Iraq has deepened my frustration that the lessons of war are learned all too slowly, too painfully, most often at the expense of other people's suffering. Those responsible for Vietnam have never apologized and apparently never will. Rather than learning the lessons, they tried to reverse the "Vietnam Syndrome" by waging dirty wars in Central America that have killed many thousands. Once the U.S. government could no longer blame the Soviet Union, they began a long war in Iraq in which their only strategies have been to keep American casualties low and Iraqi suffering hidden, to placate the young by avoiding the draft, and to tell the media and the public one fable after another. Lessons learned in so much blood leave me more angry than forgiving.

◆　　◆　　◆

THE LYNDON BAINES JOHNSON LIBRARY AND MUSEUM in Austin, Texas, sits by a grassy hill where, amid a constant stream of lighthearted students, one can reflect on the past.

The library itself is a virtually windowless brown stone building that reminds me of a vast tomb. Just past the entrance, one finds the foreign-affairs exhibit, where the visitor first learns that the Johnson years, 1963–69, were "crowded with events—dramatic, tragic, hopeful—which related to foreign affairs." Presented for display are three of those events, "each of which for a while commanded the world's attention"—Glassboro, the Six-Day War and Vietnam. A forgotten summit, an Israeli-Arab war and—Vietnam. Not "Vietnam War," not "Vietnam Tragedy," not "Vietnam Nightmare," just Vietnam—"which for a while commanded the world's attention."

The Vietnam exhibit tells us, first, that President Lyndon B. Johnson was continuing policies of Presidents Dwight D. Eisenhower and John F. Kennedy to preserve the independence of South Vietnam. North Vietnamese "triggered a conflict" by attacking us in the Tonkin Gulf, twenty-two years ago. Johnson "chose the middle course" between a pullout and all-out war. He bombed only "military targets" and busied himself "improving the lives of people." When Johnson retired, the exhibit succinctly notes, 35,541 Americans "had given their lives."

Touring the exhibit on a recent visit, I felt the ghosts of 1968 returning and said to myself: But none of these official statements are true.

The Tonkin Gulf incident was more a pretext than a cause of our bombing. Johnson hardly followed a "middle course," he unleashed more firepower than we did in World War II. He not only bombed military targets, he dropped napalm, phosphorous and anti-personnel bombs everywhere, creating millions of civilian victims and defoliating a countryside with chemicals.

Far more than the protection of a President's image is involved here. The library perpetuates a politics of denial all too prevalent in America today. Many in our nation are too easily comforted by myth and nostalgia instead of hard truth. We are far too capable of confusing Rambo and Ronald Reagan. We cover our failures with platitudes about "staying the course" and sometimes still act as if real men have no regrets.

But tragedies and failures can lead to knowledge, as the Greek playwrights tell us, and knowledge to a different sort of strength. Despite efforts to rewrite history, many Americans know Vietnam was not a proud moment but a modern Greek tragedy.

Most of the men and women of my generation want to overcome our painful past divisions. After all, we have in common, first, the fact that we all were manipulated and deceived by the authorities; and second, a growing sense that those who fought and those who resisted were both motivated by a sense of obligation, and that we have paid our dues. Many paid the ultimate price themselves; others tried to stop the killing. Some were stigmatized as baby-killers, others as traitors. Some were forced not to talk about it because no one wanted to hear and some were disavowed by their parents for years.

Very few of us could go through all that with no regrets or second thoughts. No one can feel utterly righteous about his Vietnam experience, whether he bombed a village or used a draft deferment to escape those killing fields. The strength and, one hopes, the wisdom, that only comes from second thoughts can be the lasting basis of reconciliation here in America and the protection against other Vietnams happening again.

I certainly have regrets of my own that I will always live with. I regret that Hanoi has an imperial design on Cambodia and has largely done away with pluralism in the south. I regret that I was not more critical of the cynical motives of the Soviet Union. I regret that I was infected with a hostility that alienated me from this country for years. I regret most of all that I compounded the pain of many Americans who lost sons and loved ones in Vietnam. I am sorry for the hurt I did while thinking I was trying to save those lives. There is a saying that we live two lives, the life we learn with and the life we live with after that. I will always believe the Vietnam War was wrong; I will never again believe that I was always right.

Nor should any of us become prisoners of that experience, as if it somehow contains clear lessons that are permanent guideposts in either life or politics. In fact, the supposed lessons of the past are often the pitfalls of the future.

It remains true, for example, that we cannot be the policeman of the world, but it is also true that we cannot simply withdraw from the world and believe that all conflicts can be peacefully negotiated.

It is true that a Vietnam-type war in Central America would be dishonorable and tragic, but it is also true that Third World revolutions bring their own forms of dogma and repression.

It is true that we are strengthened by democratic debate about foreign policy and weakened by an imperial presidency, but it is also true that this country needs a post-Vietnam foreign-policy consensus and doves need a defense doctrine.

These are among the questions facing us today. The Vietnam experience cannot provide answers, but it can provide the humility that we need to hear each other in the struggle for sane and honorable alternatives.

The humility I have in mind can be found by visiting a very different place of Vietnam remembrance than that afforded by the Johnson Library. I am referring, of course, to the Vietnam Memorial in Washington. Designed by a woman of Asian descent, scorned at first but finally embraced by traditional military men, this memorial is a scarred V in the capital earth. The V becomes a black mirror in which we see ourselves reflected over and behind the names of the dead, and behind us monuments to earlier glory. There is no attempt to hide the truth or repeat the lies, no euphemism about men "giving their lives," only the fact staring us in the face that they will have died for nothing until we, with an awful wisdom, turn their sacrifice into the triumph of peace.

40

Missing Mills

From Radical Nomad: C. Wright Mills and His Times
(Paradigm Publishers, 2006)

I wrote my master's thesis on C. Wright Mills in 1963–64 at the Center for Research on Conflict Resolution at the University of Michigan. It sat on a shelf until 2006 when Paradigm Publishers kindly published it under its original title, Radical Nomad: C. Wright Mills and His Times. *Mills gave graduate students like me a defiant model for working within the universities as well as without. His sociology also opened my eyes to the history of the fifties and early sixties as no one else had done. The essay below, written in 2005, looks back on Mills's meaning for our generation.*

◆   ◆   ◆

IT WAS A WARM MARCH MORNING in Atlanta, and I was sitting in bed drinking coffee. I finally had finished the draft of the manifesto of Students for a Democratic Society, which became known as the *Port Huron Statement*. The document was strongly influenced by C. Wright Mills's independent radicalism, especially his "Letter to the New Left" in which he declared that "the Age of Complacency is ending." The founding convention of SDS in Port Huron, Michigan, was three months away. The civil rights and student movements were exploding "out of apathy"—another phrase of Mills's. Epic change, we were certain, was blowing in the wind.

Then my pleasant morning was shattered: a *New York Times* headline in front of me reported that "C. Wright Mills, a Sociologist," was dead of a heart attack at age 45. I experienced chest pain and can still relive the depression that began that moment.

It was an omen of things to come. In the great movement that was beginning, euphoria and idealism would be balanced by death, and death again, by bullets but also by burnout and betrayal. Mills, it seemed, had been exhausted by a long, lonely struggle against the system he named "the power elite." Recovering from a massive 1960 heart attack, he wrote, "What we do not now know as yet is how much intellectual and moral tension I can stand. . . . What bothers me is whether the damned heart will stand up to what . . . must be done."[1]

None of us in SDS knew him, though many were followers. After Albert Camus and Bob Dylan, Mills ranked as the most pervasive influence on the first generation of SDS. He was the mentor, perhaps the father figure, I needed at the time. Even today I think of him as a sort of absent parent.

SDS members grew up either in the mass society Mills described in *White Collar* or within the Old Left he examined in *The Marxists*. More than any other thinker, he placed our lives in a meaningful context. I was the son of a divorced corporate accountant and school librarian in one of Detroit's first suburbs. My parents were those members of the new middle class Mills perfectly described as lacking any ability to connect the problems of their personal lives with larger structural causes. They were apolitical, apathetic, tending to blame themselves for any shortcomings. Mills diagnosed the serious need to somehow turn their personal troubles into political issues.

Other SDS founders, such as Dick and Mickey Flacks or Steve Max, had been raised in the culture of the Old Left, which was battered by McCarthyism, demoralized by Stalinism, and marginalized by the expansion of the suburban middle class. They, too, needed the fresh ideological beginning that Mills offered.

The growth of this fifties middle class discredited what Mills called the "labor metaphysic" of the Old Left, the dogmatic belief in one big working class. Instead, he said, American society had become a mass society whose class lines were blurred.

Out of this white-collar middle class burst the New Left, living proof that the mass society had not deadened the will to protest. The triggering revolt was the black student movement in the South, a phenomenon Mills paid little attention to, which catalyzed the larger middle-class "youth revolt" of the era. In the background was a global revolutionary upheaval starting with African liberation movements, the Cuban Revolution, and, finally, the Vietnamese resistance, all of which challenged the dangerous nuclear premises of the bipolar Cold War that Mills criticized in *The Causes of World War Three*.

With his "Letter to the New Left" and "Listen Yankee," Mills explained how the youth rebellions and anticolonial struggles were two different responses to a single, suffocating power elite devoted to obsessive anti-communism. In these later years, he both described and encouraged the revival of a "democratic public" in place of the mass society, or "democracy without publics," of the fifties. He himself was not a joiner; his old friend Saul Landau remembers Mills as an "astute observer and a man who didn't easily tolerate hypocrites, but I never saw him go to a demo or refer to having gone to one."[2] He was a radical nomad.[3] But, oh, he had a force.

The 1960 heart attack felled Mills as he prepared for a nationally televised debate over Cuba and Latin America with Adolph A. Berle, a symbol of the sort of intellectuals whom Mills accused of celebrating the status quo. Mills would live two more years, but there was little doubt that he was ground to death by a lack of support in his one-man crusade. The "furor" over Mills's pamphlet on Cuba, according to Dan Wakefield, "led to mounting pressures that clearly contributed to Mills's early death.[4] Berle himself expressed a shocking smugness over Mills's collapse, calling him a "ranting propagandist" and even claiming that "he got a heart attack—partly I think because he was frightened—and had reason to be."[5] A sympathetic biographer of Mills, Irving Louis Horowitz, in writing of Mills's death, also made a chastising reference, comparing Mills to a Joseph Conrad figure, Nostromo: "Here was a man that seemed as though he would have preferred to die rather than deface the perfect form of his egoism. Such a man was safe."[6]

I began to write a thesis on Mills for graduate school in Ann Arbor in 1963, identifying with him as a "radical nomad." Having fully absorbed his thinking and style, I then left graduate school in summer 1964, to see whether I could carry his lessons into practice, and whether practice might produce further evidence of its own. My thesis remained on my shelf until Dean Birkenkamp of Paradigm Publishers kindly offered to place it in the public domain. I am honored that Dick Flacks and Stanley Aronowitz, two of my intellectual mentors at the time, have added their perspectives to this memorializing of Mills along with respected sociologist, Charles Lemert.

Reading the manuscript today, I am struck first by how things have changed from the days of messy duplicating machines to computers. My rhetoric then was that of a graduate student full of himself. My thesis, like the work of Mills, was devoid of any reference to women, whose liberation movement would surface just after the manuscript was completed. Nor to gays, lesbians, and environmentalists, the activists just beyond the limits of my experience.

That Mills, at age 45, missed the social and public significance of women, was typical of male thinkers and activists of the time. Women were assumed to be extensions of men, often invisible, without autonomous identities. For example, while I was immersed in writing about Mills, I was hardly aware that my marriage was falling apart. Thinking only of myself, I had moved with my wife, Sandra "Casey" Cason, to graduate school at the University of Michigan. A central and charismatic leader of the southern student civil rights movement, Casey took an unfulfilling job as a secretary in Ann Arbor to support us and promptly began to wilt as I plunged into my intellectual challenges. Mills was no help as a role model here. Casey went on, with Mary King, to draft the first "notes on women's liberation" in response to the treatment of women in the early movement.

I do not blame Mills for my chauvinism, but if he had written a book describing the elite as *male* or as *a patriarchy* as powerful as the capitalists and militarists, I might have been more conscious. As a sociologist, too, Mills might have discerned the invisible disparities and contradictions faced by working women instead of describing the mass society of the fifties as hopelessly frozen and monolithic. He did not predict the women's movement as he did the New Left and anticolonial struggles. Simone de Beauvoir alone is mentioned in a 1959 Mills letter and in *Radical Nomad* as well.[7] In fairness, Betty Friedan's *The Feminine Mystique*, about the invisible suffering of women in mass society, was not published until the year of Mills's death.

The same might be said of his attitudes toward race. "I have never been interested in what is called 'the Negro problem,'" he wrote in a letter. "The truth is, I've never looked into it as a researcher. I have a feeling that if I did it would turn out to be a 'white problem' and I've got enough of those on my hands just now. . . . The US of A is a white tyranny. It will remain so until there is no distinction whatsoever drawn in marriages between the races."[8] This was a privatized view of race relations at a time when thousands of young black (and white) people were going to jail in the South to challenge elite rule. His "Letter to the New Left" did credit them as an agency of change conducting "direct non-violent action, and it seems to be working, here and there. Now we must learn from their practice and work out with them new forms of action."[9] But he went no further. While he traveled to Cuba and dramatically reported its revolution, he never visited the South during the 1955 Montgomery bus boycott or the 1960s sit-ins.

Mills felt much closer to the Mexicans, learning from his Spanish-speaking mother that "Mexicans have always formed her ideal images of the Human Being." He told his mother that "the Cubans are my Mexicans."[10]

This empathy with Mexicans is typical of Irish American Catholics, a connection that Mills never seemed to recognize. The almost total detachment from his Irish heritage limited his understanding of the price the white-collar middle classes paid by assimilation. *The mass society, after all, was the assimilated society,* producing an anxiety that had no name for most striving white ethnics (and to a lesser extent, people of color). Mills, whose Irish Catholic family was driven out of Ireland during the Famine times (a background I shared with him), never discussed being Irish except in a 1943 letter to his colleague Hans Gerth. I quote from the letter extensively, highlighting the anguished portions that appear as symptoms of the inability to assimilate into the dominant WASP culture of the time:

> Last Friday I was working at the office at night on motives chapter and sort of collapsed emotionally and "spiritually." For about two hours, I realized later, I just sat and stared at the row of books, with the light on in the office and rest of the building all dark. It was the oddest feeling and I can't explain it. Like a trance, only all

the time I was thinking about war and the *hopelessness of things.*
It was as if you were thinking—yes, you have to use that word—
with a *sequence of moods.* The polarity probably was between
helplessness and *aggressiveness* and both were, I think, rather relished! Also for the first time, except in what was, explicitly at least,
in fun, I had a self-image of being very *Irish. . . . I do not know why
because I do not know anything about "the Irish"* and I have never,
to my knowledge, been stamped as Irish by anyone particularly. I
think maybe it is all because of the *inarticulate feelings of indigna-
tion* that come up when I confront politics in any serious way and
because I cannot locate and denounce . . . such enemies as are
available. . . .

Living in an atmosphere soaked in lies, the man who thinks, at
least, that he knows some of the truth but would lose his job were
he to tell it out and is not man enough to do it anyway . . . if such
a man has built such a life around finding out the truth and being
aggressive with it, then *he suffers.* I wrote a lot more, and even
began a short story [as follows]:

> What happened was that *the self-distance and the use of self for objective
> work* which was usual with him had collapsed. It collapsed and *he saw
> another self for a while.* And what he saw was a political man. He had
> not known before that the well of indignation which had become his
> basic political feeling was masking such strong political urges.[11]

These are masked *Irish* feelings, not "Texas outsider" feelings as some
have argued. Mills died one year before the assassination of President John
Kennedy, who in 1960 symbolized the story of successful assimilation—
just before his death and the unfolding of other Kennedy family tragedies
that suggested an Irish fate rather than the immigrants' triumph. Mills
never looked at suppressed ethnic worries beneath the white collar, where
he might have discovered how the mass society served to perpetuate sta-
tus-based shame, inferiority, and feelings of helplessness. The strain of
smothering such unconscious feelings can kill a man, or so I believe today.
Instead, Mills accepted the prevalent view of the triumphal "melting pot"

that became for him the mass society, just at the moment when a *reverse assimilation* was beginning in all spheres of American culture. That is one reason that Mills became relatively forgotten amid the later emphasis on multiculturalism. Perhaps now a return to his analytic framework, including the dimensions of racial, ethnic, and gender identity, might help us achieve an integrated big picture once again.

Across the decades I still feel his loss. In retrospect, it should be said that he established in his life and work, for myself and many others, the definition of what it means to be an "intellectual," one who attempts to clarify where we fit in the larger scheme of things, and what it means to be an "agent of social change," one who participates in making history from below.

This is a time of eerie similarities with the 1950s. The Cold War framework has been replaced by that of a permanent War on Terrorism, and McCarthyism by the USA PATRIOT Act. On the other hand, new social movements, especially in the global South, threaten the glib assumptions of an omnipotent market economy and military hegemony. And where are the intellectuals? As in Mills's time, too many are occupied with celebrations of the triumph of capitalism over communism in the Cold War and the rise of a de facto American Empire. Once again they claim that there are no systemic alternatives to the status quo, that history has ended. Still others limit themselves to specialized research that has little public benefit.

Yet there is a rising global hunger for systemic explanations of our plight. Audiences as large as 25,000 listen eagerly to Noam Chomsky, Naomi Klein, and Arundhati Roy at world social forums in Brazil or India. The right questions are being asked again. Who is collecting, sorting, and analyzing the shadowy new elites of power? Has Mills's concept of the power elite now been globalized in agencies such as the World Trade Organization (WTO), and how can transnational structures be exposed and confronted by transnational movements? Are we oscillating between empire and a multipolar world, or are social movements creating space for a more participatory world of multicultural democracy?

I for one wish Mills could be present for the discussion. In his absence, I hope that his legacy of power-structure research will be revived and applied to globalization. And I hope that his infectious populist enthusiasm is communicated and carried on among those today who resist empire in new social movements, such as the Seattle shutdown of the WTO in 1999, the numerous other "Seattles" of recent years, and the unprecedented global movement against the Iraq war. These quite spontaneous movements once again surprise the elites and threaten their hegemony. They contain a clear continuity from the day that Mills's heart gave out. The causes of World War III have not been prevented so much as expanded. The mass societies today must choose between entertainment and engagement. The political parties must wake up or be abandoned. The media must begin to notice that the people are restless for independent news.

The Left is dead again; the Left is born again. As Mills said shortly before he died, we must study these new movements as "real live agencies of social change." And, I would add, join them. All movements begin at the margins, when the surface is peaceful and the pundits are sleeping. But they erupt unpredictably, march to the mainstream eventually, and become majorities in their time, clashing with the Machiavellian power elites, achieving reforms, finally fading into our blurred and brainwashed memories, exhausted, until the radical nomads find renewed resonance in the next generation.

NOTES

1. C. Wright Mills, *Letters and Autobiographical Writings,* edited by Kathryn Mills with Pamela Mills, University of California Press, 2000, p. 324.
2. Personal correspondence, 2005.
3. "I am a politician without a party," he wrote, "a writer without any of the cultural background" (of a born writer), and "a man who feels most truly alive only when working," in Mills, *Letters,* p. 303.
4. Ibid., *Letters,* p. 5.
5. Cited in Irving Louis Horowitz, C. *Wright Mills: An American Utopian,* New York: Free Press, 1983, p. 301.
6. Ibid., p. 302.
7. Mills called de Beauvior "an admirable woman . . . whom you ought read, especially if you are a woman or know any women," in a letter to Tovarich in 1959. See Mills, *Letters,* p. 276.
8. Ibid., p. 314.
9. Ibid., p. 307.
10. Ibid., p. 313–15.
11. Ibid., p. 37.

41

Enemy of the State
The Secret War against John Lennon

From Memories of John Lennon, *edited by Yoko Ono (HarperEntertainment, 2005)*

When I was asked to contribute an essay to Yoko Ono's book on her martyred husband John, I eagerly agreed. Lennon is widely misunderstood in the memory of the Sixties. Not only was he an extraordinary artist, he was directly involved in the antiwar movement, the Irish nationalist cause, and of course, the counterculture. We should never forget that he was targeted for neutralization by the FBI.

◆　　◆　　◆

JOHN LENNON CANNOT BE MEMORIALIZED without recalling his radical political attitudes at a time of roiling unrest in Britain, America and around the globe. His greatest qualities were as an artist, of course, but he would have been a different artist without the rebellious, nonconformist and subversive spirit of the 1960s. Revered by all as a great musician, John also became an enemy of the state, which future generations of fans need to remember.

The forces who targeted John Lennon—some combination of London's MI5 and J. Edgar Hoover's FBI—did so clandestinely, then waged a further war to keep their embarrassing improprieties hidden and impeccable reputations intact.

Their counterintelligence campaign unfolded, as far as we know, as the Beatles evolved from an entertainment sensation, to a fountainhead of a counterculture consciousness, to a formidable political threat in the person of John Lennon.

Five years after the Beatles had performed a last time in San Francisco in 1966, Lennon returned in his first live concert in December 1971 in Ann Arbor, Michigan. His "Give Peace a Chance" was already a peace anthem.

But this cause had a harder edge, a benefit for imprisoned poet-turned-revolutionary John Sinclair. The flower children of Motown were becoming "White Panthers," consciously emulating the Black Panther Party. According to the FBI documents obtained in a lawsuit by the historian Jon Wiener, FBI agents were in the audience of 15,000 that night and did not like what they heard, saw or inhaled. For years the spy agency had been frustrated by the rise of a counterculture; one 1966 strategy memo lamented that the "nonconformism in dress and speech, neglect of personal cleanliness, use of obscenities (printed and uttered), publicized sexual promiscuity, experimenting with and the use of drugs, filthy clothes, shaggy hair, wearing of sandals, beads and unusual jewelry tend to negate any attempt to hold these people up to ridicule." [1]

Declassified cable traffic reveals that the key reason the FBI attempted to deport John and Yoko Lennon in early 1972 for overstaying a visa was not a prior marijuana charge in London, but the upcoming 1972 reelection campaign of Richard Nixon. Antiwar sentiment had reached majority proportions in America and activism had acquired a militant edge with the siege of the White House and thousands of arrests in May 1971. Nixon's paranoia was seemingly boundless. That same year he illegally authorized the White House "plumbers" to ransack the Democratic National Committee offices in Washington, steal confidential files from Daniel Ellsberg's therapist, and lay plans to suppress the planned protests at the Republican national convention in San Diego.

John Lennon and Yoko Ono figured prominently in the plans and dreams of those hoping to upset Nixon that year. "A confidential source who has furnished reliable information in the past" advised the FBI that Lennon gave $75,000 in early 1972 toward a plan to "disrupt the Republican National Convention."

On March 1, another "confidential source" advised that I had flown into Washington for a secret meeting with Rennie Davis to discuss an election-year plan involving demonstrations, speaking tours, and a New Left–oriented "entertainment group" composed of John and Yoko whose "function [was] a stimulus to encourage youths to be in the vicinity of election candidates when they are on tour."[2]

On March 16, 1972, another FBI memo warned that "subject" Lennon "continues to plan activities directed towards RNC and will soon initiate series of 'rock concerts' to develop financial support . . ." The agent advised that the New York Bureau "promptly initiate discreet efforts to locate subject" and that any information linking Lennon to drugs be "immediately furnished to Bureau in form suitable for dissemination."

On May 21, the Bureau pledged to "*neutralize any disruptive activities of subject*" (emphasis added), in the chilling vocabulary of the FBI's counterintelligence (COINTEL) program.[3]

Somewhere between fantasy and reality, Rennie was convinced that John Lennon could transcend and unify our fragmented world with one more grand tour of protest. Abbie Hoffman and Jerry Rubin shared the same dream, and were meeting with Lennon, Rennie said. It was a time of grand and distrustful egotisms, however, despite the considerable expansion of public support for the movement's aims of peace and tolerance. One reason is that Nixon was withdrawing ground troops from Vietnam while continuing the bombing, sending police after the Black Panthers and their friends, and indicting up to sixty separate antiwar protestors on various conspiracy charges. All this was causing activists to wonder and quarrel about whether the long war was ending or heating up. One can only speculate about the role that FBI counterintelligence programs, and the plentitude of drugs, played in fostering this paranoia.

The Lennons were consumed in their government-triggered deportation hearings and could not imagine being at the storm center of a six-month crusade of concerts and confrontations to dump Richard Nixon. They would speak out, and did, being photographed in conical hats showing solidarity with South Vietnamese political prisoners. He and Yoko endorsed a protest that resulted in cancellation of the annual Armed Forces Day in New York City.[4] But on their deportation lawyer's advice, they dropped the convention concert plans by the end of 1971.

The whole bizarre history surrounding that convention remains to be told. Later documents would show that G. Gordon Liddy (of Watergate infamy) took part in a planning group that considered kidnapping protest leaders and dumping us in the Mexican desert. A vigilante group called the Secret Army Organization (SAO) fired shots into a San Diego house filled with protest planners; one bullet pierced a wrist. An FBI undercover agent sat in the car next to the shooter.

Then suddenly the Republicans pulled out, shifting their venue to Miami, for reasons never explained to this day. The effect was to undermine and weaken the protests, spurring even greater division and paranoia. A group called the Zippies was dogging Jerry Rubin and Abbie Hoffman with charges of selling out. Rennie Davis was being shunned by feminists. I was accused of burning buses when I wasn't even in town. Even the newly formed Vietnam Veterans Against the War (VVAW) was riddled with undercover agents. Inexplicably, however, FBI memos at late as June 1972 still warned that the Lennons were planning a huge rock concert outside the Republican convention hall. In July, another FBI memo urged the Miami office that the Lennons be arrested on possession of narcotics charges during the Republican convention. They even fabricated a wanted flyer for Miami police with a photo purporting to be John Lennon saying "The Pope Smokes Dope" and describing him as "a former member of the Beatles Rock Music Group." [5]

Once the convention ended, however, the FBI folded up its mythic case, reporting in several memos that the Lennons had not been seen at all in Miami, quoting a source that the "subject" had "fallen out" with Davis, Rubin and Hoffman (August 30, 1972). The Lennon counterintelligence case was put on "pending inactive status" six days after the Republican convention and closed on December 8, 1972, one month after Nixon was reelected. [6]

No doubt British intelligence was after John Lennon in that year, not because of a token marijuana charge, but because he actively demonstrated against the British Army shootings of fourteen Irish civil rights demonstrators during "Bloody Sunday" in January 1972. Cable traffic revealed that Lennon had "offered entertainment" for the Derry cause, and intense efforts were devoted to monitoring links between American activists and the republican movement in Northern Ireland. One FBI document based on "information provided by a foreign government," presumably London, was totally blacked-out apparently because the discovery of a British spy operation could provoke "retaliation" toward the spymasters.

Having attempted to defame and neutralize this "former member of the Beatles Rock Music Group," the FBI and government agencies fought fourteen years in court against disclosure of their covert campaign until 1992, when they were ordered to settle with plaintiff Jon Wiener and his ACLU lawyers. The following government officials and agencies were revealed to be in a single sinister loop to prevent an election-year concert tour featuring John Lennon: the president, the vice president, the secretary of state, the director of the Central Intelligence Agency, the director of the Defense Intelligence Agency, the Department of the Army, the Department of the Air Force, the Naval Investigative Service, the U.S. Secret Service, and the attorney general.[7]

In the end, some of the truth was revealed, but who was left to remember? Imagine what 1972 might have been with John Lennon on tour against Richard Nixon. Instead, the full weight of one, and presumably two, state spy agencies was brought down to fabricate charges, launch deportation proceedings, and discreetly set in motion a plan to "neutralize" an artist they couldn't co-opt.

Asked in a *Rolling Stone* interview about "the effect on history" of the Beatles, Lennon perhaps foresaw the future:

> The people who are in control and in power and the class system and the whole bourgeois scene is exactly the same, except that there's a lot of fag fuckin' middle-class kids with long hair walking around London in trendy clothes . . . but apart from that, nothing happened. We all dressed up. The same bastards are in control, the same people are running everything. It's exactly the same! They hyped the kids! We've grown up a little, all of us, and there has been a change and we are a bit freer and all that, but it's the same game. . . . The dream is over, it's just the same, only I'm thirty and a lot of people have got long hair, that's all.[8]

There are many ways to remember John Lennon, of course. But we should always remember the John Lennon that the FBI and MI5 will do anything to make us forget.

NOTES

1. SAC, Newark, to Director, FBI, Memorandum, May 27, 1968 (Counterintelligence Program, Internal Security: Disruption of the New Left / Re Bureau letter to Albany), May 10, 1963.
2. FBI Memorandum (Election Year Strategy Information Center), March 8, 1972.
3. Jon Wiener, *Gimme Some Truth*, University of California Press, 1999, p. 238.
4. Ibid., p. 266.
5. Ibid., p. 290.
6. Ibid., p. 298.
7. January 23, 1972 Memo from J. Edgar Hoover on "Protest Activity and Civil Disturbances," including [blacked-out] "Beatle singer John Lennon;" Wiener, *Gimme Some Truth*, p. 137.
8. Jann Wenner, *Lennon Remembers*, Rolling Stone Press, 1971, p. 106.

42

Dick Flacks
Where Caterpillars Become Butterflies

May 5, 2006

When my old friend Richard Flacks retired, the UC Santa Barbara Sociology Department organized a tribute for him and invited me to speak. There was a huge turnout, including the chancellor and a congressperson, and a fund was established to support students interested in social movements. I attended and had the honor to read this to the gathering.

◆　　◆　　◆

I RISE TO CELEBRATE THE LIVES of Dick and Mickey Flacks, perhaps my longest continuing friends since the beginning of the 1960s.

Dick's many achievements in this community will be noted by the friends who gather here tonight. I want to acknowledge his broader contributions to participatory democracy, our common project these forty years.

Dick saw and believed that participatory democracy was the moral and practical alternative to the centralized militaristic bureaucracies of the Cold War.

It was Dick who advanced the notion that another Left was possible, that instead of being subordinate satellites of the organized working class, students, intellectuals, professionals—all people of conscience—in coalition with the dispossessed, could exert a force capable of stopping wars and reforming institutions.

Believing a new Left must be grounded in everyday community life, not be a distant professional vanguard, he and Mickey fought the multinational oil companies on the Santa Barbara coast. They raised two sons, intellectuals both. Mickey became a powerful political organizer, a kind of feminist and environmental Vito Marcantonio.

Dick believed that another sociology was possible too, one that was organically linked to social movements, and helped launch a sociology liberation movement in 1968. Over the decades, he introduced thousands of university students to the history of radicalism hidden from them in the educational process.

He wrote one of the finest books ever written about the Left and social movements, asserting that making history must be about making a life as well.

I was wrong for once thinking that he would be sheltered in an ivory tower remote from the struggle. Those who hated the New Left, who hated leftist professors, perhaps Jewish professors worst of all, broke into that ivory tower and almost took his life. He soon recovered with quiet bravery, honor and integrity, and we here are blessed that his life was saved.

But the institutions do demand a price from the rebels who enter them, as I was to learn during eighteen years in the legislature. There were bright initial moments as the system opened its doors. Jerry Brown was a 35-year-old governor when we persuaded him to stop a liquified natural gas terminal right here at point conception. Jerry Brown appointed our friend Stanley Sheinbaum to the UC board of regents, and he protected the AIM leader Dennis Banks from extradition. Things could only get better and better, or so we assumed. With Dick and Mickey's help I ran for office on a platform resembling the Port Huron Statement, and won the primary in Santa Barbara County.

We did create a space for progressive alternatives and won some lasting victories along the way, but I cannot honestly that we stopped the empire, saved the planet, or closed the gap between rich or poor.

In a similar way, it was important that the study of social movements became accepted in the universities. It seemed, however, that as the energy of social movements declined, they became institutionalized, specialized, and professionalized in the university, unrecognizably so for those of us who lived them. Valuable as these reforms were, the new studies rarely if ever understood how a movement feels. I would suggest this analogy—that movements are preceded by the patient crawling of caterpillars who mysteriously weave a cocoon and transform into butterflies. This natural, inevitable, self-generating process of beauty's creation is difficult to subject to regression analysis or bureaucratic acronyms.

There was a place of distinction for Dick Flacks in the University, just as there was for Tom Hayden in politics, but those were institutional niches, not exactly launching pads of transformation.

As an example of what happens to social movements in the hands of those searching for a specialized dissertation thesis, I was teaching at Harvard's Institute of Politics on social movements a few years ago, when a young scholar approached with a question: he was working on a paper about the song "Mellow Yellow" by Donovan, and wanted to know whether there was a run on supermarkets by hippies who tried to get high on banana peels. Because it had been reported in the underground press, he felt it was significant and researchable. I couldn't recall a thing, and felt myself becoming a footnote in a thesis on how the political New Left didn't connect with the counterculture.

I took a different approach to teaching in the Big House. I took eight students, on Harvard funding, to Miami to be participant-observers at the global justice protest against the summit of the Free Trade Agreement of the Americas. They were to stay in the middle of things while journaling and interviewing the activists.

The information they discovered was interesting. Of eighty people interviewed, 54.5 percent voted for Al Gore and 45.5 percent voted for Ralph Nader in 2000. Three-fifths had never engaged in civil disobedience before. Forty-two percent believed that the WTO should be reformed, while only 21 percent thought it should be abolished altogether. Support for participatory democracy was very high, 4.72 on a scale of 1 to 5.

Five of my students were arrested as participant-observers. They were marching backwards from the troopers who pointed weapons at them, with their hands over their heads, chanting, "We are dispersing, We are dispersing." They were thrown down, pepper-sprayed, and locked up.

I spent the night bailing them out, talking to their parents by phone, and coping with Harvard's distress. Who authorized the use of Harvard's money? Who okayed Hayden taking these students into a riot zone? Would

Harvard be sued by the parents? At the time Harvard's president was a foremost advocate of corporate globalization.

At my suggestion, the students just kept journaling. It would be their most significant educational experience of their lives thus far. One of them wrote of growing up in a safe New Jersey suburb where the police were simply not a problem, but now he had learned what it was like to be a targeted enemy, an experience millions of people go through every day. He would not forget this.

There are thousands like those Harvard students in our high schools and universities across America today, sorting out their possible futures, wondering how they matter. Like us forty years ago, they yearn for relevance, for guides along the way. They want something beyond the postmodern. They want to shape their future. Students are not meant to be caterpillars for long.

Dick Flacks has served as one of those guiding mentors. He has served his time well. He will be missed, but because of him, others already are preparing to take his place in the field where the caterpillars become butterflies.

43

The Children

Los Angeles Times, *March 22, 1998*

David Halberstam died in a car crash in 2007, having just finished a book on the Korean War. He was a liberal in the best sense, a man who celebrated his country, was deeply disappointed when it failed to measure up to its ideals, and was never afraid to say so. He covered the civil rights movement as a rookie reporter in 1960, then regretted being "too clinical," not telling the story of the people behind the movement. The Children *is an important recasting of how history actually is made.*

◆　　◆　　◆

DAVID HALBERSTAM IS AMERICA'S Alexis de Toqueville. For almost forty years, he has chronicled our national life, from the tragedy of Vietnam to the triumphs in the National Football League. Now, in *The Children*, he returns to his roots as a young reporter for the Nashville *Tennessean*, where he covered the start of the civil rights movement, the sit-ins that galvanized a generation. In following a dozen student idealists through the arc of their lives in the early 1960s to the present ambiguous moment at the end of the century, he shows how people make history and how the making of that history affects their lives.

The Children is an important book, especially for today's youth, who will read in its moving and revealing pages the remarkable stories of flesh-and-blood people who were the fiber of a social movement that is at best dimly remembered and mostly associated with leaders too lofty to be emulated.

"The children" was the term used by some clergy, parents and an older establishment to characterize the daring spirit—Halberstam calls it "relentless innocence"—of the sit-in leaders whose average age was no more than twenty. It was an affectionate, if sometimes patronizing term. I remember it well, for I was one of those children, living in Atlanta in 1961. I celebrated my twenty-first birthday in jail with Bernard Lafayette, a figure in this book, who, back then, had been a student in Nashville. We had joined with others for a Freedom Ride to Albany, Georgia, where we hoped to desegregate public facilities. That year I also experienced mob violence in Mississippi, where the Nashville students led the bloodiest Freedom Ride.

Looking back on his youthful reporting, Halberstam faults himself and his colleagues for writing stories that were "quite clinical. . . . [We] did little to try and humanize the demonstrators." More than thirty years later, he seeks in this book to make up for past journalistic sterility by bringing to life some of the fascinating figures in the movement for racial justice. He does so with a sense of dramatic narrative and appreciation for nuance and complexity that moves the reader to empathy and reflection.

Halberstam's book is as much about character as it is about the vast political and cultural struggle that was waged. To taste the flavor of the courageous and compelling men and women who make up Halberstam's story, here are five typical examples:

➤ James Bevel was one of seventeen children, served in the Navy, was a singer in clubs, heard the voice of God, became a Baptist preacher and wore a yarmulke to identify with the prophets and mystify the police. It was Bevel who, in addition to the Freedom Rides, mobilized the children of Birmingham, Alabama in 1963, thought up the Selma to Montgomery march in 1965, urged Martin Luther King Jr. to oppose the Vietnam War and, thirty years later, suggested the concept of the Million Man March to Louis Farrakhan. Today Bevel lives in Chicago and, repeating his own family cycle, is father of seventeen children.

➤ Bernard Lafayette was a student at American Baptist College with Bevel and with future Congressman John Lewis. He was a Nashville Freedom Rider who took the assignment of organizing Selma, Alabama, when no one else would. The night he and his new wife, Colia, moved into Selma's

Torch Motel, they were met by FBI agents, who urged them to leave and even offered them scholarships to Columbia University. Lafayette was targeted for death and miraculously survived a vicious beating in Selma on the same night that Medgar Evers was killed in Mississippi. He eventually received a doctorate from Harvard School of Education, was a high school principal in Tuskegee, Ala., and became finally president of American Baptist College, where his activism began thirty-eight years ago. In 1991, Lafayette was presented the official keys to the city of Selma by Mayor Joe Smitherman, who unbelievably still held office thirty-two years after the violent confrontations.

➤ Gloria Johnson was a medical student at Meharry Medical College in Nashville and was forced to hide her sit-in activities from her role-model mother, whose health was failing. She married and had three kids with Rodney Powell, another medical student activist. Together, they journeyed from the sit-in movement to the Peace Corps in Africa and back to Los Angeles, where she became the first minority student in psychiatry at UCLA Medical School and he directed the Watts Neighborhood Health Center. In 1970, Rodney told her that he was gay. She struggled with the news, lived with him a few more years in Minnesota and Uganda (during Idi Amin's terror) but ultimately fell into depression and attempted suicide. Rodney formed a solid relationship with a white professor from Hawaii, and he and Gloria built their bond anew. She went on to become the first tenured black female professor at Harvard Medical School.

➤ Diane Nash was perhaps the best known of the Nashville Freedom Riders. Halberstam opens *The Children* with an interior monologue in which Nash, who had competed in the Miss Illinois beauty contest before the movement changed her life, is overcome with dread as she prepares for her first arrest. Not long after, she was forcing Nashville's mayor to publicly commit himself to lunch counter desegregation. She played the key role in continuing the Deep South Freedom Rides at a time when older civil rights leaders and the Kennedy Justice Department were pressuring participants to call them off. She entered an ill-fated marriage to James Bevel, and they had two children before their relationship collapsed. In a Mississippi courtroom in April 1962, a very pregnant Nash, defended by Bevel (who was not a lawyer), insisted on being jailed instead of pursuing an appeal. "This will be a black baby born in Mississippi, and thus wherever he is born, he will be in prison," she told the stunned judge. Eventually he ordered her release despite a two-year sentence. Years later, separated from Bevel, she raised her children in Chicago, where she continues to engage in social activism.

➤ Hank Thomas was almost beaten to death in the 1961 Anniston, Alabama, Freedom Ride and survived the terrors of Parchman Penitentiary in Mississippi only to have his hand nearly shot off while serving in Vietnam in 1966. He came out of the Veterans Hospital determined to break barriers in business, and even though he eventually became a millionaire through McDonald's franchises, he was still refused a home loan by four Atlanta banks in the 1980s because he was black. He ultimately built his home. Thomas is active in veterans affairs and has hosted North Vietnamese officers on visits of reconciliation.

The stories go on and on. Taken together, they constitute a whole that is greater than its parts, a picture in which ordinary people emerged from the oblivion of segregation to shape our national history in ways that the "best and brightest" of the establishment could not or would not do.

Halberstam also captures the moral imperative that set "the children" apart from their elders, who counseled retreat from danger: "As far as the young people were concerned, the danger was the very object of the exercise, and was what they wanted in order to push things forward. They had come to sense in some intuitive way that the things they wanted to happen would happen only if they reached and crossed a certain danger point. An intuitive philosophy of the students in the movement was being born: the safer everything was, the less likely that anything important would take place."

But Halberstam is not content to let such courage determine "the children's" place in history. By profiling more than their deeds in a singular place and time, he raises the existential question of what happens to ordinary people, whose ordinariness was extraordinarily altered, when ordinary life resumes its routine pace.

Take Curtis Murphy, who lost several years to alcoholism after Nashville before he settled as a teacher in the Chicago inner city. "Curtis Murphy hit the wall," Halberstam concludes; he was "among the first . . . who had to return to so ordinary a life, the first to learn how hard it was to be middle class."

Perhaps this experience was similar to what combat soldiers go through when they return to civilian life. As soldiers practicing nonviolence, "the children's" goal was to ride into enemy lines, to absorb the hate, violence and the real possibility of death until segregation was rendered impossible to maintain. There was constant danger but also intense love, moments of glory and deepest loss, feelings of redemption followed by burnout, then came unexpected victories, with centuries-old walls collapsing and the shock of watching politicians, who had stood on the sidelines, suddenly marching onto the battlefield proclaiming "We Shall Overcome." For some, the resumption of an ordinary life meant suffering the invisible scars of social indifference, more lasting than the bruises of police brutality.

Angeline Butler, a former Nashville sit-in leader now living in Los Angeles, describes the veterans of this singular experience as "single soldiers" today, making impacts where they can, without the presence of a larger movement.

To immerse myself locally in this Nashville legacy, I attended Martin Luther King Day services January 17 at Holman Methodist Church in South-Central Los Angeles, where the pastor is the Rev. James Lawson. In Halberstam's narrative, Lawson emerges as the most powerful connecting thread, as well he should. At 29, Lawson went to Nashville in 1958 at the call of King and trained "the children" in nonviolence workshops that led to the sit-ins. A religious pacifist, he served one year in prison as a conscientious objector in the early 1950s and three years as a Methodist missionary in India, where he became profoundly attached to the doctrines of Mohandas Gandhi. Gandhi predicted that a black man in America might bring nonviolence to the world, and Lawson was convinced that Martin Luther King Jr. was that leader and worked intimately with him until the day of his death.

Lawson's workshops enabled "the children" to form a focused community that became an instrument of action. He taught patience, knowing that at first people would feel small but, because great ideas mattered, many more would be drawn to the cause when it was seen to be serious. He transformed a legacy of suppressed shame and inferiority for being black into a passion for justice. And he trained people to accept physical assault and jail because those experiences isolated their adversaries and created public sympathy.

Lawson was a brilliant teacher and one of the most steadfast direct action leaders of all. Halberstam describes a remarkable incident in which Lawson, standing in the midst of a threatening mob, is spit upon by a segregationist. When Lawson asked him for a handkerchief to wipe himself off, the assailant complied; Lawson asked him next what kind of motorcycle he rode and turned the spitting incident into a conversation.

He was lead spokesman on the most dangerous Freedom Ride: from Montgomery, Alabama to Jackson, Mississippi, on May 14, 1961. Five years later, he remained in the center of the storm and was asked by King to regroup the 1966 Meredith, Mississippi, march after James Meredith was shot. In 1968, he was minister of Centenary Methodist Church in Memphis, rallying support for the sanitation workers' strike that became King's last crusade.

And thirty years after that madness, Lawson was presiding over the King memorial services at Holman Methodist on a quiet sunny Sunday on West Adams Boulevard. I had attended Lawson's services before, seeking to experience a memory or a flashback of those long-ago times. (I do not make it through "We Shall Overcome" without beginning to cry.) On this particular day, thinking about Halberstam's book and sitting in a virtually all-black congregation, I was struck at how in liberal Los Angeles and northern cities, the reality of segregation is entrenched in the places we worship, where we live, how we educate our children, how we bury our dead.

Still I lectured myself that we must count our blessings. There is a larger black middle class than thirty years ago, voting rights have made a difference and there are oases of genuine multicultural friendship. But segregation is not a thing of the past as we hoped it would be when we were "the children." It is the future our children face.

Only 11 percent of the students in Los Angeles public schools are white. Harvard University's Gary Orfield and Susan Eaton have shown that school segregation across the country is increasing for black students for the first time since 1954. In Nashville and the Deep South, where the Freedom Rides took place, life is freer than it was, but many conditions have worsened. Thad Kousser's analysis of census data shows that in Nashville in 1960, blacks were twice as likely as whites to be poor, but today they are three times as likely to be poor. In Mississippi in 1990, 47 percent of blacks were below the federal poverty line. In Albany, Georgia, where once I was a Freedom Rider, the average yearly black wage in 1990 was $5,904.

The ratio of incarceration of blacks to whites nationally in 1960 was five to one, while today it is more than seven to one. In the vacuum left by our failure to resolve the issues of race and poverty, youthful gang nihilism has proliferated, and multiple conflicts between blacks, Latinos and Asians cast a shadow on our future. Racism has not been defeated: the question is whether it has defeated us.

In spite of these grounds for despair, Halberstam is correct when he writes that Lawson has "remained remarkably unchanged in his beliefs after nearly four decades of social activism." After services, we talked in his book-laden study. Nearly 70, silver-maned, fit and energetic as always, Lawson remembered the events of yesteryear as a living, continuing story, suggesting people I should call in Nashville, remembering how black churches were nervous about King and "the children" in the early days and lamenting the failure to develop a "strategy for the long haul." He observed that King's "I have a dream" speech has been incorporated into American mainstream culture but that the movement's anti-militarism and anti-poverty themes have not. "The '60s are being reversed," he added, by forces that are reviving more sophisticated, even academic, rationales for white sovereignty, such as *The Bell Curve*.

Unlike Lawson, Halberstam fails to venture an opinion about race relations today or the impact of the movement overall. Perhaps this is a journalist's prerogative, though by contrast, Tom Wicker, another reporter of those days, has written of the "tragic failure" of the civil rights movement and even suggested that African American voters should abandon the Democratic Party. As a writer, Halberstam is entitled to leave to his readers the meaning of the events he describes. But throughout the book are hints that he is comfortable with, even celebrates, the workings of the very system that the movement opposed as elitist and exclusionary. Those who were scorned and beaten in 1961 are honored by Halberstam as American success stories. That is sweet justice indeed, but what about the conditions those individuals fought to change?

Halberstam left Nashville in the early 1960s, in his words, "in the middle of the story." He was ambitious for fame, meaning "serious recognition within my profession that I was a budding star." He succeeded, winning a Pulitzer Prize for his critical coverage of the Vietnam War. But his individual success in the mainstream may have led him to ignore its limitations.

Was it the mainstream that made voting rights possible, or was it "the children" who forced the mainstream to respond and concede? In his epilogue, Halberstam calls the Nashville sit-ins a shining "example of democracy at work." From the viewpoint of the Freedom Riders, however, an inclusive democracy was being outlawed for electoral expediency. Halberstam asserts that by 1964, President Lyndon Johnson had turned around J. Edgar Hoover and "completed the slow commitment of the executive branch of the federal government to the side of the activists," a judgment completely at odds with both the facts and the experience of the activists. Halberstam's conclusion is contradicted one page later, when he quotes Johnson telling King in 1965 that a voting-rights act "couldn't be done." Later, he writes that Johnson called King "that goddamn nigger preacher" for his views on Vietnam. Soon young blacks, who received little protection from terrorist bullets in the South, were dying in disproportionate numbers for freedom in Vietnam. Survivors returned to ghettos burdened with exceptional rates of unemployment and drug addiction.

Halberstam glides over these sorry chapters of history too lightly, leaving some readers to conclude that the sit-ins were a mythic example of the American Dream coming true, a case of dissidents being held up to prove that the system works. It would be interesting to know whether Halberstam sees the need for a new generation of "the children" to combat the worsening conditions of race, poverty and gang violence in our cities today. I do.

Whatever my reservations about Halberstam's analysis, I hope the lives he describes so movingly in *The Children* will inspire a new generation to see that only they can move America closer to our professed ideals.

44.

You Gotta Love Her

The Nation, *March 22, 2004*

More on right-wing America's Jane Fonda problem.

♦　　♦　　♦

I was digging into the batter's box one Saturday morning in San Pedro a couple of years ago when the catcher behind me muttered, "I'm a Vietnam vet, and I've been waiting for twenty years to say you should be dead or in jail for being a traitor." The umpire said nothing. I flied out to center. Later we talked. Then we became friends.

It turned out that his hatred was toward my ex-wife, not me, because he believed certain Web site fabrications about Jane Fonda that circulate among veterans. Twice the Republicans in the California legislature tried to block my seating because of my trips to Hanoi. But I was never a target of opportunity like my ex—more like collateral damage.

While most Americans, perhaps including that former Yale cheerleader and elusive National Guardsman George W. Bush and, I suspect, most Vietnam veterans, would like to forget the past, the Vietnam War is about to be relived this election season.

Senator John Kerry, a veteran of both the war and the antiwar movement, is causing this national Vietnam flashback. The right-wing attack dogs are on the hunt. Newt Gingrich calls Kerry an "antiwar Jane Fonda liberal, " while Internet warriors post fabricated images of Kerry and Fonda at a 1971 antiwar rally. Welcome to dirty tricks in the age of Photoshop.

The attempted smearing of Kerry through the Fonda "connection" is a Republican attempt to suppress an honest reopening of our unfinished exploration of the Vietnam era.

Neoconservatives and the Pentagon have good reason to fear the return of the Vietnam Syndrome. The label intentionally suggests a disease, a weakening of the martial will, but the syndrome was actually a healthy American reaction to false White House promises of victory, the propping up of corrupt regimes, crony contracting and cover-ups of civilian casualties during the Vietnam War that are echoed today in the news from Baghdad. Young John Kerry's 1971 question—"How do you ask a man to be the last to die for a mistake?"—is more relevant than ever.

Rather than give these reopened wounds the serious treatment they deserve, the Republicans substitute the politics of scapegoating and sheer fantasy. Most centrist Democrats, in turn, try to distance themselves from controversies that recall the 1960s. There are journalistic centrists as well, who avoid hard truths for the sake of acceptance and legitimacy. Such amnesia, whether unconscious or not, lends a wide respectability to the feeble confessions of those like Robert McNamara, who took twenty-five years to admit that Vietnam was a "mistake" and then, when asked by filmmaker Errol Morris why he didn't speak out earlier, answered, "I don't want to go any further. . . . It just opens up more controversies."

The case of Jane Fonda reveals the double standards and hypocrisies afflicting our memories. In *Tour of Duty*, the Kerry historian Douglas Brinkley describes the 1971 Winter Soldier Investigation, which Fonda supported and Kerry attended, where Vietnam veterans spilled their guts about "killing gooks for sport, sadistically torturing captured VC by cutting off ears and heads, raping women and burning villages." Brinkley then recounts how Kerry later told *Meet the Press* that "I committed the same kinds of atrocities as thousands of others," specifically taking responsibility for shooting in free-fire zones, search-and-destroy missions, and burning villages. Brinkley describes these testimonies in tepid and judicious terms, calling them "quite unsettling." By contrast, Brinkley condemns Fonda's 1972 visit to Hanoi as "unconscionable," without feeling any need for further explanation.

Why should American atrocities be merely unsettling, but a trip to Hanoi unconscionable?

In fact, Fonda was neither wrong nor unconscionable in what she said and did in North Vietnam. She told the *New York Times* in 1973, "I'm quite sure that there were incidents of torture . . . but the pilots who were saying it was the policy of the Vietnamese and that it was systematic, I believe that's a lie." Research by John Hubbell, as well as 1973 interviews with POWs, shows that Vietnamese behavior meeting any recognized definition of torture had ceased by 1969, three years before the Fonda visit. James Stockdale, the POW who emerged as Ross Perot's running mate in 1992, wrote that no more than 10 percent of the U.S. pilots received at least 90 percent of the Vietnamese punishment, often for deliberate acts of resistance. Yet the legends of widespread, sinister Oriental torture have been accepted as fact by millions of Americans.

Erased from public memory is the fact that Fonda's purpose was to use her celebrity to put a spotlight on the possible bombing of Vietnam's system of dikes. Her charges were dismissed at the time by George H. W. Bush, then America's ambassador to the United Nations, who complained of a "carefully planned campaign by the North Vietnamese and their supporters to give worldwide circulation to this falsehood. " But Fonda was right and Bush was lying, as revealed by the April–May 1972 White House transcripts of Richard Nixon talking to Henry Kissinger about "this shit-ass little country":

> NIXON: We've got to be thinking in terms of an all-out bombing attack. . . . I'm thinking of the dikes.
> KISSINGER: I agree with you.
> NIXON: . . . Will that drown people?
> KISSINGER: About two hundred thousand people.

It was in order to try to avert this catastrophe that Fonda, whose popular "FTA" road show (either "Fun, Travel, Adventure" or "Fuck the Army") was blocked from access to military bases, gave interviews on Hanoi radio describing the human consequences of all-out bombing by B-52 pilots five miles above her. After her visit, the U.S. bombing of the dike areas slowed down, "allowing the Vietnamese at last to repair damage and avert massive flooding," according to Mary Hershberger.

The now legendary Fonda photo shows her with diminutive Vietnamese women examining an antiaircraft weapon, implying in the rightist imagination that she relished the thought of killing those American pilots innocently flying overhead. To deconstruct this image and what it has come to represent, it might be helpful to look further back in our history.

Imagine a nineteenth-century Jane Fonda visiting the Oglala Sioux in the Black Hills before the battle at Little Big Horn. Imagine her examining Crazy Horse's arrows or climbing upon Sitting Bull's horse. Such behavior by a well-known actress no doubt would have infuriated General George Armstrong Custer, but what would the rest of us feel today?

In *Dances With Wolves*, Kevin Costner played an American soldier who went "native" and, as a result, was attacked and brutalized as a traitor by his own men. But we in the modern audience are supposed to respect and idealize the Costner "traitor," perhaps because his heroism assuages our historical guilt. Will it take another century for certain Americans to see the Fonda trip to Hanoi in a similar light?

The popular delusions about Fonda are a window into many other dangerous hallucinations that pass for historical memory in this country. Among the most difficult to contest are claims that antiwar activists persistently spit on returning Vietnam veterans. So universal is the consensus on "spitting" that I once gave up trying to refute it, although I had never heard of a single episode in a decade of antiwar experiences. Then came the startling historical research of a Vietnam veteran named Jerry Lembcke, who demonstrated in *The Spitting Image* (1998) that not a single case of such abuse had ever been convincingly documented. In fact, Lembcke's search of the local press throughout the Vietnam decade revealed no reports of spitting at all. It was a mythical projection by those who felt "spat-upon, " Lembcke concluded, and meant politically to discredit future antiwar activism.

The *Rambo* movies not only popularized the spitting image but also the equally incredible claim that hundreds of American soldiers missing in action were being held by the Vietnamese Communists for unspecified purposes. John Kerry's most noted achievement in the Senate was gaining bipartisan support, including that of all the Senate's Vietnam veterans, for a report declaring the MIA legend unfounded, which led to normalized relations. Yet millions of Americans remain captives of this legend.

It will be easier, I am afraid, for those Americans to believe that Jane Fonda helped torture our POWs than to accept the testimony by American GIs that they sliced ears, burned hooches, raped women and poisoned Vietnam's children with deadly chemicals. Just two years ago many of the same people in Georgia voted out of office a Vietnam War triple-amputee, Senator Max Cleland, for being "soft on national defense."

If there is any cure for this mouth-foaming mass pathology in a democracy, it may lie at the heart of John Kerry's campaign for the presidency. Rather than distance ourselves from the past, as the centrist amnesiacs would counsel, perhaps we should finally peel back the scabs and take a closer look at why all the wounds haven't healed. The most meaningful experience of John Kerry's life was the time he spent fighting and killing in Vietnam and then turning around to protest the insanity of it all. Instead of wrapping himself in fabrications, he threw his fantasies and delusions, and metaphorically his militarism, over the White House fence. That's what many more Americans need to do.

If I were George W. Bush, I would be terrorized by the eyes of those scruffy-looking veterans, the so-called band of brothers, volunteering for duty with the Kerry campaign. They look like men with scores to settle, with a palpable intolerance toward the types who sent them to war for a lie, then ignored their Agent Orange illness, cut their GI benefits, treated them like losers and still haven't explained what that war was about. They know Jane Fonda is a diversion from a larger battlefield. They are the sort who will keep a cerebral United States senator grounded, who have finally figured out who their real enemies are and who are determined that this generation hear their story anew. They are gearing up for one last battle. Chickenhawks better duck.

45

Fifty Years On the Road with Jack Kerouac

Huffington Post, *September 5, 2007*

On the fiftieth anniversary of the publication of On the Road *I gave a talk to my Pitzer College class about the 1960s. A majority of my students had either heard of Kerouac or read him in a class, but knew nothing of his life and times.*

◆   ◆   ◆

IT IS LATE—at night, and in life—and I am writing in the shadow of Jack Kerouac whose *On the Road* was first published fifty years ago on this day and I am wishing that everyone who once read him will contemplate his spirit and work again. I was a high school senior in Royal Oak, Michigan, when I read, absorbed and lived the spirit of *On The Road*. His writing was breathtaking to encounter, breaking all the conventions governing the periods and commas and paragraphs that impose false orders on the speed and flow of reality, the reality of everyday life that he observed and recorded because he believed it was all there was. His brilliant exploding frenzy and jazz-inspired pace shook and inspired our generation.

Having just returned from my fiftieth high school reunion this August, I can say that the differences from those days of "straight" and "hip" have faded over the decades. Our graduating class, the one that matured or became more immature on Kerouac, was also the class that invented cruising on Woodward Avenue, the cruising that turned into chicken contests in *Rebel Without A Cause*, the cruising that has now become an annual promotional celebration of Detroit with people proudly driving their polished 1950s cars amidst 50,000 cheering people abandoned by the automobile industry.

At first the road was Woodward Avenue, but then it became the road to the coasts, the road beyond the suburbs, the dream road, the fantasy road, the road out. It was the time of hitchhikers, when you could gather up your curiosity, stick out your thumb, jump in cars with strangers and head for exotic frontiers. Bob Dylan (then Zimmerman) hitchiked from Minnesota to see Woody Guthrie in a New York hospital. I learned all about racism and New Orleans black culture hitchhiking from Ann Arbor to Louisiana and back. I wrote poetry and short stories hitchhiking through Salt Lake City in the shadow of the Mormon Temple on my way to Telegraph Avenue where I was dumped in front of the still-there Mediterranean for a coffee where I met a girl who led me to an apartment to crash amidst the drums and excitement of the growing new radicalism. All of this was the influence of Kerouac and the times. There were tens of thousands of us, wandering, searching, experimenting, just living. One of his characters, Carlo Marx (who in reality was Allen Ginsberg) asks Sal Paradise (who in reality was Kerouac), "I mean, man, whither goest thou?," a question that was deepened in the final draft of *On The Road* into "Whither Goest Thou, America, in thy shiny car at night?," a question that just demanded an answer that could not be given from Woodward Avenue. And there, perhaps, it all started.

Or did it start in Kerouac's identification with people who were beaten down and drugged out, or with black people, who responded to oppression with church singing, jazz, bop, the hipster style? Or in Mexico, his "magic land at the end of the road" where the "Fellahin Indians of the world" stare coldly at the "moneybag Americans on a lark in their land"?

Wherever it started, in a conversation or a dream or literal experiences, being beat first meant down and out in a time of national Cold War celebration but more, "a special spirituality" which included experiencing the beatific, a reappearance of, as Kerouac wrote:

> The early Gothic springtime feeling of Western mankind before it went on its "civilization" Rationale and developed relativity, jets and superbombs and supercollosal bureaucratic totalitarian benevolent Big Brother structures—so as Spengler says, when comes the sunset of our culture . . . and the dust of civilized striv-

ing settles, the clear late-day glow reveals the original concerns again, reveals a beatific indifference to things that are Caesar's, for instance, a tiredness of that, and a yearning for, a regret for, the transcendental value, or "God," again . . .

And reading on, in his 1957 essay he says it was:

Characters of a special spirituality who didn't gang up but were solitary Bartlebies staring out the dead wall window of our civilization—the subterreaneans heroes who'd finally turned from the "freedom" of the West and were taking drugs, digging bop, having flashes of insight, experiencing "the derangement of the senses," talking strange, being poor and glad, prophesying a new style for American culture, a new style [we thought] completely free from European influences . . . talking madly about that holy new feeling out there in the streets . . .

There was this pre-political but deeply political sensibility in Kerouac's writings, a free spirit against Cold War conformity which he described in 1957 as "a handful of real hip swinging cats [who] . . . vanished mighty swiftly during the Korean War when (and after) a sinister new kind of efficiency appeared in America, maybe it was the result of the universalization of Television and nothing else (the Polite Total Police Control of Dragnet's 'peace' officers) but the beat characters after 1950 vanished into jails and madhouses, or were shamed into silent conformity . . ."

His was a quest beyond Conquest, taking enormous will as the Cold War was enshrouding the rest of us. His work was about the interior of life, the big questions of meaning and death, at a time when nearly everyone else was conditioned to face the exterior, to fall under the spell of *The Organization Man* and the *Feminine Mystique* rather than surrendering to Godless Communism. Like other minorities, Kerouac had a double-consciousness of the Great White Whale in which he lived, being French-Canadian and Catholic and a fatherless boy from Lowell, Massachusetts who lost a brother while young and another in the war of the Greatest Generation.

In keeping with the iron limits on the free society, it was nearly seven years before Viking would publish *On The Road*, and only then after many scenes and passages, especially the sexually explicit, were completely erased or rewritten. Kerouac's troubles actually began when he brought the manuscript to his publisher as a single-spaced unending scroll, to signify that the manuscript was the road itself, unfolded, just rolled through a typewriter at manic speed without paragraphs, 125,000 words and 120 feet long. The trick was that Kerouac actually taped together hundreds of individual pages before presenting the finished scroll to the publisher, saying it was delivered by the Holy Ghost. The publisher promptly rejected it. Kerouac actually lived the madness and plumbed the experiences that he extolled. Fortunately, the original scroll has been published at last but only in this fiftieth-anniversary year, by Viking, and one wonders if they will make back in profits the money they lost by suppressing the book for so many years. The back cover photo shows a stocky Kerouac, with cropped hair and a plaid shirt, unrolling the original scroll in his publisher's office.

They named him the "founder" of the "Beat Generation" shortly afterwards, a crowning that sealed him fame and perhaps his fate. Book sales soared. His alcohol and drug abuse deepened. Banned at first, now the purity of the quest was mainlined for profit: "What horror I felt to suddenly see Beat being taken up by everybody, press and TV and Hollywood Borscht circuit . . . and so now they have beatnik routines on TV, starting with satires about girls in black and fellows in jeans with snap-knives and sweatshirts and swastikas tattooed under their armpits."

Having set the stage for the 1960s, Kerouac then went missing in action, which at first I thought odd, but it made perfect sense because he defined himself as a loner on the margins. Suddenly offered the possibility of joining something, anything, he couldn't. His brilliant friend Allen Ginsberg did join movements and causes, and remained true to himself. Ginsberg's *Howl and Other Poems* (1956) became the prophecy of the 1960s while Kerouac still waited for Viking to publish *On The Road*. The black hipsters prefigured and hooked up with the civil rights movement which started with the Montgomery Bus Boycott in the same year Ginsberg first read "Howl" in San Francisco with Kerouac sitting, waiting, at a table nearby.

Kerouac, as far as I know, never joined a cause, perhaps because of his age—he was born in 1922, making him a fully conditioned 40-year-old loner by the 1960s—or because he immersed himself in the first wave of Buddhism in America. In his Buddhist/loner perspective, perhaps, he refused attachment to any side in the many sides of the culture wars of the 1960s. Nor did he sell himself to corporate branding nor to any of the seductive Machiavellians of the time. He seemed to be invisible during a time when his private alienation became publicly manifest in an alienated nation of young people trying to live like James Dean or like Kerouac himself.

In a brief 1969 essay, Kerouac—like Bob Dylan—scoffed at the idea that he was "the great white father and intellectual forebear who spawned a deluge of alienated radicals, war protestors, dropouts, hippies, and even 'beats,' when all he did was write a "matter-of-fact account of a true adventure on the road (hardly an agitational propaganda account)." The suspect father of the 1960s was abandoning his prodigy just as his own father died and left him to figure out the world in his early 20s. Kerouac didn't like what the road, for some, had become, a freeway with burgers and root beer. Nor did he like the road he perceived the Left was following. He wondered, unkindly, if he might have to obtain a university PhD in distinguishing ideological differences from "General David Dellinger in Hanoi." He speculated that the Left had ignored a key virtue of Western-style capitalism, that "I wouldn't have been able or allowed to hitchhike half broke through 47 states of this union and see the scene with my own eyes, unmolested? Who cares, Walt Whitman?"

On the other hand, Kerouac firmly rejected the road of going

"to the top echelons" of American society, all sleeked up, and try to forget the ships' crews of World War II who grew beard and long haircuts till a mission was finished, or the "disheveled aspect" of G.I. Joe in the foxholes, the "slovenly appearance" of men and women in 1930s breadlines, and understand that appearance does make the man, just like clothes, and go rushing to a Politico fundraising dinner . . . [where] every handshake, every smile, every gibberous applause is shiny hypocrisy, is political lust and concupiscence, a ninny's bray of melody backed by a ghastly neurological drone of money-grub accompanied by the anvil chorus of garbage can covers being banged over half-eaten filet mignons which don't even get to the dogs, let along hungry children of the absent "constituency."

Why, oh, why did Kerouac choose the middle between the Hippie-Yippie bloc who were his very descendants and the Military-Industrial Complex that wanted to shut down the road if it only could? "You can't fight City Hall, it keeps changing its name," he wrote, but was it a cynical Buddhist scribble or a solitary writer's distancing or a memory of his own experience in depression and war, or the deep belief in personal transcendence through the road? Was the purity he claimed too pure in the end, or was he somehow right about the 1960s, but then again, how could he be? How could all choices be the same? The question I always wanted to ask Jack Kerouac was why the road, finally, had to be so very solitary, so empty of marching as a form of human solidarity against the presence of suffering and the coming of death which so preoccupied him. In my own way, I feel fatherless without him around. Fame consumed him, one historian says, and he died of "alcohol-related hemorrhaging" in October 1969, just as eight of us were going on trial in Chicago for conspiracy to disrupt the warmakers at the 1968 Democratic Convention. Kerouac fought alone against the insanity of the world, voicing a desire that drew millions to join together, many of inspired—then and now—by *On The Road*. That he couldn't join us then cannot erase his wild example and radical inspiration in the history of those times, nor in the unfolding of the road ahead.

SOURCES OF KEROUAC'S WRITINGS QUOTED ABOVE:

Amy Charter, editor, *The Portable Jack Kerouac*, Viking, 1995.
Jack Kerouac, *On The Road: The Original Scroll*, Viking, 2007.

46

Memory and Movements
Cheney, Zinn and Beyond

January 2008

This is the introduction to a book I am currently writing about the social movements I have participated in, and where they fit in American history. It's going to be a big book—a revision of our history since the very beginning—which argues that those things most valuable to us as Americans, even including vacations, have emerged due to past social movements like those of the 1960s.

◆　　◆　　◆

WE NEED AN ALTERNATIVE to prevailing notions of how radical reforms occur in American history. The dominant view is a top-down *celebratory* one in which reform is depicted as proof of the flexibility, indeed, "genius," of the American system. A leading proponent of this view is Lynne Cheney, wife of the current U.S. vice president and head of many education commissions and initiatives since the Reagan era. Since the 1960s, the competing narrative has been a bottom-up "people's history" of forgotten uprisings, notably associated with historian Howard Zinn whose unconventional history has sold over one million copies since the early 1980s.

Conservatives tend to credit the farsightedness and generosity of Machiavellians for any reforms achieved in public policy. In its simplest form, Washington is synonymous with the American Revolution, Lincoln freed the slaves, Roosevelt gave us Social Security, and so on through a catalog of great men's achievements. The American system is eulogized as a pluralist one where a "vital center" mediates between factions in a gradually expanding success story. Often there seems to be no "system" at all, merely the play of "countervailing forces" in an open society. Like the market view of economics, the conflicts of political pluralism result in the greatest good for all. The emphasis of this good news is not that America was founded in genocide, slavery, indentured servitude, slums, social inequality, disenfranchisement, police brutality, militarism, and so forth— but that these are yardsticks to measure how far we have come, proof of our capacity for progress. It sometimes is asserted that U.S. culture, with its absence of a limiting feudal past, its open frontier, its Protestant ethic and rule of law, is ultimately inclusive and exceptional. Social movements are little, if ever, acknowledged in what one traditional high school yearbook calls "the triumph of the American nation."[1] According to the new conventional story, the benefits of social change are delivered from the top. Since the 1960s, certain leaders of social movements—Martin Luther King, Cesar Chavez, Rosa Parks—have been included in the national narrative, but only as individual leaders, and after considerable pressure, including campus rebellions. The key role story of social movements, however, is excluded from the mainstream narrative.

LYNNE CHENEY

As graduate students in Madison, Lynne and Richard Cheney stepped over striking students on their way to class during the Vietnam War.[2] Looking back, Lynne Cheney now grants that American textbooks before the sixties ignored blacks, other people of color, and women.[3] "A generation ago, students learned little about the non-European world and gained only the vaguest notion of the African-American experience," she concedes. But Ms. Cheney did little, if anything, in those fevered days about the absence of people of color in the curriculum, nor did she join student activists calling for a more "relevant" curriculum including black studies departments.[4] Many years later, as chair of the National Endowment of the Humanities under President Reagan, she crusaded against what the conservatives labeled "political correctness," a term invented to suggest that university faculty were engaged in thought control over their innocent students. Cheney frequently lamented a study purportedly showing that more high school students—83.8 percent—knew the name of Harriet Tubman than the fact that George Washington commanded the Continental Army. The survey didn't ask students to identify Washington by name, but only Tubman versus "the commander of the Revolutionary Army," which students might not have known.[5] Nor did the survey ask whether students knew anything about Harriet Tubman aside from her name; she rarely is mentioned as a friend of John Brown, who called her "the general." Instead, she is recognized more as a model of perseverance and maker of freedom quilts than an armed militant. Mention of Tubman became a "hot button for conservative critics" like Cheney and the ex-slave became a "symbolic 'whipping girl' for political correctness," according to Tubman's leading biographer, Catherine Clinton.[6] As of 2004, conservative protests in Maryland blocked a public art exhibit showing Tubman with her Civil War musket. In the eighties, the city of Macon, Georgia, named a center for cultural awareness after Tubman, but "visitors would search in vain inside for any information" about Tubman.[7] Her name, which existed in "literary obscurity" until the 1960s, was restored only when twenty-one books devoted to her life appeared in the nineties, almost 150 years since her feats of bravery.[8] It would seem that the threat of Harriet Tubman in the twentieth century was no longer to the owners of slaves but the owners of history and school curriculums. She represents the movement model of history against the model that history is made—and narrated—by the powerful.

HOWARD ZINN AND WILLIAM APPLEMAN WILLIAMS

The most forceful proponent of an alternative history has been Howard Zinn, author of *A People's History of the United States*. His work is an eye-opening radical reinterpretation of the top-down myth of American progress. Zinn brings to life the indigenous people, the slaves, the early feminists, the renters, the war resisters and all those who were rendered invisible in textbook histories for hundreds of years.[9]

Zinn has been a friend, mentor and hero of mine since we met in Atlanta during the early days of the civil rights movement, and I have assigned *A People's History* in several university classrooms. Its shock effect on students in undeniable. Most of my students pick up the book wholly unprepared for an American history that begins with genocide against native people, questions the privileged class character of the American Revolution, describes the Constitution as a "compromise between the slaveholding interests of the South and moneyed interests of the North," and reduces the two-party system to "an ingenious mode of control," all in reasonable and footnoted argument.

Read carefully, Zinn's account is one continuous, simmering, marching, rioting pattern of robust insurgencies that never win more than marginal reforms. Of renters in the Hudson Valley in 1835–45 he writes, "The farmers had fought, been crushed by the law, their struggle diverted into voting, and the system stabilized by enlarging the class of small landowners, leaving the basic structure of rich and poor intact. It was a common sequence in American history." [10] The reforms of the Progressive Era, similarly, were "aimed at soothing protest." [11] Winning the right to vote after a century of struggle didn't make that much difference for women. [12] The outcome of the New Deal, like earlier periods of upheaval, was to stabilize and preserve the capitalist system. [13] According to Zinn, the 1938 law which established the eight-hour day and which prohibited the scourge of child labor, was "enough to dull the edge of resentment." [14] Zinn portrays a system of corporate liberalism where meaningful reform only comes about when those in power are forced to make them due to pressure from below. No mention is made in *A People's History of the United States*, of Eugene McCarthy, George McGovern, Bella Abzug, Mike Gravel, Ron Dellums or other officials who were influential in the anti-Vietnam movement. Zinn does not focus on elected officials, but on the indigenous peoples, slaves, immigrants, and average citizens who have confronted injustice and organized for change.

A People's History is a powerful argument about the limits of reform, and is no doubt right in its assessment of capitalism's longevity and flexibility, as well as the two-party system's role as a shock absorber. Zinn is right that there are invisible, often classified, scaffolds of power beyond any democratic access. But the fact that Machiavellians are forced to make concessions against their will raises the theoretical question of whether power is permanent, immutable and absolute, or whether it is unstable and contingent, subject to the force of social movements, including political ones. Would John and Robert Kennedy have made no difference if they had survived the assassination attempts? Was the Eugene McCarthy campaign not worthy of mention in the history of the anti-war movement?

William Appleman Williams, another brilliant historian, even scoffed at the notion that "some people feel that ending the war in Vietnam and driving Nixon from office created a momentum for change." Would either the Vietnamese people or the Nixon Republicans agree with his assessment? Williams dismissed these major events of the 1960s as only "occasional dramatic [and marginal] victories." Evidently for radical historians like Williams there is nothing short of (undefined) revolution to be sought. After Vietnam and Watergate, he claims, the power structure remained "essentially as strong as ever."[14] That is hardly what the neoconservatives thought. They trembled at the rising of a "Vietnam Syndrome" and formed a powerful, well-financed counter-movement that prevailed in the Reagan years. The point is that these elites regarded the reforms of the 1960s as a threat to their power, hardly leaving them "as strong as ever." The history of the past forty years can be read as a continuous counter-movement, led by the neoconservatives, to erase the gains of social juctice movements.

These dismissive attitudes towards reform rob social movements of any concrete legacy and ignore the very real possibility that reform may be the only possible outcome of struggles for change in America. There is a bizarre convergence between the conservative and radical views that social change is mere accommodation by the permanent elites, offered to placate and subdue popular movements. *A new definition of reform* is required here, consistent with the critiques of those like Zinn. Real and substantive reform, first, occurs against the will of the established elites; second, it empowers previously excluded constituencies; third, such reform includes electoral politics but far more; fourth, it legitimizes previously marginal ideas; fifth, it creates powerful new cultural norms; sixth, it transfers benefits to those who have gone without them. Anything less is only token reform, not the real thing. Yes, the elites restore stability in exchange for reform and, yes, they will attempt to weaken and hollow out reforms over time. But that is not to say that the struggles for reform are meaningless. Simply consider the changes in American life generated by the forceful movements of the 1960s:

➤ voting rights for southern blacks and 18-to-21 year olds, a total of 26 million Americans;

➤ the end of the Indochina Wars in which at least two million were killed;

➤ the end of military conscription;

➤ congressional checks on the imperial presidency, the CIA and FBI;

➤ amnesty for draft evaders in Canada;

➤ normalized relations with Vietnam;

➤ the freedom of information act;

➤ the media fairness doctrine;

➤ the 1973 *Roe v. Wade* decision;

➤ tougher environmental, consumer, and health and safety laws than any passed since;

➤ participatory rights for many marginalized minorities, including disabled people;

➤ fundamental reform of school and college curriculums;

➤ freedom of sexual desire and the decline of censorship;

➤ the fall of two presidencies.

These were far from token reforms, as shown by the thirty-year conservative struggle to repeal or contain them. Nor did they amount to a revolution in the classic sense of "overthrowing" the upper classes. Between tokenism and revolution, however, are the lives we lead, which are enriched by reforms that must be fought for, achieved, protected, and passed along to future generations. A new model is needed that emphasizes the dynamic and permanent contradiction between social movements and the Machiavellian powers they confront. For many years, conservatives and radicals have visualized a world in which the dialectic ends in the triumph of one side or the other, in which the vanquishing of either the empire or its discontents is complete. But there is no end of history, nor of the dialectic.

We need a new model altogether, based on the impermanence of both power and its reform.

NOTES

1. Diane Ravitch, *The Language Police: How Pressure Groups Restrict What Students Learn,* Vintage, 2004, p. 134.
2. David Maraniss, *They Marched Into Sunlight: War and Peace, Vietnam and America, October 1967,* Simon and Schuster, 2003.
3. Lynne V. Cheney, *Telling the Truth,* Touchstone/Simon and Schuster, 1996, p. 45.
4. In Maraniss, *They Marched Into Sunlight.*
5. Lynne V. Cheney, *Telling the Truth,* p. 33. The study cited by Cheney also was employed in another book against "political correctness" by Diane Ravitz, who served under Reagan and later Bill Clinton.
6. Catherine Clinton, *Harriet Tubman: The Road to Freedom,* Little Brown, 2004, p. 217.
7. Ibid., p. 219.
8. Ibid., p. 220.
9. Of the many works complementing Zinn, James Loewen's *Lies My Teachers Told Me* is excellent and widely used. A whole generation of scholars influenced by the 1960s has excavated and written stories of the social movements described here. Some of those titles are listed in a short bibliography at the end of this book.
10. Howard Zinn, *A People's History of the United States,* HarperCollins, 2003, p. 214.
11. Ibid., p. 349.
12. Ibid., p. 503. "After 1920, women were voting, as men did, and their subordinate condition had hardly changed." Zinn approvingly cites Helen Keller and Emma Goldman who viewed the vote as a meaningless fetish.
13. Ibid., p. 403.
14. Henry Berger, ed., *William Appleman Williams Reader,* Ivan R. Dee, 1992, p. 350.

From Chicago to
Seattle and Beyond
Writings on the Global
Justice Movement

47

In the Beginning Is the Dream
Thoughts on the Zapatista Insurgency

From The Zapatista Reader, *edited by Tom Hayden*
(Nation Books, 2001)

This essay is a reflection on the rebirth of revolutionary possibilities after the decline of state socialism and the upsurge of neoliberalism promoted militarily, economically, and politically by the U.S. government in the 1980s and 1990s. The Zapatistas have helped to spark and energize a global movement that has blocked the "new international order" sought by multinational banks and corporations through the World Trade Organization, International Monetary Fund and World Bank. Today the Zapatistas represent continuing models of "revolution from below," autonomy, and community building, though they encounter predictable challenges in trying to remain entirely outside the state and institutions. I continue to believe that Mexico, Central America and Latin America are more important to our future than any other regions of the world, and that the battle begun by the Zapatistas will continue for the rest of our lives.

◆   ◆   ◆

"It is more than probable that with more time Emiliano Zapata will emerge as the great and pure man of Mexico and will take a parallel position to the Virgin of Guadalupe as the human patron of the freedom of Mexico."
—John Steinbeck, 1948

"We are the continent of desire. We are always at a rolling boil. Isn't that preferable to the rigid cold solitude of the poorly named First World, a dictatorship of technocrats and accountants that wishes to convert us into a great factory of Puritan zombies?"
—Eduardo Garcia Aguilar, 1998

THE ZAPATISTA COMMUNITY of Amador Hernández, in the Lacandon jungle of Chiapas, is as far from global markets, media centers, and metropoles as physically possible. Yet the January 1994 Zapatista rebellion, beginning in tiny hamlets such as this—mere dots in a dot.com world—has managed to survive and challenge the faraway power centers of government and finance in a pivotal test of whether the globalization of capital is prompting the globalization of conscience.

I traveled to Amador Hernández, a village of 500 indigenous Tzoltzil-speaking Mayans, and several other highlands communities under Zapatista control, in February 2000. I was flown by a beer-drinking pilot through the rainforest mist, in a journey out of Western time and space. As the small plane bumped down in a jungle meadow, I felt alternately haunted and fascinated. Haunted because I was about to witness a current-day confrontation between the indigenous of the Americas and the colonizers, militarizers, and modernizers, which had left lakes of blood in its wake for 500 years. Fascinated by the indigenous will to survive—to wage "war against oblivion"—incarnated in the Zapatista front.

North Americans like John Steinbeck have been enchanted by Mexican revolutionaries before. Like those previous gringo romanticos, I had been drawn to the indigenous cause for many years. I was raised, like most North Americans, with a dimmed and sanitized view of their genocidal fate. When discussed at all by my parents or teachers, I was led to believe that it was all a tragic misunderstanding between Europeans and the local Indians, that the fatalities were caused by accidental Western germs infecting vulnerable people, and, in any case, it was an inevitable stage of progressive development. It was not until the 1960s jarred my own sense of identity, and an Indian hand seized Alcatraz Island, that I sat down on a Berkeley floor to read *Bury My Heart at Wounded Knee* and experienced life-altering realization that America and the West had been destroying native peoples for 500 years. I then saw Vietnam for what it was, not a "mistake" or a Cold War confrontation, but a continuation of the conquest of the indigenous. The U.S. bombing campaigns had names like "Rolling Thunder," our helicopters were called Apaches. The jargon was the same, with only the labels changed: "the only good gook is a dead gook." The defoliation of crops had begun long before William Westmoreland, with Kit Carson. The Harvard-based doctrine of "forced urbanization" and the Pentagon strategy of "fighting their birth rate" were aimed at destroying ancient cultures attached spiritually to land and ancestors.

Flying over the Chiapas highlands thirty years later, I was reminded of the jungles of Vietnam, the rainforests of Brazil, the mountains of El Salvador, all the fault lines of the war between the forces of market modernity and the world of the wretched of the earth. So much starvation, so many genocides, so much overpowering technology, so many Che Guevaras dead in the long struggle to challenge the West. And as a result, so much resignation, weariness, cynicism had taken root, from the barrios of the poor to lecture halls of the left. Worst of all, the West was oblivious to the oblivion the Zapatistas were fighting. One mindset floated in the bubble of modernity while the other tried to shake off a 500-year nightmare.

But then on January 1, 1994—on the very first day of the North American Free Trade Agreement—came an armed uprising by the stones the builders forgot, in a town named for Christopher Columbus himself. Out of oblivion came thousands of masked Mayans, invoking the cultural identity of the indigenous and the land reforms of Zapata. And amidst their leadership was a masked mestizo, a spokesperson named only Marcos. Having been disillusioned all my life by cults of personality, I nonetheless became intrigued like millions of others by this subcomandante. He came from my generation, that of 1968. He was an intellectual. He chose the path of armed struggle when others were giving it up, in a time that was considered postrevolutionary despite its unending poverty and humiliation. With a handful of compañeros, he endured the utter isolation of the mountains, eating insects, repeating to themselves "we're okay, we're okay" in the darkness of the Montes Azules biosphere, the last wilderness of the Lacandon jungle.

By his mask and generic name, by becoming iconic, Marcos seemed to deflect any cult surrounding his own inaccessible personality. The most crucial aspect of his transformation seemed to come from contact with the local Indians. As he listened to their stories and followed their ways, the indigenous ghosts within his ladino identity gradually seemed to come alive. As he would later say, instead of the classic model of the guerrilla penetrating the community, the Indian communities penetrated the guerrilla until it became an Indian army in Indian time and space. To seek such a transformation, recognizing and reclaiming our collective indigenous roots—my own were Irish—was a personal Holy Grail. Just as Marcos had come to terms with the indigenous within the Mexican, by coming to know Mexico, North Americans could, in the phrase of Octavio Paz, "learn to understand an unacknowledged part of themselves."

In short, I felt slightly like another in the long line of crazy gringos seeking rebirth in Mexico.

But as a North American, I too opposed NAFTA for its assertion of commercial values over any others. As a state senator, and a former California official appointee to a binational border commission, I believed in policies that would improve opportunities for Mexican campesinos on their historic lands, not rupture their traditions for a future of emigration or maquilladoras. As a human rights activist, it seemed to me that international observers were all that stood between the indigenous communities and what they called oblivion (*el olvido*).

In that sense, we of the North were being invited, challenged, to do our part in resisting a conquest 500 years old. The past was not over. We could not lament the atrocities of "manifest destiny" as if it was finished, beyond anything we could reverse. The past was present, and we had a choice to break with it.

I realized I was in Chiapas as a meditation, to explore how resistance was possible to the New World Order first vocalized by George Bush and implemented by Bill Clinton. After eighteen years in legislative politics, I had concluded that the corporate market mentality was fast eclipsing the democratic process, human rights, and environmental concerns in a flood of campaign dollars and claims about the "inevitability" of globalization. For example, NAFTA and the World Trade Organization (WTO) threatened to negate over ninety California laws which, in NAFTA-speak, interfered with investor rights. Looking southward, American multinationals like Monsanto and Novartis were marketing cheap, genetically modified corn and seed to Mexico, disrupting the traditional Indian culture where corn is sacred, forcing countless campesinos to migrate from their jungle canyons to the cement ones of southern California. Already Los Angeles was home to 5,000 Mayans from one region of El Salvador, near neighbors of the Chiapanecos, destroyed in the U.S.-sponsored intervention of the 1980s. They huddled together in wretched apartment houses, relived their war traumas on their own, without supportive services, attended syncretic Mayan-Christian evangelical services, earned cash as day laborers, scavengers, or garment workers, were frequently stopped, searched, and sometimes deported, and raised a generation of lost children. Potentially tens of thousands would be forced to join them on the emigrant trail as their traditional lands were modernized out of existence.

Could the Zapatistas stop anything as inexorable as this? Their uprising, with the slogan "NAFTA is Death!" certainly surprised, and temporarily challenged, the NAFTA elite with its claim to invincibility. And in November 1999, just two months before my Chiapas visit, I had been in the streets of Seattle at the birth of another rebellion against NAFTA. Led by young rebels in an improbable alliance with labor unions, the "battle of Seattle" actually stopped an international meeting of the WTO from completing its business. The conflict was joined: direct participatory democracy versus the globalists with their secret tribunals who were usurping the traditional powers of elected governments. A key inspiration for the Seattle uprising was the example of the Zapatistas, whose slogans and imagery filled the air. To avoid police and tear gassing, hundreds of protestors wore ski masks like the Zapatistas, asserting that they were unmasking the invisible global trade bureaucracy. I had not seen any demonstrations on this scale since the 1960s. The poisonous pepper spray felt familiar, even bracing, after so many years of political hot air. But was it real, or were Chiapas and Seattle like the Oglala ghost dances of the 1890s, the last cry (*grito*) of history's rearguard before our fate was sealed?

And now I was staring at Mayan children running barefoot in multicolored clothing as our small plane bounced along a grassy strip in Amador Hernández. Behind them was a multicolored wall-mural of Emiliano Zapata, the revolutionary ambushed by the Mexican government—which then coopted his image, and whose political descendants, the Partido Revolucionario Institucional (PRI) were now confronted by his ghost in the jungle. Around me was a small cluster of wooden cabins—perhaps twenty-five in number—in a several-acre clearing in the rainforest. A few children ran loose with their dogs. Women in traditional Mayan dress stood in doorways. Trails ran into the forest darkness. Masked men approached on horseback and dismounted. Historically a faceless people, their masks now made them recognizable to the world while they remained invisible to surveillance cameras.

Amador Hernández was one of thirty-three autonomous "communities in resistance" that had risen in arms on January 1, 1994, and which now existed as liberated zones outside the structure of the Mexican state. On the edge of the Montes Azules biosphere, Amador became a center of rapid criss-crossing road construction as the Mexican Army sought to encircle and isolate the Zapatistas. Besides their military use, the roads were opening access to the remaining hardwoods and potentially significant oil reserves that lay below the jungle floor. Not minutes away was an Army base from which attacks could be launched on the hamlet where we stood.

We dropped our backpacks in an open-air village center and, after a drink of water, I sat on a large log interviewing two masked men about their masked history. Amador Hernández, made up of indigenous Tojolabal-speaking Mayans, had been driven from nearby lands a generation ago, and never benefited from twenty years of official Mexican development promises. For survival, they planted subsistence crops. Occasionally government representatives would try to force them out of the jungle, which contains vast untapped oil reserves.

"We started organizing resistance to the displacement on our own," one rebel recounted to me, "and then one day in 1982 or '83, I can't remember when, about a dozen compañeros came walking through the jungle and starting talking with us.

"They asked us if we were ready to stop drinking and start organizing, because the government was fucking us up with alcohol. We saw how the brothers were fighting in El Salvador and Nicaragua, so we said yes, why not?"

Those 1982 visitors to this jungle clearing were the original Zapatistas, one of them to become known as "Marcos." It was their earliest appearance as organizers among the indigenous. I tried to imagine the moment. The idea of one-to-one, patient, grassroots organizing of a movement—any movement, much less a movement toward armed insurrection—is improbable, to say the least, in this age of globalized entertainment media and technofixes. How had the Zapatistas come so far? What made them believe a rebellion could be launched from these jungle meadows? What made these Indians put down alcohol and reach for their weapons?

The Zapatistas emerged in the 1960s from disillusionment with a Mexican state that permitted the 1968 slaughter of student activists in Mexico City and likewise smothered all dissent. They chose to move to the poorest, most forgotten areas of Southern Mexico, not unlike those Americans who organized in Mississippi in 1960. In those days, any Mayan walking in the towns of Chiapas had to step off the sidewalks to let a white Mexican pass. The social order was controlled by armed ranchers employing vigilante justice. Organized paramilitary-style in groups with names like "white guards" or "peace and justice," the vigilantes often enough were Indians themselves who, through self-hate and material benefits, had become cowboys.

A tradition of Indian autonomy and resistance was still alive in Chiapas as well. They had learned to survive under many forms of oppression, but in the early 1990s their world became more threatened than ever. In preparing for NAFTA, the Mexican government cancelled Article 27 of its constitution, the cornerstone of Zapata's revolution of 1910–1919. Under the historic Article 27, Indian communal landholdings were protected from sale or privatization. But under NAFTA this guarantee was redefined as an obsolete harrier to investment. With the removal of Article 27, Indian farmers would be threatened with loss of their remaining lands and flooded by cheap imports from the United States. Thus, the Zapatistas labeled NAFTA "a death sentence," and Indian communities all over the Chiapas Highlands made preparations for war.

But it was not simply the rapidly worsening conditions that made the rebellion possible. The Zapatistas had also prepared. They metamorphosed into an indigenous army. Left behind was the vocabulary of Marxism with its primary emphasis on class; the Zapatistas constituted themselves as descendents of the original Zapata and the land reform tradition. In place of a political party, they were instigating a movement. Instead of expecting proletarian revolution, they chose to challenge and galvanize all sectors of what they called "civil society." In place of the seizure of power, they followed the Indian (and anarchist) path of disavowing power: "for everyone, everything," they declared, "for ourselves, nothing." In place of a new "Internationale" (of the Marxist or Tricontinental variety), they spoke of awaking the world's conscience. In place of a revolutionary war to overthrow the state, they used their guns to show their determination and demand attention, then turned to words and Web sites to make their case. These were armed intellectuals in a supposedly postrevolutionary time, intent on making history in defiance of the best-selling thesis proclaiming the "end of history." The Zapatistas were committed to the end of modern history as we know it, and to a revindication of the history of the indigenous whose plight is the enduring contradiction at the center of modernity's claims of "progress."

As their several "Declarations from the Lacandon Jungle" make clear, the Zapatista vision has evolved and transformed from a traditional class-based Marxism to a deep identification with the Mayan, not only in the jungles of Chiapas but the Mayan in all Mexicans and the indigenous spirit around the world. I had previously visited ancient Mayan sacred centers in the Yucatan, Guatemala, and Belize, always coming away shaken by the original, unexplained death of these ancient societies and their second death through the process of modern forgetting. Wandering amid those magnificent temples, courtyards, and ballfields—and realizing that the jungles are filled with many more as yet undiscovered—made one abandon any notion that these were primitive or backward civilizations. These were people who actually discovered and studied the cycles of time and the seasons, things we take for granted like the watches on our wrist. They lived amid myriad explosions of color, flowers, skies full of plumed birds, and survived in the dangerous world of the jaguar as well. While I offered support to indigenous struggles all over the Americas, I too assumed that the 500-year war was in its final stages, that the conquest had succeeded, that extinctions would continue their grisly toll until the end. We who cared for endangered cultures and species were only able to work within the parameters of the conquest itself, the conquest we now called the modern world, salvaging what we could of tribal cultures and fragmented ecosystems.

When Marcos and the Zapatistas showed, if only for a moment, that there was an alternative, that the conquest itself could be challenged one more time, it electrified those like myself who believed, with Carolyn Forché, that "everywhere and always, go after that which is lost." The battle of the EZLN suggested more than another resistance against repressive landowners and paramilitaries. It suggested the deeper possibility of a reversal of forced assimilation on all levels from psychic to political. It suggested that we could reclaim the indigenous roots that lie mangled beneath the architecture of our modern selves.

The declarations of Marcos and the Zapatistas are translated in several places, including the historical reader *Rebellion in Chiapas* (1999) by Harvard historian John Womack Jr. One that reflects the Indian tone and worldview is the "Fourth Declaration" of January 1996, which reads in part:

Our blood and our word lit a small fire in the mountain, and we walked it along the path that goes to the house of might and money (their march to Mexico City). Brothers and sisters of other races and languages, of another color, but of the same heart, protected our light and drank in it their own fires.

The arrogant want to put out a rebellion that their ignorance locates in the dawn of 1994. But the rebellion that today has a dark face and a true language was not born today. It spoke in other languages and in other lands. [The declaration goes on to list 70 indigenous dialects.]

Many worlds walk in the world. Many worlds are made. Many worlds make us. . . . In the world of the mighty one only the great and their servants fit. In the world we want we all fit. The world we want is one where many worlds fit . . .

The 500-year-old Cathedral of San Bartolomé de las Casas looms heavily over the charming city of San Cristóbal. A large, shabby, stone colonial structure with a dark, candlelit interior, the cathedral remains open to worshippers. On its steps, from dawn to dusk, come Indian vendors selling handmade clothing and crafts, including miniature Zapatista dolls, to European and North American tourists. Graffiti on the cathedral walls proclaim support for the armed struggle of the Zapatistas.

Bartolomé, as the locals call him even now, was a Dominican bishop sent to Chiapas in the 1540s, and one of the most fascinating figures in the history of the Conquest, representing the road not taken. He first sailed to the Americas with Columbus in 1502, returning many times. At some point he became morally repelled by the torture and exploitation of the indigenous, as recorded in vivid detail in his diaries, where he described the Indians as "the most guileless, the most devoid of wickedness and duplicity [with] no desire to possess worldly goods."[1]

In numerous religious and intellectual forums, most famously in a debate with Gines de Sepulveda in 1550 in Valladolid, de las Casas argued passionately that the indigenous people were human beings with souls (although, for whatever reason, he did not always extend the same recognition to African slaves). For his troubles, he faced scorn, harassment, and death threats as the designated "Protector of the Indians" until his death in 1566 at the age of 92.

Just as his cathedral still stands, the sixteenth-century bishop is very much alive today among the Indians of Chiapas. His name was invoked familiarly, for example, in testimony at the 1974 Congreso Indígena de Chiapas, the convention that initiated the most recent cycle of the 500-year Indian revolt. A statement from the minutes of that 1974 meeting tells the story from the native viewpoint:

Columbus came with his compañeros to know the people here and to bother them. With them came Brother Bartolomé de las

Casas [who] saw that it was very bad what his other compañeros were doing . . . Right here in San Cristóbal Brother Bartolomé de las Casas was defending the Indian. I believe we all know the church that's to one side of the Church of Santo Domingo, up from the union hall. . . . Well, comrades, now Brother Bartolomé de las Casas is no longer alive. It's only in his name that we're holding this congreso. So where is the liberty Brother Bartolomé left? We've been suffering injustice for 500 years, and we're still in the same situation.[2]

This long history nurtured the deep religious root of the insurgency in Chiapas, which blended later with the Zapatista root into the present uprising. And nurturing the spiritual root was a modern Brother Bartolomé in the person of Bishop Samuel Ruíz García—known, sometimes disparagingly as "the Indians' Prophet." Hardly a born revolutionary, Samuel Ruíz received a conventional Catholic education at the College Pío Latinoamerico in Rome before coming to Chiapas in 1960. But traveling by foot or mule through the impoverished Indian highlands changed him, as it changed the Zapatistas a decade later and de las Casas five centuries before.

In 1968 Ruíz participated in the historic conference in Medellin, Colombia, when the Latin America bishops embraced liberation theology with its "special preference for the poor." The Medellin manifesto recalled that Jesus was sent to "liberate the poor from slavery, hunger, misery, oppression, and ignorance" and mandated development of "grassroots organizations for the redress and consolidation of their rights and the search for true justice." With that in mind, Ruíz began to inspire, train, and empower a mass movement of the indigenous across Chiapas, organized by thousands of disciplined catechists. By the time of the Zapatista uprising, Ruíz had became a principal sponsor and mediator of sporadic peace talks, the only leader the Indians would trust. Like the murdered Archibishop Oscar Romero in El Salvador, Ruíz was subject to severe pressures from the Catholic hierarchy, periodic death threats, and constant scapegoating by conservative landowners who blamed him for stirring up their Indian servants and laborers. At the time of my visit, the Bishop, age 75, was entering the church's mandatory period of retirement, much to the relief of those in power.

Attempting to undermine a robed Samuel Ruíz was more difficult than raising doubts about masked Zapatistas. The most sophisticated sowing of doubts appeared in the *New York Review of Books,* a respected publication that has moved significantly to the right since the 1960s. The *Review* published a lengthy article in December 1999 by Mexican intellectual Enrique Krauze. The original piece appeared in the Spanish-language publication *Letras Libres,* with a cover drawing of a benign and lofty Bishop Ruíz standing over the bodies of Mayan peasants presumably sacrificed as a result of his liberation theology. In his magisterial 1997 history of Mexico, Krauze concludes that Chiapas will be remembered only as a "limited and isolated phenomenon."[3] Racism, he wrote, is "not a special feature of Mexican consciousness"[4] except in special cases like traditional Chiapas. Thus the acknowledged poverty and oppression in Chiapas, in Krauze's view, deserve attention but are not national in scope, an argument much like the American one in the 1960s that Mississippi's racial problems were isolated to the old Confederacy.

Krauze acknowledges that "Don Samuel" is a "true incarnation of Isaiah or Amos" whose struggle for justice has been "impressive and moving." But his *New York Review* piece also depicts the Bishop as a religious true-believer whose attitudes toward violence and compromise are "ambiguous," and who polarizes communities in ways that can lead to tragedies like the Acteal massacre of December 22, 1997, the paramilitary killing of forty-five Indians at a highlands village which caused international embarrassment for the Mexican government. The bishop's teachings serve, according to Krauze, to "intensify the exclusiveness" of the Indians, and "feed the temptation toward martyrdom as a means of triumph over injustice."

Nowhere, however, does the Krauze article mention that all forty-five victims of the Acteal massacre were praying at the time of their deaths. Or that forty-three were shot in the back, while two were bludgeoned in the head. Twenty were women—including four who were pregnant—and eighteen were children. The shootings went on for nine hours and though Mexican troops were only a few minutes away, they did not enter the site until the bloodletting was finished. The Acteal massacre was carried out through a counterinsurgency technique as old as the conquest itself—the arming of paramilitary units composed of Indians willing to kill other Indians for advantage.

I had met Bishop Ruíz in Mexico City, a stocky, jovial, plaid-shirted down-to-earth man who attended a private dinner with a group from Northern Ireland, including Gerry Adams, displaying an exhibition of the "disappeared" from the 1972 Bloody Sunday massacre. The Bishop suggested that I visit Acteal and see conditions for myself. So, after returning to San Cristóbal from the trip to Amador Hernández in the eastern highlands, I found myself caravaning north of San Cristóbal—in heavy rain through military checkpoints up winding roads—until we reached a clearing at the foot of the village. We parked next to an immense structure like a tree trunk carved from wood, which, I realized as I peered through the fog, depicted the agonized faces of Acteal's dead.

I was accompanied, guided actually, by Ophelia Medina, the respected Mexican actress who has changed her life to support the Zapatista communities with food, medicine, and solidarity. We met first inside a tent in Mexico City in 1995 where she was fasting in protest of the military occupation of Chiapas. Tall, dramatic, looking eerily like the artist Frieda Kahlo she played in a Mexican film, Medina poured out her reasons for joining the rebellion. "The most important value of this rebellion is to make us Mexicans aware that inside of us there is an an Indian that we have not allowed to talk because we think it's a stupid person. The color of our skin defines our being. But the skin is only a border. When we cross it we enter an inner world, one of community, a different way of thinking, a hope for the future." No wonder Medina is reviled or dismissed by many Mexicans, I thought. Here she was, their symbol of First World, European beauty and taste, now marching in the mud of Chiapas wearing indigenous pants, taking lessons in the native language, changing herself from the inside out. Not unlike Jane Fonda transforming from Barbarella to friend of the Indians at Alcatraz, the Black Panthers, and the Vietnamese peasants.

I followed Medina down fifty yards of steps that had turned into a small waterfall, and walked uncertainly into the village. It reminded me of entering the heavy, unchanging emptiness of Wounded Knee where the Sioux were slaughtered in 1890 (and where, incidentally, the Sioux staged protests in solidarity with the Acteal victims). Before me was an unoccupied, open-walled community center used for religious services and assemblies. A small child stood in a doorway, nose running, sobbing, and I remembered someone saying that newborn babies in Acteal are becoming smaller due to the lack of medicine and malnutrition. It seemed to be raining tears. There were low ravines on both sides of the path where I stood, the places where villagers were hunted down and shot on that day in December. Except for the little girl, the inhabitants of the shanties around me were shuttered inside. Unlike Amador Hernández, Acteal was loaded with grief.

We passed a red brick building, the only one of its kind, and entered a one-room structure nearby—Acteal's "city hall." Inside sat a circle of survivors of the massacre to tell us their story. The room had a dirt floor in which numerous Pepsi bottle caps were pressed. The light came through an open door. I noticed a photo of Archbishop Romero, a calendar, maps of the mountains, and a large poster of a black and yellow bee pollinating a flower.

The community was known as Acteal of the Bees (*las abejas*) to distinguish it from an adjacent Acteal controlled by the Zapatistas. The difference between the neighboring hamlets is that *las abejas,* while supporting the goals of the Zapatistas, is a devout religious group that prays constantly and practices strict nonviolence—a fact that couldn't have escaped the paramilitaries responsible for the massacre. Two years later, the community still had not recovered its pre-massacre population. Nearby communities—Pohlo and Juan Diego de X'ovep were two we visited—are filled with refugees from the time of the massacre, still unable to move back to lands taken by landlords and paramilitaries.

These were the people who, in the account of Enrique Krauze, were manipulated by Bishop Ruíz and liberation theology into their own martyrdom. They sat in a small circle, wearing combinations of tattered jackets with traditional Indian garb. They looked down or away. They were prepared to speak, however, and brought notebooks to record the occasion.

Amid this melancholy, I asked them about their religious beliefs and, in particular, why they remained so nonviolent. They answered readily, in both Tzoltzil and Spanish, while still looking away. A dark-skinned man wrapped in a heave blue blanket said "the bees" began organizing seven years ago. "We knew the government didn't recognize us, and since the authorities won't protect us, we put ourselves in the hands of God. We call ourselves "the bees" because bees are unified—they diversify their labor but they all work together. We knew the government was giving weapons to the paramilitaries. Christmas was near, so many of us were praying all the time, hoping our Lord would help them see the light. For two days we fasted, but we could not finish because they came to kill us. We were completely surprised. Some stayed in prayer, and others tried to run into our canyons. They hunted us all day long while we prayed."

Their account was confirmed by eyewitnesses. During the massacre, one *abeja* ran up the very road from which we had descended, begging an Army commander to intervene. Nothing was done. During the same hours, an Army spokesman told a reporter there was no news, *sin novedad.*[5]

How could a Krauze cast blame on these people, or Bishop Ruíz, for provoking their own massacre by their devout nonviolence? If they had been armed Zapatistas, the massacre would have been unlikely. Only a profound discomfort with liberation theology, and with Indian autonomy, could cause Krauze to blame the victims for stirring such genocidal passions. The scene they described brought to mind Picasso's *Guernica* painting, the photographs of My Lai, and, of course, images of frozen bodies at Wounded Knee. I put down my notebook, feeling as much like an intruder as a witness. There was a stoicism about these people, based in the centuries, that would sustain them. But would there be a global conscience large enough to add Acteal to its long list of unanswered wrongs?

It finally stopped raining, so *las abejas* led us a few yards over to the brick building I had noticed before. Inside was a chilly rectangular chamber decorated with flowers and small family photographs of Indian faces. Below our feet, I realized, under a cement landing, the bodies of the firty-five dead had been laid to rest. The killings had been barbarous. I remembered reading an autopsy report on "Corpse #16," for example, a "female cadaver, approximately 32 years old, who died of perforation to her abdominal viscera by a cutting instrument—the abdominal cavity was opened up and the product of approximately 28 weeks extracted."[6] Corpse #16 and her baby were beneath my feet. We all knelt down. Medina spread newly gathered flowers in a ceremonial arrangement on the floor. Not everyone's photo was on the wall, they said, because some of the victims had never had a photograph taken in their lives. They asked if I would tell people on "the outside" what had happened here. I felt like the question came from 500 years before. I could not speak, so I nodded yes.

An unresolved issue is how far up the Mexican ladder of power the official complicity in Acteal extended. Human rights observers had documented the links between paramilitaries, the army, and Chiapas landowners and government officials. John Ross calls the vigilantes the "Frankenstein love children" of the Mexican army and landowners. But what of the U.S. role? How could one know in an age of "plausible deniability," covert operations, or low-intensity warfare? Instead of holding liberation theology responsible for this tragedy, why didn't publications like the *New York Review* explore whether American advisors and officials foster a mentality of bloodletting by the extremists on "our side?" Thousands of Mexican army officers, after all, were trained in counterinsurgency techniques at the School of the Americas, known to critics as the "School of Assassins." Our military advisors and strategists blinked at death squads in El Salvador, our CIA hired thugs in Guatemala. President Clinton had even apologized to the new Guatemalan government for our part in that dirty war. How long would it take to establish the murky truth in Chiapas?

President Clinton wrote me about these concerns on March 25, 1994, just after the Zapatista uprising. The relevant part reads as follows:

> I assure you that my administration is working hard to protect human rights in Mexico and other countries. In meetings with President Salinas and Foreign Minister Camacho, Ambassador Jones stressed the importance of Army restraint and respect for

human rights in dealing with the recent skirmishes. As I continue
to monitor the situation in Mexico, I will keep your ideas in mind.
Sincerely,
Bill Clinton

I am sure there is some truth in this reassuring letter. But not the whole
truth. Chiapas has become more than the "skirmish" Clinton originally
imagined. Even if the White House counsels restraint, even if a massacre
like Acteal was the handiwork of isolated thugs, it is clear by now that the
U.S. government is implicated through NAFTA in a simmering crisis in
Chiapas which can explode into more Acteals at any moment. The U.S.
administration persists in sinking us deeper into a brave new world of
globalization that requires counterinsurgency if it is to prosper. America
remains the policeman of the world, this time wearing masks of our own,
masks far more effective than those of the Zapatistas: the masks which are
the uniforms of the armies we train and the mercenaries we foster.

While I was in Chiapas, President Zedillo was in Davos, Switzerland,
speaking at a WTO conference on the aftermath of Seattle. His speech was
a classic example of the new corporate globalizer's mantra. The low wages
of workers in developing countries—and how long developing countries
have been developing!—represent a "step toward better opportunities" as
well as an escape from "extreme rural poverty or a marginal occupation."
The environmental price is acceptable, he added, since more trade equals
more growth without which the funding to clean the damaged environment would be unavailable. We wreck the environment, in other words, to
generate the capital necessary to restore it. [7]

Zedillo zealously branded all opponents of the WTO "globalphobics,"
a turn of phrase surely applauded among the besieged insiders of the
WTO. The dismissive label served two purposes: first, to brand the critics
as antimodern and therefore irrelevant, and second, to politically blame
North American (white) protectionists and environmentalist zealots for
holding back Mexico's development.

To which Subcommandante Marcos responded over jungle Internet
that the Zapatistas welcomed all "Zedillo-phobics, all global-phobics, even

all phobic-phobics" to join the struggle against neoliberalism. It was not a question of globalization versus protectionists phobias, he understood, it was a question of global corporatism versus global conscience.

Memories of Chiapas can make one lonely in America. The process of forgetting is seductive when the alternative is grief. I left the gravesites of Chiapas and returned home to California. I wrote a letter summarizing my trip to the Mexican consul-general, and received no answer. I wrote James Carville urging him to lobby the PRI for a Chiapas pullout, but there was no answer. To my surprise, the most conservative presidential candidate, Vicente Fox, did respond to questions I submitted through a Mexican reporter in Sacramento, Xochitl Arellano. On May 8, 2000, Fox said straightforwardly, "we could remove the two great obstacles that exist to reach an agreement. One has to do with the military presence, which we are willing to take out from their original positions, and number two, use the agreements of San Andreas Larrainzar as a point of departure for this negotiation. I think we are ready also if an interview with Comandante Marcos happens."

I was not surprised, therefore, when the newly elected Fox took the bold initiative to invite the Zapatistas to present their case in Mexico City and begin negotiations after prisoner releases and troop withdrawals to passive positions. In March 2001, hundreds of thousands of Mexicans welcomed Marcos and the other comandantes to Mexico City in a scene reminiscent of the August 1963 March on Washington. While a historic moment of opportunity, however, it was neither a love feast nor an end to the conflict. President Fox's own party unanimously opposed letting the Zapatistas into the halls of power which the Panistas had seized after eight years of PRI domination. Marcos sparred with Fox, suggesting that the Presidente was trying to co-opt the Zapatistas. Others feared a new Chinameca, named after the place where Zapata was ambushed and assassinated. After an extraordinary week of celebration, oratory, and negotiations, the EZLN comandantes left the city for Las Canadas of Chiapas once again, this time with discreet security from the Mexican Army.

No one can say what the future holds, but then no one expected the rebellion to come this far.

Marcos and the EZLN, while raising hopes for a settlement of the 500-year-old question of Indian autonomy, continue to remain infectious irritants in the body of the globalizers. The Zapatistas hope that world opinion will not only protect their struggle but challenge the New World Order. They do not want to become merely the reform wing of that New World Order, not even modern day Bartolomés railing against the conquest. They seem deeply satisfied for now to insist on the relevence of dreamers—armed dreamers to be sure—against the visionless nightmares of modernity.

For precisely this reason, both the media and many influential observers write them off as a romantic fringe. Jorge Castañeda, the respected Mexican author chosen by Fox to be secretary of foreign affairs, is one of those. On several occasions Castañeda has predicted the demise of the Zapatistas, blaming Marcos for missed opportunities to enter the political process (as Castaneda, a man of the left, has done by joining the Fox regime). By not joining the "political game," Castañeda has written, Marcos is bungling his chance and in danger of fading to the margins.[8] In his biography of Che Guevara, *Compañero*, Castañeda made the same argument, that the fate of revolutionary leaders is to become at best cultural icons, not political or military winners.

This argument, however, understates the achievements of revolutionaries like Marcos who have shaken Mexico, shaken NAFTA and the WTO, and once again raised the question of the indigenous out of the dustbins of history. From a narrower revolutionary perspective, Marcos and his comrades have succeeded where others, even el Che, have failed, in truly modifying and adapting themselves to the Indian world. In his perceptive 1992 book on the Maya, *The Heart of the Sky*, Peter Canby interviewed a Guatemalan Indian about the guerrillas in his country so close to Chiapas.

> The guerrillas used efficacious methods. They spoke to the Maya in their own languages. But their approach had one fundamental flaw. Their interest in the Maya derived from a theoretical conclusion that the Indians had a revolutionary potential that the guerrillas could use. They therefore wanted to proletarianize the

Indians until they were not longer Indians. To them, it was all about a conflict of classes. . . . Because of this, many Indians felt that if the guerrillas had won, it would only have been a change of masters.[9]

In the 1960s, we learned that the role of an organizer is to organize himself or herself out of a job, to awaken the powerless to dream of their possibilities of leadership and self-determination. We were to be *a catalytic* vanguard but not an organizational vanguard seeking power, for power, as we chanted, was "to the people." We were a mystery to the establishment always hungry to identify leaders for purposes of co-optation or elimination, and a mystery as well to those liberals and leftists who believed in institutionalized agencies of change. I learned much later that these debates were at the center of many efforts to change the world long before the 1960s, including the Mexican revolution.

Marcos and the comandantes appear to be the latest incarnation of the same dream. And even if Castañeda is proven right in his political realism, we all should wonder if that is a good thing. Should utopianism be cauterized from the souls of those who oppose injustice? Or is Marcos right, that dreams are a function of the human character worthy of defending? Zapatismo takes the risk of becoming "just another organization," he has said, "or on the contrary, contributing something truly new."[10]

Having experienced pragmatism for forty years since the utopian blessed communities and youthful visions of the 1960s, I can testify that the world needs "something truly new." Not that social reforms should be rejected or scorned, but those reforms lose their vitality, their meaning, if they lack all connection to dreaming. They become means of co-optation which finally sap all our righteousness. We in the West have lost the dreaming capacity that evolved as a spiritual and survival resource among our native predecessors over many thousands of years. Now, dialectically, the dreamless tides of globalization are giving rise to a new global resistance on behalf of dreamers.

In the beginning is not the party, not the program, not the constituency, and certainly not the weapons. In the beginning is the dream, which parties, programs, constituencies, and weapons must serve. Without the dream, the means become the ends and the world of power is reproduced. That is the message from Chiapas that the globalizers can neither understand nor suppress.

NOTES

1. Bartolomé de las Casas, *The Devastation of the Indies: A Brief Account*, Johns Hopkins University Press, 1992, pp. 28–29.
2. John Womack Jr., editor, *Rebellion in Chiapas*, New Press, 1999, p. 150.
3. Enrique Krauze, *Mexico: Biography of Power: A History of Modern Mexico*, 1810-11, HarperCollins, 1997, p. 794.
4. Ibid., p. 787.
5. John Ross, *The War Against Oblivion*, Common Courage Press, 2000, pp. 241–242.
6. Ibid., p. 240.
7. See *Los Angeles Times*, March 7, 2000, for the full text.
8. See Yve Le Bot interview with Marcos, citing Castañeda, in John Womack, *Rebellion in Chiapas*, p. 321.
9. Peter Canby, *The Heart of the Sky*, Kodansha International, p. 339.
10. John Womack, *Rebellion in Chiapas*, p. 326.

48

Seattle: It Was Bigger than Chicago

Washington Post, *December 5, 1999*

Written on the run, this Washington Post *op-ed was an attempt to announce the birth of a new movement, much like my excited accounts of the student movement at the beginning of the 1960s. The issues raised by Seattle—the need for democratically decided trade agreements with enforceable labor and environmental standards—have passed into mainstream American politics. Despite being eclipsed by 9/11 and the U.S. "War on Terror," the global justice movement continues to produce "Seattles"—fiery confrontations wherever the WTO attempts to meet. The corporate trade agenda has been derailed, an incredible achievement for social movements around the world.*

◆　　◆　　◆

COMPARISONS BETWEEN the World Trade Organization protests here and the protest movements of the 1960s became a media micro-industry last week. One reporter even asked me, is the pepper spray helping you relive your youth? My response was that it beats taking Viagra.

My serious take on the question might surprise you. Based on five days of joining in protests, marching, being gassed myself, sitting on cold pavements and hard floors, I have to say I am glad to have lived long enough to see a new generation of rebels accomplish something *bigger* here in 1999 than we accomplished in Chicago in 1968 with our disruptive protests at the Democratic National Convention.

Unfortunately, the public has been given a picture of the protests that's as foggy as the tear gas. While the scattered violence got most of the media attention, the protesters were overwhelmingly committed to nonviolent action. Of the 587 people arrested, virtually all were committing acts of peaceful civil disobedience, such as violating curfew or entering the no-protest zone.

Events get magnified at close range, and it's impossible to know whether the protests here have discredited the WTO fatally or will have any lasting effect. But consider the difference a week can make. I came to Seattle as a state legislator concerned about the WTO's impact on state and local government, and it seemed to me that most Americans knew nothing about the WTO. Now I hear people talking about it with suspicion. Many Americans said that Generation X was apathetic until last week. Then, in Bill Gates's backyard, protesters, most of them young, stopped the organization of the new global economy in its tracks—however briefly—and sent the pundits looking for new generational labels.

The 1968 protest in Chicago was the crest of a wave that had been rising for eight years, through thousands of protests from the civil rights movement to the antiwar movement. The Seattle protest, rather than riding a wave, allowed a whole new generation of activists to surface, bringing attention to one of the world's most powerful organizations.

In 1968, people expected Chicago to be Chicago—you could see the protest building. Here, the city and the authorities seemed generally stunned; the protesters accomplished more with less.

Seattle will have greater consequences. In Chicago, we were dealing with a single issue, the Vietnam war. The Seattle activists were confronting the very nature of the way economics, environmentalism and human rights are going to be shaped for the rest of our lives. The so-called New World Order has to do with everything: exports, prevailing wages, sweatshops, sea turtles, the price and quality of food. The Vietnam War was going to end eventually, but the New World Order will not. You'll either be part of it or you'll be frozen out.

Clearly another major difference is that the issues that brought the protesters to Seattle had such broad-based support from labor *and* environmentalists—the traditional base of the Democratic Party. President Clinton, while distancing himself from his own role in shaping the WTO, expressed support for the protesters' goals. This is quite different from the attitude thirty years ago of President Lyndon B. Johnson—or the actions of Mayor Richard Daley—towards us antiwar rebels in the streets of Chicago.

The Seattle protesters' confrontation was forceful, effective and innovative. They shut down the WTO meeting, albeit temporarily, by chaining themselves together in the streets for as long as twelve hours last Tuesday. Bicyclists recorded the scene with hand-held cameras, enabling the organizers to broadcast live on the World Wide Web. They managed to maintain an attitude more buoyant and carnival-like than violent. Hard hats walked with nature lovers. Students mobilized with action teams with names like the Radical Cheerleaders, the Dot.Commies and the Unarrestables, whose marches were led by a giant puppet of a crying Buddha. American campuses are still more silent than they were in the 60s. But the Seattle protesters represent the breakthrough of the vast hip-hop generation into a public effort to challenge the system.

To the young people who fasted in jail and froze in the streets, the WTO represents all they fear about the future. They will not find a home in the market globalism of Clinton, who appeared tone-deaf by referring to the protests as "hoopla" while endorsing their goals in the same breath. Still, they are just as unlikely to be part of Pat Buchanan's anti-WTO model and narrow nationalist constituency.

For the first time in memory, the patriotism of the corporate globalizers is in question, not that of their opponents. Do the Clinton administration's investor-based trade priorities benefit America's interest in high-wage jobs, environmental protection and human rights? Are American democratic values and middle-class interests secondary to those of transnational corporations? As a grassroots movement seeking the overthrow of what its sees as an oppressive system, Seattle 1999 was more like the Boston Tea Party than the days of rage we knew in the late 1960s.

49

Cancun Files
WTO Opens to Tragedy and Protest

AlterNet, September 11, 2003

After leaving the California state legislature in 2000, I was fascinated to follow and report on the new "anti-globalization" movement born amidst pepper spray and puppets in Seattle. It seemed to be the rebirth of the sixties but somehow on a global scale. Several of these urgent online dispatches remind me of my early writings from Mississippi.

◆   ◆   ◆

A SOUTH KOREAN FARMER, Kun Hai Lee, committed ritual suicide during the WTO's opening day to protest the organization's agricultural policies.

Witnesses said Lee stood in front of police lines, declared that "the WTO kills farmers," and then slashed himself to death with a blade. His suicide came on South Korea's Day of the Dead.

Few at the demonstration realized what had occurred until later in the day. As word slowly spread of the suicide, supporters of Kun Hai Lee vowed to protest his martyrdom throughout the coming week, possibly starting with a tent city at the barricades where the death occurred.

The WTO Secretariat issued a one-paragraph statement of "regret" at the death that they described as resulting from a "self-inflicted" wound. Lee's supporters condemned the WTO for the callous description of his death as self-inflicted, which absolved the organization of any responsibility in his death or the fate of thousands of farmers suffering from its policies.

Lee was known for a previous hunger strike outside the WTO Secretariat in Geneva. A decade ago, three South Korean farmers attempted to immolate themselves, and one died, in anti-WTO protests.

Lee's suicide marked the tragic end of a day of loud and sometimes violent protest. Earlier in the day, twenty global-justice activists peacefully disrupted today's opening ceremony, sealing their mouths with masking tape to represent the voiceless, but left before they were arrested. Carrying bilingual placards proclaiming "WTO anti-development," "WTO obsolete," and "WTO undemocratic," they visibly ruffled the feathers of the trade organization's director-general, Supachai Panitchpakdi of Thailand.

Hours later, thousands of campesinos, marching from Cancun's barrio towards the posh hotel zone where the WTO is headquartered, were blocked by a wire-mesh fence and heavily armed police. Immediately, more militant members of direct action affinity groups from the so-called Black Bloc swarmed the fence to unsuccessfully tear it down.

Black Bloc describes itself as a tactic rather than an organization—a loose and changing collection of anarchist groups who come together for a specific action. The militants appeared to include Mexican students, Europeans with black flags, Koreans and a few from the U.S. As they raged against the fence, twenty-five members of Seattle's Infernal Noise Brigade, dressed in black peasant costumes and armed with painted wooden rifles, played drums and chanted. Chac, the Mayan rain god, blessed the dehydrated throng with a twenty-minute shower.

The protesters threw rocks and water bags and attacked the line of police with sticks and poles. They even hurled themselves against the shielded police phalanx, bouncing back into the crowd, then charging again. They were successful in shaking and bending—but not breaking—the police fence at the intersection of Kukulcan and Bonampak boulevards, placed as a barrier to the hotel zone. As a result, traffic was blocked for several hours across the city. "Why aren't there wire-cutters?" asked one frustrated militant. Several protesters suffered head wounds during the confrontation, but there were no immediate reports of injuries from the police side.

The confrontation, in clear view of the world's media, demonstrated the deep divisions that continue to bedevil the anti-WTO movement.

While a minority believes in storming the barricades physically and symbolically, larger coalitions prefer peaceful confrontations highlighting the grievances of local community-based movements, such as the farmers who belong to Via Campesina. Wednesday's public rift came after a promising late-night meeting between Via Campesina and Black Bloc members. According to Via Campesina leader, Rafael Alegria Moncada, the Black Bloc agreed not to "intervene" at the fence and remain in the rear ranks of the march. In addition, Alegria negotiated a three-kilometer extension of the march with the police, allowing the campesinos to enter the hotel zone that was previously off-limits. The Via Campesina wanted to march on the convention center itself, but the three-kilometer proposal was seen as at least a partial victory.

Both agreements collapsed when Black Bloc groups began attacking the fence. After a three-hour standoff, the Via Campesina contingent pulled back. It was their last scheduled effort to mount a march, and many began boarding buses to return to their villages this evening. About 2,000 remain encamped at the Casa de la Cultura outside the hotel zone.

Alegria was disappointed but philosophical about the day's outcome. He told AlterNet, "Our objectives were not achieved, unfortunately. But what can you say, the others were young people, who came to fight, and it does no good to criticize them." He planned to meet with the remaining Via Campesina contingent tonight to explore their options for the remainder of the week.

Other organizers of the week's protests, including members of Public Citizen and Global Exchange, were seething at the disruption of the campesino march. "Who gives them the right to interfere and impose their agenda on indigenous people?" one prominent activist asked. "Was this what the campesinos took a two-day bus trip for?" asked another. Months of planning and thousands of dollars had been invested in the march, designed to show the human face of the Mexican countryside to the media and WTO delegates.

On the one hand, the small group using Black Bloc tactics succeeded in creating a media spectacle questioning the legitimacy of a beseiged WTO hiding behind military protection. On the other hand, the episode divided the movement and diluted any message being sent by the global South.

But it would be a mistake to conclude that the protests are "marginalized," as a recent *New York Times* editorial suggested. At this point, Cancun 2003 certainly does not compare to Seattle 1999, Washington, D.C., 2000, Prague 2000, Genoa 2001, Quebec 2001, Lazarc (France) 2000, or the antiwar protests of this spring, all events that drew tens of thousands people taking unprecedented mass action. While Cancun is not as isolated as Qatar or the upper Canadian Rockies (where WTO and G-7 meetings have been held in the past), it is difficult terrain for protests, both from a tactical and logistical point of view. Yet as many as 10,000 indigenous people have streamed in from the Mexican countryside to join global non-governmental organizations in a broadening alliance against the trade agreements that leave them out.

In addition, the impact of the movement gathered here has greater influence than ever before. For example, five years ago, Argentina was a poster-child for corporate globalization before its economic collapse. In response, social movements began blocking roads, taking over factories, besieging banks, and forming popular neighborhood assemblies to reclaim their lives. Unexpectedly, this year they elected a populist president, Nestor Kirchner, who, on the eve of the WTO's conference opening, dropped a bombshell by refusing to pay a $3 billion loan to the International Monetary Fund (IMF). Heeding the social movement, Kirchner refused the IMF's demands that he slash social programs, increase middle class taxes, allow foreign-owned utilities to raise rates, and banks to foreclose on homeowners without savings.

It was a dream come true for the anti-globalization movement—all because of an election that the cynics dismissed as meaningless. The Argentina developments followed on the heels of the election of Lula in Brazil, and other populist victories across Latin America.

In an another victory for the movement, on the day the Cancun conference opened, the European Union's high court ruled that European states can ban genetically modified foods for health reasons, delivering yet another blow to U.S. chemical companies, agribusiness, and the WTO.

The mass protests against the WTO will continue in Cancun and beyond. But what we are seeing behind today's headlines is the growing strength of global-justice ideas, which are moving from the outside margins of protest to the mainstream of public opinion in many countries. A poll of Americans released Wednesday found that a majority believe the Bush administration is overemphasizing military approaches and should stress economic reform and diplomacy.

Paradoxically, the movement could encounter more isolation and division right as it reaches the moment of critical mass, just as the anti-Vietnam and civil rights movements fell apart in the 1970s as their message gained acceptance and their leaders were canonized in a new establishment consensus.

It is far too early to predict this next phase of the global justice movement, except to say that it will need an internal review and course-correction if it is to keep up with the history it has helped unleash.

50.

Harvard in Miami

Z-Net, *November 23, 2003*

In fall 2003, I was an associate at Harvard's Institute of Politics, teaching a seminar on students and social change. In that capacity I took a delegation of Harvard and Massachusetts Institute of Technology students to participate as eyewitnesses in an expected confrontation between global justice protesters and the Miami summit conference of the Free Trade Area of the Americas (FTAA). It turned into a dramatic educational experience, rattling Harvard in what I hope were healthy ways.

♦ ♦ ♦

THE POLICE FORCE seemed to operate with the brains and appetite of a carnivorous shark today as city officials promoted "the Miami model" of suppression even as protesters and trade ministers were leaving the city.

At an afternoon press conference, Thea Lee, the chief international economist of the AFL-CIO, spoke of feeling terrified yesterday as police fired pepper gas and plastic bullets at peaceful marchers. Other labor leaders, including AFL-CIO president John Sweeney, expressed "outrage" over the police blocking of a permitted gathering, and cited specific abuses such as a union retiree being denied medication after an arbitrary arrest.

Global Exchange cofounder Medea Benjamin and others were pulled over last night by a dozen officers who pointed guns at them. The Sierra Club's Washington, D.C. advocate, Dan Seligman, also described officers holding a weapon to his head and that of another colleague. Mark Rand, coordinator of a group of foundation funders, displayed a large bluish bruise on his back leg from a rubber bullet.

When 100 protesters ventured to the county jail today to speak out against yesterday's arrests and detentions of some 145 people, one-third on felonies, the very cycle of avoidable suppression they were describing unfolded yet again.

David Solnit, one of the founders of the Seattle movement, attributed the harsh police measures to Miami's character as a center of the South's "vulgar capitalism." Unlike other cities, where authorities may appear to assimilate dissent for political reasons, he said, Miami has attempted to sweep it away as a foreign curse. AFL-CIO leader Ron Judd speculated that the police suppression deflected public attention away from working-class trade issues, while Medea Benjamin accused authorities of "trying to get the people of this city and county used to this militaristic model" instead of the relatively benign model of policing shown at Cancun only two months ago.

I came to Miami with eight students from Harvard University, where I have been teaching a study group on social movements this semester. Though they carried surveys to sample the opinions of protesters, they received a firsthand education in police suppression today. After the press conference outside the county jail, about 200 marched a few hundred yards, stopping in a parking lot across a street from several hundred heavily equipped police. Negotiations between a police commander and activist lawyers produced a peaceful coexistence for an hour late in the afternoon. There was high spirit, even humor, among the protesters who invented chants like "There ain't no riot here, take off that stupid gear!" singing "We all live in a failed democracy."

The protest could easily have been contained by a handful of officers, or might have simply faded as the day ended. Instead, at approximately 5 p.m., the commanding officer summoned the activist lawyers to announce that those milling in the parking lot had become an "unlawful assembly" with three minutes to disperse. In addition, he said with a straight face, there was "intelligence" that some in the crowd had rocks. There was no evidence backing the secret intelligence and no rocks were seen in the events to follow.

Instead of resisting, the crowd began dispersing along 14 Street, the only egress route available. With the Harvard students I was among the last to leave, along with camerawoman Ana Nogueira and reporter Jeremy Scahill from *Democracy Now!* Crossing a driveway I met David Solnit again, who had decided not to take it any more.

"Come on, Tom, here's your historical moment," he waived, "we need civil disobedience to say no to all this."

I replied with words to the effect that I was writing about this, not leading it, feeling slight pang of nostalgia and guilt. There was no more time for talk. The police were advancing only a few feet behind us. I stayed with my Harvard students, having warned them that they might be caught up or hurt in the police sweep.

Solnit and six others sat down suddenly on the sidewalk, holding their hands up in V-signs. A phalanx of twenty-five police closed in on them as we took photographs and notes from a few feet away. In moments they were handcuffed and led away. More police were swarming everywhere, overwhelming the protestors by ten to one.

One block away the dispersing crowd was walking backwards as more police approached with helmet visors down and guns and clubs drawn. By now five of my students had joined their witness, holding their hands over their head and chanting "We are dispersing!" again and again. How could the police not notice how young they were, how utterly unthreatening, how innocent?

I moved alongside the advancing and retreating lines to take a photograph when I noticed that a policeman was aiming a shotgun straight at my chest. Fear leaped in me, then he pointed the weapon down. But a moment later he was looking down the barrel at me again. I was holding a camera, notebook and pen. Suddenly I found myself asking him, "Are you really pointing that fucking gun at me?" Nothing happened, and I turned back to look for the students. They were on the public sidewalk, but by now more police had arrived to prevent them from walking any further.

The last I saw of them—Anne Beckett, Maddy Elfenbein, Jordan Bar Am, Rachel Bloomekatz, and Toussaint Losier, all undergraduates—their hands were still up as they were swallowed up by the black-and-brown-uniformed horde. When they were on the ground, one officer added a final squirt of pepper spray. How brave they look, I added to myself.

Two of my other students avoided arrest by happening to turn in another direction and, minutes later, Toussaint, a tall African American with dreads and a video camera, magically walked free because the police were too busy with their already-downed quarry. A minute later, I learned that *Democracy Now!*'s Ana Nogueira—and her camera—were enveloped and arrested too.

Police informed the larger world that a mob of menacing protesters had disobeyed orders to dissolve an unlawful assembly and were treated accordingly.

In truth they may have radicalized a whole new generation of America's future leaders.

◆   ◆   ◆

A few months later, my students paid fines and charges were dropped. They would have prevailed in court, but didn't want to live under the shadow of Miami any longer. Back at Harvard, the rumor could not be dispelled that this was a pre-planned conspiracy. Harvard students didn't act this way any more. Little or no blame was directed at the Miami police, and the students had to grapple with the realization that there was little if any sympathy from the authority figures in their lives. A few months later, we reported the results of the survey (see Chapter 42: "Dick Flacks: Where Caterpillars Become Butterflies"). The young people who we interviewed bore a great resemblance to the early SDS activists of my generation.

51

Out of the Melting Pot

AlterNet, *January 23, 2004*

♦   ♦   ♦

Bobby Jindal was elected governor of Louisiana in 2007 with less than 40 percent of the vote, a political victory for the right-wing effort to promote token people of color who will shoulder the White Man's Burden. Stirrings among youth and students are invisible in the media today, but here's a glimpse.

♦   ♦   ♦

INDIAN AMERICANS are a prime target of opportunity for conservatives seeking political headway among people of color. The author Dinesh D'Souza, funded by conservative foundations, attacks campus liberals and affirmative action, becoming an Indian American version of Ward Connerly, the conservative African American who wishes to legislate color blindness. In Louisiana this year (2004), a 29-year-old, born-again Christian Republican, Bobby Jindal, was almost elected the first Indian American governor of any state.

But at the World Social Forum this week, young, progressive Indian Americans have surfaced everywhere, all with stories to tell. The forum experience may be seen as a turning point in building their confidence to challenge the conservative leadership of their communities, according to one of them, Rinku Sen, 37.

Sen, a Brown University graduate, directed the Oakland-based Center for Third World Organizing before becoming the publisher of *ColorLines* magazine. She came to the U.S. with her parents in 1972, part of the wave of Indian professionals encouraged by 1965 immigration reforms.

"We grew up in white suburbia," she recalls, "with no desis [Indian nationals] to relate to." She was encouraged by her professors to study literary criticism, but chose to do something about social justice instead. She became involved in student movements, then was trained by longtime organizers at the Midwest Academy. Last year she published her first book, *Stir It Up*.

Sen's consciousness initially was radicalized by African Americans and feminists more than other South Asians. As the Indian immigrant community became larger and more diverse, an identifiable constituency began to search for definition, including where they fit on the color spectrum. While there were only 387,000 Indians in the United States in 1980, estimates today are as high as two million—still only six-tenths of one percent of the American population, but 16 percent of Asian Americans.

D'Souza's arguments extolling upward mobility would be favorably received by this first generation of Indian professionals, with nearly twice the median incomes and college degrees of other Americans. But the growing Indian community still experienced the color line, political isolation and, especially after September 11, hate crimes and hostility towards immigrants. They began to address their political invisibility, having only three elected officials at state legislative levels when their population ratio should result in forty-five.

For Sen, the World Social Forum has been a marker on her journey. "It's a perfect mix of my identities. It's about my political work. About spending time with my family and not feeling the divisions of identity. I pass as all Indian, it's important to have that in one's life. Otherwise we are constantly negotiating the fragments inside us."

Sen believes that the more her community has this experience of integration, "it builds the community confidence so that progressive south Asians might take on the conservatives" now trying to dominate and speak for the whole community.

And Rinku Sen is not alone. There are other Indian Americans, most in their mid-20s, attending the forum:

➤ Sarita Gupta, who spent last week sleeping on the ground and listening to the stories of Adivasis (indigenous) and Dalits (untouchables) brutally displaced for the construction of the Narmada Dam. Gupta is a former president of the United States Student Association (USSA), and an organizer with the Jobs with Justice campaign;

➤ Anuradha Mittal is a researcher and director of Oakland-based Food First, which provides policy support to small farmer movements across the globe;

➤ New York-based Monami Maulik is with the Desis Rising Up Movement (DRUM), which works on INS immigrant-detention issues;

➤ Saket Soni, who grew up in India, is an immigrant rights organizer in Chicago;

➤ Mallika Dutt, formerly with the Ford Foundation, is trying to promote a human rights culture through the group Breakthrough in New York;

➤ Anannya Bhattacharjee is involved with South Asian working-class and feminist communities in New York, and worked all year on preparations for the WSF;

➤ Swaroopa Iyengar, from Bangladore, came to the San Francisco Bay Area four years ago and works on living-wage campaigns. She recently traveled on the immigrant workers' coast-to-coast Freedom Ride.

These days there are fewer "ABCDs" (American-born Confused Desis) than ever before. The new generation marched among 100,000 in their Indian homeland at the World Social Forum, before returning to their lives and struggles in America. They may come to apply the radical traditions of their Indian heritage in a unique form of progressive assimilation into American political culture.

52

Post-Marx From Mumbai

AlterNet, *January 27, 2004*

As a new century unfolded, I found myself fascinated with the growth of new global networks resisting U.S. corporate domination of trade and international relations. The new networks arose in the void left by the end of the Soviet Union and its allied communist parties. A great rethinking began about possible alternatives to the American bid for superpower dominance, known as the neoliberal model to most of the world, and described as "free markets" in official U.S. national-security doctrines. The new movements included revived strains of anarchism, democratic socialism, and reform communism, but were distinguished by political and intellectual struggles to think anew, not be bound by centralized industrial models that preceded the new age of global information technologies. As an American, it was mindboggling to be surrounded by as many as 100,000 diverse revolutionaries gathered in places as different as Porto Allegre, Brazil, and Mumbai, India. This is a summary account of the forces represented at those immense transitional gatherings. Already, the "anti-globalization" phase of these movements has been followed by newer dramatic events, including [1] the strategic stalemate of the U.S. in Iraq, including its plans to forcibly impose a Western-dominated market economy, [2] the popular election of left-nationalist governments across Latin America who reject the U.S. neoliberal model of privatization and the dictatorial legacies of the 1970s, [3] the intellectual discrediting of the neoliberal model by much of the global community, including prestigious members of the American establishment from Joseph Stiglitz to Al Gore, and [4] the derailing of programs by institutions once considered invincible, like the World Trade Organization and the International Monetary Fund. It is not only clear that "another world is possible" but another world already is being constructed, though step by step in piecemeal fashion, across Latin America on issues of trade, within the European bloc on issues of environmentalism, and globally on issues of human rights in response to dictators like Pinochet. Another empire is impossible. A complex multipolar world, rather than an American-dominated unipolar one, is evolving rapidly in the wake of the bipolar Cold War. A third alternative, that led by global social movements interacting in complex ways with political parties and progressive governments, shows continued vibrancy too. I agree with Fidel Castro's prediction in his 2007 autobiography, Fidel Castro: My Life, *"If a solution is not found for these problems quickly—and the Free Trade [Area] of the Americas is not a solution, and neoliberal globalization is not a solution—more than one revolution may occur in Latin America when the United States least expects it. And there'll be no one to blame [i.e. Fidel Castro], for promoting that revolution."*

◆   ◆   ◆

MUMBAI, INDIA. The World Social Forum successfully channeled the energies of global justice and antiwar forces last week, while continuing to struggle toward a positive alternative that gives further meaning to the phrase, "another world is possible."

The Forum was born in opposition to the entire alphabet soup of neoliberal institutions like the WTO, IMF and World Bank, and the imposition of those neoliberal policies by force in Iraq. It serves as a crucial outreach venue, or space, for action networks like Our World Is Not for Sale, which has led recent campaigns in Cancun and Miami against proposed trade agreements.

In addition, the Forum has touched a deep chord of global solidarity, as shown by the enthusiastic dancing, chanting and marching through Mumbai's streets at the close of this year's event. It is a rare achievement to bring together cosmopolitan intellectuals from the *New Left Review* with traditionally voiceless Dalits (untouchables), Adivasis (indigenous), and Brazil's landless movement.

The Forum seemed to realize, however awkwardly, that it cannot create a better world and once again leave out the Dalits or Adivasis, or demand that they change their cultural traditions as a condition for participating. In turn, the Dalits and Adivasis seemed to know from experience that there is another world filled with potential friends who support their survival. The result was a solidarity that went beyond the usual speeches and resolutions, a solidarity—between the privileged and the damned, between people who might have inhabited different planets yet whose fates are interconnected—that seemed too fragile to maintain, yet too precious to give up.

The fact that the Forum, which originated in Brazil, could plant itself in the center of South Asia was an achievement in itself. The WSF organizers plan to return to Porto Alegre, Brazil, next year as the controversial deadline for concluding the Free Trade Area of the Americas (FTAA) nears. The following year, the WSF expects to meet in Africa, perhaps in Egypt.

A NEW INTERNATIONAL

Since its inception, the Forum has raised expectations that it might become a "new International" replacing the traditional parties of the left, or a coordinating center for solidarity campaigns with workers, the landless, and indigenous groups excluded from the benefits of neoliberalism.

Now the criticism is becoming public. From the ideological left comes the claim that the WSF has "no ideology, no organization, no alternative, no militant struggle, no program," and is a tool of the Ford Foundation (which provided $500,000 to the first Forum and $300,000 for the second, but was rejected by the Indian organizers this year). Whatever their impatience with the Forum, however, most participants seem deeply averse to slipping into doctrinaire Marxism.

A wider criticism is that the new world is being made with too many old-world habits. Speeches are invariably pedantic and too long, the ground covered is already familiar to the audience, and the time allotted for questions inevitably evaporates. Some leading Forum participants, like Naomi Klein, who did not attend this year, have proposed that anyone who speaks at a Forum should be forced to be a listener at the next one.

Others, like Vandana Shiva, complain that the WSF is beginning "to imitate the giganticism and centralized control of the dominant structures being challenged by citizens." Still others question the dominance of well-funded nongovernmental organizations (NGOs) compared to struggling but effective grassroots organizations. Many assert that the annual nature of the Forums drains and diverts resources from their local campaigns. They are promoting regional forums on every continent.

The most tender issue is how to manage the differences between those who ultimately favor political action with all its contradictions, like Brazil's triumphant Workers Party which grew out of social movements, and those who identify with the forces of direct action, land seizures and road blockades for the homeless, and disruptions of the WTO, FTAA and other bodies considered illegitimate.

These differences arise from real experiences and are grounded in a history sometimes forgotten. The Workers Party was the voice of Brazil's oppressed majority for several decades before the successful election two years ago. Its leadership, once in power, felt forced to accommodate to the IMF for global financing, and to challenge the WTO and FTAA from within, rather than confronting the American empire directly. A similar path in power was followed by the African National Congress (ANC) after its victory over apartheid.

These neoliberal accommodations have left the social movements in Brazil and South Africa increasingly frustrated in the search for answers, wondering if another world is possible without another approach to politics altogether. Cuba and Venezuela represent still another circumstance, one where Yanqui imperialism is challenged directly. Countries like Argentina may be in between. The result is a complicated crisis in strategy oversimplified as "reform" versus "revolution."

The WSF was created to address just such issues in an open, pluralistic process, but its floundering, bureaucratic process and 2,100 separate scheduled events make any consensus difficult to reach.

Thus the organizational challenges seem twofold: first, how to achieve consensus on a positive alternative to corporate globalization without splitting into warring factions, and second, how to achieve creative participation on local levels without grooming a permanent, globetrotting elite of its own.

It would be tragic if the effort fails, but not the first time in the history of the left. At this critical juncture, some history is in order to facilitate greater understanding of the challenges, starting with the actual history of the WSF and its roots in the history of social movements going back 150 years. The story will show that while the WSF is "post-Marx," that is, arisen with the end of the Cold War and the Soviet Union, its heritage lies in the solidarity movements originally created by Karl Marx long before Marxism was institutionalized.

A BRIEF HISTORY OF THE WSF

The emergence of the United States as the "sole superpower" after the Cold War led to a new architecture of projected governance over future generations, symbolized by the centralized, undemocratic, secretive, business-dominated machinery of the World Trade Organization and NAFTA, along with the International Monetary Fund and World Bank. The globalization of economic power globalized resistance, beginning with the Zapatista uprising against NAFTA in 1994. The 1999 Seattle confrontation brought to greater visibility a global uprising that already was underway. The corporations and media frantically minimized the threat as merely "isolated," but the rebels kept reproducing themselves at Quebec City, Quito, Genoa, Cancun, etc.

At the same time, the World Social Forum was being conceived in the vacuum left by the Cold War, mainly by groupings in Europe and Brazil. The first was associated with the publisher of *Le Monde Diplomatique*, Bernard Cassen, who also chaired a coalition that embraced a "Tobin tax," named after the American economist James Tobin, who proposed taxation on speculative currency transactions. The assertive name of the group was ATTAC, for Association for the Taxation of Financial Transactions for the Aid of Citizens, and it was funded with $8 million in European Union funds. But the French realized that a resumption of progressive initiative after the Cold War would require new linkages with the South, among groups like Brazil's social and political movements.

Brazilians associated with the Workers Party were moving in the same direction. Their party had survived the twists and turns of Cold War politics, was radical at its core, had succeeded on municipal levels, recognized the importance of "civil society," and become deeply connected with the landless movement sweeping Brazil. They conceived of a broader dialogue toward creating a post–Cold War left, based on a Brazilian approach known as *construção*, a process of consensus-building rather than the withering debates of the Old Left.

The French and the Brazilians met in early 2000 and the Forum was born officially. They obtained official support and funding from the municipal government of Porto Alegre and the state of Rio Grande do Sul, both controlled by the Workers Party at the time. Those government bodies committed U.S. $1.3 million to the event.

The first WSF was held in January 2001 in Porto Alegre, with 5,000 registered attendees from 117 countries. It was overly intellectual, criticized for whiteness, and yet seemed to meet a rising global need. Coming after Seattle in 1999, the decision to be an in-your-face counterpoint to the elite Davos World Economic Forum seemed ingenious.

The second Forum saw a doubling of delegates. By the 2003 Forum, there were more journalists registered (4,000) than the total delegates at the founding one two years before, and over 75,000 turned Porto Alegre into a dream experience for radicals awakening from isolation. The continuous cycle of militant confrontations at WTO summits fostered the expectation that the Forum might become an intercontinental center of a new Left, post-communist, more inclusive than before.

The WSF was controlled by an internal organizing committee, which consisted of key leaders of the CUT (Central Unica dos Trabalhadores) and the MST (Movimento dos Trabalhadores Rurais Sem Terra) among others. Its larger steering committee, the International Council, has evolved to include representatives of the different organizations represented in the Forum. The bodies proceed by consensus, but leadership has rested with the organizing committee so far. The success of the Forum model, and the source of the emergent complaints as well, is that it avoids platform fights in favor of discussions, excludes political parties and groups supportive of armed struggle (except as individuals), and is a "guided" democracy instead of a participatory one.

But where to go with a body so internally diverse? Some clues were suggested during the Forum in an article by a Brazilian sociologist and civil society leader, Candido Gryzbowski, who called for a careful deepening of the Forum in "galvanizing the world." The Forum's greatest deficit, Gryzbowski concluded, is political. "We engage in a fully political act, but it seems that we fear the consequences." He described the tension as between "an old style of leftist politics" and an "anarchic force, impossible to condense," on the other. The only remedy, he seemed to suggest, is further dialogue and networking, in process rather than political conventions.

POST-MARX?

History suggests that these questions have been faced before, perhaps most interestingly—and unexpectedly—by Karl Marx and his partner Friedrich Engels, who created the equivalent of a World Social Forum in their time. This will seem retro, obsolete, or politically correct to some, a history to be kept in a lockbox. Why dredge up a communist memory that the vast majority of movement participants, myself included, left behind long ago or never learned?

But Stalinism and the Soviet model should not be allowed to bury the story of what Marx originally set out to do. A recent essay by August Nimtz, a professor at the University of Minnesota, rescues the history of Marx and Engels from the dustbins of both communism and anticommunism and revives what C. Wright Mills once called "plain Marxism" as distinguished from its dogmatic descendants.

Nimtz reminds us that Marx and Engels created the original "transnational movement of workers," or First International, organized as the International Working Men's Association (IMWA) which Marx led from 1864 to 1872. These efforts led to the eight-hour day and the formation of the first workers' parties in Europe, from which the Brazilian Workers Party descends. What occurred during and after the Soviet Revolution should not erase the process begun decades earlier.

Marx and Engels sought to create a "proletarian" and democratic consciousness among workers to transcend the narrow boundaries of nationalism and religion. They believed that the globalization of capital in their time could not be checked by local movements alone. In 1845, they formed a transnational network called the "Society of Fraternal Democrats" with its goal "to succor the militant democracy of every country." They next formed the Communist Correspondence Societies, based on Thomas Paine's legacy of transnational networking. Finally, they wrote the manifesto for a new organization, the League of Communists, in 1848, a time exploding with revolutions on their continent.

It is interesting that these first networks were premised on discussion rather than explicit programs, so that space would exist for participants to "clear things up among themselves," as Marx wrote. There was a major emphasis on "drawing lessons" by documenting and discussing class struggles in given countries. Engels alone clipped some twenty-seven papers each week, an international "indymedia" in his own right.

The American Civil War was an immediate reason for the creation of the First International, which campaigned against British intervention on the side of Confederate cotton growers. Marx's letters appeared in the *New York Daily Tribune* and were cited in congressional debates at the time. The anti-intervention movement was successful. Soon the IWMA became a "de facto worldwide strike center," aiding bronze-workers in Paris, the building trades in Geneva, coal miners in Belgium, and pressuring British trade unions to support Irish self-determination.

Marx and Engels favored campaigns around single issues, such as the Reform League which demanded the extension of suffrage to male heads of households and, most importantly, the eight-hour day, which the IWMA embraced in 1866 and became the repeated focus of coordinated campaigns on the First of May. Marx believed the "limitation of the working day," as he called it, would free workers for intellectual development and political action.

Marx and Engels saw two dangers on the political front. On the one hand the British trade unions "flirted" with the government of liberal prime minister William Gladstone, which amounted to "class collaboration." On the other hand were the anarchists led by Mikhail Bakunin who advocated abstaining from politics in favor of direct power for workers. The first was a "bourgeois trap" of reformism. While Bakunin's path sounded more revolutionary, Engels wrote, simple abstentionism would leave the workers no alternative but to be pushed into the same bourgeois fate.

Their alternative was the organization of the working class as an independent political force, including the formation of workers' parties. It was, according to Nimtz, "the first explicit call for what would eventually be Europe's mass working-class political parties." The eventual empowerment of the European working class was critical "for the final breakthrough to democracy."

The rest, as some say, is history—or is history repeating itself? Setting aside the legacy of Stalinism, which cannot be blamed on Karl Marx, the original endeavor of Marx and Engels was an example of transnational networking with repercussions for generations to come. The U.S. New Deal and the European welfare states were built not only as alternatives to communism, but from the very traditions that Marx and Engels initiated in the nineteenth century.

Now that those traditions appear weakened, or absorbed into coexistence with corporate power, it is no wonder that so many contemporary activists feel contempt for politics as usual. But capitalism never forgets, which is why the corporations are campaigning today not only for increased access to developing countries' economies, but to roll back the gains in wages, health benefits, pensions, vacations and overall quality of life achieved in earlier decades by socialist or social-democratic movements and political parties. The fall of authoritarian communist states should be celebrated by democrats, but the danger today is that the vacuum is being filled by arrogant multinational corporations, rapacious oil companies, mafias large and small, arms traffickers, and sordid scavengers for profits of any kind. If social democracy—including Left electoral parties, trade unions and nongovernmental organizations—is rejected by many in the new social movements as too "reformist," what option is left?

Can decentralized social movements alone stop the pillage of the global commons?

If not, can the World Social Forum become an international coordinating center for solidarity campaigns, lobbying, boycotts and civil disobedience? Or will it fade away as its original purposes are served?

If the eight-hour day was achieved by a transnational social movement, who today will similarly achieve a global living wage, a reversal of the arms race, and participatory democracy?

If the progressive parties of the past have achieved their purposes and entered a terminal phase, will political parties of a new type replace them? If not, how will enforceable workers' rights become law or global environmental treaties be enforced? Or does democracy exist only in the streets?

How is it that movements so frequently arise from mystery, first appear at the margins, march into the mainstream, achieve a new majority, only to fade again like waves of the ocean?

Those are the questions facing the World Social Forum today. It may be helpful to know they have been asked and answered before in the heat of battle by our radical forebears, that there is a history to be learned from and enriched by, even as history now begins anew.

53.

A New Bolivian Diary

The Nation *Web site, January 27, 2006*

I encourage North Americans seeking a new U.S. policy toward Latin America to visit the countries with new progressive governments, beginning with Bolivia where the daily struggle is both vivid and large-scale. Steady opposition to U.S. intervention in Bolivia, Venezuela and Cuba is crucial, as are people-to-people cultural exchanges. One of my fantasies is to mobilize heart patients like myself to demand the legalization of coca for medicinal purposes, along the lines of medical marijuana. This blow against the drug war would be hugely beneficial for Bolivia.

◆　　◆　　◆

TODAY IS DAY ONE of the new Morales government in Bolivia. No one predicted the tectonic shift which resulted in a 54 percent victory for the man everyone knows as Evo, the Aymaran Indian, leader of the Movement Toward Socialism (MAS), and longtime head of the coca growers union. "It's like the slaves have elected the president, for the first time in 513 years," since the death of the last Inca king, said one community leader in El Alto, the vast Indian community that looks down upon this Spanish colonial city.

When he organized a guerrilla base here in the 1960s, Che Guevara wrote in his Bolivian diaries of awakening the indigenous people around him. Today, a new Bolivian diary is being written by Morales and the newly empowered people who elected him.

Bolivia's population mainly consists of Aymaran and Quechua people; they are among the poorest in the Americas. They won the right to vote only fifty years ago, in a 1952 nationalist revolution that left them culturally and economically subordinate.

What are the immediate prospects and long-term implications for Morales's new Bolivia? On day one there was widespread exhilaration, but there were also creeping worries. Social activists were delighted by some of his promises, for example, his inaugural declaration that the privatization of water violates a "basic human right." Only days before, the Bechtel Corporation had dropped its suit against Bolivia for alleged losses in a water-management project that ended when protesters from Cochabamba drove Bechtel from the country. Corporate insiders admitted that a major factor in Bechtel's retreat was "reputational," a desire to save its corporate image from further tarnishing.

Pablo Solon, a close friend of Morales and the country's leading critic of corporate-driven free-trade pacts, was delighted by the news on water, almost giddy at the new possibilities, but worried that the United States already was moving behind the scenes to thwart Morales's vision of an independent democratic socialism, a kind of New Deal for the indigenous.

When we spoke, Solon sat in his foundation headquarters amid dozens of exquisite sketches from the collection of his father, a well-known muralist. Images of tin miners with skeletal faces, and of Don Quixote being tortured, looked down from the walls. Solon, whose brother was murdered during military rule, was contemplating the new relationship between Bolivian social movements and the new government they had been pivotal in electing. The State Department reportedly already was moving to force Bolivia into an Andean Free Trade Agreement (AFTA, as in NAFTA or CAFTA) that would lock Morales's new government into subordination to the multinationals. U.S. Undersecretary of State for Western Hemispheric Affairs Thomas Shannon was signaling privately that while Washington might be open to "dialogue" on the issues of hydrocarbons and coca planting, the issue of free trade itself was non-negotiable.

THE COST OF FREE TRADE

In its effort to head off Morales, the U.S. is allied with Bolivian businessman Marcos Iberkleid, the descendant of Jewish immigrants from Poland, and owner of a textile consortium known as Ametex (America Textil SA).

Previous U.S.-dominated Bolivian governments have envisioned Ametex, which employs 4,500 workers, as the motor of a textile-based exports strategy. For Iberkleid, this requires winning an extension on tariff preferences for textile exports to the U.S., currently due to expire at the end of this year. The U.S. says that it will favor the extension only if Bolivia signs off on an overall free-trade agreement.

One graphic example of how free-trade pacts work is that the U.S. plans to assert a right to patent plants and animals under intellectual property-rights provisions. "It's against Andean policies and traditions," Solon almost shouts. Further, U.S. drug companies and agricultural interests will seek to extend their patent rights from twenty to twenty-seven years. And Bolivia will have to surrender its judicial sovereignty over trade disputes, declared in Article 135 of its constitution, to closed-door AFTA arbitration panels dominated by corporate property interests.

Enter Iberkleid, the Bolivian point man for the free-trade agenda. His credit rating was a "D" on December 30, according to the Fitch Ratings Index. He desperately seeks to keep filling the orders of his principal corporate client, Polo Ralph Lauren. The U.S. embassy in La Paz has opened its doors three times to welcome Iberkleid's workers in their campaign in support of AFTA. By contrast, when Bolivian citizens petition the embassy for the Bolivian government's own request to extradite former President Gonzalo Sanchez de Lozada from Miami to prosecute him for the deaths of dozens of demonstrators in 2004, they get only as far as the security blockades at the embassy gate.

Iberkleid brandishes a threat that Morales fears—the possibility that Ametex workers will protest or, worst of all, begin a hunger strike on the streets of El Alto, demanding their jobs be saved. In an ominous sign of Morales's potential direction, on day one the new president appointed the union leader at Iberkleid's plant as the minister of labor.

Working conditions at Iberkleid's factory, while not technically those of a typical maquiladora, are still based on the competitive advantage of offering the cheapest possible labor, says La Paz economist Tom Kruze.

"We have failed in the public debate to break the false belief that we have to export or die, " says Kruze, who specializes in labor economics. Fabric and clothing exports to the U.S. represent only $35 million in total. "That's all, with this one man, Marcos Iberkleid, controlling 75 percent of them," says Pablo Solon. Hardly the basis for an economic miracle, Solon and Kruze also question Bolivia's future as a textile exporter when quotas are lifted on Chinese manufacturers in 2008. Any immediate benefits in extending U.S. preferences for Iberkleid will be at the sacrifice of Bolivian sovereignty under a free-trade agreement.

Evo Morales knows all this. "You are right, but there is huge pressure," he has told his friend Pablo Solon.

Solon hopes that Evo will denounce the U.S. pressure as blackmail. But to illustrate the new president's vacillation, Solon swerves his hands back and forth. "They are trying in the next thirty days to convert Evo into a Lula," complained Pablo, referring to Brazilian President Luiz Inacio Lula da Silva's acceptance of international financial rules after years of campaigning against the "neoliberal" agenda. As recently as November 2005, Morales returned from an Argentina summit to declare his opposition to free-trade agreements, for either the Andes or Latin America. But in his inaugural remarks in La Paz, the new president declared only that he would "analyze" the agreement, an equivocation that adds to Solon's worries.

ENDING "EL MODELO"

Such are the practical problems confronting any radical movement that achieves political power. Evo Morales has yet to define where Bolivia will stand in the spectrum of new Latin American nationalisms, which range from Cuba and Venezuela, which so far oppose any free-trade deals with the United States, to the more reformist Brazil, Argentina and Chile, which see themselves as driving bargains for their domestic industries in a free-trade context. In part these differences reflect different economic realities—Cuba is under U.S. embargo, while Venezuela is a source of oil—rather than ideology alone. But Morales has preached a "communitarian socialism based on the community, a socialism, let's say, based on reciprocity and solidarity. And beyond that, respecting Mother Earth, the

Pachamama. It is not possible within the [neoliberal] model to convert Mother Earth to merchandise."

When I interviewed Morales in 2004, he said the "struggle is not only in Bolivia, because *el modelo* [the neoliberal model] fails especially for the poor," adding that multinational domination "is not going to happen" because "it's a clash between two cultures, the indigenous versus the U.S., sharing versus individualism."

Morales's vice president is Álvaro García Linera, a former guerrilla leader, political prisoner, academic researcher and public commentator. He describes the Morales-MAS coalition as one on the "center-left." Socialism, he says, is not possible in a Bolivia where a proletariat is "numerically in a minority and politically non-existent," and where the economy has imploded into family and community structures, "which have been the framework within which the social movements have arisen." Linera favors an "Andean capitalism," which will build a "strong state" to transfer the surplus of the nationalized hydrocarbon industry to "encourage the setting up of forms of self-organization, of self-management and of commercial development that is really Andean and Amazonian." In other words, modern economic development would be embedded in, or allied with, the traditional communal structures of the indigenous people, instead of replacing those structures with vertical forms of control.

In an interview with *Monthly Review* before the election, Morales described socialism as "something much deeper" than the class-based model, founded on the indigenous values. It is likely that Bolivia will contribute to this indigenous framework to the ongoing debate over a Latin American alternative to neoliberalism. That suggests that he will avoid surrendering to the free-trade model Washington demands. Instead, he is proposing a "constituent assembly" that will transfer even greater power to communities excluded by the colonial Bolivian state. He has said, "a new integration is possible," borrowing from the global justice movement's refrain that "another world is possible."

There is another factor in the equation, a North American one, often ignored by the analysts. "We need support in the United States, not only about our image but especially about these trade agreements," Pablo Solon said. There is so far only a fledgling network of Bolivian solidarity activists, compared with the U.S. movements during the Central American wars of the 1970s and 1980s. And despite remarkable but unheralded work by fair trade activists like Global Trade Watch in the United States, demonstrations and lobbying have so far only dented, but not prevented, congressional acquiescence in the U.S. administration's drive to assure corporate property rights over labor and environmental standards. When I interviewed him two years ago, Morales said he sided with "the many movements in the United States struggling against neoliberalism, and we must struggle together."

In sum, a far stronger alliance between Latin American and North American social movements, based on a common anticorporate, pro-indigenous, pro-democracy agenda, might become a crucial factor in expanding the possibilities of what leaders like Evo Morales feel able to achieve. Twenty years after Bolivia was plunged into chaos by U.S.-imposed privatizations, there is an incipient rethinking of free trade in U.S. establishment circles. For example, *Newsweek* reported in January that a "new consensus" is developing that "trade is not enough to end poverty" and that "what's needed is more government intervention in economies, not less. Call it a new New Deal, and get ready to hear much more about it in 2006."

But there is little sign of this welcome development in the U.S. approach to the new Bolivia. It is likely that multinational oil companies will accept greater sharing of their wealth, and the transfer of controls over industrialization, to Bolivians. But that is because their profit margins are in the range of 30 percent, according to a corporate attorney I talked to who had fifteen years' experience in Bolivia. But a World Bank official I interviewed repeated the official dogma that development depends on unfettered private foreign investment. Her key suggestion for Evo Morales was that Bolivia's street vendors—about 70 percent of Bolivians are employed in the "informal sector," selling Fresca and toothpaste on the streets—should be licensed and registered so they can be taxed. It is a trickle-up policy sure to be resisted.

INDIGENOUS ICON

Whatever Evo Morales decides on the immediate question of textiles, it would be premature to categorize the Bolivian revolution as over, or to dismiss it as merely "neoliberalism with an Indian face." But this is the thrust of some on the Left, as in the recent *Democracy Now!* interview with James Petras, a longtime expert on the region, who says that Morales is only a social democratic reformer Washington can live with. Petras may be right that the new Bolivia will seek to avoid the kind of confrontation with the United States exemplified by oil-rich Venezuela, but such criticism underestimates the moral and political importance of the Bolivian revolution for the indigenous poor. What Petras may be underplaying is the large, radical-left indigenous movement in Bolivia—such as the movment led by Felipe Quispe—that is evaluating his every policy move. The "Indian question" has rarely been an emphasis of the Left, but it still remains the central question in Bolivia, in the Andes, in Chiapas, and much of Latin America.

Few whites or mestizos understand this as well as García Linera, whose life has been devoted to what he calls the "decolonization of the state" so that indigenous people will govern, ending a fault line that has existed between society and the state in Bolivia for 180 years. "Fifteen years ago, we thought that it could come about through an armed uprising of the communities. Today, we think it is an objective that we can attain through a great electoral triumph." He calls for a new dialogue between "indigenism" and a Marxism which only perceived the Indians as reactionary or the dependent clients of humanitarian nongovernmental organizations.

Nothing illustrates the profound importance of this shift more than the inaugural ceremonies over the past weekend. Since García Linera was sworn in as vice president first, it became his duty to place the presidential sash over the shoulders of Morales. In a moment that millions watched on television, Morales visibly shed a tear, buckled slightly, then embraced his friend and became Bolivia's first indigenous president. Not only had the indigenous majority voted for him, but also at least one-third of the white or mestizo privileged classes, an outcome that ended centuries of brutal discrimination and marginalization.

Even more important was the ceremony on Saturday, when indigenous spiritual leaders inaugurated Evo Morales in their own way, at the pre-Inca ruins known as Tiwanaku, on the remote *altiplano* near Lake Titikaka. There, as 30,000 or more waited and witnessed, Aymara leaders changed Evo's clothes into native ones, removed his shoes so that he would stand on Pachamama (Mother Earth), and gave him a walking stick decorated in gold and silver, representing the transfer of authority for the first time in five centuries.

There the world watched the rising of another kind of power, one more cultural than political, that of a postmodern Indian icon. Garbed in a red ceremonial robe and holding the staff of power, Evo Morales stood in a portal cut from a single block of stone ten feet high, eleven feet wide, estimated to weigh ten tons. Like the ancient portals at Newgrange in Ireland or Maya sites in Central America, the stone portal was designed to receive the rays of the sun at the equinoxes, a reminder of pre-Inca science and cosmology.

The image flooded the world, over the heads of the technicians of power and stenographers in the media, a visceral reminder that another globalization is possible, and that the "Indian question" is not over, not for the United States, not for Western culture, not for the progressive Left, but only beginning again.

54

Who Are You Calling An Immigrant?

Truthdig, *May 3, 2006*

One benefit of living in Los Angeles is witnessing its transition to a Latino metropolis as the rest of North America grapples with the implications. While issues of multiculturalism are being debated abstractly by pundits and politicians, here in L.A. and many other cities around the country, they are being experienced by most people on a daily basis. These issues will increasingly divide and define our politics, shape the progressive agenda, and drive North America's identity in the future.

◆   ◆   ◆

I WORE THE MULTICOLORED Aymaran flag of Bolivia to the May Day march in Los Angeles, the same day that Evo Morales, the first indigenous president of Bolivia, nationalized the oil and gas fields. It seemed right to recognize the reappearance of the indigenous in the Americas. I gazed at Marcos Aguilar, one of the UCLA hunger strikers for Chicano studies in 1993. Now he stood bare-skinned and feathered, leading a traditional dance below the edifice of the *Los Angeles Times*. Rather than becoming assimilated into gringotopia, he was forcing the reverse, the assimilation of the Machiavellians into the new reality of L.A. Another hunger striker from those days, Cindy Montañez, was chairing the state Assembly's rules committee. Another UCLA student, a beneficiary of 1960s outreach programs, was mayor of the city.

Contrary to most mainstream commentary, these protests were part of a continuous social movement going back many decades, even centuries. And yet the commentators, especially on the national level, once again summoned the stereotype of the lazy Mexican, the sleeping giant awakening. For years it was convenient to blame apathy and low participation rates on the Mexican Americans and other Latinos, ignoring the racial exclusion that prevailed east of the Los Angeles River. In 1994, the same "sleeping giant" arose against Pete Wilson's Proposition 187. It previously awoke in the 1968 high-school "blowouts," the 1968–69 Chicano moratorium and the farmworker boycotts, which were the largest in history, and, in an earlier generation, the giant awoke in the "Zoot Suit Riots" and Ed Roybal's winning campaign for City Council. The giant never had time to sleep at all.

In the Great Depression, in the lifetimes of the parents and grandparents of today's students, up to 600,000 Mexicans, one-third of the entire U.S. Mexican population, many of them born in the United States, were deported with their children back to Mexico, their labor no longer needed.

OUT OF NOWHERE?

There is a frightening gap between the white perception of this fifty-year trauma of deportation and the experience of Mexicans and other immigrants, like the Salvadorans who were driven here by the U.S.-backed civil wars of the 1970s. Somewhere between amnesia and a self-induced lobotomy, the gap needs to be closed in the dialogue that may come of these historic protests. The mere passage of time may erase white memories and guilt, and induce acceptance among Mexicans, but it does not legitimize the occupation itself. The wound will not disappear under American flags, searchlights and border walls.

The fundamental issue still shaping attitudes down to the present is this: either the Mexicans (and other Latinos) are immigrants to a country called the United States or the U.S. is a Machiavellian power that denies occupying one-half of Mexico for 156 years. During the 1846–48 war against Mexico, at least 50,000 Mexicans died. The fighting took place across many cities considered pure-bred American today; in Los Angeles, a revolt temporarily drove out the U.S. Army. Guerrilla resistance by Mexican fighters left a mythic legacy of those like Joaquin Murrieta and Tiburcio Vasquez, names still alive among Mexican-American students today. Meanwhile, the

New York Times was declaring in 1860: "The Mexicans, ignorant and degraded as they are, [should welcome a system] founded on free trade and the right of colonization so that, after a few years of pupilege, the Mexican state would be incorporated into the Union under the same conditions as the original colonies."

After unilaterally annexing Texas in 1845, despite massive protests, the U.S. president sent troops 100 miles into what previously was Mexican land. When the Mexicans retaliated, the U.S. declared war on the pretext that Americans had been attacked on American soil. When it ended, the U.S. took 51 percent of Mexico's land, including California, where the discovery of gold had been kept secret from Mexican negotiators. At least 100,000 Mexicans and an additional 200,000 indigenous people lived on those lands. Ever since, those people and their descendants have lived in a split-consciousness similar to that of African-Americans described in W. E. B. DuBois's *The Souls of Black Folk*. Each new generation of immigrants fuels that consciousness all over again.

Under the Treaty of Guadalupe Hidalgo, the imposed settlement of the 1846–48 war, the inhabitants of the occupied territories were granted legal, political, educational and cultural rights as citizens, not as immigrants. Some of the earliest official documents of California were required under the treaty to be printed in Spanish and English. This treaty, which was unenforced, became the basis for later movements stretching into the 1960s, movements that gave the Southwest an Aztec name (Aztlan) and demanded the return of former land grants. It was not unlike Radical Reconstruction, the period after the Civil War when Gen. Sherman's official promise of "forty acres and a mule" was withdrawn.

Today's demonstrations are not demanding implementation of the Treaty of Guadalupe Hidalgo. Modern Mexican Americans have made the legalization of undocumented workers as United States citizens their consensus demand. But there remains an unspoken difference between two states of mind regarding the meaning of the border. In every generation, immigrant workers and youth have claimed their American rights without abandoning the memory of their deeper historical ones.

A significant number of white Americans, especially among the elites, still hold to nativist definitions of American identity, in contrast to those multinational corporations that tend to be more interested in cheap foreign labor than in keeping American white.

Conservative journals like the *American Outlook* publish articles glorifying "the Anglosphere" as the standard of globalization. Kevin Phillips is quoted in the article as still longing for an American culture whose "core thought is a kind of English revivalism." Regarding this month's demonstrations, the black neoconservative Thomas Sowell has criticized the "demanding" and "threatening" tone of "people who [want] their own turf on American soil. . . ."[1]

No one lends an Ivy League luster to the minuteman mentality more than Harvard University professor Samuel Huntington. A proud "Anglo-Protestant," Huntington previously advocated the "forced urbanization" of the Vietnamese peasantry into a "Honda culture" as a formula for ending the nationalist uprising. In the 1970s, he complained that an "excess of democracy" threatened Western authorities. More recently, he formulated the strident doctrine of "the clash of civilizations," decreeing that Islamic culture is incompatible with democratic civilization. Finally, he has weighed in on "the Hispanic challenge," arguing that Latino immigration is "a major potential threat to the country's cultural and possibly political integrity."[2] Huntington argues that Mexican Americans are too close to their traditional culture to become assimilated as patriotic Americans. By this he means, of course, that they cannot become imitation WASPs, whose identity he sees as basic to the American nation. For Huntington, assimilation seems to mean submission and disappearance into the master culture, a viewpoint still held by many. We defeated you, and now you should become like us.

Largely forgotten in the current debate, too, are those among the elites who still consider Mexico itself a strategic long-term threat. The late Caspar Weinberger, a secretary of defense under Ronald Reagan, wrote in 1998 of planning for a theoretical "next war" against Mexico, opting for the military option in case "it becomes necessary to go down in and try to catch [a] rebel leader in Mexico and restore democratic rule to Mexico."[3] The Harvard historian of Chiapas, John Womack Jr., has written that in the

1990s "the U.S. government, in particular the Defense Department . . . wanted 'low-intensity' warfare in Mexico."[4]

But the U.S. has historically been the destabilizing force in Mexico, most recently with the North American Free Trade Agreement (NAFTA), which has flooded the country with corn and other products and replaced indigenous manufacturing with the maquiladora economy, thus displacing at least hundreds of thousands of Mexicans, many of whom seek survival in *el norte*. Perpetuating the cycle is absolutely crucial to neoliberal economics. But it also perpetually stimulates rebelliousness, in fact and memory, among those who take to U.S. streets today, and who shortly will be the urban majority in a new America.

As people of color, mainly immigrants, edge closer to majority status in key states, their relatives to the south are becoming nationalist, populist majorities in country after country, with interests that sharply conflict with the disintegrating U.S. Monroe Doctrine of 1823. If the populist mayor of Mexico City is elected president of Mexico this fall, NAFTA itself will die or be renegotiated. This is the first time in many decades that the interests of Latinos in the United States are closely converging with the governments and people of the nations of the south. As seen even in the recent international baseball championships, the willingness of America's major-league Latino players to join the lineups of their homelands shows the fluid nature of borders and solidarity. A policy beyond the Monroe Doctrine will have to be crafted for the United States, with Latinos in the lead. As Evo Morales of Bolivia is suggesting, "another annexation is possible," the annexation of the United States into peaceful coexistence with Latin America.

Some would argue that the United States must simply follow the path of previous immigrant generations, like my Famine Irish ancestors. It is true that the slum-dwelling Irish, Jews and Italians rose in time to the middle class, and the same future may lie ahead for the new immigrants. We can see signs of the past in the growing ranks of Latino trade unionists and mayors and other politicians. But the difference in the histories is race and class. If neoliberalism has failed to widen the American middle class since 1973, how will it expand to provide decent jobs for the aspiring immigrants in today's underclass? Is there another New Deal just over the horizon, or a hardening defense of the status quo?

Huntington's Anglosphere is dying, if only through demographics. It is a matter of time—of when, not whether. The newcomers have neither the need nor the capacity to assimilate into a declining Anglosphere. They will remain multicultural of necessity, the hybrid multitude arising from the depths of empire and its resistance. The real question is how the rest of the United States, the rest of us, can assimilate and find belonging within all the Americas, where so many flags are fluttering in the gusts of self-determination.

NOTES

1. Thomas Sowell, *L.A. Daily News*, April 29, 2006.
2. Samuel P. Huntington, "The Hispanic Challenge," *Foreign Policy*, March–April 2004.
3. Interview with "Chuck Baldwin Live," February 17, 1998.
4. John Womack Jr., editor, *Rebellion in Chiapas*, New Press, 1999.

XI **Writing Against the Iraq War**

55

It's Empire versus Democracy

AlterNet, *September 10, 2002*

I wrote this article as the first anniversary of 9/11 was approaching, the war in Afghanistan was raging, and the Bush administration was preparing to invade Iraq. The tone and carefulness reflect the anxieties I was sensing in people. Certain national peace leaders had explicitly told me that one could not question the framework of the war on terror and expect to be taken seriously by anyone in Washington. It was the beginning of the leading Democrats' tactical argument that Iraq was a "diversion" from taking up the "real" war on terrorism, an argument I never understood. It would turn out that, just as Vietnam was the key to unraveling Cold War thinking, the quagmire in Iraq would become the key to challenging the assumptions of the war on terror, a task that is still before us.

◆　　◆　　◆

IN THE AFTERMATH of September 11, American conservatives launched a political and intellectual offensive to discredit any public questioning of the Bush administration's open-ended, blank-check, undefined war against terrorism. The conservative message, delivered through multiple media outlets, was that dissenters from the Bush administration's war were those who allegedly "blamed America first," that is, dared to explore whether bin Laden's terrorism was possibly rooted in Western policies toward the Islamic world, the Palestinians, and the oil monarchies of the Middle East.

The strike against domestic dissent was a preemptive one, since most progressives were too stunned, traumatized, and confused by the September 11 attacks to dissent anyway. But Susan Sontag was targeted for a right-wing stoning for an article in the *New Yorker,* and Bill Maher for not being politically correct. Vice President Cheney's wife helped monitor college classrooms for dissenting voices. Rapid articles appeared in the *New Republic.* Intimidating full-page ads by William Bennett announced plans to expose anyone who "blamed America first." White House spokesman Ari Fleischer added an official warning when he 'crafted an "offhand" remark that Americans should "watch what they say." Chief Republican political strategist Karl Rove proposed that his party's candidates make the war on terrorism an election issue. Senate Republican leader Trent Lott accused Democratic Senator Tom Daschle of being soft on Saddam Hussein (because Daschle opposed Arctic oil drilling). The chairman of the Republican House Campaign Committee declared that all questioners were "giving aid and comfort to the enemy."

Civil liberties were rapidly becoming the domestic collateral damage of the war on terrorism. It almost could be said they died without a fight, except for a brave but ineffective handful of stragglers in their progressive enclaves.

Some will ask, so what? Isn't the right to dissent a secondary concern when thousands of innocent Americans have been killed in terrorist attacks? A fair question. The truth is that Osama bin Laden set the stage for this political shift to the right by his strategy of targeting civilians. And bin Laden is no aberration. Radical Islamic fundamentalism has risen in the vacuum created by the failures of political Arab nationalism (and the end of the Soviet Union, which, whatever else may be said, supported non-religious revolutionary movements). The radical religious-based movements are here to stay.

So it is understandable that the vast majority of Americans responded to September 11 with existential cries for public safety and a military response. And if bin Laden or his successor carry out further attacks against American civilians, the politics of repression will deepen. The problem is that conservatives inside and outside the Bush administration are seeking to take advantage of America's understandable fears to push a right-wing agenda that would not otherwise be palatable. In short, they are playing patriot games with the nation's future.

The *Wall Street Journal* gave the secret away in an October 2001 editorial declaring that September 11 created a unique political opportunity to advance the whole Republican-conservative platform. Worse, the real conservative agenda is to create an American empire, not simply rout out the Al Qaeda organization. No sooner had the September 11 attacks occurred than the *Wall Street Journal*'s editorial writer, Max Boot, published "The Case for American Empire" in the conservative organ, the *Weekly Standard*. Boot endorsed a return to nineteenth-century British imperialism, this time under American hegemony. "Afghanistan and other troubled lands today cry out for the sort of enlightened foreign administration once provided by self-confident Englishmen in jodhpurs and pith helmets" (see the *New York Times,* March 31, 2002). The orchestrated call for empire was "out of the closet," according to conservative columnist Charles Krauthammer, and was echoed in the works of historians Paul Kennedy and Robert D. Kaplan (who found nice things to say about Emperor Tiberius, namely that he used force to "preserve a peace that was favorable to Rome").

The skilled but immoral and deceitful machinations of these would-be Romans have been described by David Brock in his confessional bestseller, *Blinded by the Right: The Conscience of an Ex-Conservative.* Brock should know the game. He consciously distorted the facts to gun down Anita Hill and protect Clarence Thomas's nomination to the Supreme Court. Not satisfied, he invented the "Troopergate" allegations against the Clintons. He admits that the conservative agenda was to impeach Clinton even before there was a Monica Lewinsky scandal. He describes in detail the "vast right-wing conspiracy" of investigators, muckrakers, pundits, talk-show hosts, and hard-line Republican congressmen who made Newt Gingrich Speaker for two years, instigated the Iran-Contra scandal, nearly brought down Clinton, and eventually mobilized the ground troops which shut down the Florida recount for George Bush.

With the Cold War ended, these conservatives asked what the new enemy threat was that would justify the continuation of a growing military budget and an authoritarian emphasis on national security. The answer, brewing long before September 11, was the threat of "international terror"—sometimes described as Islamic fundamentalism, sometimes as the drug cartels—but in any event suitably nebulous and scary to justify the resurrection of priorities not seen since the Cold War.

Let us review those Cold War priorities for those who didn't live through the era of the fifties and sixties, the era that shaped—indeed, finalized—the consciousness of the Bush family, Dick Cheney, Donald Rumsfeld, and many others fingering the military trigger today. The fundamental paradigm of the Cold War era was that an innocent democratic America was threatened by a shadowy communist conspiracy representing two billion people in countries with nuclear capabilities and an amoral disregard for human life. This fearful paradigm justified America's first permanent military establishment, alliances with despotic right-wing dictators around the world, and a domestic politics that smeared dissenters who were charged with being "soft on communism."

Those are exactly the dynamics in play again today. The difference is that, with the fall of the Soviet Union, the U.S. government and our multinational corporations are bidding for global preeminence. According to interviews with White House officials by Nicholas Lemann in the *New Yorker*, the new American strategy is to transcend traditional balance-of-power politics by an assertion of American military dominance, which incidentally would lay the foundation of empire. One example of this imperial thinking is the leaked Pentagon strategy paper of January 2002 which called for a new reliance on usable nuclear weapons targeted for possible use against China, Russia, and several other countries. The previous nuclear strategy of "mutual assured destruction" was dangerous enough, but this radical new U.S. doctrine—never publicly debated—introduces the ambition of nuclear dominance.

What can be done about this journey from Afghanistan to empire? For now, counting on an electoral alternative seems like wishful thinking. The Democratic Party, whatever doubts it may harbor, will remain devoted to the war on terrorism, including spending for a new generation of weapons and reinvigorated intelligence programs, as long as it is popular. The framework of the war on terrorism will be accepted as the litmus test of political legitimacy, and partisan differences will be limited to social security, unemployment benefits, Enron-inspired regulatory reform, and the like. Those differences are not unimportant, but the truth is that spending alone on the war on terrorism will cause permanent underfunding of important social programs for many years to come. For the Democrats to offer themselves as simply a liberal version of the war on terrorism will not address the root causes nor protect programs for which earlier generations of liberals, unionists, and Democrats have struggled.

The same bipartisan lockstep politics dominated the Cold War era of the fifties. Democrats stood for civil rights and progressive domestic issues, but blindly accepted the doctrine that "politics ends at the water's edge" until the anti–Vietnam War movement finally shattered the consensus. It will take the same popular discontent in the years ahead to shake the Democrats and challenge the framework of the war on terrorism. At first, that discontent will arise from a prophetic minority.

How to make it a mainstream issue? Conservative crusades have a way of backfiring when, unchecked by effective dissent, they go too far. McCarthyism began to unravel when the Wisconsin senator started searching for communists in the army. The Nixon administration, teethed on McCarthyism, repeated the same extremist folly with Watergate. Inevitably, the same fate awaits the unchecked war on terrorism. A combination of military quagmire abroad and neglect of priorities at home will sooner or later shape an opposition.

The U.S. military is involved in more multiplying fronts of the war on terrorism (the Middle East, Afghanistan, the southern Philippines, Colombia, Georgia, Indonesia, not to mention threats of future action against Iraq, Iran, and North Korea) than it can sustain without eventually causing domestic repercussions. These interventions are being carried out—thus far—with little or no congressional oversight or fiscal accountability. The Bush defense budget augmentation request of $50 billion—which itself is larger than the military budget of any other country—when combined with massive tax breaks for the wealthy will steadily erode funding for Social Security, health care, education, and the environment.

At the same time, a new human rights movement is sweeping the planet, with protests against corporate globalization and militarism. Before September 11, North American protests, especially those in Seattle in December

1999, were more forceful than any I can recall since the 1960s. While that American protest energy has been drained or divided since September 11, the battle continues to explode globally in places like Quebec City, Genoa, and Porto Allegre. Corporate globalization, led by the U.S. government, has spawned a new globalization of conscience. For a valid comparison of the historic impact, one would have to revisit the global confrontations of 1968 and, before the sixties, the period of the 1840s in Europe, when the world order was last threatened and rearranged by revolts from below.

The war on terrorism is simply incompatible with serious efforts to alleviate world poverty, just as it was impossible for President Lyndon Johnson to afford both "guns and butter" in the sixties. There are two billion people on the planet working for daily wages of less than two U.S. dollars. At ten hours a day in degrading workplace conditions, without health benefits, without union protections. A recent appeal by workers in Bangladesh, a Muslim country that supplies most of North America's apparel, pleaded for thirty-four cents in wages from every seventeen-dollar U.S. baseball cap, up from twenty-four cents. Global sweatshops are among the petri dishes in which anti-Western violence is grown.

The conservatives strain to deny any connection between world poverty and terrorism. That is what their bullying tirades against "blaming America first" are all about. They fear the blame. But they cannot deny that humiliation fostered by poverty and arrogance is a long fuse leading to the suicide bomber.

Take the story of Laura Blumenfeld as an example. A young reporter for the *Washington Post*, her father, a rabbi, was shot and wounded by a Palestinian militant in Jerusalem in 1986. The assailant simply wanted to kill a Jew, and Laura Blumenfeld's father was available. At first seeking revenge, Laura Blumenfeld concealed her identity and began a correspondence with the imprisoned Palestinian gunman, finally revealing herself and confronting him in a courtroom. She then came to know his family, ventured into a complicated reconciliation, and wrote a book on her experience. Reflecting on the Israeli-Palestinian conflict, she told the *New York Times* on April 6, 2002:

I think for them [the Palestinians], humiliation is sometimes more important than the actual offense. Humiliation drives revenge more than anything . . . They feel honor and pride are very important in their culture, and they feel utterly humiliated, whether it's by roadblocks or just by the sheer wealth and success of society that's set up right next to them . . . I found that feelings of humiliation and shame fuel revenge more than anything else.

Blumenfeld's thoughtful analysis distinguishes mere poverty from shame and degradation. Poverty is sometimes bearable if the poor feel respected or hopeful; for example, the Aristide government in Haiti has campaigned on a slogan of "poverty with dignity." But usually the policies that allow poverty to grow as if it were a natural condition of market economics are accompanied by a rationale that transfers blame from the rich and powerful to the poor and powerless. That shaming inherent in globalization is the triggering source of violence, as shown in numerous studies such as those of James Gilligan at Harvard. The syndrome we can call the *will to empire* (like Nietzsche's famous *will to power*) is wrapped into a need to shame others.

Instead of recognizing the reality of global interdependence, the will to empire seeks American independence by plunging other nations, cultures, and classes into dependence, which in turn triggers a spiral of resentment and resistance. Actually, the conservatives who condemn thinking about "root causes" as "blaming America" have a root cause in mind themselves— the belief that all terrorists and the cultures that spawn them are incorrigible enemies because they are "evil." American conservatives substitute theology for sociology, psychology, and history. Since the evil they seek to purge is defined as innate to human nature, and satanic, it arises from no causes that can be addressed politically or economically. The only option for Pentagon planners when confronted with evil is war, which is the secular equivalent of exorcism, or conversion to the American Way of Life.

That this is actually a logical crutch, a rhetorical device, is shown by the ease with which the stamp of evil is applied and removed. Mujahideen, including Osama bin Laden, were not "evil" when the U.S. government supplied them with weapons and funding in the 1980s, because then the Islamic fundamentalists were battling true "evil" in the form of the Soviet Union. But the label of evil has its uses. It serves to shut off rational debate, for example. It stimulates public fear. It justifies the killing of people whose annihilation might be problematic if they were classified as simply desperate. Fighting evil is good politics.

A domestic analogy might be useful in understanding how this process works. In 1988, George H. W. Bush was battling for the presidency against Michael Dukakis. Bush's media consultant then was Roger Ailes, now the top executive at Rupert Murdoch's Fox television news. The Bush campaign concocted the famous "Willie Horton" ads, depicting a shadowy and menacing black figure, and blamed Dukakis for being soft on crime. The attack, which manipulated fears of black violence, served the purpose of the Bush campaign. Taking advantage of the formula, the Republican conservatives ushered in a law-and-order politics that justified the drug wars, disproportionate sentences for powder versus crack cocaine, and the largest prison build-up per capita in the world. In the process, job training and numerous social programs were slashed, private investment was drawn toward speculative mergers instead of the inner cities, and the oppression of the underclass became so severe that fully one-third of all African-American males between the ages of eighteen and twenty-five were ensnared in the criminal justice system. As politics, the law-and-order campaign was successful, while the long-term consequences of worsening the racial divide in America were left for a future generation to sort out.

The current war on terrorism is the internationalization of the Willie Horton campaign. Instead of going along with the conservative agenda out of fear or expediency, it is time to outline an alternative.

The litmus test for political bravery at present is whether one questions the framework of the war on terrorism. Progressives might still disagree about whether a U.S. military response against Al Qaeda was justified, but all can agree that while seeking to demobilize Al Qaeda is one thing, using September 11 as a pretext for an open-ended war leading to a new empire is, to say the least, a policy worthy of debate. Even if one supports the right of U.S. self-defense against Al Qaeda, there should be broad consensus on the need for congressional hearings and oversight. Patriotism should not mean the restoration of the imperial presidency.

Were there flaws or biases in U.S. intelligence gathering that made September 11 more likely? Have the Taliban actually been defeated, or simply faded into the mainstream population? Are Afghan women better off under warlords? Will a global glut of heroin result from greater opium reduction "expected to enrich tribal leaders whose support is vital to the American-backed government"?[1] Is Texas-based Unocal's oil pipeline across Afghanistan now "feasible once again"?[2] Should Bush have appointed a former Unocal consultant the new U.S. ambassador to Afghanistan? The nearly one year of silence in Washington on these reasonable questions is a measure of the fear that has eroded the democratic process already.

Beyond Afghanistan, the political questions are whether this war should be conducted unilaterally by the executive branch, whether its budget should be unlimited, whether congressional oversight should be waived, and whether the battle should be conducted wherever undefined terrorists are alleged to be based, whatever their threat to the American people.

Is the Bush administration, intoxicated with gladiator fantasies, trying to build a new Roman Empire by neutralizing the checks and balances intended by having a vigorous legislative branch? (It should be remembered that the Russell Crowe character in *Gladiator* was committed to defending the Roman Senate and the Republic against the imperial designs of the emperor—this is one case where Washington should definitely mimic Hollywood.)

How to challenge this imperial framework cloaked, with apparent legitimacy, as the war on terror? My advice is: carefully, thoughtfully, but deliberately and for the long haul. For demonstrators interested in mass outreach in a time of manipulated patriotism, it may mean calling for a process of greater oversight, greater attention to priorities, and greater tolerance of dissent, instead of, for example, calls for military withdrawal from Afghanistan. For Democrats in the mainstream, it will mean provoking debate in the party over how to challenge the Bush framework, then nurturing and promoting a new generation of Democrats for peace.

In either scenario, here are some fruitful issues to raise that will resonate with a majority of voters. First, progressives and Democrats should take the position that those in power have failed over the years to make America safer from terrorist attack. There should be full public disclosure of what Condoleezza Rice has called the increased "chatter" of intelligence cables concerning a possible Al Qaeda attack before it happened. Questions should be asked. For example: why did the Federal Aviation Administration (FAA) make a finding that bin Laden was "a significant threat to civil aviation" in late July 2001, but do nothing about airline security regulations which were so lax that knives with four-inch blades could be carried on planes? These questions go to the heart of the bipartisan special-interest nature of the state that has strangled accountability and democracy for a very long time.

Public questioning is urgently needed about the unprecedented U.S. strategy of making nuclear warfare feasible in the future. This classified military strategy represents the return of Dr. Strangelove to the Pentagon, and is certain to make Americans less safe from an uncontrolled nuclear arms race.

Another key question that needs to be addressed concerns budget priorities. In concrete, easy-to-understand terms, the costs of the war on terrorism need to be conveyed to a public now shielded from the facts. For the Bush administration and the military-industrial complex, the moment has come for a massive increase in Pentagon spending. Nongovernmental organizations and Democrats must make clear to the public that the daily spending on terrorism means less funding for everything from family farms to inner-city schools.

Next, progressives and Democrats should question whether the massive intelligence failure surrounding September 11 really justifies returning to the Cold War policies of hiring as operatives or allies the same unsavory elements that brought us the Bay of Pigs and the Central American "dirty wars" of the 1970s and 1980s.

The war on terrorism should not become pretext for undermining the Freedom of Information Act and preventing disclosure of presidential files from the first Bush era. Bush's solicitor general is arguing in court that government has a right to misinform and disinform the American people.

Nor should the war be a further excuse to advance the agenda of the oil industry, whether drilling in Alaska, protecting Occidental pipelines in Columbia, enmeshing ourselves with the Saudi royal family, or launching joint ventures for Unocal on the old Silk Road through southern Asia.

Before any further subsidies are granted to the Bush-Cheney friends in the oil industry, the government should take the lead in charting a transition to energy conservation and renewable resources. A modest fuel-efficiency increase of 2.7 miles per gallon would eliminate the need for any Persian Gulf oil. In the Middle East, the U.S. should promote a settlement that results in a viable Palestinian state, the end of Israeli occupation, and a military guarantee of secure Israeli borders. Instead, the war on terrorism is being used as the new rationale for the use of U.S. weapons in assisting an Israeli occupation.

Finally, the "new world order" should be based on living wages, not starvation sweatshops, and the United States should lead the G-7 powers to meet the aspirations of the United Nations to double foreign aid by 2015. So-called "free trade" and "fast track" agreements now blatantly being justified by the war on terrorism will reinforce divisions between the rich minority and the poor majority. Demanding peace is not enough. What is at stake is a conflict in the American soul between empire and democracy that will shadow our lifetimes.

NOTES

1. Tim Golden, "A Nation Challenged: Drug Trafficking," *New York Times*, April 1, 2002.
2. Ibid.

56

Billy Graham's Legacy: A Crusade in Iraq?

I was solicited by Professor Michael Long of Elizabethtown College to write this essay for a book he was editing. The essay was rejected by the publisher, Westminster John Knox Press, on the grounds that it did not "fit easily with the other chapters in the book." Expressing embarrassment, Long said the publishers "got burned by a group of conservatives" over an earlier book, "and now they're running around with their tails between their legs." The incident reflects a larger failure of the mainstream media to report critically on the role of Christian fundamentalists in promoting the war in Iraq.

◆　　◆　　◆

I WAS VERY YOUNG INDEED, just out of high school, and I was searching, for ideals to live by, for love, and some sort of transcendence. There was a young woman from my hometown, bright, funny, cute, and resistant to my awkward adolescent advances. Like me, she was different, a bit strange, in our very conformist suburb, and I didn't quite understand why. But it made us soul mates. So in our freshman year, when she called asking me to come visit her at Wheaton, the college she was attending, I was primed. But there was a condition, she emphasized. I had to attend a Billy Graham campus crusade with her.

I wanted to see her, not the preacher. But I was an aspiring young journalist and thought there might be a story. Soon I found myself at Wheaton College, the very bastion of conservative Christianity, and I quickly discovered why the feelings between us were so complicated. Simply put, she couldn't make out like the other girls I knew, because that was giving into temptation, to satanic impulses, which is why she chose to begin the sixties at Wheaton and not, say, in Ann Arbor.

I was reared in the Catholic parish of Father Charles Coughlin, the famed "radio priest" of the thirties who turned anti-Semite and was silenced politically in the forties. His thundering sermons instilled a blind fear of sin during my childhood, but I eventually gave in to adolescent desires and lived in the shadow of sin, reading deeply such works as Joyce's *Portrait of the Artist as a Young Man.* Nor could I bring myself to believe that my non-Catholic friends would be consigned to hell.

I was prepared for the Billy Graham experience, you could say.

When the time came, I was sitting close beside my friend in a vast complex with thousands of other young people. I don't remember the words he spoke that day, but I do remember an internal pressure building toward the moment known as the call to Christ. Would she rise from her seat, arms outstretched, leaving me behind? Would I have to accompany her? If I held back, would she or I be ostracized? And what if it all was true, that Jesus Christ was calling?

I stayed in my seat, uncomfortably, watching in amazement as hundreds of young people surged forward. She stayed with me. Afterwards, somehow, I did get my backstage interview with Graham. Again, I remember none of his words, but his eyes were unforgettable, blue and eternal.

OUT OF TOUCH

The needs of the sixties generation simply couldn't be met by the calls of Graham or Coughlin. We of the civil rights, student, and peace movements were motivated spiritually, but it was a spirituality with no name. It came from dissatisfaction with religions that stressed the eternal more than the immediate, that stressed the drama of the individual encounter with God more than the individual encounter with a suffering humanity and earth. A surprising number of those who wrote the *Port Huron Statement of Students for a Democratic Society* (SDS) in 1962 were spiritual refugees from institutional religion.

From the beginning, we thought Billy Graham was out of touch. Worse, as the years passed, he seemed less transcendent than self-interested in the power of Caesar, more comfortable with golf clubs than carrying the crucifix. When many clergy were protesting the crucifixion of Vietnam, he was providing spiritual succor to presidents, promoting the defeat of godless communism, and lamenting the degeneration of hippies and draft resisters.

"I have been extremely careful not to be drawn into either the moral implications or the tactical military problems of the Vietnam war," he often said.[1] It was as if taking a stand would be breaching the line between church and state, when all it would really mean was fewer invitations to the White House. "What can people expect me to do? March in protest? Carry a sign? If I do that, then all the doors at the White House and all the avenues to people in high office in this administration are closed to me."[2]

My high-school girlfriend dropped away from such religion, married and divorced, became an established poet, and now lives in New York City. Hers was a typical sixties journey, finding her soul on her own.

A LONG-DISTANCE WARRIOR

When I next met Graham, it was the eighties and I was a member of the California legislature and married to Jane Fonda. Some of my colleagues were of the evangelical stripe and would occasionally seek me out, as I had become demonized into a somewhat satanic figure for Republican campaign purposes. One of these colleagues, for example, approached me on the Senate floor to have lunch. "I was asking myself this morning," he said, "What would Jesus do? And I realized Jesus would want me to take Tom to lunch." It was a kindly evangelizing, and who knew, perhaps it would lead to a bipartisan vote down the road.

In the same spirit one day, another of my Christian colleagues asked if Jane and I would join his family at a small lunch with Billy Graham. We met in his room at a motel in Sacramento, where Graham was crusading. The room-service meal was hamburgers, and once again, I remember little of the conversation except for its main point. It was a gesture of reconciliation and dialogue, I felt, signifying that the wars of the sixties were over. For me, politically, the lunch meant legitimacy of a kind against the raging right-wingers who still sought my expulsion from the legislature. He offered no apologies for Nixon and Vietnam, and none were asked.

For his gesture, I was appreciative. I joked about how he had tried and failed to convert me twenty-five years before at Wheaton College. In the back of my mind, I couldn't help but wonder if he was offering redemption, especially to Jane, who at the time was still the focus of venomous right-wing hatreds. (Later it turned out that there was a whole network of powerful Christian conservatives praying and working for her conversion, and that they nearly succeeded. It was during the trauma of her later divorce from Ted Turner, when, on her knees, she almost accepted Jesus Christ as her lord and savior. The conservatives were giddy at the prospect of converting this powerful symbol of sin, communism, and excess. But feminism apparently saved her.)

What I realized that day in Sacramento was that Graham was a long-distance warrior for Christ, for whom ups and downs, trials and tribulations, were in the nature of the battle. Far more than the progressive Christians to his left, Graham was fostering a culture and institutions that would deeply impact American society long after he was gone. He was the reassuring, seemingly otherworldly, father of the Christian Right that became empowered in the 1990s, deeply intertwined with the Republican Party, corporate America, and perhaps most importantly and quietly, the Pentagon and military culture. Indeed, as the Christian conservative moment begins to founder politically, in part due to scandals of hypocrisy and fundraising, and partly due to positions many voters consider too extreme, the unexplored legacy of Graham's long tenure seems to be the steady integration of Christianity and the military.

FUSING WAR AND CHRISTIANITY

Relations between the Pentagon and Christianity were not always comfortable. Protestant military chaplains were 40 percent Episcopalian and drawn from other liberal denominations during the 1940s, for example.[3] But during the storm-tossed sixties, when conservatives and the military were threatened by a pervasive antiwar counterculture, the evangelicals found a receptive host culture in militarism. According to historian Anne Loveland, "their participation in the debate over the [Vietnam] war provided them an entrée into national politics."[4]

Starting in the late 1960s, evangelicals became rooted in the military academies, including a born-again football team. By the seventies, prayer breakfasts and Bible studies were routine throughout the Pentagon, and a group called Christian Men of the Pentagon was busy evangelizing young officers.[5] Christian book-racks in the Pentagon and worldwide Christian broadcasts to the armed forces also became institutionalized.[6]

Graham was thoroughly part of this Christian militarism. When receiving a prestigious West Point award as a symbol of "duty, honor and country" in 1972, he delivered an acceptance speech condemning antiwar protests as undermining the "delicate balance between freedom and order."[7] As late as 1972, he was defending a "holy war against the Vietcong" at Expo '72, an evangelical event that Graham chaired, highlighting support for the armed forces.[8]

Perhaps the primary symbol of the fusion of war and Christianity was Ronald Reagan's 1983 speech attacking the Soviet Union as an "evil empire," delivered not from the Oval Office but at the conference of the National Association of Evangelicals.[9] Graham, the informal leader of the evangelicals, had introduced the term "crusades" to define his ministry; now the war against evil and the Cold War against the Soviet Union were becoming one, with ominous implications for wars around the corner.

THE CHRISTIAN CRUSADE IN IRAQ

The alliance of the evangelicals and the Pentagon has only grown during the wars against Iraq, starting in the 1990s, and its background theme has been "the clash of civilizations," a term introduced by Harvard professor Samuel P. Huntington.[10] It is not entirely clear that President Bush meant to use the term "crusade" in describing the Iraq war—he denies it—but it is a fitting term for the goals of the evangelicals and their military allies in the Middle East today, now linked theologically and politically with Jewish and Israeli neoconservatives in a struggle over the biblical lands between the Tigris and Euphrates, the location of Eden.

Graham's legacy today lives on through his son, Franklin Graham, who blessed the war to come at Bush's inauguration in 2001, condemning Islam as a "very evil and wicked religion."[11] Such words, when coupled with U.S. military action in the Middle East, led to the appearance of a crusade by force. In many Muslim countries, according to one analyst, "the American military and its dominant religion appear inseparable . . . you have the image of a deeply religious president essentially giving Christians a green light to come into Iraq."[12]

Come they did. In the first year of war, at least nine evangelical churches opened in Baghdad.[13] Nearly one million bibles were dispatched in Arabic in that same year. One hundred fifty evangelical missionaries came to visit. "God and the president have given us the opportunity to bring Jesus Christ to the Middle East," one said. It was, for many, the end time. "Iraq fits like hand in glove," said the editor of *Endtime* magazine in an article headlined "End-Time Believers See Prophecies Fulfilled in Iraq."[14]

Bush periodically demurred from the biblical implications; after all, such rhetoric would inflame the Muslim world. But official support for this new crusade came directly from the top of the Pentagon, from the point person for intelligence and once head of special operations, under-secretary and lieutenant general William "Jerry" Boykin. His intelligence capability was revealed in presentations where he depicted dark smudges in aerial photos of Mogadishu as evidence of "a demonic presence . . . that God revealed to me as the enemy." A steady speaker at prayer breakfasts and meetings of the Christian Right, Boykin made statements that were embarrassing to the administration, particularly his revelation that Bush was "appointed by God." The Christian God is a "real god," Boykin announced, whereas Allah is an idol. "Satan wants to destroy us," he frequently declared, because "we are a Christian army [fighting for] a nation of believers."[15]

In his Pentagon role, Boykin has exonerated elite special-operations forces accused of beating Iraqi prisoners at a top-secret "black room" detention facility in 2004. Boykin was asked by the White House to investigate published charges that the secret Task Force 6-26 was abusing insurgent prisoners before sending them to Abu Ghraib. Slogans posted at the secret facility including placards proclaiming "No Blood, No Foul," which meant "if you don't make them bleed, they can't prosecute for it." Despite a lengthy account in the March 19, 2006 edition of the *New York Times*, Boykin found no pattern of misconduct at the facility. Apparently, his was not a merciful God.

Despite these openly provocative declarations, Boykin has never been disciplined much less removed from his powerful Pentagon office, revealing the power of evangelical presence in both White House and the military. One other Pentagon crusader who, unlike Boykin, ran headlong into scandal, is the Pentagon inspector-general, Joseph E. Schmitz. Before being snared in a contractor scandal, Schmitz was a hardcore Christian proselytizer whose Web site identified him with the Sovereign Military Order of Malta, an eleventh-century Crusader group whose mission was to "defend territories that the Crusaders had conquered from the Moslems."[16] The Order of Malta membership is shared by several executives of the military contractor Blackwater, all of whom share, fund and promote the Christian agenda.[17] That Christian presence became deeply institutionalized and intertwined with militarism during the past few decades. Despite being pledged to minister to everyone, for example, the military chaplain corps is filling with evangelicals, their numbers appearing to double between 1994 and 2005, while chaplains from more mainline religions have declined, according to a 2005 *New York Times* survey.[18] "We reserve the right to evangelize the unchurched," said the deputy chief of chaplains for the Air Force. When Capt. MeLinda Morton, a chaplain at the Air Force Academy, reported "systemic and pervasive proselytizing" based on a careful study, she was forced to resign.[19] An evangelical quoted in her report told cadets that they would burn in the fires of hell if they were not born again.

In a related controversy, James Yee, the Muslim U.S. chaplain at Guantánamo, was pilloried for his apparent understanding of the religious sentiments of the inmates. He was charged falsely for taking classified documents, detained in isolation for seventy-six days before the charges were dropped. Next, he was accused of an extramarital affair, which he acknowledged, and was discharged from the military. Yee claimed in speeches and writings that Muslims were subject to extreme hostility based on their religion.[20]

In summary, it is impossible to deny a *concealed crusader dimension* to the American occupation of Iraq. One particular instance is most illustrative. At the sentencing phase in the court-martial of Charles A. Graner, Jr., convicted of torturing inmates at Abu Ghraib, his key character witness argued for leniency because the defendant spent time off-duty handing out Bibles to Iraqis.[21] This example demonstrated how Christian love could excuse the worst forms of torture. Graham himself had made the point decades earlier when he expressed sympathy for Lt. William Calley, convicted of the killing of Vietnamese women and children at My Lai, South Vietnam, on the grounds that we all have "a little Calley" in our souls.[22]

If there is good news in all this, it is that the government, the military, and the media have largely avoided public mention, much less scrutiny, of this crusader mentality for fear of global public opinion, including American opinion. Even as it fights a war tinged with religious implications, both Christian and Zionist, the U.S. government strives for a nonsectarian face. How could the United States deplore sectarian killings between Sunnis and Shi'a while its armed forces are a vehicle for the end-time schemes of neo-crusader militias? How would the war be packaged and sold to the American people, including tens of millions of Christians? One can be thankful for a public opinion so tolerant that the neo-crusaders are made to work in the shadows.

Where are the Christian faithful today in the battle against those hijacking their religion in the name of a *fanatical premillenial dispensationalism*? Institutional religion has been relatively quiet. There are encouraging signs of a backlash among some evangelicals against the aggressive right-wing crusader profile of their majority sistren and brethren. It is possible the evangelical-military complex has gone too far, finally producing a backlash.

What would Billy Graham counsel today? I think he might have questions, as he did about nuclear war when his friend Ronald Reagan contemplated the end of nuclear weapons in the 1980s. But if history and the path of his successor son is any guide, his doubts would be too little and too late to rein in the extremists that emerged from the cradle of this crusade. He would express regret over Abu Ghraib, regret over the demonizing of Muslims, but certainly he would bless the Iraq enterprise as a whole.

Those who believe that the Iraq war means that God's judgment is imminent, that the Great Tribulation is at hand, are only taking Graham's crusades to their apocalyptic fulfillment. According to prophecy, the kings will move their armies from the Euphrates Valley to Megiddo in northern Israel by the present cease-fire line with Hezbollah. They will battle Abaddon, the releaser of locusts, whose name the end-timers associate with Saddam. Four angels of the Euphrates then will unleash agents of death to kill one-third of mankind. This is the heart of the evangelical "Left Behind" novels of Tim LaHaye and Jerry Jenkins, published just as the new crusade against Iraq was building momentum, and read so far by forty million American Christians.

If other Christians lack faith and will, it will remain the responsibility of the rest of the world to assure that, after 500 years, the crusades are over in any form, and a new spirit is safely born. It is perhaps too late to hope that the Nazarene is remembered as a foe of empire, not its official agent, but it is not too late to avert an apocalypse in his name.

NOTES

1. Billy Graham to editor, *Christian Century*, May 17, 1967.
2. Cited in Paul Boyer, "Praise the Lord and Pass the Ammunition," *Reviews in American History* 25, no. 4 (Dec. 1997), p. 689.
3. Ibid., p. 687.
4. Anne C. Loveland, *American Evangelicals and the US Military, 1942-1993*, Louisiana State University Press, 1997, p. 164.
5. Ibid., p. 166.
6. Ibid., p. 171.
7. Ibid., p. 166.
8. Ibid., p. 177.
9. Boyer, "Praise the Lord," p. 686.
10. See Samuel P. Huntington, *The Clash of Civilizations and the Remaking of the World Order*, Simon & Schuster, 1998.
11. Quoted in "Should Christian Missionaries Heed the Call in Iraq," *New York Times*, April 6, 2003, p. A14.

12. See comments of John C. Green, University of Akron, in ibid.
13. *Los Angeles Times,* March 18, 2004.
14. "Direst of Predictions for War in Iraq: End-Time Believers See Prophecies Fulfilled in Iraq," *Washington Post,* March 8, 2003, p. B9.
15. *Los Angeles Times,* October 16, 2003.
16. Jeremy Scahill, *Blackwater,* Nation Books, 2007, p. 299.
17. Ibid.
18. "Evangelicals Are Growing Force in the Military Chaplain Corps," *New York Times,* July 13, 2005, p. A1.
19. "Air Force Chaplain Submits Resignation," *New York Times,* June 22, 2005, p. A12.
20. "As Chaplain's Spy Case Nears, Some Ask Why It Went So Far," *New York Times,* January 4, 2004, p. A1; *Los Angeles Times,* March 23, 2004.
21. "U.S. Soldier Found Guilty in Iraq Prison Abuse Scandal," *New York Times,* January 15, 2005, p. A1.
22. "Billy Graham: On Calley," *New York Times,* April 9, 1971, p. A31.

57.

Antiwar Movement Deserves Some Credit

San Francisco Chronicle, *November 26, 2006*

These thoughts were expanded in my book Ending the War in Iraq *(Akashic, 2007)*

◆　◆　◆

ALTHOUGH RARELY CREDITED, the antiwar movement has been a major factor in mobilizing a majority of the American public to oppose the occupation and killing in Iraq.

To many observers, the movement seems feckless and marginal, its rallies an incoherent bazaar of radical sloganeering. Yet according to Gallup surveys, a majority of Americans came to view Iraq as a mistake more rapidly than they came to oppose the Vietnam War more than three decades ago. So how could there be a peace majority without a peace movement?

Foreign Affairs, the journal of the foreign policy establishment, wondered about this riddle in a 2005 essay by John Mueller reporting a precipitous decline in public support for the war even though "there has not been much" of a peace movement.

In January, when congressional opinion was shifting against the war, a *Washington Post* analysis made eight references to "public opinion," as if it were a magical floating balloon, without any mention of organized lobbying, petitioning, protests or marches. That was consistent with a pattern beginning before the invasion, when both the *New York Times* and National Public Radio reported that few people attended an October 2002 rally in Washington, only to admit a week later that 100,000 had been in the streets.

It is not in the nature of elites to acknowledge people in the streets. Foreign policy is seen as the reserve of the privileged and sophisticated, protected from populist influence. But if antiwar sentiment is truly unimportant, why has there been so much government secrecy and domestic spying?

Two years ago, San Francisco voters supported withdrawal from Iraq by a large margin. Last year many activists sought an antiwar candidate to run against Representative Nancy Pelosi. Shortly afterward, she shifted from a vague centrism to support for Representative John Murtha's call for withdrawal.

When Senator Hillary Clinton was booed at a liberal preelection rally recently, it wasn't accidental that she chose to begin supporting Senator Carl Levin's proposal to start a phased withdrawal by year's end. Understandably, she didn't want booing throughout her presidential campaign.

Little reported in this month's electoral upheaval were the referendums demanding immediate withdrawal that passed in Chicago and several Illinois suburbs. One year ago, antiwar resolutions passed in forty-nine of fifty-seven cities in Vermont.

Perhaps these events go largely unnoticed because of a false paradigm that antiwar protesters must be isolated, howling, fringe figures. That doesn't fit Cindy Sheehan or the military families who have turned against the war.

Even defined as a street phenomenon, the antiwar movement has commanded significant numbers. The global movement surely succeeded in pressuring foreign governments against supporting the U.S. invasion in 2003. The February 2003 protests were the largest turnouts in history before a war began. The August 2004 demonstrations at the Republican convention in New York were unprecedented in convention history, including the 1,800 arrests (approximately three times the number arrested in Chicago in 1968.)

It is true there have been periodic lapses in street protests since 2003, but these can be explained by the surge of activists into antiwar presidential campaigns like that of Howard Dean. Not only were thousands involved, but MoveOn's voter fund raised $17 million in 2004, most of it from 160,000 contributors averaging $69 donations.

In this year's election, MoveOn activists made one million calls to their elected officials, and poured thousands of dollars and volunteers into campaigns. New Hampshire elected to Congress Carol Shea-Porter, a woman previously known for pulling up her outer garment to display an antiwar slogan.

To disregard forces such as these in the definition of the antiwar movement is a sleight-of-hand, something like eliminating Eugene McCarthy's New Hampshire campaign in March 1968 from the history of the anti-Vietnam movement.

The phenomena of the Netroots and Indymedia, new since 1999, have opened up vistas of dialogue, resistance and confrontation far beyond the streets and teach-ins of college towns.

This resistance is more remarkable when one considers the establishment's post-Vietnam strategies to terminate the spread of the Vietnam Syndrome, which supposedly had weakened the nation's resolve for war.

The 18-year-old vote was delivered along with the end of the military draft by a White House bent on domestic pacification. But now, as *Foreign Affairs* warns, the inoculation has failed and an Iraq Syndrome is replacing the Vietnam Syndrome.

Based on a disease-control model, this Iraq Syndrome will cause Americans to question the supposed benefits of having the largest military budget in the world, an imperial presidency or policies of policing the world, according to *Foreign Affairs*. But it seems healthy, not a sign of sickness, for the citizens of a democratic state to question government secrecy or the use of their taxes for torture.

An irreverence toward power, too, is a healthy sign, in a country showered with fear-inducing propaganda, where not a single mainstream media organ has called for bringing our troops home either now or within a year.

If history is any guide, the recommendations of the elite Iraq Study Group may well be designed to placate, or divide, the antiwar sentiment that was a driving force in the November 7 election.

Alongside a military crackdown in Baghdad and possibly a strongman government, there will be talk of beginning a "partial withdrawal" in several months, depending of course on "conditions on the ground." There may be an attempt to carve up Iraq (politely known as "partition"), but none of these plans is likely to stop the insurgency.

If ever consulted, antiwar voices might propose the following:

First, seek a dialogue with anti-occupation forces in Iraq, from politicians to insurgents, to work toward a cease-fire and a longer-term conflict resolution process.

Second, announce the withdrawal timetable that about 80 percent of Iraqi people and 60 percent of the American people want.

Third, initiate a diplomatic offensive, beginning with Iran, to seek regional global assistance in dealing with security, reconciliation and reconstruction issues.

Because the antiwar movement remains voiceless in the debates, the only recourse is to prepare widespread demonstrations and ground organizing in the key presidential primary states, to make it impossible for any candidate to become president in 2008 without pledging to end the war and occupation. If there is no peace movement, there will be no peace.

58.

Iraq is Dying

The Nation *Web site, August 9, 2006*

The Biddle Plan described below was being implemented by Gen. David Petraeus in the so-called surge of 2007. I firmly believe the U.S. strategic goal is to dissolve Iraq as a strong Arab nationalist state, thus creating easier post-war access to Iraqi oil and fortifying Israel's military position in the region. The most feasible way to destroy the Iraqi state is by forced partition, as advocated by many liberal politicians like Joseph Biden and Barbara Boxer. Whether or not their plan succeeds, the outcome will favor Iran in the short term, which may then become the next battlefield.

◆　　◆　　◆

THE POSSIBILITY OF SAVING IRAQ as a viable Arab nation is in question, even if American public opinion forces the withdrawal of U.S. troops. For some American hawks, a dismembered Iraq may not be ideal but would no longer be a strategic threat.

Those were the morbid impressions I formed after two days of discussions with Iraqis gathered in Amman, Jordan, at an unprecedented meeting initiated by Code Pink and attended by Cindy Sheehan and a smattering of peace activists that included Iraq Veterans Against the War and United for Peace and Justice.

That so many Iraqi representatives wanted to meet with antiwar Americans was a hopeful sign. Attending were official representatives of the Shiite coalition now holding power, the minority Sunni bloc, the anti-occupation Muslim Scholars Association, parliamentarians, and torture victims from Abu Ghraib. Their broad consensus favored a specific timetable for American withdrawal combined with efforts to "fix the problems" of the occupation as the withdrawal proceeds. Recent surveys show that 87 percent of Iraqis hold the same views.

Dr. Habib Jabar, carefully balancing the divisions within his majority

Shiite parliamentary bloc, stated, "We don't need American forces to protect us from each other. We have been here 1,000 years. My wife is a Sunni. I don't need the Americans to protect her from me." He is seeking a Shiite consensus to demand that the United Nations Security Council formally end its authorization of the U.S. occupation when it meets this December. At the same time, the U.S.-backed Shiite representative was diplomatically noncommittal on dissolving death squads or the Badr Corps now operating with little or no restraint by the Interior Ministry. Nor did he acknowledge the plans of dominant Shiite leaders like Abdul Aziz al-Hakim for an autonomous Shiite region running from Baghdad south to Basra, which would require mass removals of the Sunni population.

Even Sunni political representatives, while demanding a timetable for withdrawal, increasingly worry that they will be more exposed to vengeful Shiite and Kurdish militias when the Americans leave. The Sunni bloc representative, Salman al-Jumaili, said with frustration, "We want the Americans out tomorrow. But we want negotiated timetables to fill security gaps and prevent a power grab." He indicated that the nationalist insurgency "is looking for recognition . . . and a road map to ending the occupation through negotiations."

These are more nuanced positions than the demands for immediate withdrawal that Code Pink's Medea Benjamin recalls hearing in Baghdad street interviews three years ago. The qualified Iraqi demands for withdrawal reflect the virtual civil war that has arisen in the wake of the U.S. occupation. Like victims of repeated battery, many Sunnis fear escalating attacks on their civilian population if the streets are dominated by the Badr militia after the Americans leave. They feel pressured by the Americans to abandon their aspirations for a unified Iraqi state, accept minority status in a partitioned country, or join as partners with their American occupiers to fight against pro-Iranian or Al Qaeda forces in Iraq.

The raging war in Lebanon has reinforced Iraqi paranoia that the United States, Britain and Israel intend to divide the Middle East into quarreling sects. Dr. Saleh al-Mutlaq of the Sunni-based Iraqi National Dialogue Front, which lost 100 campaign workers in killings during last year's election, said, "Lebanon could be even easier to send into civil war than Iraq." On the other hand, the U.S.-backed Shiite coalition in Baghdad is loudly supporting its Shiite brethren in Lebanon's Hezbollah.

Not only are the complexities mind-boggling, but the pressures on the insurgents and Sunni organizations are beyond anything described in the mainstream American media. For example, on the flight home I met an American contractor with thirty years of security experience, who is a counselor to the top Sunni official in the new Iraqi government. "There are 10,000 or 12,000 Sunnis, mainly teachers, lawyers and professionals, being held without charges in Iraqi prisons, and the [Iraqi] guards are drilling holes in them," he said bitterly. Of course, there are Sunni or foreign militias attacking the Shiite population as well, but the Sunni minority neighborhoods bear the brunt of attack. One member of Parliament, a Sunni, told us that "half of my friends have been kidnapped." She lives most of the year in Jordan, returning only for parliamentary sessions.

At least four million Iraqis like this parliamentarian have become refugees since 2003, with three million sheltered in Syria, one million in Jordan and many thousands more living in various places from the United Arab Emirates to Europe.

It is difficult to estimate to what extent all this carnage is intentional, a cycle of revenge, blowback from the U.S. occupation—or all three. Iraqis at the meeting complained of their country becoming a battleground in America's war against Syria, Iran and jihadists in general. The U.S. case for a divide-and-conquer strategy has been supplied by Stephen Biddle who advocates using military threats to maintain leverage with both the Shiite majority and the Sunni minority.[1] He writes that the United States could remove the current constraints on Iraqi security forces and provide them with tanks, armored personal carriers, artillery, armed helicopters, and fixed-wing ground-attack aircraft, enlarging the capacity of the Kurds and Shiites to "commit mass violence against the Sunnis . . . dramatically . . . threatening such a change could provide an important incentive for the Sunnis to compromise [their withdrawal demand]."

At the same time, Biddle believes that "a U.S. threat to cease backing the Shiites, coupled with a program to arm the Sunnis overtly or in a semi-clandestine way, would substantially reduce the Shiites' military prospects."

Biddle's goal would be to "keep U.S. troops in Iraq as long as would be necessary to protect the parties who cooperate." A perfect equilibrium for the occupiers, in other words. But for Biddle, there is one bothersome factor: "recent polls of U.S. public opinion are not encouraging." That could be a problem, Biddle believes, if voters can be convinced of the importance of keeping U.S. troops in place. "Sacrificing U.S. lives now could save many more later, and staying is an imperative."

Biddle's worries about public opinion are justified. Few Americans share his enthusiasm for sending troops into the midst of an Iraqi civil war. The very phrase "civil war," delicately hinted by U.S. generals in recent Congressional testimony, is code for the tipping point in Iraq. Even Thomas Friedman called for a "Plan B," meaning a withdrawal strategy, in the *New York Times* this week.

Despite all its complexity, the Iraq debate now heating up in American politics should favor opponents of the war. The White House's insistence on "staying the course" sounds bankrupt given the daily news from Iraq. Antiwar candidates, alongside the peace movement, can offer a defensible alternative, as the interviews in Amman show, including:

1. A declaration by the United States of its intention to withdraw troops within a fixed timetable, including no permanent bases.

2. A parallel commitment to fix as many mistakes as possible in the same timetable.

3. An amnesty for Iraqi nationals who have fought against the occupation. If a U.S. withdrawal timetable is agreed upon, the foreign jihadists will lose the margin of support they currently have.

4. An end to Paul Bremer's de-Baathification policy and restoring former military and other professionals to security and civic roles.

5. Termination of U.S. support, training, financing or advising of sectarian militias.

6. A paradigm shift away from neoconservative extremism toward diplomatic and political solutions to the region's problems.

7. International efforts to rebuild Iraq after fifteen years of sanctions, bombardment, invasion, war and civil war.

The most contentious of these points concerns amnesty for Iraqis who have fought the occupation. But it should be remembered that the American Civil War ended with an amnesty for Jefferson Davis. Amnesties always are included in negotiated settlements, and this endgame looks to be no different. If we don't achieve this, we will face a future of faith-based militarism until, as they say, the end of days.

NOTE

1. Stephen Biddle, "Seeing Baghdad, Thinking Saigon," *Foreign Affairs*, March/April 2006, and "What to Do in Iraq: A Roundtable," *Foreign Affairs*, July/August 2006.

59

The New Counterinsurgency

The Nation, *September 24, 2007*

If we are to become a critical force against U.S. doctrines of global aggression and dominance, I believe that we in the peace movement need to study not simply ethics, theory, and political economy, but the classics of war and counterinsurgency. The Pentagon anticipates a "long war" against Islamic radicalism, in the shadows of obscure battlefronts, far from the cameras, using counterinsurgency techniques borrowed from the British, the French, and the experience of Vietnam and Central America. It may become more difficult to inform and arouse American opinion against these secretive wars, but the experience of the peace and solidarity movements during the Central American wars makes me believe it is possible. This article was written to warn of a coming transition from conventional war in Iraq to a battle that resembles Afghanistan and Central America.

◆　　◆　　◆

AMERICAN OFFICERS CALL THEM the Kit Carson Scouts: Sunni military units prowling the desert to hunt down Al Qaeda in Mesopotamia and other extremist jihadi groups. The original Kit Carson fought ruthlessly to repress the Navajo on their reservations by employing rival tribes like the Ute in one of the American military's first counterinsurgency campaigns. Even today, America's favorite weapons—the Apaches, Comanches, Kiowas, Black Hawks and Tomahawks—testify to the military's most formative memories.

Now counterinsurgency is back in favor, the cure for Iraq as implemented by General David Petraeus and an assortment of Ivy League advisers. By enlisting Sunni Iraqi insurgents to turn their guns against jihadis, Petraeus is claiming tactical progress in the "surge." The Bush administration is using that claim in its campaign to continue the surge for another six months, and the war itself for a few years longer. There may also be a high-stakes internal coup against Prime Minister Nuri Kamal al-Maliki, which could be coupled with U.S. appeals to allow more time for political progress. August was spent on feverish promotion of the Petraeus plan, when several dozen members of Congress were wined, dined and personally briefed in Baghdad's Green Zone. Pundits Michael O'Hanlon and Kenneth Pollack, who promoted the 2003 invasion, wrote a widely circulated *New York Times* op-ed piece titled "A War We Just Might Win" after a recent trip to Baghdad. FOX News then featured O'Hanlon in an upbeat hour-long special about Petraeus and counterinsurgency. Secretary of State Condoleezza Rice gave O'Hanlon an appreciative audience as well. (The PR campaign is having some effect: in late August 2007, 29 percent of Americans believed the surge was "making the situation better in Iraq," up ten points from July. And $15 million is now being spent on Republican television spots to shore up support for the war.)

While FOX is doing the flacking, the Petraeus plan draws intellectual legitimacy from Harvard's Carr Center for Human Rights Policy, whose director, Sarah Sewall, proudly embraces an "unprecedented collaboration [as] a human rights center partnered with the armed forces." Sewall, a former Pentagon official, cosponsored a "doctrine revision workshop" at Fort Leavenworth that prepared the army and marines' new counterinsurgency-war-fighting field manual. The manual is the most widely read of several new and reissued works on counterinsurgency, or COIN, with two million downloads in its first two months on the Internet. The other influential works are John Nagl's *Counterinsurgency Lessons From Malaya and Vietnam: Learning to Eat Soup With a Knife* (2002) and David Galula's book on Algeria, *Counterinsurgency Warfare: Theory and Practice* (1964). Not only are both books endorsed by Sewall in her introduction to the field manual but the field manual and the 2006 reprinting of Galula's book both contain introductions by Nagl, a Rhodes scholar from West Point and a former commander in Iraq who predicts counterinsurgency warfare for the next fifty years in an "arc of instability" in the Middle East, Africa, and Central and South Asia.

The attraction of intellectuals to counterinsurgency certainly isn't new. The maxim about eating soup with a knife, a reference to the messiness and difficulty of counterinsurgency campaigns, was coined almost a century ago by Lawrence of Arabia, who encouraged Arab nationalism against the Ottoman Empire (on behalf of the British, who after the Ottoman defeat refused the Arabs the independence they'd been promised). President John F. Kennedy promoted the Green Berets with the "best and the brightest" in 1961 in response to the Cuban Revolution. A Special Forces expert in Iraq is quoted by Nagl as saying that "counterinsurgency is not just thinking man's warfare—it is the graduate level of warfare." Nearly half the field manual reads more like Max Weber than Carl von Clausewitz.

Much of the difficulty with counterinsurgency derives from its ends. Usually it seeks to coerce populations into accepting a repressive regime or foreign occupation—and sometimes both. Translated to modern Iraq, eating soup with a knife means persuading a majority of nationalist and Islamist Iraqis to accept the U.S. occupation or, in Nagl's words, "winning the Iraqi people's willingness to turn in their terrorist neighbors." The goal of COIN is to replace Arab nationalism with a subdued, fragmented culture of subservient informants split along tribal and sectarian lines, like the mercenary Ute manhunters against the Navajo.

Separating the insurgents from the population is indeed eating soup with a knife. In practice, that means breaking down doors in the middle of the night, creating barricaded and tightly controlled enclaves where residents live behind concertina wire and blast walls and beneath watchtowers, surveilled constantly by U.S. and Iraqi troops who control ingress and egress with eye scanners and fingerprinted ID cards. Residents stay home at night and are pressured to report anyone who is missing. Mass displacements, roundups and detentions of Iraqi civilians have all nearly doubled since the surge began in February 2007. The Pentagon's euphemism for this coercive program is "gated communities," a new name for a very old tradition.

In the days of Kit Carson, native people were herded into reservations while U.S. troops destroyed the insurgents and their natural resources. In

Malaya in the 1950s the British destroyed the Chinese communities at the base of the insurgency while herding civilians into "new villages" behind barbed wire. In South Vietnam the enclosures were called "strategic hamlets," and the assassination campaign to root out Vietcong guerrillas was called the Phoenix Program. To empty the countryside of potential Vietcong sympathizers, Harvard's Samuel Huntington advocated "forced urbanization."

Yet Sewall of Harvard's Carr Center suggests that intellectuals have a moral duty to collaborate with the military in devising counterinsurgency doctrines. "Humanitarians often avoid wading into the conduct of war for fear of becoming complicit in its purpose," she writes in an introduction to the field manual. In a direct response to critics who argue that the manual's passages endorsing human rights standards are just window dressing, she adds, "The field manual requires engagement precisely from those who fear that its words lack meaning."

One would think that past experiences with death squads indirectly supported by the United States, as in El Salvador in the 1980s, or the recent exposure of abuses at Iraq's Abu Ghraib, Afghanistan's Bagram facility and Guantánamo, would justify such worries about complicity. But Sewall defends Harvard's collaboration through a pro-military revisionist argument. She says, "Military annals today tally that effort [the war in El Salvador] as a success, but others cannot get past the shame of America's indirect role in fostering death squads." Can she mean that the Pentagon's self-serving narrative of the Central American wars is correct, and that critics of a conflict in which 75,000 Salvadorans died—the equivalent of more than 4 million Americans—most of them at the hands of U.S.-trained and -equipped security forces, including death squads, simply need to "get past" being squeamish about the methods? Instead of churning out self-deluding platitudes about civilizing the military, Harvard would do well to worry more about how collaboration with the Pentagon impairs the critical independent role of intellectuals.

The most fitting metaphor for Iraq today might be that of Dr. Frankenstein's monster. The effect of the "gated communities" and Kit Carson Scouts—indeed, the effect of much of the U.S. occupation since 2003—

has been to grind native populations into a state of anarchic fragmentation, with the vacuum filled by multiple sectarian militias. Consider the following evidence:

➤ A bombshell Pentagon report in September 2007 recommends "scrapping" the sectarian Iraqi police force and starting over.

➤ According to a July 2007 *Los Angeles Times* analysis, the current Interior Ministry, heavily funded and advised by Americans, is run by loyalists of the Shiite Supreme Islamic Iraqi Council and is responsible for secret prisons and torture. An average of one to two employees are killed each week, with Sunnis now "almost entirely purged from the ministry."

➤ The prestigious Baker-Hamilton Iraq Study Group noted last year that the Iraqi police "routinely engage in sectarian violence, including the unnecessary detention, torture and targeted execution of Sunni Arab civilians."

➤ The White House's own July benchmarks report noted "evidence of sectarian bias in the appointment of senior military and police commanders" as well as "target lists emanating from the Office of the Commander in Chief that bypassed operational commanders and directed lower-level intelligence officers to make arrests, primarily of Sunnis."

➤ According to the *New York Times*, as of the end of 2005, in Baghdad there were eight to ten secret prisons operated by militia units that reported directly to the Interior Minister.

➤ BBC television reporter Deborah Davies showed footage of torture and ethnic cleansing against Sunni civilians in late 2006, reporting that "it's all happening under the eyes of U.S. commanders who seem unwilling or unable to intervene."

➤ The United Nations has accused the Iraqi government of failing to address allegations of torture inflicted on the several thousand new detainees rounded up during the current Baghdad security plan.

➤ According to the U.S. Government Accountability Office, since 2004 190,000 U.S.-made AK-47s have gone missing, with many thought to be in the hands of various Iraqi militias.

The United States has spent $19 billion on the Iraqi security forces since 2003. The results are blatantly illegal under the government's Leahy Amendment (1997), which forbids military assistance to known human rights abusers. Why hasn't that amendment been a greater focus of Congressional attention? A key Senate consultant suggested in an interview with the *Nation* that there is widespread Congressional avoidance of the Frankenstein problem. In any other conflict, a regime like Iraq's would be termed a police state. In America, such talk makes people cringe. The dominant paradigm is that the "new Iraq" is a fledgling democracy that needs our nourishing protection before it "stands up." Although political talk shows frequently discuss Iraq's problems, rarely do they focus in depth on the death squads and militias embedded in the U.S.-funded security forces.

Perhaps this is more than a case of avoiding an ugly, unwanted phenomenon that is difficult to shut down. One explanation is hard to discount, however unnerving it might be. Soon after the 9/11 terror attacks, Vice President Cheney spoke of working "the dark side," doing apparently unspeakable things "quietly, without any discussion." Neoconservative military analyst Robert Kaplan has argued that counterinsurgency should be conducted "off camera, so to speak." The divide-and-conquer strategy was articulated by President Bush himself, who declared in his 2001 address on confronting terrorism that the United States would "turn them one against another."

Bernard Lewis, perhaps the dominant neoconservative voice advocating the Iraq War, proposed dismembering Arab nationalism back in the early 1990s, writing that "if the central power is sufficiently weakened, there is no real civic society . . . the state then disintegrates—as happened in

Lebanon—into a chaos of squabbling, feuding, fighting sects, tribes, religions and parties." In 2005 a longtime Israeli foreign ministry official wrote in a *Los Angeles Times* op-ed titled, "Israel Could Live With a Fractured, Failed Iraq," that "an Iraq split into three semi-autonomous mini-states, or an Iraq in civil war, means that the kind of threat posed by [Saddam] Hussein . . . is unlikely to rise again."

The specter of forced partition is directly accelerating with the U.S. troop surge, and sectarian civil war is already at hand. What is lacking is recognition that the United States is the driver of both; the surge has doubled the number of Iraqi refugees, and the civil war features American funding, weapons and advisers on all sides. "We sit back and watch because that can only benefit us," said one top commander of insurgent groups battling each other in 2006.

More evidence for this exploitation of sectarian chaos comes from Stephen Biddle, a Harvard PhD now at the Council on Foreign Relations and an on-the-ground adviser to General Petraeus in Baghdad. The Biddle plan, as described in a 2006 *Foreign Affairs* essay, called for playing both sides of the sectarian divide, something like the colonial defense of occupation as *the only way to* keep the barbarians in balance. After the United States had put the Shiites (and Kurds) in power, Biddle advised manipulating their behavior by "a U.S. threat to cease backing the Shiites coupled with a program to arm the Sunnis overtly or, in a semi-clandestine way . . . substantially reduce the Shiites' military prospects" against the Sunni insurgents.

Alternatively, Biddle proposed that the United States might unleash greater Shiite military power by providing tanks, armored personnel carriers, fixed-wing attack aircraft and the like to increase the Shiite capacity to "commit mass violence against the Sunnis dramatically." The reason? To provide an "important incentive for the Sunnis to compromise" on their longstanding demand for an American troop withdrawal.

This is dangerous territory, playing the "devil's game," in the apt phrase of author Robert Dreyfuss. One danger is that it can be played both ways. Iraqi militias are not only using the Americans to go after their rivals but seem to have turned their weapons on the occupiers. Just where and how

564 Writing Against the Iraq War

did those 190,000 AK-47s disappear? After routing their local rivals, who might the Kit Carson Scouts turn against next?

It is dangerous for American democracy to rely on policies based on stealth and deception. American Special Operations Forces carry out secret attacks in Baghdad's Shiite neighborhood of Sadr City or against Al Qaeda suspects "in the shadows of the troop increase," according to the *New York Times*. No one—not the media, Congress or the public—can be fully aware of what happens in such shadows. Biddle worries about a major obstacle: "Recent polls of American public opinion are not encouraging." Rather than bow to democratic public opinion, those like Biddle, Petraeus and Bush are rushing forward with exaggerations, fabrications and manipulations to defuse antiwar public opinion as the 2008 elections approach. The subtext is clear: the war itself must be masked and the media fed a false narrative once again.

One reality that will be hard to avoid is the exhaustion of the U.S. Army. Military commanders have made it clear that present troop levels will become unsustainable after April 2008. If this is so, the pressure for low-visibility counterinsurgency will only increase, with some brigades of American combat troops coming home during the presidential season and increased numbers of Americans advising and training Iraqi security forces as well as engaging in secret operations. The problem is that the media and leading presidential candidates have already internalized the paradigm shift from a combat mission to a training one. The Senate antiwar proposal with the greatest support, for example, allows explicit exemptions for trainers and operations against Al Qaeda. The Baker-Hamilton Iraq Study Group recommended 10,000–20,000 advisers, up from the current 3,000–4,000. The Center for New American Security, a hawkish Democratic-leaning think tank, advocates an increase to 20,000 advisers. The center, which includes former officials from Raytheon and Lockheed Martin as well as former Secretary of State Madeleine Albright and former Deputy Secretary of State Richard Armitage on its board, is especially worried about the home front:

The transition from President Bush is getting more and more problematic as the American people continue to lose confidence in the Iraq War and step up their pressure on candidates from both parties. If no bipartisan consensus is reached before the Democratic and Republican primaries, the next President will likely be elected principally on a "Get Out of Iraq" platform. The political space to do otherwise is shrinking by the day.

Only one think tank of well-connected insiders, the Center for American Progress (CAP), has evolved from supporting U.S. advisers to advocating their phaseout along with nearly all U.S. troops by the end of 2008. CAP is led by Bill Clinton's former chief of staff John Podesta—who also sits on the board of his more hawkish rivals at the Center for New American Security. But the differences between these insider advocates could not be more stark: leave the American troops engaged in the midst of a sectarian civil war, or bring them home in twelve months. The most interesting CAP proposal is for Congress to enforce the Leahy Amendment. Shortly after CAP issued its report advocating total withdrawal, the leaders of Congress's Out of Iraq Caucus (Representatives Maxine Waters, Barbara Lee and Lynn Woolsey) introduced HR 3134, which prohibits funding, training and transferring arms to the Iraqi security forces, and any militias or local forces, unless specifically authorized by Congress. Hearings on this legislation might uncover the bloody realities involved in the counterinsurgency campaign. If so, members of Congress who have been reluctant so far to end funding for the troops may be less willing to ratify taxes that abet secret prisons and Interior Ministry death squads.

For those who can still get past the shame of death squads, as Harvard's Sewall seems to urge, and who still believe a better world lies ahead for Iraq under U.S. tutelage, Congress could ask the Navaho and Ute to testify. These believers might then learn that the hidden shame behind the counterinsurgency in Iraq is the same one that has compromised America's identity for centuries.

60.

Our Gulag
The Secret State of Torture

Huffington Post, *October 5, 2007*

Torture, I believe, is an inevitable dimension of fighting counterinsurgency wars against popular nationalist or revolutionary movements. This is the reason why so much Pentagon attention is devoted to denial and the use of Orwellian terminology. The media, the clergy, and the civil liberties communities must serve as public watchdogs to prevent America from sliding further into the dark alleys of dirty war—at home as well as abroad.

◆   ◆   ◆

LIKE A SHARP RAZOR cutting through the fog of war, the *New York Times* headline reads, "Justice Dept. Said to Back Harshest Tactics After Declaring Torture Abhorrent." The article could not be clearer. The Bush Justice Department has secretly authorized "the harshest interrogation techniques ever used by the Central Intelligence Agency."

Simulated drowning. Fear of suffocation. Blows to the head. Naked men held in freezing cells. Sleep deprivation. Noise assaults. All secretly legalized, from Guantánamo to Abu Ghraib. As long as it doesn't "shock the conscience," anything is permissible up to organ failure or death.

In defense of silence, one might claim it is impossible to be shocked at horrors that are not known. But if we know, and still are not shocked, there are lessons.

It's all in the 1960 classic, *The Battle of Algiers*, in the dialogue between the press and the general:

JOURNALIST: Excuse me. It seems that out of an excess of caution, my colleagues keep asking you indirect questions. It would be better to call a spade a spade, so let's talk about torture.

THE GENERAL: The word "torture" isn't used in our orders. We use "interrogation" as the only valid police method. We could talk for hours to no avail because that is not the problem. The problem is this. The FLN wants to throw us out of Algeria, and we want to stay.

Even with slight shades of opinion, you all agree that we must stay. We're here for that reason alone. We are neither madmen nor sadists. We are soldiers. Our duty is to win. Therefore to be precise, it is my turn to ask a question.

Should France stay in Algeria? If your answer is still yes, then you must accept all the consequences.

Are the torturers winning? The October 4, 2007, *New York Times* front-page headline surrenders the struggle over words. "Severe interrogations" replaces "torture" as a description of our behavior. Nonetheless, the *New York Times* has the courage to lay bare the entire truth of the Bush administration's secret policies.

If torture is winning on the field of rhetoric, it must be stopped in reality. Otherwise, we will be accepting America's status as an emptied democracy that cannot put an end to its own gulags. Two weeks ago, an eminent Pentagon commission reported that the Iraqi security forces are engaged in brutal sectarian violence against civilians. The White House acknowledged the same findings in July. The Baker-Hamilton Report made the same findings almost two years ago. The torture runs deep. And it continues, with American advisers and $19 billion in taxpayer funding.

We must learn a painful lesson, that torture is not out-of-control behavior by an isolated handful of poorly trained soldiers, but is *integral*, sooner or later, in any policies aimed at suppressing a popular insurgency. And secrecy is not limited to a handful of over-enthusiastic bureaucrats, but is integral, sooner or later, to any state pursuing an unpopular war. Torture and secrecy are embedded in America's policies in Iraq. And so we must paraphrase the French general's question to the media and public, by asking: *Should America stay in Iraq?* If your answer is still yes, then you must accept *all* the consequences.

Permissions

◆　　◆　　◆

I. BUILDING A NEW LEFT: STUDENT ACTIVISM & CIVIL RIGHTS IN THE EARLY 1960S

CHAPTER 2

"A Letter to the New (Young) Left," from *The New Student Left* by Mitchell Cohen. Copyright © 1966 by the Activist Publishing Company. Reprinted by permission of Beacon Press, Boston.

CHAPTER 3

"SNCC in Action: Dignity for the Enslaved and for Us All," from *The New Student Left* by Mitchell Cohen. Copyright © 1966 by the Activist Publishing Company. Reprinted by permission of Beacon Press, Boston.

II. THE VIETNAM WAR, THE ANTIWAR MOVEMENT, AND THE CHICAGO EIGHT

CHAPTER 8

Boston Globe, "North Vietnam Stands Defiant under Storm of U.S. Bombs," January 1, 1973. Reprinted by permission of the publisher.

III. INSIDE VIEWS: ELECTORAL POLITICS, PUBLIC POLICY, AND THE CALIFORNIA STATE LEGISLATURE

CHAPTER 16

The Nation, "California Cracks its Mortarboards," September 18, 1995. Reprinted by permission of the publisher.

IV. DIGGING FOR ROOT CAUSES: ENDING GANG VIOLENCE

CHAPTER 20

The Nation, "Gato and Alex—No Safe Place," July 10, 2000. Reprinted by permission of the publisher.

V. PERSONAL ROOTS: THOUGHTS
ON IRELAND

CHAPTER 25

"The Famine of Feeling" from *Irish Hunger*, ed. Tom Hayden. Copyright © 1997, 1998 by Roberts Rinehart Publishers. Reprinted by permission of Rowman & Littlefield Publishing Group.

CHAPTER 26

San Francisco Chronicle, "Drumcree 1998 Is Mississippi 1963," July 21, 1998. Reprinted by permission of the publisher.

VI. PERSONAL LIFE

CHAPTER 28

Modern Maturity, "Your Son Became a Defendant Instead of a Lawyer." Copyright © 1996 AARP. Reprinted by permission of the publisher.

VII. PRESERVING THE ENVIRONMENT

CHAPTER 31

"The Politics of Nature," from *The Soul of Nature: Visions of a Living Earth*, ed. Michael Tobias and Georgianne Cowan. Copyright © 1994 by Continuum International Publishing Group. Reprinted by permission of the publisher.

VIII. LESSONS LEARNED: PROGRESSIVE POLITICS
AND FOREIGN POLICY

CHAPTER 38

The Nation, "An Exiled Son of Santiago," April 4, 2005. Reprinted by permission of the publisher.

X. REFLECTIONS ON THE 1960S

CHAPTER 41

"Conspiracy In the Streets," from *Conspiracy in the Streets: The Extraordinary Trial of the Chicago Eight*, ed. Jon Weiner. Copyright © 2006 by The New Press. Reprinted by permission of the publisher.

CHAPTER 43

"Missing Mills," from *Radical Nomad: C. Wright Mills and His Times*, by Tom Hayden. Copyright © 2006 by Paradigm Publishers. Reprinted by permission of the publisher.

CHAPTER 44

"Enemy of the State: The Secret War Against John Lennon," from *Memories of John Lennon*, ed. Yoko Ono. Copyright © 2005 by Yoko Ono. Reprinted by permission of the editor c/o Bill Adler Books.

CHAPTER 47

The Nation, "You Gotta Love Her," March 22, 2004. Reprinted by permission of the publisher.

XI. FROM CHICAGO TO SEATTLE AND BEYOND: WRITINGS ON THE GLOBAL JUSTICE MOVEMENT

CHAPTER 50

"In the Beginning Is the Dream: Thoughts on the Zapatista Insurgency," from *The Zapatista Reader*, ed. Tom Hayden. Copyright © 2002 by Avalon Publishing Group, Incorporated. Reprinted by permission of Nation Books, a member of Perseus Books Group.

CHAPTER 56

The Nation, "A New Bolivian Diary," January 27, 2006. Reprinted by permission of the publisher.

XII. WRITING AGAINST THE IRAQ WAR

CHAPTER 57

San Francisco Chronicle, "Anti-War Movement Deserves Some Credit," November 26, 2006. Reprinted by permission of the publisher.

CHAPTER 58

The Nation, "Iraq is Dying," August 9, 2006. Reprinted by permission of the publisher.

CHAPTER 59

The Nation, "The New Counterinsurgency," September 24, 2007. Reprinted by permission of the publisher.

Index

♦   ♦   ♦

POWs, 114, 121,124, 275, 446, 448
Pacem in Terris encyclical, 251, 377
Paine, Thomas, 11, 27, 265, 312, 376, 405
Paisley, Ian, 261
Palestinians, 355–361 passim, 532–533
Papandreou, Andreas, 347
paramilitary massacres, 476–480
Parchman Penitentiary, 438
Paris peace talks, 1968, 123, 124
Park, Brad, 65
Parker, Charles Mack, 33
"participatory democracy," 373–374, 376–380 passim, 393, 469
    Internet and, 395
    unsurprising support for among activists, 433
Partido Revolucionario Institucional (PRI), 470
partition
    Iraq, 551–554 passim, 563
passports, 91, 96–97, 109
Patriot Act, 345, 380, 382
Patton, Joel, 260
Pauer, Jan, 334
Peace and Freedom Party, 142, 151
Peace Corps, 75–76
peace movement, 55–57, 91, 116, 359, 360
    condemned by Billy Graham, 542
    Iraq war and, 548–551, 552
    Nixon and, 402n56
    political theater and, 271
    repression against, 270–271, 410
    See also Moratorium to End the War, 1969
Peace Now, 356, 358
Pelosi, Nancy, 549
Pentagon
    prayer breakfasts, 542
Pentagon Papers, 276, 402n56
People's History of the United States, A (Zinn), 405, 457–458
pepper spray, 409, 411, 469, 486, 494, 497
Pérez Jiménez, Marcos, 351
Pérez Jiménez, Monica Mercedes, 351–352
permits, 126, 128, 129, 132
Persian Gulf Crisis, 338–340
Persian Gulf War, 171
personal computers, 394–395
Pesonen, Everett, 315
Peter, Paul and Mary, 144
Peters, Rose, 219
Petraeus, David, 552, 557, 558, 563, 564
Petras, James, 517
petroleum industry. *See* oil industry
Pham Van Dong, 107–109
Phillips, Kevin, 522
physicians, 205
Pico-Union, Los Angeles, 219, 221, 226

pigs ·
    nomination for president, 134
"pigs" (label), 159, 165
Pinochet, Augusto, 341–354 passim
piranha, 294
Pitzer College, 20n2
plastic surgery
    Vietnam, 173
Podesta, John, 565
Podhoretz, John, 381
Podhoretz, Norman, 381
poetry
    Chicago conspiracy trial and, 163–165
police
    anti-gang units, 222, 225–227 passim, 230
    anti-protester actions, 133–155 passim, 389, 391, 408–412, 494–497
    brutality, 78–79, 150–154 passim, 222, 226, 389, 411
    Chicago, 126, 133–134, 144–145, 147–149
        riot, 149–154, 389, 391
        collusion with INS, 227
    funding and growth, 181, 230
    high-tech weapons of, 409, 411
    in fiction, 95
    informers, 165
    Julian Bond thinks of calling "pigs," 159
    Los Angeles, 217, 222, 225–227 passim, 408–409
    Miami, 494–497
    Mississippi, 28, 31, 32
    need for more of, 215
    Newark, New Jersey, 65, 77–81 passim, 85
    Oakland, 141
    psychology of, 166
    rogue practices of, 222, 226–227
    See also secret police
political action committees, 197, 357
political campaign platforms, 177–187
political commercials, 199, 534
political correctness, 456–457
political economy, 311
political endorsements, 255–261 passim
political theater, 271
political trials, 278. *See also* Chicago conspiracy trial, 1969–70
politics and nature, 308–314
Pollack, Kenneth, 558
polls, 136, 390, 548, 558
    in Iraq, 553
Poor People's Caravan, 152
Pope John XXIII, 251, 377
population growth, 51, 321
Port Huron Statement, 11, 19, 369, 373–402 passim
    excerpts from, 35–64
    Pope John XXIII and, 251
    writing of, 375

ABOUT THE AUTHOR

TOM HAYDEN began writing as a high school editor and has never stopped. He has written or edited fifteen books and hundreds of published op-eds and essays.

Hayden entered the University of Michigan in time to be touched by the Southern student civil rights movement, the John F. Kennedy campaign, and the Peace Corps. He was chosen editor of the *Michigan Daily*, but passed up a journalism career to work on the front lines of the civil rights movement. He was a Freedom Rider in southern Georgia in 1961, and wrote blazing dispatches for national audiences, including *Mademoiselle* magazine.

He drafted what became the *Port Huron Statement* from an Albany, Georgia, jail cell in late 1961. The document became the founding manifesto of the Students for a Democratic Society, and has been hailed as the greatest document of the New Left era.

Hayden left university life to become a community organizer in the Newark ghetto, 1964–68. When Vietnam was bombed and invaded starting in 1965, however, Hayden began opposing the war as a derailment of the fight for social justice in America. He was an early traveler to Hanoi and opponent of the war and draft.

His opposition to Vietnam led Hayden to participate in the Columbia student strike in April 1968 and the militant street protests in Chicago that same year. He was indicted with seven others by the Nixon administration, convicted in 1969, and acquitted on appeal in 1973. He was married at the time to actress Jane Fonda, with whom he has a son and stepdaughter.

After the war, Hayden entered California politics for two decades, winning seven out of eleven races, and chairing legislative policy committees on natural resources, higher education and labor. He authored over 100 measures that became law, and was described as "the conscience of the Senate" when he retired in 2000.

Hayden still writes prolifically, and has taught in recent years at Pitzer College, Occidental College, and the Harvard Institute of Politics. His most recent books are *Ending the War in Iraq* (2006), *The Port Huron Statement* (2006), *Street Wars* (2005), *The Lost Gospel of the Earth* (2005), and *The Zapatista Reader* (2003). His website is www.tomhayden.com.